Early praise for *Lillie's*

"...a good teaching tool for anyone who [has been sexually] abused and [is] unable to speak of it... carefully wrought, and deceptively simple (in other words, not)..."

Emily

"The characters were well-drawn and quickly familiar, and the action kept me eagerly turning pages. I truly could not bear to put the book down until I had finished it...it seemed to have an overall cadence that allowed for a stretch at appropriate intervals, yet I could hardly wait to move on to the next to find out what would happen to the heroine, her lover, her dad...Abigail...Oh my goodness, I came to care deeply about all of them...

"Do I want more? Oh, YES!"

Wendyl Ross

"...though sometimes difficult to read, it was cathartic...after 35 years, *Lillie's Redemption* opened my eyes to the pervasive impact betrayal by a trusted spiritual leader at a vulnerable time has had on my ability to embrace life and joy...I finally realized the reason I had never been able to forgive myself was that I wasn't the one who needed forgiveness..."

Marie, victimized at 17

"A real page-turner...You have boldly taken on a topic that has rarely been discussed in an open, objective, and honest way. I saw many parallels between the behavior of the perpetrator in the book and my own experience as a former congregant in a church with an abusive pastor. I particularly appreciated your description of the efforts of the supporters of the pastor to suppress any discussion of the abuse through threats of lawsuits, etc. I experienced similar behavior firsthand...It amazes me that some church-goers can behave like that and yet continue to fill the pews on Sunday morning...

"...an important exposé and compelling love story deserving wide dissemination and discussion..."

Ron Frantz
Prosecuting Attorney

Lillie's
Redemption

Lydia Waring Meyer

Michelle,
May this
story speak to
your heart!
Lydia M

PRINCIPIA
MEDIA

Lillie's Redemption

© 2012 Lydia Waring Meyer

Published by Principia Media, LLC, Wyoming, MI

www. principiamedia.com

ISBN-13: 978-1-61485-305-3

Principia Media, LLC

1853 R W Berends Drive SW

Wyoming, MI 49519

Cover photograph courtesy of the author.

Quote on page ix from the book:

Gift of Story: A Wise Tale About What Is Enough by Cynthia Pinkola Estes, Ph.D. (Ballantine Books, 1993)

Printed in the United States of America

18 17 16 15 14 13 12 7 6 5 4 3 2 1

To those who have yet to be empowered
&
to those who empower them

Acknowledgments

My entire life, everything I've done and everyone I've known, even being an insatiable people watcher, has prepared me for writing this book. There are more people than I can name here to thank for their impact and part in that preparation and I send my gratitude to all of them. The idea of writing a book mulled in my soul for years before the morning, three days before Christmas in 2006, I sat at my journal to write and I began instead to write this novel. I credit the Divine Spirit with the idea that this story needed to be told. I felt somehow chosen to be the teller. I have been in awe of the serendipitous ways in which the right people, opportunities, insights and ideas have been provided. I am humbled and grateful for this experience, which has launched me into a whole new world of writing. At times I have railed against this task as it felt like a burden. At other times I have never felt closer to my God. Although real experiences do inform this story, all the people, places, names and details are my own creation, fictional in every way.

I would like to thank my parents Thomas Waring and Theodora Elkinton Waring for raising us in the Quaker tradition and creating a place for us in nature which taught me to love the outdoors; Nancy Martin who showed me what loving wild flowers looked like; my ornithology professor Bill Buskirk who taught me how to identify birds and Gregg Godsey who taught me to love birdwatching. I thank my sons for their ongoing support, ideas and encouragement—my oldest, Matthew Meyer, for encouraging me to write the book I'd always talked about writing, and my youngest, Ried Meyer, and Camilla Fulvi, for patiently responding to my early need to read aloud when the book was in its first throes of life and I wasn't yet sure I was a writer; Virginia Sobel for being an author I could talk with about what it meant to be an author and share the experience of writing when it was still new to me; Clayton Pauer and Martha Plantenga, who met with me faithfully each week the whole first year as I wrote the story, and who kept my passion for the project alive— Clayton who read the book at every stage and witnessed its development, who brought his unique perspective through hours of discussion and laughter and his vulnerable, honest and hilarious sharing, Martha who went with me into the presence of the Divine Spirit and offered her spiritual and earth wisdom, her knowledge of healing, medicinals, and recovery and who helped me see symbolic elements I had not realized I had written into the story. I thank Margret Bazany who validates my earth-based spiritual practice and that I talk with trees, and who saw the vision of completion, shared her love of books and writing and was my final reader, and all those who taught me about Native American history, experience and spirituality.

I thank Jean Martinelli whose enthusiasm for my commitment to the project and her mutual love for writing inspired and supported me; Nicole Fisher, who read and loved this book when it was still raw, unedited material, who believed in me and supported me in many ways; Melanie VerDuin, who, as a member of my congregation, and a colleague in the church, brought her perspective of personal and professional understanding of me and my work as a pastor, and the congregation I served as pastor, who allowed me to learn first hand about the church.

I thank Jonathan, my nephew, who was the first to read the manuscript on a Blackberry and gave me the most important piece of feedback I received; Marie Waring, my sister-in-law who gave her stamp of approval boosting my confidence during revision and who saw "Quaker genius" in the story line; Katharine Scheusner, my niece who brought her faith, experience and intelligence to bear on this book and gave me insightful feedback in the later stages; Kristin Aardema-Faigh whose spiritual acuity allowed her to grasp the full message of this work and encourage my purpose; Mike Spalsbury, who brought an intellectual proficiency and perspective to the characters and themes of the book that made his feedback indispensable; and Audra Allen, whose reading was reliably thorough and capable of ferreting out discrepancies and inconsistencies.

I thank all my soul sisters who helped me develop the system of healing I use and teach, and now demonstrate in the book, and especially Pam Bennett, Elaine Leigh, Jennifer Hudson, and Cindy Johnson for reading parts of the book and listening to me talk ad nauseum about my novel without turning away from me, and all my clients for teaching me about the human condition and the elements of the healing process that I witnessed and learned to facilitate. It is my hope that I have accurately rendered the experience of abuse, faithful to the realities of the pain and wounding therein.

I thank Jim Dana, Margaret Willey, Erik Stoneburner, Scott Stewart, and Sarah Cowhey, for their expertise, advice and support; Dirk Wierenga for showing up at the perfect moments along the way with the right question or piece of wisdom to guide my process; and Vally Sharpe, my editor, who joined me in this project with equal passion, lived in my mind, taught me many things about writing and transformed my manuscript into a book. Her wisdom and instinct to know when I needed to talk and be reassured, and our laughter, sustained me in the hardest parts of the editing process.

Finally and most of all, thanks to my husband Tim Meyer, who learned to believe in my work and became my greatest supporter, advisor and cheerleader, who held things together as I became a writer, who helped me capture elements of the plot that he knew better than I did, who got excited with me and brainstormed about marketing as the businessperson he is and who celebrates the product of my labor with a joy, born of his love for me, that matches my own.

Preface

I began life in New England instilled with the Quaker values of seeking justice, recognizing the equality of all people, speaking with honesty, living in simplicity of heart, of language and of lifestyle, experiencing and expressing a love of Nature and listening to and following the guidance of the Spirit within. I have sought work and opportunities that have taught me much about the ways of humanity. As the youngest of five, I learned to observe people as well as live in the woods, build fires, paddle a canoe and chase my sisters and brothers in the treetops. I attended Quaker schools growing up and met my husband at Earlham College in Indiana.

We moved to Michigan where I received my Masters of Social Work degree and worked in foster care dealing with family dysfunction, sexual abuse and teenage delinquency. After starting our family, I continued my education by fitting in a Masters of Divinity degree. In various ministry settings I lead youth groups, taught women's bible studies and provided pastoral care. As a social worker, a pastoral intern, and an ordained minister, working with children, teens, adults and the elderly, and serving as the solo pastor of a church, I have learned much about the goodness and wisdom of human beings as well as the dynamics of power, control, and abuse.

In these professional roles I have been privy to the existence and the cover-up of predatory behavior rampant in this culture. From personal experience I have learned to develop an inner wisdom, therapeutic tools and healthy boundaries that allow me to examine my own issues and protect myself. At my private counseling practice, La Loba, Inc., through individual counseling, small group work, retreats and wilderness trips, I seek to teach what I have learned and work to empower others to retrieve their intuition, become their own healers, and develop the ability to recognize and protect themselves from predatory behavior. In 2006, a journal entry turned into the beginning of this novel. I was compelled to share what I know in even larger circles.

As I have lived my 53 years, I have come to learn that life is riddled everyday with the need for maintaining healthy boundaries between people. We push across the line constantly in personal, familial, employment, and organizational settings into inappropriate areas of connectedness with one another. It is our lot as human beings to learn how to navigate these nuances in relationships. We are all capable and often culpable of stealing one another's innocence, forcing our agenda onto others, making people feel obligated to us, and manipulating others to their own demise. It is also possible to misunderstand what we see. In our fervor and effort to identify dangerous predators we run the risk of falsely accusing someone of doing something they did not do. Perception and evidence are illusive and even the justice system can mishandle them from time to time. So, I believe, we must all carefully examine our selves, our motives, and our behavior.

This is a book about hope and second chances as much as it is an honest take on what happens in the church and the surrounding community at the hands of predatory pastors. My hope is that this story will show the best of humanity, will demonstrate the healing that I have learned is possible and will offer catharsis to all who read it. May it spawn conversations that usher in redemption.

Lydia Waring Meyer
Grand Haven, Michigan
April 2011

"Stories that instruct, renew, and heal provide a vital nourishment to the psyche that cannot be obtained in any other way. Stories reveal over and over again the precious and peculiar knack that humans have for triumph over travail. They provide all the vital instructions we need to live a useful, necessary, and unbounded life—a life of meaning, a life worth remembering."

Main Characters

The Farmer Family
Martin and Melodie (deceased) Farmer
Violet (Farmer) and Kevin Parks and their children
Ben, age 10, and Samantha, age 7,
(called Sassy for short and Sassafrass by her grandfather)
Bruce Farmer
Lillie Farmer, age 25

The Crumley Family
Miriam and Samuel (deceased) Crumley
Joshua Crumley, age 25

Abigail

Reverend Lane Richardson (Pastor Lane)
former pastor of Hopeston Church / current pastor of Broadley Community Church

Support Group Members
Heidi Spellworth
Rebecca Jones
Gail Ligatho
Ruth Turner
Elizabeth Hallman

Hopeston Congregation
Reverend Terrance Bunker (Pastor Terry)
Mike Johnston, chairman of the church board, and Penelope, his wife
Marie Calsik – church secretary
Dorothy Banks
Jerry and Julia Bomont
Barbara and Ralph Stacey

The Nelsons
Delbert and Pamela Nelson – members of Hopeston Church
Mary Anne Hodge, third of Delbert and Pamela's five children

Ned

The character of Abigail in the story was raised within the Quaker tradition, and speaks with the "plain language" typical of the early Quakers. In England, where Quakerism was born in the 1600's, believers chose not to follow the custom whereby one referred to equals or inferiors with "thee" and "thy" and to superiors with the more proper "you" and "yours." Believing that all human beings are equal in the sight of God, and offering witness to the fact through their language, they addressed everyone, including the monarchs, using "thee" and "thy." The custom is still used today within some Quaker families and the Quaker community at large.

Abigail uses it still with all who cross her path, as a continuing witness to her belief that all people are of equal value.

Part One

The Diary

1

June 10, 1985

I know people think I am a proper lady, a good Christian woman, a loving mother and a devoted wife. But I am none of these. I must be evil, for I have abandoned my children, refused to let my husband touch me. A lady would not be as anti-social and uncooperative, and as for being a Christian... I have failed in all of these, so there is no doubt about it, I must be evil! I wonder if this is what hell is like? I hope I have not led my children astray by my poor example.

Lillie is especially sensitive and was around during the worst of it. Dear God, she has been so depressed. I know it is all my fault! But I don't know what to do for her. I am incapable of helping her. Please, God, keep her safe, keep her safe from me! And give her happiness.

I don't know what I would have done without Abigail! I think I would have gone totally insane or tried to end it all if it weren't for her. She always seems to know what's bothering me and talking to her helps. I don't know how I found her the first time. I certainly don't deserve her. God must have sent her to me!

But, do you think God knows about Abigail? I'm not sure He would approve.

Ten Years Later

L illie Farmer closed her mother's diary. Normally, sitting on the porch with a nice cup of tea brought a sense of peace—when she visited her father, she liked rising before everyone else and watching the dawn paint the sky in an ever-changing masterpiece of color and light. But this morning was different. Instead, a mixture of fear and sadness weighed heavily on her heart.

A gentle breeze blew cool on naked calves, fluttering the hem of her cotton sundress but all she could feel was the buzz of locusts that vibrated through her. She brushed strands of her shoulder-length light brown hair from her face, and breathed in the sweet mist-filled air rising from the meadow in front of her, hoping it would save her from the darkness of the depression that had visited her on and off since her mother's death. Vaguely uncomfortable, she adjusted her medium frame in the soft cushions of the wicker chair.

She pressed the small book between her palms and drew it to her chest, then opened it to read again. Just at that moment, a hermit thrush, deep in the woods at the side of the porch, broke into its flutelike trill, and reminded her she was not alone.

Though Lillie wondered if, by reading her late mother's diary, she was trespassing on holy ground, she felt comforted at the same time. The slightly yellowed pages, which were filled with Melodie's carefully penned script, brought large tears of equal joy and sadness. So familiar was the delicate handwriting that memories washed over the young woman, and she succumbed to them.

As a child and young adolescent, she'd received most of her emotional support from her mother. No matter what happened, Melodie had always seemed to make it better for Lillie. Playful and sensitive, she'd had a way of making her daughter laugh about the things that happened during the day—home-baked cookies always awaited Lillie's return from school in the afternoons, and Melodie was always a ready partner for board games.

4

Lillie had loved nothing more than running and playing in the woods with her brother Bruce—she'd never liked playing house and Barbie and experimenting with make-up. By the time she reached middle school, the majority of girls were consumed with boys and who liked whom, while she'd been more interested in sports and reading.

The boys she'd grown up with had suddenly become uncomfortable having her around, so she'd struggled even more to belong. She had depended on her mother's steady presence to make it through those days of adolescent angst. But in an instant, everything had changed.

She had come home from playing in the woods one afternoon to find the kitchen dark and empty and had called out to her mother. When no response had come, she had run through the house calling for her. Finally, when she'd reached the door of her parents' bedroom, she had found it locked.

Lillie closed her eyes and saw herself in her mind's eye, standing outside the door.

A small voice responded from within the room.
"Lillie, please. Please go away."
"Mother? Are you sick? What's wrong?"
"Just go, please. I can't talk to you now."

Puzzled, she'd complied with her mother's request, and done what she'd always done when she was upset—she'd buried herself in a book. Later that evening, when her father had come home from work, he had found her fast asleep on her bed, the book clasped in her arms.

God had always been at the center of her mother's life, and worship had been yet another special thing she had shared with Lillie, but after that day, she had refused to go back to the little church in Hopeston they had attended. Lillie had continued going alone but she had finally stopped too—the pats on the head she received from well-meaning folks had felt patronizing in a way.

As time had gone on, Lillie's mother had continued to withdraw from her husband and daughter, and eventually became a shell of her former self. Lillie's once kind and cheerful mother was no longer capable of offering her family the warmth and hospitality for which she had been famous—and her daughter resigned herself to the fact that she would never again be able to depend on Melodie as a source of comfort. Not old enough to understand what had happened, Lillie sank into depression, and Martin, ill-prepared to handle the devastation of both his wife and his daughter, had consulted their family doctor and found a therapist for Lillie. He'd failed to get through to his wife.

Several years passed, with no real change. Lillie finished high school and went away to the city. Her parents remained together, going through the motions of the marriage they had once had. And then tragedy had struck—at the young age of 51, Melodie Farmer had died of a massive heart attack.

Two years later, the family had, in a word, disintegrated. No one had seen Lillie's brother Bruce since the funeral, and though she'd tried to get close to her older sister Violet, the chasm between them, which had existed long before their mother's death, had widened.

Home for a week to visit her father, Lillie had found the diary lying on the hall desk upstairs. Glancing through it, and seeing the dates of the journal entries, she had felt herself drawn through a narrow door—a door through which the answer to what was still a mystery might finally be revealed. With mixed emotion, she had quietly taken the book to the porch and begun to read. Old wounds had reared their heads almost immediately.

Swallowing hard to subdue the hurt that rose in her throat, she looked out over the meadow and breathed in again. Three raucously cawing crows, black against the pastel sky, offered her momentary relief. The magical mist of the early morning began to recede as the heat of the day set in and her attention wandered as she felt a first trickle of perspiration between her breasts.

The screen door creaked and a step fell heavy on the wooden porch. Startled from her reverie, Lillie glanced over to find her father facing the meadow, and she nervously closed the diary and slipped it under her thigh. Smoothing her dress, she turned back to look at him.

Though small in stature, Martin Farmer was clearly a working man, his cologne a mixture of wood chips, aftershave and pipe tobacco. His profile revealed a sharp nose above narrow lips and a strong chin, attributes Lillie had only recently begun to admire. She noted too that her father's hair had thinned at the crown, a fact usually hidden by a faded John Deere cap.

"Tea?" he offered, without turning around.

"Yes, thanks," she replied softly.

Martin retreated into the house and she sat perfectly still, though the diary seemed to burn a hole in her leg. She listened as a clank of dishes began in the kitchen and waited for the tea kettle's whistle. When it sounded, she hid her mother's diary under the cushion and headed through the door. Her reading would have to wait.

The tile of the dark hall was cold under her bare feet as she padded quietly into the kitchen. Lowering herself to sit at the table, she watched as her father poured hot water into twin teacups—delicate, no-longer-used teacups that had belonged to her mother. Silence lingered so long that Lillie thought at first that her father hadn't noticed her entrance. But she was mistaken.

"You've been reading," he said. It was not a question.

"Yeah," she replied.

"How is it?" he asked, his back still toward her.

"I don't know yet. I...I...just started," she stuttered.

Martin turned and brought their tea to the table, and Lillie watched, silently incredulous. After years of coffee mugs and a stated dislike for tea, her father was serving Earl Grey, her mother's favorite. He gently slid her cup and saucer toward her with his large, calloused hand.

Bringing the cup to her mouth absentmindedly, she gulped the hot liquid. It scalded her tongue, and she dropped the cup. It clattered onto its saucer. Embarassed, Lillie tried to sound nonchalant.

"What are you going to do today, Dad?"

"I thought I'd let you read."

Lillie was stunned, disconcerted even. The taskmaster of her childhood sat calmly in front of her, his lips touching flowered porcelain, now encouraging her to read—something he had often fought with her about when she'd been a child and the chores weren't done. In those days, all she'd wanted to do was curl up in a chair and read a book, but he had thought it a waste of time.

"I'll take the kids into town so you can read in peace," he continued. "Violet and Kevin come back tomorrow, so this is a good day for reading."

Lillie loved spending time with Sassy and Ben, her sister's children, but she knew her father was right. It *was* a good day for reading.

Martin sipped from his cup and set it down. "I'm glad you found her diary."

She sat back, startled, and then it dawned on her. "You left it out for me…"

He nodded, examining his fingernails so as not to make eye contact. "I thought you should know what happened."

She wanted to ask what he meant, but she also feared the answer. Reading the pain on his daughter's face, Martin responded with tenderness.

"Just read it, Lillie. What happened to your mother affected us all. But…I think it hit you the hardest. I didn't know…when it happened, Lillie. I don't think I handled things very well." He picked at his fingernails again.

Lillie shook her head as if to remove the cobwebs.

"When *what* happened?"

Martin sighed and closed his eyes. "Just read the diary, Lillie. We can talk about it later." Before she could respond, he got up from the table, placed his half-empty teacup on the counter and went out of the house. The slam of the screen door behind him jarred her to the bone.

2

The ceiling creaked loudly overhead. The children were getting up—they always woke early when they were visiting, just so they could traipse along with their grandfather as he mowed the lawn or worked in the barn.

Still stunned that her father had actually planned the day so she could read her mother's diary in peace, Lillie realized he wanted her to uncover the mystery of what had happened.

But did she want to? She considered hiding the diary away. Why had her father gone to such trouble? She'd been fifteen years old when her mother had written in this diary. A lifetime ago, it had been a year she'd worked hard with her therapists to overcome.

The noises from upstairs spread and Lillie shook herself from her thoughts just as Sassy, her seven-year-old niece, came flying on bare feet into the kitchen, cotton nightgown streaming behind. Forcing a ready grin, she turned to offer her open lap and Sassy jumped into it with abandon, wiggling and settling in like a purring kitten.

"Good morning, Sas," said Lillie, pressing her lips to her curly head and breathing in the aroma of a sleepy child.

"Hi!" exclaimed Sassy.

"Where's your brother?"

"Coming. He's slow!"

The little girl wriggled free, slid off her aunt's lap and ran toward the porch. Lillie called after her. "Grandpa's in the barn!"

As Sassy bounced down the steps, her breakfast order trailed back like the tail of a kite in the wind. "I want scrambled eggs!"

Lillie smiled again, flooded with warm affection for her wild little niece. She stood, gathered up her mother's cup and saucer, and sent up a prayer of gratitude for the rare beauty of Samantha Parks.

Another creak was heard and a few seconds later, Sassy's older brother, Ben, shuffled in. More asleep than awake, he plunked himself down at the kitchen table and rested his curly blond head on his arms while Lillie quietly washed and dried the teacups and gently set them back in the cupboard. She flushed with warmth, remembering the time spent with her father earlier. Looking out of the kitchen window, she saw him emerge from the barn and head across the yard with her niece close behind, in tall green boots that extended well above her knees. Lillie chuckled at the sight of Sassy stumbling and lurching, hair and nightgown floating around her, an angel with huge, green frog legs. Martin had never allowed bare feet in the barn, and to cover all contingencies, he kept boots for offenders. She had worn them herself as a child.

Ben raised his head from the table. "What's so funny?"

"Your sister! You should see her in Grandpa's boots!"

He lifted his head again and placed it heavily between his fists, leaning his elbows on the table. "Do I *have* to share a room with that brat? She keeps me awake all night and gets me up too early! I can't sleep at all with her around!"

Lillie ruffled her nephew's tousled, sleepy head and sat down next to him. "I know what it's like. I had to share with *my* sister in that very same room every day for years…until your uncle Bruce moved to the basement."

"You shared a room with *Mom*?"

"Yup, you got it!" Lillie said. "Only I was the little one and she always complained about *me*."

"You couldn't have been as bad as Sassy!"

Lillie laughed. "You've got a point there." She reached out and patted his hand. "How about some breakfast?"

"Got any Cocoa Puffs?"

"Are you kidding?" She scuffed his head with the heel of her hand.

He grinned and pushed back in his chair. "Okay. Cheerios, then."

Lillie watched as Ben shuffled down the hall toward the stairs. She felt the urge to lay her own head on the table, but instead started breakfast for the children, grateful for the distraction. She was excited, but also nervous—even a little giddy—at the idea of a whole day free to explore her mother's life.

3

Once fortified for the day, the kids threw on their clothes while Martin drove his pick-up truck from the barn to the house. As they pulled away, Sassy yelling good-byes all the way down the lane, Lillie sank to the porch steps. Though the locust drone made her sleepy, the diary, still tucked under the cushion, beckoned to her. She had put it off long enough.

❧

June 12, 1985

I need to go see Abigail. She wants me to write down what happened. Supposedly it helps you get better if you tell your story to someone and since I can't tell this story to anyone ever, I guess I'll have to tell my diary.

It all started two summers ago when I was helping with the Summer Bible Series at church. I loved teaching the kids, and Pastor Lane needed help. He told me I was a good teacher and my knowledge of the Bible exemplary.

At first it was great. I enjoyed finding ways of making the Bible understandable to the little ones. I found they loved it when I told Bible stories, acting them out. Pastor Lane would listen and watch too. He often smiled at me and at the children listening so intently.

After the children went home, Pastor Lane would help me clean up the craft supplies. He gave me tips on how to share the Bible so the children would learn how not to sin and how to behave like good Christians. I remember feeling so blessed to have these personal tutorials.

There were days when Pastor Lane would teach the children and I watched and listened. He made the precepts and promises of the Bible come to life. I remember feeling very secure in my salvation and looking forward to going to Heaven back then...

I felt totally safe around Pastor Lane. He was my shepherd, my guide and mentor.

Oh God! Abigail, I can't do this!

June 15, 1985

I went to see Abigail today. She says I have made a good start in writing my story. She promised again that it will help. But I don't think there can be any help for one such as me!

June 20, 1985

Today is a good day. I hate to ruin it, but I think I must write today.

I'll never forget the day that Pastor Lane hugged me. I felt his support and affection as a teacher. I remember feeling that he was like Jesus must have been, with a deep *affection for a beloved disciple. It filled me with joy and pride.*

Joshua Crumley, one of the boys in my class, often hung around after. I'm not sure why exactly, but I think I was like a second mom to him. So I took Joshua under my wing and he became my little helper.

June 29, 1985

It's been over a week and I haven't been able to write anymore. I need to see Abigail again.

I can't stand it here! Marty and Lillie hate me, I know it! And Violet and Bruce seem too busy to pay me any mind. I guess I'm grateful for that. I'd rather not be noticed at all than feel those accusing eyes!

Lillie lay the diary in her lap, remembering. She had attended the Summer Bible Series at Hopeston Church that summer and could still picture the one large basement room where they'd always held the lessons. In the heat of summer, it was nice and cool there.

Her father had never accompanied the two of them to church—he'd always said he was too busy with chores. Now, Lillie thought he probably couldn't stand the hellfire and brimstone style and had chosen to stay away.

She wondered what it was that had changed her mother's feelings about God. Having had doubts herself in recent years, Lillie found she longed for the blind faith of her childhood, and thought perhaps her mother had, too. But she was confused. Now there was this part about Joshua Crumley. She remembered him well—they had gone through school together. What did that little pest, who'd always wanted attention, have to do with anything? Whatever it was her mother was referring to, Lillie felt no pity for Joshua. He had been mean to her after she'd quit going to church—he'd even called her awful names at school. She had never understood the abruptness with which his attitude had changed. Had that all happened at the same time?

The bit about her father hating her mother confused her too. She was fairly sure he hadn't felt that way. She certainly hadn't. She recognized a new feeling that had begun to grow in her, a connection with her father that had not existed before. Whatever this was, they were clearly in it together.

She put the diary face down on the wicker table next to her chair and went into the house, letting the screen door slam behind her. She refilled her glass, drank the lemonade down, and stood looking out the kitchen window. Hungry, she opened a loaf of bread and made herself a peanut butter sandwich.

When she had finished eating, she made her way back to the porch and sat down once again in the wicker chair. A solitary crow flew soundlessly overhead and landed in the top of the tallest tree, a silent observer silhouetted against the sky. She picked up the diary and began to read again.

❧

July 5, 1985

Seeing Abigail was as good as always, and I think I can write some more, so here we go.

One day, after the children had gone outside to play and Joshua was helping me clean up, Pastor Lane called me into his office. I told Joshua I would be right back.

Pastor Lane asked me to sit down. He explained that, as teachers of the faith, we had to live lives of perfect example and I had a few things to learn in order to reach perfection.

He told me in a very kind voice that he didn't believe I was being very attentive to my husband as a good Christian wife should be. He said I needed lessons in how to be more attentive and, as my spiritual guide, it was his duty to teach me. I remember feeling I had let him down, how disappointed he must have been. It upset me to disappoint him.

I told Pastor Lane I would work on my responses to my husband. But he insisted I learn to initiate, not just respond. He said he would start by showing me how to kiss. I remember thinking it a little strange, but I agreed.

When he kissed me on the mouth. I was shocked and surprised—it felt good, and I was confused. But I was grateful for his willingness to teach me. He explained then that I should go home and start kissing my husband. I agreed.

As I left the office, I noticed Joshua was close to the open office door. It occurs to me now that he might have been listening.

July 7, 1985

I surely hope Abigail is right—that it will eventually help me feel better by writing this evil story down. Probably all it will do is send me deeper into Hell. But she insists it will help the pain and fear begin to go away if I get it out onto paper.

After that first day when Pastor Lane kissed me, he and I had regular "lessons in affection," as he called them. He *introduced new kinds of kissing, and new kinds of hugs. The whole time he explained carefully what he was doing and how this would help the man in a marriage. He explained that I needed to know what my husband needed and had the right to expect from me.*

I remember now that Pastor Lane always very kindly reinforced that I would be sinning and in danger of eternal damnation if I didn't learn to give what my husband expected from me in our marriage bed.

He also told me not to tell anyone that we were having these lessons. He explained it would be arrogant for him to get credit for being my teacher and that one should learn to be humble. He said I would be helping him be a humble, godly man by not telling anyone, especially my husband. It's all pretty incredible now that I believed him.

And then one day he said I needed to learn how to offer my body and he unbuttoned my blouse!

The diary slid through Lillie's fingers and dropped to the floor as an old, familiar heaviness crept through her and her chest grew tight. Her mind raced. What do I do when I feel like this? She could hear her therapist's voice reassuring her and after a moment began to get her breathing under control.

She picked up the diary and started up the stairs to put it away—she'd had enough for the moment. As if on cue, her father's truck came rolling down the driveway, and Sassy's high pitched greeting pierced the air.

Feeling suddenly faint, Lillie reached out and held onto the hall desk for support, breathing deeply again until she regained her composure. The sound of footsteps hit the porch, and Sassy came bounding through the screened door and down the hall. "Aunt Lillie, where are you? AUNT LILLIE!!"

"I'm here, Sas, upstairs." Lillie quickly stashed the diary away in the desk drawer and turned just in time for her niece to leap into her arms. She hugged the little girl, a little bit harder than she meant to, and Sassy pushed away and wriggled to the floor.

"You're hurting me, Aunt Lillie!"

"Sorry, Sas. I'm just glad to see you." Oblivious, Sassy had already turned on her heels, and grabbing Lillie's hand, proceeded to drag her down the stairs. Glad once again for the distraction, Lillie's thoughts flashed to the diary again. There would be another day.

Don't worry, Mother, she thought. I'll be back.

Lillie joined her niece and nephew in a game of catch in the back yard with the new baseball and bat their grandfather had bought them in town. Between plays, she received excited bursts of information from Sassy about the day's adventures.

After an hour had passed, the heat became unbearable and Lillie offered to make them all lemonade. Once she had called the kids in and given them their drinks, she headed back to the porch, hoping to find her father there, and she was not disappointed.

Martin sat on the steps smoking his pipe, a habit Lillie now knew he saved for times when he needed to think. He turned slightly as she came through the screen door and greeted her with a grunt, which she took as an invitation to join him. They sat quietly side-by-side for a long while, until Lillie broke the silence. "Dad, have you read *all* Mother's diaries?"

"Yes," he said simply.

"After she died?"

"A few months ago."

"What made you do it?"

Martin tamped his pipe. "I could never figure out why she suddenly abandoned her church, her faith, even herself. I guess I just needed to know."

He glanced over at Lillie. "Plus, I thought I was losing you again. I was searching for clues to help you."

"Is that why you wanted me to read it?"

"Well, Abigail seemed to think writing the truth would help your mother. I thought knowing the truth might help *you*."

In all her life, Lillie had never seen her father look so vulnerable. She reached out and touched his knee.

"It's hard to read," she said, after a long pause.

"Yes, it is."

The peacefulness of their moment together was short-lived, however, as a shriek was heard from the kitchen. Sassy burst through the screen door onto the porch and reflexively, both her aunt and grandfather readied for her to fling herself at them. Instead, she stopped dead in her tracks and stared. "What are you doing?" Before either could answer, she frowned.

"You look sad!"

Lillie and her father exchanged a secret look. Martin smiled and reached out for his granddaughter. "We've been talking grown-up stuff, little missy. That's all."

They all laughed when Sassy jumped into his arms and his tickles were met with screeches and giggles.

Ben, who seemed always a step behind his sister, peered through the door. "What's so funny?"

Lillie put her arms out for her nephew and took him onto her lap. She leaned forward and whispered softly into his ear.

"It's just Sassy thinking she knows everything."

4

The next morning, Lillie woke to the sun pouring through her sheer bedroom curtains. She lay still for a while, looking around the room, soaking in the comfort of her childhood bed. The scents of pine, fresh air-dried cotton sheets and sun-warmed wood wafted through the room, reminding her of days past.

Then an image of her mother's diary popped into her mind and a flutter of nervousness entered her stomach. Closing her eyes to ward it off, she fell back asleep and dozed until Sassy and her brother burst in the door.

Ben climbed onto the bed and curled up by Lillie's feet while Sassy shook her by the shoulder. The little girl screamed with excitement, bouncing on her toes at the edge of the bed. "Mommy and Daddy are coming back today!"

"Yes, Sas!" Lillie said, cringing, "they are." She pictured her sister, all about order and schedule and rules. She knew she often got into arguments with Sassy, but in spite of her controlling tendencies, she knew too that Violet was a kind woman and a good mother.

On the other hand, her brother-in-law, Kevin, was a large gentle man who exuded warmth. She had decided that Ben had come by his personality honestly—his father always had something helpful to say when he deemed it necessary. Otherwise he was quiet.

Raising up on one elbow, Lillie turned her niece toward the door and gave her a nudge. "Go see if Grandpa's got breakfast ready."

Sassy was off and running in a flash, so Lillie called after her. "Yell up if he does, okay?"

A muffled noise was heard from the end of the bed. Lillie jostled the lump with her feet.

"Are *you* ready for Mom and Dad to come back?"

"Yeah," answered Ben. "I want to show them the ball and bat Grandpa got us." He climbed down from the bed and wandered out of the room, still asleep.

Lillie lay in the bed for a moment longer, collecting herself, then rose, dressed in a fresh cotton dress and went downstairs. As she entered the kitchen, she was greeted by a big grin from Sassy, now perched on the kitchen stool—she was helping her grandfather. As he poured pancake batter on the griddle, it was her job to drop fresh blueberries in the puddle. Lillie grinned back—Sassy's blue face and hands and Grandpa's big smile were quite a sight.

Recalling the "tea party" with her father, Lillie headed for the cupboard and one of her mother's cups. As she reached for it, tears came unbidden—Melodie had been just like her teacups—delicate and beautiful.

At about that time, Ben came into the kitchen, carrying the ball and bat. Sassy started to climb down from her stool, a protest forming on her face.

"Not so fast, young lady," said Martin. "The assistant cook has to make sure the pancakes come out just right." Pouting, Sassy reluctantly returned to her job. Lillie gave Ben a pointed look and he retreated into the hall to stash the toys safely out of sight. When he returned, pancakes and syrup awaited him on the table, and everyone present dug in.

As usual, Sassy was the first to finish eating, and when excused, flew outside like a dog chasing something in the bushes. The three still at the table burst out laughing. At the sound, Sassy reappeared, her hands and nose pressing flat against the screen. "What's so funny?" she demanded.

As if designed to interrupt the little girl's frustration, a crunch of tires on the gravel driveway signaled the arrival of her parents. In a flash, Sassy disappeared once again, and then returned, hauling her father behind.

Kevin looked at the trio at the table, still wiping their eyes, and smiled knowingly. "Our little lightning bug entertaining us again, is she?" he said, and the laughter started all over again.

Lillie's sister pushed past her husband into the kitchen, and just as quickly, the joyful moment was gone. Violet looked at the group, shook her head, and charged into the hall with a suitcase in each hand, barking orders all the while. "Ben, help me unload the car! Sassy, get the dogs out of the back seat!"

They had never been close, but it seemed to Lillie that Violet had become even more severe since their mother's death. Her sister had refused to go to church with them during those early years, which had troubled their mother, but curiously, not long after her death, the Parks had started attending services at a large Presbyterian church in the city, one which bore no similarity to the small country church with the kind pastor Lillie had attended with her mother as a young girl. Well, she mused, I *thought* he was kind.

Jarred once again by a reminder of the diary, Lillie pushed back her chair and stood up. Her sudden movements escaped neither Ben, Kevin nor her father, but none of them said anything. She turned and stood at the sink, looking out the window and focusing on the concreteness of the sunlit barn to steady herself. Within a matter of minutes, life had changed dramatically at the Farmer homestead.

The next few days were a blur of activity—baseball games in the backyard, arguments, family meals, trips into town in the back of Grandpa's pick-up truck, raucous baths. The dogs were constantly underfoot and Sassy was always whining. There were no opportunities for Lillie to pick up the diary again, though she was as aware of it in the desk drawer as if she carried it in her hip pocket.

At sunset one evening, in search of a quiet moment, Lillie found Violet alone on the porch and sat down in the wicker chair next to her. A long silence ensued with the vibration of locusts as a backdrop before Violet acknowledged her. "Kids okay while we were gone?"

"Yup!"

"Good. I appreciate your taking care of them—Kevin and I haven't had a get-away in a long time!"

Lillie almost did a double-take in response. It was the first "thank you" she could remember receiving from her older sister, and it startled her—their mother's death, it seemed, was softening them all and bringing them closer.

Bruce, their brother, had always been gentler and more approachable to Lillie than Violet had been, but since their mother's death, he had been scarce. Lillie wondered when the three of them would be back together again. Her thoughts drifted to Abigail. She wondered if the woman was still around. Then she thought of Joshua Crumley.

Violet interrupted her thoughts. "So, what have you been up to, Lil?"

"Well…we played baseball…had Sassafras pancakes."

"No baths or proper bed times, I take it."

Lillie shook her head. "I guess not. But we had fun!"

The glint of tears appeared in Violet's eyes. "You know, I used to sit out here with Mom on summer nights—just like this—and watch the sun disappear with her before I went to bed."

"I don't remember her ever doing that with me."

Violet wiped her cheeks with the back of her hand. "I guess it was the one thing she reserved for me."

Lillie reached over and touched Violet's shoulder, and the tears fell in earnest. "I miss her, Lil," she said finally.

"Yeah," said Lillie, nodding softly, "so do I."

5

Two days later, in the cool of morning, Lillie and her father stood, waving goodbye to Violet and her family. Sassy's arms and glistening curls flailed chaotically out the window; Ben was already deep into a book.

Lillie smiled even as tears trickled down her cheeks—she would miss the kids. She went to her father, gently touching his shoulder, and he covered her hand with his large rough one until they saw the car disappear around the bend. Almost a week had passed since Lillie'd last read her mother's painful writing.

Before ascending the stairs, she made herself a fresh cup of tea. When she reached the hall desk she opened the drawer, lifted the diary from its hiding place and held it to her nose. The smell of old leather, ink and roses, coupled with the feel of the teacup in her hands, roused a mixture of emotions.

Now carrying both of these precious remnants of her mother, Lillie headed for the porch and settled in to read once more.

❧

July 9, 1985

Okay, Abigail, here I go.

I was vaguely aware that Joshua was always near when Pastor Lane and I had our "lessons." I thought of him almost as part of the classroom—it was not unusual for him to be there. I was struck by his growing devotion for me. When Pastor Lane would call me into his office Joshua would look at me with sad, pleading eyes.

I tried hard to apply what Pastor Lane was "teaching" me in my relationship with Marty. It wasn't the same.

When Pastor Lane touched me and kissed me, I felt such happiness! I had never felt that way with Marty.

I wondered what was wrong with me that I couldn't apply what the pastor took such pains to teach. He was always so kind and gentle. I felt safe. I felt joy and I actually felt I was being a good Christian woman to try to learn how to please my husband.

Then one day Pastor Lane called me into his office as usual. I was ready—I loved the personal attention and the blessings from God that I experienced. Pastor Lane had explained that feeling pleasure was a gift from God to be shared between a man and a woman.

Before I headed to his office Joshua gave me his forlorn look, and whispered, "Don't go!" I told him I wouldn't be long, that I would help him clean up when we were done. He shook his head violently, but I left him standing there. Now, that young boy was so aware. How could I just ignore him like that?

In the pastor's study, with the door slightly open, Pastor Lane kissed me. He touched me and caressed me, and my body was tingling all over. I felt he was Jesus and I was his beloved disciple.

He lifted my skirt and put his hand down below. Just then the door opened and there stood Joshua, yelling, "Stop!"

What happened next I will never forget. Pastor Lane quickly pulled away and walked over to Joshua leaving me standing embarrassed, trying to straighten my clothing. I heard him say: "Oh Joshua I'm glad you've joined us."

And then he locked the door behind him.

He said he was just teaching me how to be a good Christian woman, and Joshua yelled at him, "No you weren't! What you're doing is wrong!"

Then I saw a look come into Pastor Lane's eyes that I had never seen before. The kindness was replaced by a look I can't even describe. He grabbed Joshua by the back of the neck, pinching so hard it made him squeal.

And he said, "Oh, but she is an evil, sinful woman and she has tried to take advantage of my kindness."

My head started spinning. I couldn't believe what he was saying. My kind, gentle teacher had changed. His face looked angry. Then he said something about teaching me a lesson. In one stride, he came back to me, grabbed my hair and pushed me to the floor. My blouse was still unbuttoned. I lay frozen with fear. Then he was pulling Joshua to him where I could see.

I can't even write about what happened then.

Pastor Lane pinned my arms above my head and held my wrists so tight they hurt. He yelled at me to shut up, calling me awful names, and I was afraid to fight. Then the pastor had his way with me.

The whole time Joshua huddled nearby crying and sniffling and with that evil look back in his eye, the pastor said awful things, calling me more awful names. He said: "You're going to hell for this, for not paying enough attention to my teachings. This is what you get."

When he was done with me he used my blouse to clean himself. I lay there crying and shaking. He looked at me and then at Joshua, who by now was crying uncontrollably, and said: "If either of you even think of telling anyone about this, you'd better think again. Who would believe your word over mine?"

Then he unlocked the door and left. Just like that. I'll always remember how softly he closed the door behind him. I lay there stunned, feeling very alone and too scared to move. Then I heard Joshua's sobs.

I sat up and covered myself. I told him I would take him home. There was nothing else to say. I offered him a tissue from the pastor's desk and we both tried to clean up our faces. Then we went to my car and I drove him home in silence.

Later, I realized we had left the craft supplies all over the room. We exchanged a look, which still breaks my heart, when he got out at his house. I drove home, went straight upstairs, and locked myself in my room. Although I took a bath, I have not felt clean since that day.

Lillie lurched to the railing, and retched until her stomach had no more to give. Wiping her mouth on her arm, she returned to the chair, numb, and after another moment, forced herself to finish the passage.

That was the last time I saw Joshua and the last time I went to the church. I hated God for letting it happen to me, to us, Joshua and me. Joshua had figured out what Pastor Lane was up to and tried to stop him. That kindness stays with me to this day.

All I've heard about Joshua since then has been from Lillie. She tells me he is mean to her and calls her names at school.

I pulled away from all my church friends. No one understood. But I couldn't be around any of them anymore. They believed in a God and a pastor that I hated and I couldn't discuss it with them.

I haven't been intimate with Marty since. He has been kind to me and sometimes angry. I know he wonders why, but I've never mentioned what happened that day to him. I couldn't.

I think Lillie has suffered the most. I pulled away from her too. I didn't know how to teach her about boys and love and intimate relations. She and I had shared our churchgoing as a special bond and I couldn't tell her anything. I couldn't even talk about religion or God or faith in general. I did her a huge disservice by teaching her to trust Pastor Lane.

I know Lillie feels forgotten, but there is nothing I can do about it. Everything I had believed about my life was a lie.

Lowering the diary slowly to her lap, Lillie stared into space. She yearned for her mother, to talk to her, to reassure her. "Mother, I'm fine!" she cried. "It's not your fault that you couldn't be there."

Feeling the depth of her sorrow reach into the bowels of the earth, she began to weep again. As she sat back, wiping the tears away, a movement caught her eye. A mouse stood on the top porch step looking at her, nose and whiskers twitching. Aware of the smell of pine on the breeze, she felt strangely calm.

After a moment, the mouse quietly scurried away, and Lillie rose woodenly, made her way to the desk upstairs, and tucked the diary away.

6

artin had watched from the barn as Lillie made a beeline for the house. He thought he understood his daughter's compulsion to read the diary but he was also concerned. Not finding her in the kitchen when he stepped inside the house, he quietly climbed the stairs and stood watching the rise and fall of his daughter's breathing from the doorway of her bedroom.

Though he had grieved for himself after Melodie died, he had worried desperately about Lillie. She had dipped into profound depression again, but thankfully, she had stuck it out with her psychiatrist and pulled through.

The decision to share the diary with her had been a difficult one because of his fear that she would sink into depression again, so he had sought advice from Abigail. Melodie's counselor had supported his instinct to give Lillie the diary. The new information about her mother's trauma, she had said, would be painful for Lillie to process at first, but it would answer important questions about her own life. So, based on the strength of Abigail's support, Martin had invited Lillie home for a week. But he hadn't been able to give her the diary directly. Instead, he had placed it where she would find it.

Now he stood silently watching his daughter sleep, curled up in a fetal position on her bed, dried tear streaks on her face. He tiptoed into the room, tenderly moved a strand of hair from her face, and spoke a silent prayer before leaving her to rest.

Lillie awoke to the slant of afternoon sunlight shining across the floorboards and a cool breeze blowing gently through her bedroom window. Grateful the day had proven to be less humid than the one before, she felt more peaceful and rested than she had at any time during the week.

Then, she was jerked into full awareness, recalling the diary and what it had revealed. Instantly, all she could think about was her mother lying on the pastor's floor, and fresh and angry tears returned to her eyes.

Lillie had loved her pastor—had implicitly trusted him and his pastoral wisdom. At first, she had missed going to church and being with everyone she knew there. But now she was glad she hadn't continued to trust this minister who had raped her mother.

Though it was warm outside, she shivered when she rose from the bed. She wrapped herself in the bedspread like a winter robe and padded into the hall. She looked at the desk and, for a moment, wished she had never found the diary. But the feeling soon passed.

Descending the stairs to the kitchen, she found her father once again making tea, and sat down at the table, her wrap pulled close. Lillie watched him in silence—though glad for his company, she felt no compulsion to talk. It would be he who spoke first.

"How you doing, Lil?"

"I don't know," she said, looking down. Tears threatened again. "I just read about...the rape." She choked on a sob.

Uncertain what to do, he pushed a cup carefully toward her and waited. Hunched over it, she felt the warmth of the tea rise to her face, and the calm steadiness of her father's presence. She looked up to find him quietly crying and touched his hand. He clasped her hand in his.

"Anything you want to ask me?"

Lillie nodded. "Have you met Abigail?"

"Yes," he said. "She's the one who encouraged me to have you read the diary."

"You told her about *me*?"

He was apologetic but determined. "Yes, Lillie. I had to. I didn't know what to do. You had such a hard time with your mother's death, and after I read the diaries, I thought they might help you."

"So you asked Abigail what to do?"

"I needed to know if giving you the diary was the right thing to do—for you, I mean. I didn't want to...to cause you to..."

"...go off the deep end!?"

"You could put it that way."

A long silence ensued. Lillie finally spoke. "What's she like?"

Martin smiled. "A bit odd, but wise. I like her."

"Did you talk to my psychiatrist about this?"

He smiled ruefully. "Yeah. He wasn't sure it was a smart thing to do, but I needed more than that. I figured Abigail was right." He paused. "But it was *my* idea, Lillie, and ultimately my choice. Did I do wrong?"

Fingering her teacup, she responded softly. "No, Dad, you didn't do wrong."

He sighed audibly, as if he had been holding his breath for a lifetime.

Lillie looked back up at her father. "Did you ever hate Mother after she changed, after it happened?"

Martin weighed his response carefully. "I know she *thought* I did. But, no, I didn't hate her. I was hurt, sometimes angry and…honestly…quite lonely, but never did I hate her. I could never have hated your mother. I missed her, mostly." He looked down, struggling to say the right words.

A chill came over Lillie, as though clouds had passed over the sun, and she pulled the bedspread up around her shoulders. She couldn't handle her father's pain in addition to her own. She got up from the table, and started to leave the kitchen.

Martin cleared his throat. "If you need to get away for a while, I'll be right here when you get back."

"Thanks."

Numb, she climbed the stairs to her bedroom and sat on the bed staring out the window for a long time. Finally she roused herself, and got dressed. As an afterthought, she grabbed a five-dollar bill she'd left on the dresser and stuffed it into her pocket.

Then running from the room and out by way of the front porch, she disappeared into the woods.

7

Having grown up playing long hours in the woods, Lillie had learned to know and love them. Throughout her childhood, she had encountered many forest animals and they had taught her much.

She walked at a determined pace with no destination in mind—it just felt good to her to walk hard. Following a path she knew well enough to walk blindfolded, she was comforted by the familiar sounds of small animals rustling in the undergrowth and the gentle breeze in the trees overhead. As she walked, the sun shone through the canopy of leaves and cast its golden light on the path.

After she'd walked for a while, she came upon one of her favorite clearings, and sat down on a stump, bathed in the dappled light of the deep woods around her. Pulling fresh air deeply into her lungs, she listened and watched, seeking to open her sore heart.

As if summoned, a white-tailed deer came into view some fifty yards away. The doe stared at Lillie and stomped her hoof. For a number of minutes, the dance continued—the doe inching closer and Lillie, sitting completely still, watching through the trees. Then, as suddenly as she had come, the doe turned and bounded off into the woods, white tail flashing.

Lillie was touched by the holiness of the moment and felt the sting of tears in her eyes. Glad she had come to this sacred place, she rose and headed toward home, more slowly this time.

Thoughts of her mother drifted through her mind and she let herself feel how desperately she missed her. She wished she could talk with her mother about what had happened and how both their lives had turned out. The mental image of the day her mother had gone away passed across her mind. Eventually, her thoughts turned to the boy, Joshua.

Though she thought she now understood what had been the cause of his cruel attention back in high school, she felt nauseous as she visualized what might have happened the day her mother had been assaulted. She daydreamed about what it would be like to see Joshua now, to talk to him, to know what he knew—and she thought of Pastor Lane, who had been so kind to her and the other children. Fury began to rise in her like a raging fire.

Why hadn't *any* of them seen his evil side? Why hadn't *they* realized how cunning and two-faced he was? Then it struck her, like a swift kick.

Perhaps one of them had.

Lillie had always thought Joshua Crumley a somewhat awkward boy and had never sought him out to play even though he had seemed rather attached to her mother. Guilt filled her now for that transgression. In school, they hadn't interacted because their interests kept them in separate circles. It hadn't been until after her mother left the church that Joshua had paid attention to her at all.

Her mind drifted and she wondered what it had been like for him after it had happened. She surmised that he would never be able to forget what the pastor had done—that to Joshua, she had been, and would always be, a reminder of her mother and a source of pain.

The opening in the canopy overhead woke her to her surroundings, and she was disoriented—all her attention focused inward, she had inadvertently taken the path to the road that led into town. She was further from home than she had been at the clearing.

On impulse, she turned toward Hopeston. It was not long before she approached the center of the town, where there stood an ancient grocery store, a café that had been there since World War II, an equally old and tiny post office, two shops—one that sold clothing, the other souvenirs—and around the bend, across the river, the church. She dug her hands in her pockets and discovered the five-dollar bill she had grabbed from her dresser. Thirsty, she headed toward the grocery store.

As she came through the automatic doors, she was greeted by the warm, booming voice of its owner, Bill Hadley. "Well, Lillie Farmer! How are you? Sure has been a long time since we saw you in these parts!" He grinned, his crooked teeth showing beneath a bushy mustache.

She felt both embarrassed and glad to be remembered and mumbled something back to him in greeting.

"So what are you looking for today?" he asked.

33

Though she knew Mr. Hadley meant groceries, it struck Lillie that she was actually looking for something—some*one*—else. "I'm looking for Joshua Crumley," she blurted, surprised at her own admission.

Bill contemplated for a moment, as if examining an apple before putting it on the shelf. "I haven't seen him myself, but I've heard he's in town."

Lillie flushed, suddenly regretting having been so impulsive. If she found Joshua, what was she planning on doing?

She felt Bill's eyes on her. Not wanting to give away any more information, she quickly changed the subject. "Have any bottled water?"

Bill pointed his gaze down aisle three, motioning with his brow and giving her a big grin.

As she grabbed a bottle of water from the shelf, determination settled in— she had taken on a mission, a quest to complete unfinished business.

8

The old farmer whose property adjoined her father's ambled into the store, and once Lillie had paid for her water, she hitched a ride home with him. He dropped her off at the road and she walked down the driveway. Her father was sitting on the front porch, smoking his pipe.

"You hungry, Lil?" he asked, getting to his feet. She nodded and followed him into the kitchen. While Martin made dinner for the two of them, Lillie sat at the table watching the sky out the window. She told him about her walk, about the clearing and the doe, about how being in nature had soothed and comforted her. She told him about her accidental foray into town but she did not tell him she had asked about Joshua.

They ate quietly and ravenously, as neither had eaten anything of substance all day. While they sipped their tea at the end of the meal, Lillie sensed a change in her father's mood. An old feeling of dread filled her as it had when she had been a girl awaiting the guillotine to drop.

Martin wiped his mouth with the back of his hand. "Your brother called." He paused. "You know, he hasn't been home since your mother died."

Lillie's head snapped up. "Bruce's coming home?"

"Yup. He'll be here the day after tomorrow," he continued. "He plans to spend the night. He said he thought he'd stop by on his way through."

Lillie and her father smiled conspiratorially. They both knew he wasn't going *through* to anywhere.

After dinner, Lillie took her tea to the porch. It now made her feel close to her mother and, surprisingly, to her sister. Dusk was especially beautiful in the summer—the fragrance of flowers perfuming the warm air, the cicadas singing in the fading light seemed to lift a weight from her heart.

With renewed joy, she went to bed. Her brother was coming home and she was on a mission. For the first time in days, she drifted peacefully into a deep sleep and began to dream.

The doe met her in the clearing in the woods and beckoned her to follow. They wound their way for hours along narrow paths until they came to another large clearing. A bright fire burned at its center and there were many ghostly beings gathered around it. She couldn't make out who the people were but they seemed strangely familiar—she wanted to join them but something held her back.

Lillie sat up. Unable to return to sleep after the dream, she lay awake until just before the break of day and then made her way silently down to the kitchen. Since her father's reintroduction of them to her, she always used her mother's teacups as a matter of sacred ritual—they made her feel connected to both of her parents now.

In bare feet and loose cotton nightgown, she wandered out onto the porch into the darkness and mist of the morning. The cold dampness hit her face and arms, and goose flesh rose on her skin. It was too early even for locusts and the sky still shone with the deep, dark blue of night.

She curled up in the wicker chair, tucking her feet beneath her. Unseeing, she took in the beauty that surrounded her. Smelling the scent of dew-filled grass and honeysuckle, she listened to the first chirpings of birds as they began to wake up. Gradually, the sky lightened, revealing a covering of clouds. It would be an overcast day.

It had been years since she'd last seen Joshua Crumley. Just after their graduation ceremony, he had walked past her too close on purpose, knocking her roughly aside and she had been furious. Now she saw it differently—without saying anything, he had made contact with her in the presence of her parents, and she realized it had been the only contact he could make with her—or her mother—without being painfully reminded of whatever had happened. She wanted to know if that had changed.

The mist floated away, replaced by warm air, and morning began to show itself. A few brave locusts and crickets began to chirp but the song sparrow of the meadow and the hermit thrush of the forest were already in full melody. Restless, and ready to start her quest, Lillie jumped up, returned her teacup to the sink and headed upstairs to dress.

Martin woke to the sound of his truck being fired up in the barn. He was now aware of Lillie's every move.

As he had adjusted to his role as the sole surviving parent to his children, his life had undergone a transformation. At first, it had been a very painful time of grieving and loneliness. But he had felt some relief for himself and for Melodie. They had become quite distant in the years before her death, and she had finally moved out of their bedroom to sleep in the room that had once been Violet's.

Intimacy gone from their marriage, all they'd had left were the everyday chores, household decisions, meals and discussions of the weather. His efforts to get his wife to talk to him or go for counseling had failed and she had retreated even further into herself. He had finally come to accept things as they were, and had found that there was more interaction between them, albeit somewhat meaningless, if he just let her be.

It had been a year and a half after Melodie's death before he had decided to read her diaries, all in an attempt to reclaim the good years they'd shared. At first, he'd felt as though he was prying into her privacy. But he had come to believe it a gift he had earned by being her faithful husband. It was helpful to read about her inner thoughts and experiences—he had cried and laughed and found his heart mending slowly.

When he'd come to the diary in which the rape had been described, he had experienced a murderous rage. For days, he had smashed dishes, thrown tools in his shop, and mowed erratic edges into his otherwise perfect lawn. He had yelled at God and cursed the church in violent protest. He had thought of tracking down the pastor and killing him and had prowled around the small church in his pick-up truck. And, distracted, he had chopped wood obsessively until his carelessness had resulted in his embedding his axe into the toe of his boot.

He had limped, axe in hand, to the porch and had sat for hours gripping it, white-knuckled across his lap, like a man holding a rifle ready to shoot. By sheer act of will, he had finally put the axe aside and gone to bed, and had lain awake for hours, turning the whole thing over and over in his mind. Finally, he had given in to sorrow and had cried tears born of his powerlessness to change the past. Somehow, in the morning, his rage had shifted in focus—though it was still alive, he knew he would not kill the man, but he would go to his grave wishing he had.

While Melodie had still been alive, he had wondered if he was to blame for what had happened between them. After all, he had never supported Melodie's churchgoing or her faith. He rejected the idea of a strict, authoritative God and had made that clear on numerous occasions. He couldn't stand the idea of any man, any minister, having the right or the authority to tell others what to believe or how to behave. And he'd been right—he could see how confining, even crippling, it had been for his wife and Lillie.

For him, a sit on the porch smoking his pipe or taking a walk in the woods or the meadow—even mowing the yard was a way of connecting deeply with his spirituality. It was at those times that he felt most content and connected with himself and with God. That was why he had chosen a place in the country to raise his family. He was delighted that his children would grow up with a chance to love the outdoors as much as he.

He had found that his original hunch had been right—it had been the church that had come between them. As far as he knew, no one from the church had reached out to her after that fateful day. No one had seemed to care that faithful, devoted Melodie Farmer had dropped away so suddenly. It confirmed for him the falseness and hypocrisy of the Christian church and its believers. He had no respect for the organized church—there was no one else to blame.

He had felt a certain victory in discovering that she had finally turned away from the church and its oppressive teachings, but the price she—and he—had paid was unbearably high. He had found himself bargaining with Melodie's God, saying he would go to her church and act like he believed it all, if only God would turn back time, and bring her back to life.

But it was, of course, not to be. After her death, he had felt closer to Melodie than he had in life, a fact that made him both deeply sad and profoundly grateful. He was grateful, too, that what he'd hoped for his daughter seemed to be coming true—now knowing the truth, Lillie appeared to find solace and peace.

9

Lillie drove into town and stopped at the café for breakfast. Betty, the owner, greeted her warmly and slid a menu along the counter, and Lillie ordered a large breakfast of scrambled eggs, hash browns, bacon and raisin toast.

When she was done eating, she walked to the post office, not knowing exactly what she was doing but following her nose. Audrey Powers, the pinch-nosed, beady-eyed postmistress who ran the place single-handedly, looked up as she entered. "Well, what d'ya know! Lillie Farmer! We've been hankerin' for the sight of you around here," she said.

Lillie blushed and grinned in response. Audrey asked about her job and whether she was "meeting men" in the city. Lillie blushed again, uncomfortable at Audrey's intrusion and about the whole subject in general.

After a few more minutes of socializing, Lillie asked to borrow the phone book, and turned aside for privacy while she looked up the number for the Crumley residence. After copying down the address and number on a piece of paper from her hip pocket, she returned the thin book to its owner. Thanking Audrey, who she knew had watched her out of the corner of her eye while she worked, Lillie slipped out of the post office. Once outside, she sauntered across the street to the grocery store. A phone booth stood at the back of its parking lot.

Sandwiched safely in the phone booth, Lillie hesitated for a long time before dialing, then waited in suspense while the phone rang and rang. She was about to give up when someone answered.

It was a woman's voice. "Hello?"

Lillie gulped. "Is Joshua there?"

"Not at the moment, no. Who is calling, please?"

"This is Lillie Farmer. Can you have him call me?"

There was a long pause. "Oh. Is this Lillie from high school?"

"Yes. Is this Mrs. Crumley?"

40

"Yes, this is Joshua's mother. I'll give him your message."

They hung up and Lillie realized she hadn't left her own phone number. She considered calling back but decided finally that if Joshua wanted to talk to her, he could find her number as easily as she had found his.

She chuckled nervously to herself. The cat was out of the bag—she had started something that she wasn't sure she could finish.

A knot formed in the pit of her stomach and she suddenly regretted having eaten so much. Deliberately shifting her focus, she stepped out of the phone booth and went into the grocery store to buy milk, bread, detergent and a few special things she knew her brother loved to eat, and then headed home.

Miriam Crumley wrote a note for her son and went back to her cleaning. As she vacuumed, she wondered what Lillie wanted with him—there had been some kind of trouble between them in high school, but she couldn't remember what it was about. She did recall clearly, though, that when Joshua had said anything about Lillie Farmer, it hadn't been good.

She thought about Melodie Farmer, too—she had both resented and been grateful to Lillie's mother for taking Joshua under her wing. In some ways, she'd felt displaced by her.

But, after the death of Samuel, her husband and Joshua's father, she had ceased all Jewish training and practice in their home. Since they'd been the only Jewish family in Hopeston, the church had been the only option; the closest synagogue was in the city. She herself would never have attended a Christian church, but she had wanted Joshua to have a religious foundation.

She had liked the pastor of the Hopeston church and had also trusted him to offer her son a male role model. And until Joshua had reached his teenaage years and elected not to continue attending the church, everything had seemed to go according to plan.

Though she hadn't liked Lillie because of what Joshua had said about her, Miriam saw no reason to try and block her from contacting him now. Though Melodie Farmer herself was dead, she had been kind to Joshua when he'd needed it most.

41

The shock of learning about the assault on her mother had begun to subside, and Lillie found herself still drawn to the diary—there were questions yet to be answered. After putting the groceries away, she removed the diary from its hiding place in the hall desk and lay on her bed reading.

July 12, 1985

I think Abigail was right. It does feel better to write down what happened. It's like I've let it go a little bit.

July 14, 1985

I think about Joshua a lot. I'm worried about him. As I allow myself to look back at that fateful day, with Abigail's help, I see it more clearly. Joshua tried to stop the pastor. He tried to stop me from going to the pastor, for that matter.

That boy was the only one in the world who saw what Pastor Lane was up to. He is also the only one, as far as I know, who knows what the pastor did to me that day, other than Lane himself, who carries the secret with him like I do.

Abigail suggested I consider writing Joshua a letter, that it might help both of us. She says we each need to find closure and some kind of communication between us might help. I don't know if I can. But I'll try.

July 19, 1985
I finally wrote a letter to Joshua that I've put in the
back of the diary. But I haven't been able to send it.

Lillie flipped quickly to the back of the diary. There was nothing there. She flipped again through the pages and still nothing. Frantic, she turned the diary over and shook it vigorously. A thin piece of paper, folded in half, fell to the floor.

She picked it up and hesitated for a moment, but then opened and read it. When she finished, with fresh tears in her eyes, she tucked the letter back between the pages of the diary for safekeeping, and put the book away.

10

Lillie and her father spent the rest of the afternoon doing chores in the house and around the grounds of the homestead. They both enjoyed the physical nature of the tasks—washing dishes and laundry, mowing the yard, making up Violet's room, cleaning the bathrooms, running the vacuum. After all, Bruce was coming and all would be ready.

By sundown, they were tired and ready for a break. The sky had cleared and it was much warmer than it had been when the day had begun. They sat peacefully on the porch before going in to make supper. In their silent vigil together, nature spoke to them in tones of birdsong and insect drone and the soaring grace of the turkey vulture riding the wind currents overhead. This was their meditation.

The phone rang. Lillie jerked at the sound and her stomach filled with butterflies. At the second ring, she rose and went to answer it. "Hello?" she said, her heart beating wildly in her throat.

"Lil? Is that you?" It was Violet.

Both disappointed and relieved that it wasn't Joshua on the other end of the line, Lillie realized how unsettled she was about the idea of talking to him. "Yes, Violet. How are you?"

"Fine. I just wanted to call to say hi and to thank you again. The kids had a great time with you and Dad."

"Oh, good! We all enjoyed it!"

"I hear you plan to stay longer at Dad's."

"Yes, Bruce is coming tomorrow." Lillie regretted having said it as soon as it had cleared her mouth.

"Oh," replied Violet. After a long, almost painful pause, she spoke again. "Well, tell him I said hi." She paused again. "Can I speak to Dad?"

"Yup. Just a minute," Lillie said, "he's out on the porch." Lillie laid down the phone and went to get her father. From the porch, she heard his end of the conversation, a series of two-word answers between long bouts of listening.

As the conversation continued, Lillie's mind wandered. She took in a deep breath of pungent evening air and exhaled, consciously releasing the nervous tension that had built up in her body. She was glad not to have to talk to Violet, to leave that job to her father.

Once she heard her father hang up and the sounds of him banging around in the kitchen, Lillie took in their empty glasses. Two thin steaks were marinating on the counter, ready for grilling, so Lillie busied herself making a salad. The two had just sat down to eat when the phone rang again. Lillie answered it on the second ring. "Hello?" she said, heart pounding.

"Is this Lillie?"

"Yes." Silence. Lillie took the phone into the hall to get as far out of earshot from her father as she could.

"Well, this is Joshua. You called?" There would be no beating around the bush in this conversation. He was as matter of fact as ever.

Lillie pulled courage from deep inside. "Yes, I did. Would you meet me for coffee sometime?"

A long pause ensued and then Joshua answered. "Okay…but why?"

"I don't know. I just heard you were in town and since I am too, I thought maybe we could catch up with each other." Lillie suddenly wanted to forget the whole thing. "But if you don't want to…that's okay."

"No, I'm just surprised you give a shit!"

"Where and when?" she said, ignoring his tone.

"How about Flanigan's in Broadley? Tonight. We could get a beer."

Lillie's heart pounded hard against her temples. "Yeah, I'll meet you there, at…nine?"

"Okay." Click.

Back at the table, she resumed eating without saying a word. Her father asked nothing about who had called and she was glad to divert his attention. "What did Violet want?"

Martin chewed and swallowed a bite of steak. "She wants to bring the kids back here sometime soon. She's trying to figure out how she can get Bruce to stay longer or come back for a visit when they're here too."

Though she told herself that it didn't matter what Joshua thought of how she looked, Lillie took a long time to select the clothes she would wear. After several changes, she stood before her bedroom mirror in jeans and a tight black tank top with a low scoop neck and a white tailored shirt. She pulled on high-heeled black boots and fluffed her hair one last time before putting on eyeliner and lipstick. She stood back and looked at her reflection and pronounced it good.

Lillie said goodbye to her father as she bounded off the porch and jumped into her compact car. As she drove the 25 miles to Broadley, along tree-lined roads and open meadows filled with white moths and wildflowers, she tried to imagine how the meeting with Joshua would go. She pictured him the way he had been in high school: skinny, tall, a big mop of dark brown curly hair, pimples on his face, and glasses. He had started to grow out of his awkwardness by the time they had graduated. She wondered how much he had changed since then.

The lights of Broadley came into view and she made her way along the streets until she found "Flanigan's," known as a hangout for young people from all the towns nearby. Several cars were parked in the lot, and she breathed a sigh of relief. The place would not be uncomfortably empty.

She pulled into a spot and turned off her engine. Still anxious, she reminded herself that she was an adult, and that this was not a date. She wanted to see Joshua and talk with him—and that was all.

Gathering her courage around her like a cloak, she grabbed her purse and got out of the car before she could change her mind. Making her way into the bar, she looked around.

There he was, with his back to her, at the bar, already most of the way through a beer—she would have recognized him anywhere. He was taller and broader in the shoulders. His hair was cropped short but still very curly. She approached slowly and slipped onto the barstool next to him, and he turned to look at her, acknowledging her presence. Not nearly as damning as they had been in high school, his dark eyes were cool and examining, free of glasses.

Lillie suddenly felt self-conscious—she hadn't expected him to be handsome. She turned to the waiting bartender who brought a cocktail napkin for her yet unordered drink. "I'll have a Budweiser, please."

She hung her purse on the hook below the bar. Since it did not appear that Joshua was going to say anything to her, she cleared her throat and steeled her heart. "Hi, Joshua."

He responded without looking at her. "I thought I'd be on my second beer by the time you got here."

She looked at her watch—it was five minutes past nine. Fashionably late. "Well, if you hadn't started so early, you wouldn't be grumbling now."

The old bantering was back. "Thanks for agreeing to meet with me," she added, smiling.

"No problem." He spoke without conviction, and downed the rest of his Heineken before ordering another. Lillie just watched.

"So what have you been doing with your life since we graduated?"

"Not much. Work," he said, still looking at his beer.

"What kind of work?"

"Legal. What about you? What do *you* do, Lillie?" He spat out the words.

Was there contempt in his tone? She wasn't sure, but she plowed on. "I work for an insurance company. Rather boring, really."

"I'd say." They both took a swig of their beers.

"What kind of legal work do you do?"

Joshua turned to look at her for the first time. "Why do you care?" Something flickered in his eyes for an instant and then it was gone.

"Well, are you a lawyer or a legal secretary?"

He smiled slightly, appreciating the humor. "A lawyer."

"Wow, that's cool!"

He continued. "In the prosecutor's office. I send bad people to jail."

"So…you protect people?"

Joshua considered what she'd said. "Yeah. Actually, that's what turns me on."

"I bet you're good at it."

He reached into his shirt pocket, brought out a pack of Marlboros, procured a silver lighter from his pants and proceeded to light a cigarette.

Lawyers, she thought. They all smoke. He offered her one. Though she wasn't a smoker, she took it anyway and let him light it for her, and was struck by the intimacy of the moment.

"Actually, I am," Joshua said.

Lillie squinted her eyes at him. "You're what?"

"Good at it."

She racked her brain. "Oh, yeah. At being a lawyer."

"Yeah. I hope to be prosecutor some day."

They spent the next hour talking about their work, and then they began to reminisce about their high school days.

"Why did you hate me so much back then?" asked Lillie.

The question blindsided Joshua and he attempted to cover his reaction. "I didn't hate you. I just found pleasure in tormenting you."

"Why, though, all of a sudden, in our seventh grade year?"

"Isn't that when puberty kicks in?"

"I suppose." She took another swig of her beer.

"I guess you got in my line of vision right when everything was the most confusing."

"What do you mean…got in your line of vision?"

Joshua laughed at her apparent naivete. "Boys get tunnel vision when their hormones kick in, Lillie. Kinda like a bull in heat."

"Are you saying I was like a red cape for you?"

"Something like that."

"Let me get this straight. You liked me and tormenting me was the only way you knew how to show it? That's hard to believe."

"Why?"

"Because I never once thought you liked me and I think I really did hate you for being so mean." She paused before her next comment. "I used to complain to my mother about you all the time."

He remained silent for some time before speaking. "I did kinda like you. I just wasn't sure you could ever like me back."

They talked for a few more minutes about the normal high school angst and how glad they were not to be there anymore, until Lillie looked at her watch. "I gotta go. My brother'll be here early tomorrow." She knew Bruce would probably not arrive until midday or later, but suddenly feeling tired, she needed an excuse to get going. She paid for her beer, and started for the door.

"Lillie?"

She turned to look back at him.

"Do you want to do this again?"

"Yeah, that'd be great. Call me in a few days."

On the drive home, Lillie marveled at what had transpired. Though it had been hard at first, she and Joshua Crumley, of all people, had actually reconnected in a good way and would see each other again. They had moved beyond being locked in each other's adolescent horns and had actually enjoyed one another's company.

He still seemed a bit rough around the edges but she had seen something in his eyes that made her want to be careful not to hurt him. And despite herself, she was attracted to him. Whatever transpired, she needed to be clear with herself about what she was doing and why.

11

The next day, Lillie stayed on the porch all morning and read a novel she'd brought with her. She was anxious for Bruce to arrive, but there was nothing to do but wait.

After eating a light lunch, she took a short nap, and was awakened by the sound of a car on the gravel drive. Leaping from her bed, she glanced out the window, ran down the stairs—skipping steps in her haste—and dashed out to the shiny red Corvette. She leapt into a hug as her big brother unfolded his tall body and got out. Bruce laughed out loud, his eyes shining. "Easy girl! You remind me of Sassy!"

"I'm *so* glad you're here! I can't believe it!" Lillie jumped up and down, confirming her brother's reference to her niece.

"I thought it was time to come visit the old homestead."

Bruce looked past Lillie to their father, who now stood quietly with his arms crossed, a big smile on his face. In two strides, Bruce reached Martin's side. "Hiya, Dad! Good ta see ya!"

The two men hugged each other and Lillie joined them. The three stood admiring one another for several minutes, until Martin finally gestured for his children to follow him into the house. When Bruce turned to get his duffle bag out of the car, Lillie offered help and then followed him into the house, pushing him from behind. Their father poured lemonade for the three of them and they sat down at the table to catch up on news.

Lillie related to Bruce that Violet and her family had been there earlier in the week; Martin filled in details about the kids. Bruce asked Lillie about her job and Martin about work that needed to be done around the place. Bruce answered questions about his work and life in the city. But no one said anything about Melodie. No one was ready to tackle that subject yet.

When they'd finished their lemonade, Lillie took Bruce upstairs to Violet's old room. "We thought you could stay here instead of the basement this time. I hope it's okay."

"I don't care," said Bruce. "I'm just sleepin' here." He squeezed Lillie's shoulder and plunked his bag on the floor at the end of the bed.

Though he had chosen to live in the city and claimed to prefer it to country living, when Bruce was out among trees, he was in his element. One could visibly see the city peel away from him.

The old beech tree had finally come down next to the barn during a spring storm and needed to be moved. Bruce was handy with a chainsaw and both Lillie and Martin enjoyed being with him, so the three Farmers spent the rest of the day outside. After supper, they sat on the porch in the mild evening air.

Lillie wanted to talk to Bruce about what she'd learned from their mother's diary, but felt hesitant to begin. As night fell, Martin started to yawn, and excused himself to go off to bed.

Brother and sister sat for a while in comfortable silence. Then Bruce stretched out his long legs. "Do you find it strange to be here with Mom not around?"

Lillie was surprised that Bruce had brought up the subject of their mother himself, and she was pleased. "Yes and no. She's here…in little ways. But I miss her too."

Bruce's voice cracked. "I'm still not used to it, ya know…"

Lillie nodded. "I know what you mean, but I think it's good being here. It helps me get used to her being gone."

"Yeah." Bruce's thoughts seemed a million miles away.

Lillie continued. "You know, Bruce, Dad's changed a lot."

"In what way?"

"Haven't you noticed? He's so sensitive and, I don't know, always around. Like he wants to know how you're doing or what you're thinking. He doesn't pry though. I like that."

Bruce took in what Lillie was saying, but didn't respond, and she continued. "I think Mother's death changed him. I feel like he treasures us more or something."

"That's cool."

"Bruce, he gave me one of Mother's diaries to read. I guess he thought it would answer my questions about what happened to her…the year I was in seventh grade."

"And has it?"

"Yes." Lillie stopped. How much should she tell him? "She met a woman—a healer—who helped her deal with stuff."

"Cool." Bruce said, seeming to drift off in his own thoughts again.

Lillie kept on. "After Dad read the diaries, he went to see the healer too. Abigail's her name."

Bruce sat up, frowning. "*Dad* read Mom's diaries?"

"Yeah. Before she died, she retreated into herself and I guess he needed to understand why."

Bruce shook his head and settled back in his chair. "I guess I wasn't around much then. Not enough to see how bad it was, anyway."

"Well, I, for one, felt abandoned."

Bruce loved his sister and was concerned, like Martin, about the years of her debilitating depression. She'd seemed to recover and then, with no warning, their mother had died and she had dipped her back into depression for months. A question popped into his head.

"Have *you* met this healer woman?"

"Abigail? No, but I think I'd like to."

He nodded his head. "I think you should."

The two siblings sat, lost in their own thoughts once again, as darkness deepened around them.

Tired from the day, first Bruce and then Lillie headed up to bed. Warmed by the assurance of her brother's love, she drifted into a sound sleep, and before long, began to dream.

The doe took her through the labyrinth of paths again to the fire in the clearing. As Lillie approached the same ring of people, she saw Joshua and Bruce and her father smiling at her. She tried to join them but hung back as if by choice, and they resumed their dance around the fire. She found a stump to sit on so she could watch from a distance. An older lady watched her from the shadows.

12

Martin looked up from fixing his lawn mower as Lillie approached. She smiled. "Whatcha doing, Dad?"

"Something on your mind?"

"Yeah. How did you get so good at reading me?"

A hint of a smile appeared on Martin's face and his eyes glistened.

"I guess I've learned a lot since your mother died," he said. "I'd been trying to stay out of her inner world for so long just to keep her near me. I think I wasn't able to really be present to anyone, even myself."

Lillie took this in and considered it carefully.

Martin paused, wiping his hands. "Your mother and I lost touch with each other and also with ourselves, Lillie. I've come to realize true closeness is sharing your soul with someone. You don't need to be physically present to have that kind of closeness. You can feel it even when you are hundreds of miles apart."

He took a deep breath. "You can *also* live in the same house with someone for years and never feel close if you don't open your souls to each other."

Lillie thought of Joshua, but pushed him out of her mind. Her parents had lived a shell of a life together for so long and now her father seemed to be coming back to life. His new life and wisdom seemed to have sprung out of the death of his marriage and then his wife.

"The amazing thing is that I feel closer to your mother now than I ever did," he said. "After her death and after reading her diaries."

"Me, too," Lillie said. Feeling her throat tighten, she looked at the ground and scuffed the dirt floor with her sandaled toe. "Dad, will you tell me about your visit with Abigail?"

"Well…" He stopped to think for a moment. "I called her and told her who I was. She seemed delighted to hear from me. It had been a while since she had last heard from your mother."

"Did she know she had died?"

"No, but she suspected it." He shook his head, recalling how intuitive Abigail was. "We agreed that I would come see her so we could talk. She didn't want to talk on the phone. You know, that woman listens with every bit of herself...I remember her eyes never left me."

He chuckled. "So, I went to her house and we spent the afternoon talking...and she served me tea." He smiled sheepishly at Lillie.

"So *that's* when you started being a tea freak!"

"Yeah. It's how I feel close to your mother now."

Lillie understood. She had felt it too. "Do you think I should go to see Abigail?"

"I do."

"Did you go and see her more than once?"

Martin shook his head. "I didn't feel the need to."

"I went to see Joshua, Dad."

He said nothing but a knowing smile appeared on his face.

She fiddled with the tools on his workbench. "I think I'm going to give him the letter Mother wrote to him—the one in her diary. I think it might help him."

Martin looked down at his lawn mower and spun the blade. "I hope you're right."

"Do you think I am?"

"I think you'll know if it's the right thing to do. Trust yourself, Lillie."

Martin watched as Lillie crossed the yard and went back into the house. She had grown up so much, even in the past week. He hoped she would let some wonderful man into her inner world and share a life with him sometime soon. He thought about how difficult dating had been for her—after a few painful experiences, she had thrown herself into work, and begun building a solitary life for herself. Musing, he went back to working on the lawn mower.

An hour passed and Lillie returned to the yard with her brother. Together, they worked on the outside of the house, repairing the back steps and washing windows—during which the siblings threw soap at each other.

Martin stood inside chuckling. Bruce and Lillie were capable of serious and intimate conversation and had often helped each other through rough points, and he was glad. They clearly had the rare and wonderful ability to play and tease and gallivant around.

He was sad that it was a quality their older sister did not share. She was too serious—too controlling and rule-conscious for play. He wondered what had happened to Violet that had made her turn out so differently, and then it occurred to him that between Melodie and him, he'd been the serious one. He'd rarely had time to play with his children when they were growing up. His work and sense of responsibility to provide for his family had occupied him thoroughly.

It had been their mother, in her innocent, trusting, playful way, who had taught them to enjoy life. She'd had a simple faith in the good in life and had passed that on to them. It was suddenly obvious why the drastic change in her had been so traumatic. He brought his thoughts back to the present and focused on his two children in front of him, thankful that they were adults who brought out the best in one another, adults able to show love and playfulness.

After a hearty supper, the three of them headed out to the porch for what had become a regular evening vigil, and sat quietly listening to the symphony of dusk. The air was still warm, but it had cooled from the intense heat of the day. Bruce broke the silence. "I'm leaving in the morning."

They all sat quietly for a while, and then Bruce cleared his throat. "So, Dad, Lillie said you read all Mom's diaries." A hint of accusation was apparent in his voice.

Glancing at Lillie, Martin waited a while before answering. "I have."

"So, you found out what made her tick?"

"Your mother was a fragile and beautiful flower and she was so thoroughly crushed that I wonder if it killed her in the end."

Lillie was stunned. It had not occurred to her that her mother's heart attack had been brought on by the trauma.

Bruce was confused. "What do you mean…crushed?"

Lillie looked at her father and then back at her brother. "Bruce, Mother was raped. She never truly recovered."

Bruce closed his eyes, trying to compose himself. "*What* did you say?"

Lillie repeated herself. "Mother was raped."

"What the fuck!" Bruce threw up his hands as though he had been backed against the wall at gunpoint.

Martin tried to interject something, but his son interrupted him. "Dad, who did this? *Where? How?* Tell me!"

Martin tried again. "Son, wait…"

Bruce jumped to his feet, overturning his chair. "No Dad!" he yelled. "Don't wait! TELL ME, goddamn it! I wanna know! Who raped my mother!!?"

Martin remembered his own rage as he watched his son's reaction to the news. "Calm down, son, and I'll tell you." Lillie sat frozen, fearful she had made a big mistake by bringing up the diary. She had never seen the extent of her brother's anger and it was frightening to behold.

Bruce sat down and leaned forward, his head in his hands and listened as, between them, Martin and Lillie told of the horrible details of Melodie's rape. They told of her work with the minister and his advances. They told of his entrapment and the final violation. By some unspoken agreement, they chose not to mention Joshua.

The muscles in Bruce's shoulders and back flinched as he received each new bit of information, as if he were feeling a blow.

When they were done, Martin and Lillie fell silent. The sound of Bruce's crying was audible.

Suddenly, Bruce lifted his head and wiped the tears from his face. "Where's the fucker now?!"

"Gone," was all Martin felt it was wise to say. He knew how his son felt. It had taken him months to begin to deal with it all—Bruce would need time too.

"God, Dad!" Bruce said, flinging his arms over his head, his voice cracking with emotion.

"I know, son. I know."

Bruce stared out into the meadow, his hands on his head, fingers intertwined. After a long silence, he stood up. "I gotta go, I gotta get outa here."

His father and sister stood with him. Tears ran down Lillie's face, and she wanted to hug her brother but she knew he needed space. Bruce went inside, slamming the door violently behind him. Moments later, he thumped back down the stairs with his duffle bag, and called to them from the kitchen.

"I'll talk to you guys later. Sorry. I just gotta go. I gotta go *now*."

And in a matter of seconds, he was gone, the tires of his sports car squealing and spraying gravel on his way out the lane. Martin and Lillie stood stunned in the ringing silence that followed.

13

The phone rang three times before a woman answered. Lillie hadn't realized she had expected an old, frail voice until she heard the strong, youthful quality in the voice on the phone.

"Hello," Lillie responded. "Is this Abigail?"

"Yes, this is Abigail."

"Hello. This is Lillie."

"Lillie Farmer?"

"Yes. Melodie Farmer was my mother."

"I was wondering when I might hear from thee."

It had not occurred to Lillie that Abigail would be expecting her call. "You were?"

"Thee's read thy mother's diary, hasn't thee?"

Why, of course! Abigail had encouraged Martin to let Lillie read her mother's diary.

"Yes, and I was wondering if I could come talk to you." Lillie felt hopeful and a little nervous, suddenly feeling as though she was requesting an audience with the Dalai Lama.

Abigail's voice was warm. "Yes, Lillie. I'd like that."

"Are you available in the next day or two?"

"How about tomorrow?"

Surprised, Lillie giggled. "Thank you."

"Does thee need directions or can thy father give them to thee?"

"Oh, Dad can give me directions. What time should I come?"

"Is thee an early riser, Lillie?"

"Yes, I love to get up before dawn."

"Perfect. We'll watch the sun rise together."

Lillie thought quickly. "Is there anything I should bring?"

"Thee may bring a small candle if thee wants. I'll see thee in the morning."

Lillie was stunned. She was in awe of this woman who knew about her mother's death without being told. What was she, a psychic? Did she know Bruce was in pain? Had Abigail known how much she loved to watch the sunrise?

She set about preparing a special breakfast for her and her father: poached eggs on English muffins with slices of fresh tomato and basil, drizzled with hollandaise sauce. Carefully placed slices of mango, avocado and lime adorned the plates of her mother's special china.

Earl Grey steeped in the teapot with matching sugar bowl and cream pitcher along side. Lillie felt her mother would be happy they had made contact with her friend and healer. The use of her mother's fine china was to celebrate.

She turned to set the vase of wildflowers she had dashed out to the meadow to cut in the center of the table as a finishing touch, and saw her father standing in the doorway with a sweet expression on his face.

"It's like your mother is here!" He looked at her with glistening eyes.

She grinned broadly. "I feel that way too. What *is* it about her china?"

Martin chuckled and seated himself before the feast, laid out so artfully on his usually ordinary kitchen table. A few years ago, he wouldn't have appreciated the beauty of what lay before him. But things were different now.

"Your mother is very much with us. It's more than our memory. It's her presence, her spirit. I don't know how to explain it." He looked up at Lillie with an otherworldly radiance on his face.

Lillie's hands shook as she lit the candle. She sat and gazed at her father, who had closed his eyes in prayer. When he opened them again, she smiled. "Let's eat before it's cold."

They ate in silence for a while, making only sounds of pleasure, until Lillie pushed back and laid her napkin aside. "Dad, I called Abigail. I'm going to see her tomorrow morning, before dawn."

"Wow," he responded, as he took a bite of English muffin. "You don't wait around!"

Lillie shook her head. "Not anymore. I guess I'm on a roll. Now all I need are directions."

After breakfast, Lillie went for a walk in the woods. As she followed the well-worn path of pine needles, dead leaves from winters past and velvet summer moss, she mused peacefully. Gratitude and humility spread through her. She spoke out loud to her mother.

"This is a strange thing to be thankful for, Mother, but...somehow since your death, we've all begun to live again."

Lillie settled herself on a moss cushion in the greatest cathedral of all. The mild air caressed her skin, as warm shafts of sunlight glimmered around her. She heard the chortle of a flicker deep in the woods, chickadees peeping nearby and blue jay calls slicing the silence. In awe of everything, Lillie began to think. What would she talk with Abigail about?

When Lillie returned to the house, her father told her that Joshua had called and left his number. After a long drink of water from the kitchen tap, she called him back. The phone rang twice and Joshua answered. Their conversation was short and sweet—but they arranged to meet at the bar in Broadley again the next evening.

Before their evening vigil on the porch, Lillie went to her room to ready a small backpack for her visit with Abigail. On her bed, she collected items to take: her mother's diary, a sweater, the slip of paper with her father's directions, a flashlight, a small white candle wrapped in tissue paper, a pen and paper for notes. Lillie carefully placed the items in her pack, leaving the sweater out to put on when she woke in the morning.

At this time of year, the sun rose at six, so she planned on waking at five. There would be time to dress and eat before leaving. Lillie was nervous, but excited at the prospect of seeing Abigail *and* Joshua, all on the same day. Life hadn't been so interesting and mysterious in a very long time.

14

illie looked at her watch by lamplight—it was 5:01 a.m. She discarded her nightgown and stood naked in the dim light. Goose bumps covered her flesh, so she quickly donned jeans and a T-shirt, the sweater she'd left out, and the sneakers she kept for walking on forest paths.

After brushing her hair, she took her backpack and quietly tiptoed down the stairs to the dark, empty kitchen. While the tea kettle heated, she poured herself a bowl of Cheerios and milk.

What was she getting herself into? Who *was* this healer who invited people to visit her in the darkness of morning? Lillie rinsed her dishes and left them in the sink, dismissing the thoughts. A sense of adventure ran through her veins.

As she drove, winding her way through mysterious night tunnels, she followed the directions on the slip of paper clutched in her fingers. After nearly half an hour, she turned off the blacktop onto a gravel road that led into the woods. Shortly thereafter, she came to a stop sign and turned down a dirt road that seemed to disappear into the thicket.

Soon, a hand-painted sign that read "Abigail's House – Lake Osampi" came into view in her headlights. Across the road from the sign she saw a small shed and a rusted, yellow Volkswagen Beetle parked in a crude clearing.

Lillie pulled in next to the Beetle, cut her engine and turned off the headlights. Grabbing her backpack, she emerged from her car, and stepped into the blackness of morning. She stood listening and smelling the forest odors that enveloped her: damp earth, pine, rotting leaves and a hint of water—Lake Osampi was nearby. She heard a mourning dove coo overhead and the rustle of a small creature in the forest.

Rummaging for her flashlight and casting the beam around, she found the trail her father had said would lead into the woods. Her backpack over her shoulders, she hugged herself against the morning chill. She stretched her eyelids wide to see in the dark, and gingerly followed the flashlight's beam.

Soon the trail narrowed into a well-worn path, and she found she could now see somewhat better with the flashlight off. Before long, the black silhouette of a small cabin in a clearing appeared and the lake beyond dimly reflected the first light of day.

As she approached the cabin, she heard the laughing call of a loon echo from the lake, and her heart leapt with joy at the haunting sound. Overhead, she heard the flap of huge wings and the identifying rattle cry of the great blue heron. Smiling at their welcome, she came to the cabin and paused a moment, aware of her heavy breathing.

The cabin was dark. Had she come too early? Was Abigail still sleeping? Gathering her courage, she knocked forcefully, and waited. After a few moments, she heard a faint voice call from within. Assuming it bore invitation for entry, she opened the screen door, and the hinges scolded loudly. She turned the wooden knob and opened the inner door.

Stepping inside the dark cabin, she was enveloped in warmth and the mixed aroma of wood smoke and herbs, something baking and the clean smell of soap. A voice called out to her. "Come in, Lillie. I'm on the porch."

She made her way carefully through the room to the far side of the cabin, where the flickering light of a candle beckoned through an archway. As she came through the archway, she saw the woman she assumed was Abigail. Abigail faced the lake in a chair to the left of a small table that was adorned with a long shimmering cloth and a number of objects around a candle in the center. A second chair to the right of the table was clearly intended for her.

Abigail greeted Lillie with a warm smile. "Welcome to my home." She gestured with her hand to the empty chair.

Lillie took the seat, lowering her backpack to the floor, and snuggled under the welcomed warmth of an afghan draped over the back of her chair. Once settled, she noticed another small table in front of them with hot tea and biscuits.

Closing her eyes, she took a deep breath and let out a long sigh—she was instantly at home and at peace in this place. She sat in silence for a long time, watching the dark sky and the lake, listening to the cry of the loon and the croak of bullfrogs along the near shoreline. It was an eerie sound, but music to Lillie's soul and she relaxed into it.

Out of nowhere came a high-pitched, undulating sound. A wailing that reminded Lillie of the songs Native Americans sang at powwows erupted from Abigail's throat. The song grew and faded and grew again.

Words unfamiliar to Lillie were spoken, and as she listened to their ancient sound, she watched the sun rise in front of her. First came the deep colors of purple and orange on the horizon, reflected on the glassy surface of the lake. Then peach, turquoise and lavender replaced the earlier richness as the sky lightened. Finally, the sky turned mostly light yellow as the bright orange edge of the sun itself appeared above the dark trees on the far side of the lake. More birds began to chirp and sing—a chorus of birdsong joining Abigail.

Lillie was thoroughly absorbed in the sensual beauty of the place. Drawn into the colors and their changes, her body hummed. For a while, she was so caught up in the waking up of the woods and sky and water and by the sound of song that seemed to emanate from her own soul, that she forgot where she was.

When the sun had reached its full size and pulled away from the anchor of the tree line, Abigail's song stopped abruptly, and the birds stopped their singing too. The whole forest was still, as if in awe of the huge circle of orange light that hung in the softly colored morning sky. And then, just as suddenly, all the sounds of the woods resumed.

Abigail began to pray, *"O Great Spirit, we are humbled before thy power and beauty. Thank thee for this new day full of promise and opportunity. We seek to be made whole and to follow the paths that will help us to fulfill our destinies in this earthly life. Thee has brought Lillie here to join me in my home. We ask thee for all the power and purpose of thy love to be placed upon us and for that which thee has placed within us to come alive. Thank thee. Amen."*

When she was done they sat quietly. Lillie felt a vibration through her whole body. She had been deeply touched by the sunrise ritual and the prayer. Without saying a word, Abigail leaned forward, took the tea cozy off the teapot and poured a pungent herbal brew into their cups. She placed a steaming raspberry biscuit on each saucer and handed Lillie hers before taking her own tea and biscuit. They ate and drank in a comfortable quiet for some time.

Lillie wasn't sure where to start. Millions of questions flooded her mind. She knew then she would have to come many times to visit Abigail in order to learn all she wanted to know, so she decided to start with her mother. "Abigail, how did my mother know you?"

"Melodie?" Abigail smiled warmly at Lillie and then, with a reflective, far off look in her eyes, she glanced out over the lake.

Lillie waited. She knew somehow there would be no rushing Abigail. She felt content to wait while sipping her tea.

"I came across Melodie lost in the woods one day. Over there." Abigail pointed into the woods to her left. "She was crying and scared. I brought her back here and gave her hot tea and a blanket to warm her." She went silent, reflecting.

It became evident that Abigail was done. Lillie tried to take in the details of her appearance without staring at her. She was a kind looking woman, probably in her sixties. She had shoulder length wavy dark brown hair and hazel eyes. Her face had wrinkles that spoke of character and expressiveness, and she wore a colorful cape-like dress. A large bosom supported a beaded necklace.

Lillie asked another question. "Why was she in *your* woods?"

"These woods," Abigail motioned with an affectionate sweep of the hand, "are not *my* woods, Lillie. *We* belong to the land—the land does not belong to us." Her eyes crinkled at the corners as she paused to let what she'd said sink in.

Lillie had the sense that Abigail would be imparting many nuggets of wisdom, so she quickly filed this one away.

"Thy mother had run away," said Abigail.

An involuntary grunt erupted from Lillie's throat.

Abigail continued. "She was desperate to find herself."

"So, she drove here and walked into the woods to find herself?" Lillie repeated, incredulous.

Abigail nodded in response. "She was in a great deal of emotional pain, desperate to get away from it. She had lost all sense of herself."

Lillie looked down at her teacup. "My father said that too. He feels we lost her after her rape."

Abigail looked deeply into the young woman's face. "So thee's read about that," she stated with tenderness.

"Yes. Have *you*?"

"Thy mother read it to me. She needed to tell someone."

"So, you took her in that day. Then what happened?"

"She stayed with me for a few days. I took care of her to build up her strength and then I encouraged her to return home."

After a pause, Abigail continued. "She made me promise to let her come often to see me, which she did."

Lillie sighed, looking out over the sunlit lake. She noticed a green canoe overturned on the bank just below the cabin. Looking around the porch now lit by daylight, she saw a single paddle standing in the corner. She took a bite of biscuit and washed it down with tea. "Mother wrote that you helped her."

Abigail nodded. "We had many powerful moments together."

"Did she ever talk about Joshua?"

"Yes. Often. She hadn't stopped worrying about him since that day."

Tears came to Lillie's eyes and her throat tightened. "Is *that* why she wrote the letter to him?"

"She needed to let him go and bring some closure for herself."

"Did that work? I don't think she ever sent it to him."

"I think thee's right about that, but I do think she felt some release from that particular burden."

"What about Joshua? Did he feel some release?" Lillie felt her throat constrict.

Abigail looked closely at Lillie's face. "I don't know much about Joshua. Does thee?"

She knows I've met with him, Lillie thought with a sting of self-consciousness. She nodded her head slowly. "I've seen both sorrow and coldness in his eyes. I don't think he's had closure—I suspect he's never told anyone about what happened."

Abigail pursed her lips in thought, which caused the flesh on the tip of her chin to wrinkle and rise up. She let the silence stretch out, allowing Lillie to continue when she was ready.

"Do you think I should reach out to him?"

"I think thee should follow thy heart, Lillie. This world has need of as much love as it can get. Just remember to pay attention to thy own feelings and needs. He's a very wounded young man, I suspect."

After a long pause, she went on. "It helps if thee can always be honest with thyself and with others."

Lillie smiled to herself as she watched the sun sparkle on the water before them. She's a wise one. I must remember that: Always be honest. Lillie turned and looked at Abigail, who smiled at her.

"Be careful not to take on thy mother's burden, Lillie," she said gently.

The years rolled backward in Lillie's mind. "Why couldn't she tell us what happened to her?"

A sad expression appeared on Abigail's face. "She was deeply traumatized. She was filled with fear and paralyzed by shame. She could hardly deal with it herself, let alone talk about it with others."

Lillie felt heavy pain fill her chest. "But, I needed her! She left me all alone! I never felt like I could get to her after that! I became depressed. I even wanted to kill myself!"

Abigail saw the past cloud Lillie's eyes. "Did it feel as though she abandoned thee, Lillie?"

"Yes! It did! She wasn't there for my prom! She never answered my questions about boys, and I sure could have used some help with boys. I needed my mother. It felt like she fell off the face of the earth."

"It hurts a lot to lose a mother like that," Abigail said.

Lillie nodded. "I still have dark days sometimes. Her death hit me hard." She sat in glum silence, trying to let the pain in her chest subside. "There was nothing anyone could do for her then, was there?"

"No." Abigail let the silence soothe and then went on. "She did what she could with her diary and the letter to Joshua. But it became clear one day that she could go no further."

Lillie looked out at the lake, and cradled her teacup in her hands. She was suddenly very tired.

Abigail spoke again. "Lillie, thy depression and the desire to end thy life were directly related to thy sensitivity to the traumatic events in thy life.

Now that those events are past, thee can direct thy own emotional and psychological well being in a positive direction. Thy depression need not haunt thee any longer. I know thee's done a great deal of work on this in therapy. From now on thee can be thy own healer."

Abigail took up a bundle of silvery green herbs tied with string from the small table between them and lit the blunt end in the flame of the candle. Chanting softly and using her hands to gently pull the rising smoke over her head and shoulders, she pushed it in Lillie's direction. With closed eyes, she hummed another soft, undulating, wordless song. Lillie's nostrils filled with the strong scented smoke that curled around her in the air, and felt as though she had been washed clean.

Abigail finished the song and doused the herb bundle in a handmade clay bowl filled with sand. For the first time, Lillie noticed the other objects on the table: a few beautiful stones, a large black, white and brown striped feather, a small polished bone, a shell, a string of colorful beads and a clay figurine of a woman in prayer. This must be some sort of altar, she thought.

Placing her afghan on her chair, Abigail picked up the tea tray and made her way into the cabin. She was not tall, Lillie noticed, but she had a strong presence.

Lillie rose too. "May I come see you again, Abigail?" she called out.

"Yes, my dear, anytime."

Abigail's kind voice wafted from the kitchen, where she had begun to wash the dishes. Lillie stood for a minute with her backpack over her shoulder and turned for a last look at the lake. The dancing light on its shiny, rippled surface seemed to wink at her.

Remembering the candle in her pack, she took it out and gently set it on the altar. Was it a gift or a way for Abigail to remember her? She wasn't sure.

Lillie walked quietly into the kitchen where Abigail stood wiping her hands on a dishtowel.

"May I give thee a hug?" asked the older woman.

Lillie allowed herself to be enveloped in the healer's soft arms and bosom, and rested there until Abigail released her. They smiled at one another and Lillie made her way to the door.

"I'm glad thee came, Lillie," Abigail said. "I look forward to thy next visit."

Lillie nodded in silent agreement, and then let herself out and made her way down the path through the forest to her car.

15

L illie found Joshua at the bar, already a little tipsy. Disappointed, she hoped it wouldn't destroy their time together.

They continued their discussion from before, talking about what they'd each done after high school. It was obvious that Joshua had gone to law school. Lillie had attended community college, but because of her depression, she had finally dropped out and taken a job with an insurance company in the city. They talked about what it was like to come back to Hopeston, and each of their families and the conversation drifted to Melodie.

Strengthened by her visit with Abigail, Lillie took a deep breath. "I went to see the woman my mother used to get help from before she died."

Joshua stilled, as if frozen in place. His face betrayed no emotion.

"I needed to see her myself. I have a lot of questions about my mother."

She stopped to let what she'd said sink in, remembering Abigail's words: *Be honest.*

Joshua took a long swig of beer and set the bottle down slowly. He looked at it for a long time, saying nothing. He took out a cigarette and lit it, without offering one to Lillie this time. She watched him take several long drags before he finally turned to look at her. "Did you get any answers?"

Lillie studied his eyes. They held no evidence of emotion or pain. "Yeah. But now I have more questions."

"Why are you telling me this?" he asked softly.

She was sure she caught a trace of sadness in his tone and considered her words carefully before taking the plunge. She had decided it would not be fair to Joshua to wait too long as their friendship developed without letting him know that she knew about the day her mother was raped. Yet she knew that by telling him she risked causing him even more pain. But from her own recovery, she had learned that healing comes from facing old wounds and working through them.

69

"I know what happened that day."

He was quiet, looking at his beer.

"With my mother and the pastor and you," she continued.

Joshua inhaled smoke from the last of his cigarette, blew it out and scrubbed the butt into the ashtray. He turned and looked at her. "I don't know what you're talking about."

"You *must* know, Joshua," she said.

He sipped his beer. "Why did you get me to come here?"

"I come in friendship. I came because my mother wrote you a letter," Lillie said.

Joshua turned to look at her, struggling not to reveal the panic rising in him. She waited for him to say or do something and when he didn't, she bent down to her purse and took out the envelope. She placed it gently on the bar next to his arm.

"I want you to have this. I think my mother wanted to send it to you."

When he still didn't respond, she spoke again. "I'll understand if you never want to see me again. But know that I'll be here for you."

She placed her money on the bar, gathered her things and slowly walked out of the restaurant.

Joshua left the letter on the counter, letting minutes go by before he picked it up. He looked at the envelope for a long time, feeling a roiling mix of nervousness, curiosity, and fear. Then he put it down again. Old, familiar, long forgotten emotions threatened to surface. He swallowed hard, steeled himself, and grabbed the letter, stuffing it roughly into his hip pocket and ordered another beer.

When he returned home early in the morning, quite drunk, he was too tired to do anything more than fall into bed. He slept well into the next day and awoke with a hangover.

After arriving home, exhausted, Lillie went straight to bed. She had done what she needed to do, but she was now worried about Joshua and felt sadness at the thought that she might never hear from him again. She wondered if she could leave it at that.

Trying to imagine what he must have been feeling, her heart ached for him—it would be a restless night.

Lillie looked for the doe to guide her down the path to the fire in the clearing, but the doe didn't come. She wandered aimlessly through the forest, searching. She noticed crushed flowers everywhere and wondered what had happened.

She finally caught up with the cause of the destruction—a teenage boy, Joshua with grotesque features, deliberately crushing the fragile, beautiful flowers and laughing in an evil, hideous way.

She awoke and the smell of bacon and onions cooking filled her nostrils. She could hear her father moving about in the kitchen. The clink of pots and pans strangely reassuring to her, she got up with a smile on her face. It was raining—one of those gentle rains that lasts all day—and warmth flowed into her heart. She resigned herself, with some relief, to a day indoors at home—she would bury herself in a novel.

For two days after he'd met Lillie at the bar, Joshua had been unable to bring himself to face the envelope in his pocket, but finally, he drove to a deserted scenic lookout at the top of a hill overlooking a valley. As it had rained the day before, everything was green and lush. The life bursting out before him was in stark contrast to the deadness he felt inside. The letter "burning a hole" in his hip, he lit a cigarette and stared out over the valley. He had waited for this moment for years—both wishing for it and dreading it.

He had often wanted to talk with Mrs. Farmer about what had happened to them but he had never been able to muster the courage. Convinced she hated him and wanted nothing to do with him, he still felt forever linked to her by the horror they had gone through. Hell was something we experience during life, no matter what they said in the Christian church!

Joshua had worried about Lillie's mother. He'd heard she never returned to church. He had seen her only a few more times—once across the street in town, once at the bank, and then, for the last time, at the high school when he and Lillie had graduated. He had been too afraid, in too much pain to really look at her, let alone speak to her. And then he'd heard she had died.

He'd been unable to bring himself to go to her funeral. Unable to face her family, he had tried to forget her and everything that had happened. Now, his heart ached as he recalled her gentleness and her kindness to him at church—her sweet voice came back to him and he felt ashamed.

The feelings consumed him as he sat on his car. A tsunami, they overwhelmed him, and he supposed they would either pass or kill him outright.

A breeze caressed his cheek and the shame he felt ebbed slowly away. His heart filled first with relief, and then gratitude—and then a small glimmer of hope grew like a tiny seed buried deep in the earth.

Listening to the breeze in the trees, he heard the far off call of a crow and the answering call of another. He thought of Lillie and the courage it must have taken for her to call and meet with him, to help her mother reach out to him. He pictured her in his mind and a lump rose in his throat.

After a bit, he flicked his cigarette butt onto the pavement and reached into his pocket for the letter. Gingerly opening the rumpled envelope, he pulled out the folded stationary with Mrs. Farmer's delicate writing on it. Taking a few deep breaths, he unfolded the letter and began to read.

July 10, 1985

Dear Joshua,

I hope you are well. In the past two years, I have often thought of you.

I am sorry that I never spoke to you again after that summer. It was a very painful summer for both of us and I am very sorry it happened. I have often wished we could go back to before that time and re-write our lives. But unfortunately that is not possible.

I want you to know that I do not blame you in any way for what happened that day. It was not your fault!

The biggest hurt I experienced was from the deep sense of betrayal I feel. The pastor did an evil thing and violated my trust and destroyed my faith. I know now that you tried to protect me and to stop him from...I thank you for that.

Please do not worry about me. Know that you did what you could. I have found help, and I hope you have too.

Take care of yourself, Joshua, and live a happy life.

Sincerely,
Mrs. Jarmer

By the time he was done reading, Joshua was sobbing. He had held back the pain for far too long. Now, in his heart, he made the apology to Mrs. Farmer he had always wished to. It came to him that because she was no longer alive, she could hear his apology spoken genuinely within his heart. He felt her as though she were sitting next to him.

Guilt came over him for having wished he'd never tried to stop the pastor. Mrs. Farmer had come to accept what had happened rather than fighting to pretend it hadn't. Both she and he had gone through similar stages to try and make sense of the trauma and go on with their lives. Only she had finally come to acceptance. His tears subsided and he wiped his face with his wrist.

Like a cleansing rain, it washed over him that it was possible for him as well, that there was hope for him to arrive at acceptance too. While sitting on the hood of his car, with Melodie Farmer's letter in his hands, the seed of hope began to grow within him.

He thought about Pastor Lane. He had respected and trusted, even loved him. He had felt so thoroughly betrayed in the horrific events of that day that it was as if his soul had been stolen. Anger rose within him that a man of the "cloth" could so completely destroy two people's lives. The pastor had earned trust from unsuspecting congregants and used his power to perpetrate violence.

He looked again at the letter. Mrs. Farmer had seen his attempt to stop what he had somehow understood was developing. He had spent weeks trying to drum up the courage to confront the pastor. She had been grateful to him for what he'd tried to do— however failed it had been in the end. She had seen that he was a boy of just and good motives.

How many years had he spent thinking because of what had happened that he was somehow bad, perverted? The one person in the world from whom he had needed empathy and forgiveness had given it to him from beyond the grave and a terrible weight had been lifted.

Through the letter, she had given him a blessing, a call to get on with his life, to be good to himself. He realized she was right, but he had punished himself for so long he wasn't sure how to stop.

I've allowed that bastard to keep me down by hating myself for what he did, he thought. No more, bastard! He mouthed the words. And then he bellowed them. "NO MORE, BASTARD! NO MORE!!" His voice echoed across the valley.

Slipping off the hood of his car, he stood holding the letter to his chest, breathing in the healing aroma of the rain-fed forest around him. He had the power to forgive himself and she had encouraged him to claim it. Bringing the letter to his lips, he kissed it softly. Thank you, Mrs. Farmer.

Looking over the valley for a long time, he carefully refolded the letter, returned it to its envelope and stowed it in his pocket again. Exhausted, he lay down on the seat of his car and fell into a deep sleep.

16

"I'm glad to hear your voice, Dad."

Martin sighed. Bruce hadn't called since the night they'd told him about Melodie's rape. "Same here, son."

Bruce's voice trembled. "She never told anyone?"

"No, son. She just wrote about it in her diary."

"You mean, no one knew about it 'til after she died?"

Martin cleared his throat of emotion. "I tried everything in my power to help her but she kept me out."

Bruce choked out a sob. "I'm so sorry, Dad. I didn't know what you and Lillie were going through—I wasn't around much in those days. But I knew something was different because the house went kinda flat."

Martin heard the sounds of crying. "I think you picked it up on some level...and stayed away, son. It was a very painful time for all of us."

"I'm so sorry, Dad!"

Martin felt pressure in his chest, but spoke kindly to his son. "Your mother is free of her pain and fear now."

❧

Lillie had done what she could to keep busy and to help her father around the homestead. She'd gone into town for groceries and mail and had driven to the bank in Broadley. Not quite ready to leave her father or Joshua, she had called her office in the city to let them know she was going to take an additional week of vacation.

Joshua seemed to be on her mind all the time now, just under the surface as she went about her day. She wondered if he had read the letter and, if he had, how it had affected him. She realized she had waited, expectantly, moment after moment, day after day, for his call. But three days had gone by and no call had come.

On the evening of the third day, Lillie sat on the porch reading when she heard the crunch of footsteps on the gravel drive. In the dusk of the evening, she could barely discern a solitary figure standing there. She tried to make out who it was, her heart pounding.

It was Joshua! Her heart leapt into her throat. She sat frozen in place, watching him approach, and searched his face as he came into the light of the porch. Something was different about him.

Each looked at the other for a long time without speaking. Finally, Lillie blurted out, "You're here!"

"May I come up?" he asked, with a slight incline of his head toward the porch.

This was the first time Lillie had seen Joshua standing up, and her eyes surveyed him. He was taller than she remembered, maybe six feet, and his legs were long. He wore a button-down white shirt with the top button undone and the sleeves rolled up, tucked into jeans that were worn. Bare ankles showed over his soft leather loafers. Full lips and a slightly bowed nose adorned an angular face, and the eyebrows above his dark brown eyes matched his curly, close-cut hair. "Yes, please...come." She gestured towards the chair next to hers.

Just as he started to mount the steps, Lillie's father came out the door. For a long moment, Martin and Joshua stood looking at one another, and Lillie cringed, not knowing what to expect.

"Hello, Joshua. Nice to see you...here," said Martin.

Joshua bowed his head ever so slightly in submission. "Mister Farmer, I wanted to speak with Lillie, if I may...sir."

Martin reached out and put his hand on the young man's shoulder. "Call me Martin." Glancing at Lillie, he turned back towards the door. "You two go ahead. I'll read inside." Smiling, he retreated into the house and closed the wooden door behind him.

Joshua waited until the door was closed and then moved to sit in the chair. He sighed and settled, looking out over the meadow, breathing in the balmy evening air.

Lillie was unable to take her eyes off him. She smiled slightly, touched by his effort to appear calm.

Finally Joshua cleared his throat. "Lillie, I want to thank you for the letter…" He paused and turned to look at her, and she saw something in his eyes she had not seen before. She couldn't quite put her finger on it—sadness, humility, gratitude perhaps.

"You're welcome. I thought you should have it."

"Yes," he said. "But why did you go to the trouble of giving it to me?"

"What happened to you and Mother…well, I thought it was the least I could do."

His face blanched. "How do you know what happened?" His voice sounded small.

"Joshua, my mother wrote about it in her diary and I read it, every word…" She breathed deeply before going on. "Abigail, the healer I mentioned, encouraged her to do that in order to get it out of her. Sometimes you have to tell someone what happened to you in order to get over it." Lillie knew this well from her own experience with therapy.

"I've never told anyone," he said quietly.

"I wondered if you had." They sat in silence for a while looking out over the meadow and listening to sounds in the growing darkness.

Joshua spoke so softly that Lillie could hardly hear him. "I don't think I could."

"It might help. Maybe you should go see Abigail, too. She already knows about it from my mother. It might help you to tell her."

He leaned forward and put his head in his hands. She could see the muscles in his back and shoulders flex under his shirt. He remained in that position for a long time.

"Joshua, if you don't mind my asking, what was it like for you to read Mother's letter?"

He lifted his head and looked out into the darkness. "I think I've been wishing for something like that all these years."

He turned to look at Lillie, and she smiled. Her face shone.

"I'm really glad you came," she said softly.

He grinned sheepishly. "I'm sorry I took it out on you in high school."

"It's okay," Lillie said, looking at him.

Joshua saw her attraction to him in her eyes, and fear crept over him. He stood abruptly. "I should go." He nodded at her and turned, took the steps in a single stride and walked quickly away into the darkness.

Overwhelmed by his feelings, Joshua drove away. He was attracted to Mrs. Farmer's daughter…and she was attracted to him! Ancient shame and disgust came over him—he could no longer hide the horrible truth about what had happened that day. How could he face Lillie again? How could she face *him*? Did others know? Did *Mr.* Farmer?

Since that day, he'd felt shame every time he had become sexually aroused. He had explored the realm of his own sexual response with abandon, but he had always done it alone and it had always left him with a mixture of sadistic pleasure and self-loathing.

Just the thought of it caused his body to respond and he slammed his fist against the steering wheel. He had no idea what to do other than what he usually did—take the road to his favorite bar and drink until he could make it all go away.

But he couldn't do it. Lillie's shining face came to mind and strengthened his resolve to drive straight home. He crept into his mother's dark house, trying not to cause the wooden steps to creak. When he reached his room, he carefully locked the door, a long-practiced habit aimed at keeping his mother away.

He exhaled and released the tension in his body. As he undressed, he began to feel aroused again and sat down on his bed. Shuddering with pleasure, he took care of his needs, and then disgusted with himself, he curled up naked in his bed and went almost immediately to sleep. It would be Joshua who dreamed this night.

He was a boy walking to church, but was having trouble walking. An overly large penis dangled between his legs. He was very scared, but felt obliged to go to the Bible study, even with his embarrassingly large appendage.

When he arrived, only Pastor Lane, Mrs. Farmer and Lillie were there, but Lillie was a grown-up—not a child like him. They all looked at him with warm smiles but when he approached them to sit in his seat, their smiles became evil. He was frozen with fear.

Soon Mrs. Farmer rose, and turning her back on him, walked away toward the back of the church. He watched her until she disappeared into the shadows.

Then, Pastor Lane got up and came to Joshua with an evil smile. Would he beat him or rape him? He wasn't sure which.

At the last minute, Lillie appeared between them. She smiled with empathy at Joshua and stretched out her hand to him. He hesitated, but took her hand. Within moments his organ shrank to a normal size.

Though he was very self-conscious that this had occurred in front of Lillie, her kind smile did not change, and he responded to the gentle pull of her hand. Feeling that he could trust her, he allowed her to lead him out of the church's big front doors and into the light.

17

When Joshua awoke in the late morning, the dream was still vivid in his mind. He thought about his visit with Lillie and felt a strong need to put it all behind him. By giving him the letter, she had offered him a chance for peace and a sense of closure. He had thanked her, and now it was time for them to get on with their lives.

It was clear that Lillie reminded him too much of the past. He had become very good at pushing it out of his mind. There was no need to mess with what had worked for him so well—he would bury himself in his work, drink when he had to, and satisfy his own sexual needs. There was nothing wrong with that. And through his work, he was doing some good in the world.

Lillie, too, woke with a sense of discomfort. Though admittedly she found him attractive and had seen a gentle, respectful quality in him that she had liked, she couldn't imagine them being together. Why was it that in the end, she was always the one who was hurt?

Her mission was complete. She would put Joshua out of her mind.

July 20, 1985

I asked Abigail today why I was so easily sucked in to the pastor's deception. Why did I think it was okay for a pastor to teach sexual touching to a parishioner? I feel so stupid! He would never have gotten as far as he did with me if I had been smarter.

Abigail says one has to be wary because there are predators out there, that people need to be taught to have a healthy suspicion and to question things that don't feel quite right. She says our intuition is what guides us to know what's going on around us and helps us take steps to protect ourselves.

That's what Lane is – a predator! And I was his prey.

Lillie put down the diary. She too had a tendency to be too trusting and naïve when it came to men. Joshua's face flashed into her mind, but she quickly pushed him out.

When it came to sex, Lillie had never felt comfortable opening up to anyone. She thought about her mother—as far as she knew, she had never been with a man before her father. Her parents had both been naïve.

She thought of how her father had been since she'd come home, and realized that he was actually quite intuitive. She wondered how he had figured out all that he had and then remembered that, just like her mother, he had been guided by Abigail. Lillie wanted to learn more from Abigail, too.

Joshua packed hastily, said goodbye to his mother, and returned to his apartment in the city. It would be good to get back into his work.

When he'd taken time off to visit his mother and the small town of his childhood, he had not expected to have his past shoved into his face. He certainly hadn't expected to run into Lillie Farmer or to find himself thinking about her in that way.

He convinced himself that to pursue a relationship with Lillie—even a friendship—would be too complicated and painful. It would be best for both of them if they simply forgot they had met. He would keep to himself, and everything would be okay again.

It had been several days since Lillie had seen Joshua, and she had been unable to get him off her mind. She *had* to see him again, although she wasn't sure why. She gathered up her courage and made a phone call to his mother's house to find he wasn't home. Another day went by before she called again and learned that he had returned to his apartment in the city, and had no plans to come back to Hopeston.

Lillie asked Miriam to have him call her when she next talked to him, and his mother agreed to pass on the message.

The rest of the day Lillie was troubled and distracted. She tried to resign herself to the obvious, that Joshua didn't want to be involved. But she had seen a look in his eye, and she wouldn't rest until she knew for sure he didn't care about her.

There was only one place to go, one person to talk to—Abigail.

A week had gone by and Joshua was angry. Unable to concentrate on his work, he was frustrated—his old routine was no longer satisfying. He tried to drown his emotional rawness with deeper isolation and even heavier drinking than usual. Now when he relieved his own sexual tension, Lillie would pop into his mind and his anger would flare. The more he tried to stop thinking about her, the more she remained on his mind. Because he was drunk nearly every night, he'd begun to let his work slide. Finally, in desperation, he called home.

"Hello?" His mother's voice was of surprising comfort to him.

"Hi, Mom."

"How are you, son?"

He had kept his mother at arm's length all of his adolescence and young adulthood. He hadn't wanted her to get too close for fear he would crack and confess his pain. Now he was desperate. He would be honest.

"Not good."

"Why? What's going on?"

He heard the concern in his mother's voice. He had always known she loved him, although she had not been particularly affectionate. He had needed to be independent after his father died and had sought his nurturance elsewhere. But now, he needed his mother. "Well, it's a long story. But, basically, I've met a girl and I can't get her off my mind." He hoped that would be enough.

"Well...dear...I can't see anything wrong with you being distracted by your interest in a young woman."

"Yeah, but...the girl is Lillie Farmer."

"Oh. What's the problem?"

Here goes, he thought, fear rising in his throat. He pushed himself to speak. "Do you remember the summer I helped Mrs. Farmer with Summer Bible School? Back in 1983?"

"Yes..." she said slowly, trying to pull up any memory that would help her now.

"Well...I got into some trouble that summer...which has left me feeling... very uncomfortable around the Farmer family."

Miriam stretched her brain, trying to grasp what her son was saying. "Okay...so what do you want to do about it?"

Joshua thought for a minute. "I think I need to see someone...like a counselor or something."

Wow, she thought. This must be big if he is willing to see a counselor. She had tried to get him to talk to someone during a particularly dark time in his high school years and he had never been the least bit willing to give it a try. "I think that could be helpful, son."

"But what do I do about my interest in Lillie in the meantime?"

"I think you must follow your heart."

She pulled from deep within her the feeling of being interested in someone, in loving someone. She realized that since her husband had died, she had stuffed those feelings.

They had not been a perfect match, she and her Samuel, but they had loved one another. She had held onto that after his death in order to keep herself afloat in her grief and loneliness.

Joshua interrupted her thoughts. "I'm scared, Mom!"

"Dear, you have to be faithful to your own feelings or you will one day find you have no feelings at all anymore." As she spoke, she realized she was talking about herself. "Lillie's called a few times since you left. I think she'd like to see you too."

Joshua's heart skipped a beat. "Really? What did she say?"

"She asked me to have you call her."

Joshua felt elated, like a schoolboy with a crush on the class beauty. "Really?"

"Yes, honey, she seems to want to talk to you."

"Then, I'm coming back home, Mom. I'll be there in time for supper!"

Miriam chuckled. "Okay, hon. I'll make your favorite."

"Pot roast! Great! I'll see you in a couple hours."

When they hung up, Miriam felt as hopeful as if a light had been turned on within her own heart.

18

Lillie all but ran up the path to Abigail's cabin and pounded on the door. Hearing a voice from within, she opened the door and made her way quickly to the porch. It was early afternoon and the sun sent shafts of golden light through the trees and onto the surface of the lake so that the trees, underbrush and water all sparkled and glowed.

Abigail sat in her chair looking out at the lake. Lillie slipped off her sandals, let her backpack slide to the floor and sat in the chair that awaited her. She entered the silence with her healer, grateful for the calm.

After a few moments, Abigail leaned forward. "Would thee like some tea?"

"Oh, yes, please!"

A hint of a smile appeared on Abigail's face as she poured Lillie a cup of her herbal blend. "It'll calm thee."

Lillie giggled. "I am pretty hyper, aren't I?"

Abigail laughed in response. "I could feel thy energy before thee even got out of thy car." She gestured with her chin down the path up which Lillie had galloped moments before.

Lillie felt as if she were literally jumping up and down in front of the woman. She reminded herself of Sassy and smiled as she recalled Bruce's comparison. "I have so much to talk about."

"Well, hold onto it for a bit, my girl. We need to call upon the Goddess to give us audience first."

Lillie looked at her, puzzled, and she explained. "We are not alone in this world. As we struggle to understand life—or just to live it—we have the constant help of the Divine Spirit. Some call that God. But there are many names." She paused to let Lillie keep pace with her.

"When we gather to share with one another and to tell our stories in order to make sense of life, the Goddess is with us. But we must honor Her by asking Her to let us come into Her presence. We will always begin our sessions in this way."

Lillie nodded. Abigail turned to the altar between them and took up a bundle of sacred sage from a ceramic bowl. She lit it in the glowing flame of the candle. The sage began to smoke, filling the porch with its aroma.

Abigail stood and beckoned for Lillie to stand as well. Beginning a chant deep within her throat, she pulled the smoke over her body with her left hand as she held the smudge stick in her right. Lillie watched the smoke as it curled and danced around Abigail's head and face and down her body like the morning mist.

Once Abigail was finished she handed the smudge stick to Lillie. "Now thee do it. Cover thy whole body with the smoke. Blow on the embers to keep the smoke coming."

As Lillie started to follow her directions, Abigail explained. "Thee is cleansing thy aura and bringing purification to thy soul in order to prepare thyself for an audience with the Great Spirit."

Lillie did the best she could with the smudge stick. Though she didn't fully understand, she felt confidence in Abigail and trusted that this was a necessary thing to do before entering into any kind of "healing work." She assumed that Abigail had gone through this smudging ritual with Melodie too—if her mother had practiced these strange and ancient rituals and found help and healing, then Lillie would trust anything Abigail introduced.

Once done, she handed the stick back to Abigail. Holding the bundle of sage in front of her, Abigail faced the lake and closed her eyes, and began to pray in a singsong voice. Lillie turned towards the lake and closed her eyes too, following her lead.

"Oh, Holy Goddess of all the Universe and of all the Earth, we come into thy presence now in humble petition. We ask that thee honor our desire to be in communion with thee and with one another. We come seeking wisdom, clarity and guidance for Lillie's life and we need thy help, support and abundant blessings upon us to be able to do this sacred healing work. We open our hearts, our minds, our souls and our bodies and lift ourselves up to thee as a holy and precious offering. Thank thee. Amen."

At the end of the prayer, Abigail returned the smoldering smudge stick to its bowl, scrubbed it out in the sand and sat down. Lillie also sat down again and watched as Abigail ceremoniously lit two candles cradled in tiny ceramic dishes. Flecks of color sparkled in the light.

"These candles each symbolically represent our souls, Lillie. Our souls encircle and reflect the light and presence of the Divine Spirit just as these candles encircle the center candle on this altar."

Lillie took in everything Abigail said, and savored the awe that filled her. She felt her body vibrate and sensed that she was in the very presence of God.

Once Abigail had settled herself with teacup in hand across the altar from Lillie, she glanced at her with a peaceful look. "Now, tell me what's on thy mind."

By now, Lillie was considerably calmer than when she had first arrived. She took time to carefully consider what she wanted to say and knew Abigail would wait with infinite patience until she was ready to speak.

"I've never had much luck with men," she began. "In fact, all of my dating relationships have failed miserably. Now I'm gun-shy. I don't want to get hurt again."

Abigail listened and watched closely as Lillie continued.

"Since I saw you last, I went to see Joshua and gave him the letter my mother wrote to him. He later came to my house to thank me for giving it to him," Lillie said, "and now, I find I'm attracted to him and very interested in him. I can't get him off my mind." With a plaintive look on her face, she waited for Abigail to respond.

After a pregnant pause, Abigail spoke. "So thee has been honest with him? He knows thee has read thy mother's diary?"

"Yes."

"It seems thee is paying attention to thy own feelings and needs, as I encouraged thee to do. So, what does thy heart tell thee now?"

Lillie considered the question. "It tells me that I want to see him again and get to know him, if I can."

"Yes, go on."

"I don't know him well enough to know if there is anything there for us. This is so complicated, Abigail."

"Yes, thee's right," she said. "So, what does thee plan to do?"

"I'm willing to try to work on a relationship if he's willing."

"And if he's not?"

"Then I guess I'll have to leave him alone." Lillie noted the great sadness she felt when saying this. "But, I won't know if he's willing unless I ask."

Abigail smiled broadly, but said nothing.

"What if I, what if *both* of us get hurt in trying? Both of us have been hurt before. *Him* especially!"

"Well now, that's the question, isn't it? Is it worth the trying if one ends up getting hurt?"

The look in Abigail's eyes told Lillie she had experienced her share of hurt. She wondered if Abigail had ever loved or married—perhaps she had a husband hidden away somewhere behind her curtains. At that thought Lillie chuckled softly.

"Thee must ask thyself if thee cares enough about him to navigate all the waters ahead, both calm and troubled. This cannot be a selfish thing." Abigail paused to let Lillie think about what she'd said. "But neither can thee neglect thy own needs when weathering such an experience." Abigail sipped her tea. Lillie followed suit. "Thee will need to make a commitment up front...to be true to thyself...and honest...and patient with him."

Lillie drank the last of her tea. She knew with clarity that she needed to pursue Joshua and see what would happen. She realized she had already started to care about him enough to commit to riding the waves and being patient with his process. She felt ready to need and seek the same from him.

"How will I know he's committed enough to care about me?"

Abigail smiled and looked deeply into Lillie's eyes as if viewing her soul. "What would thee look for as signs to let thee know that?"

Lillie thought hard and couldn't think of a thing. After a time she looked to Abigail for help.

Abigail spoke gently. "Let the wisdom of thy soul speak now." She patted her solar plexus, the place above the stomach and below the diaphragm. "What lets thee know he has patience?"

Lillie remembered the moment when Joshua stood below the railing of her porch waiting for her permission to come up and join her. "If he asks permission before he acts and then waits for me to grant it?"

This brought a rewarding smile from Abigail. "Now what is a sign that he cares about thee?"

Lillie knew immediately. Joshua had come to her at her home, in person, to thank her for the letter and talk openly with her about it. "When he is willing to take risks and to step out of his comfort zone to reach out to me with honesty."

Abigail smiled again. "Am I correct in saying that thee has already seen these signs in thy interactions with Joshua?"

"Yes!" Lillie exclaimed.

"So, what is the next step? What's keeping thee from taking it?"

Lillie thought the next step was to find him and meet with him. She knew what she needed to do. "I think Joshua needs to talk to someone about what happened with the pastor and my mother. Could he come and talk with you?"

Abigail let this sit in the air before answering. She had held the hope in her heart for a long time that Joshua would find his way to her. Perhaps Lillie would be the one to bring him. "If he is willing and ready to come, then thee may bring him, Lillie. I think he would appreciate thy company. But when thee does, bring along something to do while he and I talk. And set aside plenty of time to be here."

Lillie smiled as she looked at the kind and glowing face of this woman and flushed with gratitude. How grateful she was that Abigail had been there for all of them: her mother, her father, her…and now possibly for Joshua. She wondered how many other people had found this wise woman, this healer.

"Thank you, Abigail, for everything."

Abigail rewarded her with a brilliant smile and took up a drum the size of a dinner plate from beside her chair. She began to use her fingers and the heel of her hand to project a rhythm that settled Lillie into a meditative state. She closed her eyes, and felt the hum and buzz of the vibration and the rhythm. Again she heard the squawk and rattle of the great blue heron and the responding laugh of the loon far out on the lake.

All of nature responded and participated in these sessions with Abigail. Lillie found herself sending up an inner prayer of hope and thanksgiving. When the drumming ended, Abigail sat in silence for a moment and then blew out the blood red candle on the altar, indicating that Lillie do the same. After blowing out her pure white candle, Lillie spoke. "I brought you something."

She bent down and retrieved a bundle from her backpack, and gave it to Abigail to unwrap. Lillie saw a childlike excitement in her eyes. Sensing it was fragile, Abigail unwrapped it very carefully. Soon a delicate teacup and saucer with hand-painted roses rested in her sturdy hands. She gazed at them with delight and awe as if she had never seen anything more beautiful in her life.

Lillie said simply, "My mother's."

A long moment passed and Abigail whispered, "Thank thee, Lillie. Thank thee!" Her eyes gleamed.

Lillie swelled with happiness. It had been the perfect gift, the perfect payment for healing work.

19

Joshua arrived home to the delicious aroma of pot roast cooking in the oven. He walked in the kitchen door, kissed his mother on the cheek and went upstairs with his duffle bag to get settled and ready for supper. Before going downstairs, he picked up the phone to call Lillie.

Lillie's voice came on the line. "Hello?"

Joshua froze.

"Hello?" she said again.

"Hello, Lillie."

"Joshua! I was hoping you would call!"

"Yeah, imagine that."

"I've been wondering how you've been doing," Lillie blurted, unable to help herself.

"Okay," he lied. "Do you want to get together…sometime?"

"Yes! Yes, I do."

Lillie could scarcely hold back her excitement, and worried she might scare Joshua away for good if she didn't tone it down.

"When and where. You choose," he said.

It's a *sign*, she thought, recalling her conversation with Abigail. "How about a picnic…tomorrow?"

"Okay…" he said. "How 'bout I pick you up. I'll drive. Can you make the lunch?" Joshua didn't have the slightest idea what to make for a picnic. He wasn't even sure he would like a picnic, but, at this point, he was willing to do anything Lillie wanted to do.

"Great! I'll be ready at ten."

"Okay. See you then." Joshua was stunned. Lillie had seemed happy to hear from him. The self-critical voice in his head spoke up. Don't screw this up, Crumley! For now he would focus on his mother and…pot roast.

He knew his mother would have questions. And she deserved to be let in on things, even though he knew he couldn't tell her what *really* happened. Not yet. Maybe not ever. But he was glad to be home. He went to the bathroom, washed his hands and face and combed his hair before going back down to the kitchen.

Miriam hummed as she set the table. She wanted to enjoy this evening with her son. When Joshua came to the table looking as though he was keeping a secret, it made Miriam smile. "I know we haven't practiced our faith much in our home, hon, but would you mind if I said a prayer?" she asked after sitting down.

"That's fine." Joshua bowed his head as he had been taught in church as a boy, and his mother began to pray:

"Blessed are you, Lord, our God, king of the universe. We thank you for this evening. We are gathered, grateful for the love of family and for life. We ask for your help and blessings as we try to live well. We offer up this food and thank you for the blessings of your abundant provision. Bless our sleep this night. Amen."

They ate in silence for a moment until Miriam laid down her fork and leaned back in her chair. "Joshua, I was thinking today after you called that I spent a long time hiding away from life after your father died. It occurred to me that as a result, I've not been particularly available to you. I'm deeply sorry for that. Will you forgive me?"

Joshua let her words sit with him for a while. She was right, and he was glad she had figured it out. He looked at her and nodded. "It's okay, Mom. I think I've done the same thing." He paused. "Only I don't deserve to be forgiven." The look on Miriam's face made him wish he hadn't said it.

"What's bothering you, Josh? Why do you say that?"

"Oh God, Mom…I'm not sure I can talk about it now. I'm going to look for a counselor tomorrow, though. Thanks for listening earlier."

She produced a smile but her heart ached. Joshua turned the conversation to lighter things. Soon they were laughing and enjoying themselves again.

He had long before developed the ability to make his mother laugh to keep her from crying after his father died. He saw that he was still capable of doing that…and he was glad.

Lillie bounded down the stairs in search of her father and found him on the porch reading a book. She flopped heavily into the wicker chair beside him.

Martin chuckled to himself. "What's up?"

Lillie pretended to be shocked. "Oh, I didn't know you were there, Dad!"

"I'm not really here. It's just a mirage."

"A pretty conversational mirage!" Lillie exclaimed.

"Oh, yes! Even to be a *mirage* in this family one must keep up conversationally!"

"Well, in that case, Mirage, what would you pack for a picnic with an unsuspecting fool?"

"It depends on the tastes of the unsuspecting fool unless one wants this fool never to go on picnics again."

Lillie laughed. "It's Joshua! I don't know what he likes!"

Though he appeared to try to hide it, Martin's face fell. Lillie looked away. She knew they were going to have to talk about her involvement with Joshua. She figured now was as good a time as any. "I like him, Dad. I need to give it a chance."

"I'm just concerned. I don't ever want to see you get hurt again."

Lillie softened at the thought of how much her father loved her. "Neither do I. But if I don't follow my heart, I'll never know if there is something special for us."

Martin knew from experience that there is little rhyme or reason to the finding of lovers and friends. He wasn't sure he had much to offer his daughter by way of guidance. Before he could respond, Lillie spoke again.

"I went to see Abigail about this."

Martin instantly felt some relief. Abigail would be a big help, he thought. "Good. How will the trauma he went through with your mother affect things?"

"I don't know, Dad, but he came to thank me for her letter the other night." She recalled Joshua's face. "And I know I want to get to know him."

"Okay, but please come to me if you get stuck. And keep in touch."

"Okay, Dad. I will." She gave him a glowing smile.

Seeing how it lit up her face, he thought with a shiver, Watch out, Joshua. You are doomed to fall in love with this daughter of mine.

Standing up, he started for the kitchen. "Let's see about that picnic!"

20

Showered and dressed, with hours to kill, Lillie puttered around in the kitchen preparing their picnic lunch. At her father's suggestion, she cut carrots and celery into sticks, boiled four eggs and put salt and pepper in a baggie, sliced a pile of roast beef and made sandwiches with catsup on slabs of homemade bread. For dessert, she picked out two apples and a milk chocolate bar. To top it off, she filled a thermos with white wine and a bottle with cold well water.

Martin, who by this time had wandered in for his morning tea, watched with delight. She had pulled her hair into a ponytail with the ends curling at the nape of her neck, and was lovely in her light blue tank top, soft tan sweater and blue jean shorts.

Lillie packed the lunch she'd prepared in a basket, and added silverware, paper plates, napkins, cups, and a large checkered red and white tablecloth. Still with hours to spare, she took a stroll in the woods. Upon her return, she reported to her father that she had seen a pair of redheaded woodpeckers.

Martin was planning to greet Joshua when he arrived—he wanted to observe the boy to see if he was putting off any strange vibes. There were so many areas of parenting and life in general that required wisdom he didn't feel he had. Out of necessity, he'd begun to let his gut guide him. Suddenly, as he stood at his workbench, something caught his eye.

❧

A huge red bird, the size of a heron, with brilliant feathers that shone and shimmered like fire, rose up out of the ground. It seemed to hover and look back at him. Its human-like eyes met his and in that moment he felt power surge through his heart and body. The bird flew up high and circled overhead three times, then emitted a loud cry and disappeared into thin air. It was gone as suddenly as it had come.

Martin stood very still watching out the window, struck dumb by the vision he had seen. It left him both awed and a little troubled.

At exactly ten o'clock, Joshua pulled into the drive. Nervous, he had been up for hours, too, and had almost called off the picnic on the pretense of not feeling well. His stomach was tied in knots, but he knew Lillie would have been disappointed if he'd backed out.

Joshua realized he had no real idea how to relate to a woman as a friend… or anything else for that matter. He had steered clear of intimacy, finding it easier to keep his distance. That way he wouldn't risk making a wrong move or doing anything unpleasant or hurtful.

He was easily turned on by things—sometimes things strange and cruel, and it both frightened and excited him. As a result, he had developed a private sexual world that he didn't feel comfortable revealing to anyone. It had always been much safer to stay away from women altogether. Besides, he thought, he hadn't met anyone he felt interested in anyway. Until now.

He had even wondered if it was men he was interested in sexually. During the act of masturbation, his thoughts of the pastor gave him mixed emotions about being sexually active with other men. He'd had an encounter with a gay man he met at a bar once. They had done things together that really stimulated him, but he was disgusted with himself afterwards and felt dirty all over again. After that, he never again entertained homosexual possibilities and chose instead to isolate himself from both men and women. It had become much easier just to handle it all himself.

Martin walked out of the barn and headed toward the shiny black BMW. Joshua, seeing him coming, got out of the car to meet him, steeling himself on the inside to meet the challenge he knew lay ahead.

Martin offered his hand. "Good morning, Joshua."

Joshua dipped his head slightly and thrust his hand out. "Good morning, Mr. Far…Martin." He blushed.

"I understand you're going on a picnic."

"Yes, sir."

"Where are you going?"

"I don't know. That's up to Lillie, sir."

Martin looked him over. "Well…have a good time."

"Yes sir, we will!" With that Joshua bowed his head and backed away. Unnerved, he nearly ran into Lillie as she approached him from behind, carrying the picnic basket and a blanket.

"Bye, Dad. We'll see you later."

21

Joshua grinned. "I never thought I'd be going on a picnic with Lillie Farmer."

Lillie looked at him and smiled.

"Never thought I'd be here with you either." They rode on another mile.

"Your mother said you weren't coming back. But you did. Why?"

Joshua waited, unsure of how forthcoming he should be. "I don't know exactly. I guess you just got under my skin."

Lillie sensed Joshua's nervousness. Remembering Abigail's advice to be patient, she waited.

"Mom told me you called," he continued. "And I felt like I needed to come back."

"I'm glad," Lillie said simply. They rode on again in silence.

"So, where are we going?"

"There's a couple places—the park by the river or Monroe's Hill…"

"I have an idea. We've got time before lunch. Do you mind if I take you somewhere else first?"

"Where?" Lillie narrowed her eyes and looked at him with mock suspicion.

"It's a secret. You'll like it though. I promise."

"Oka-a-a-y…." Lillie looked closely at him to see if he would give anything away. He stared straight ahead, hiding his amusement.

After a couple of turns, Joshua pulled the car into a scenic lookout along the side of the road. A sunlit valley stretched out below them. From where they stood, one could view the panorama of rolling hills and pine forests, meadows of different hues, and homesteads nestled among outbuildings with animals roaming nearby, all dissected by a serpentine river flashing silver in the sunlight.

Lillie breathed in the fresh air. "It's beautiful here!"

Joshua nodded. "I've always liked this place." They stood quietly together taking in the beauty.

"This is where I came to read your mother's letter."

Lillie glanced at him in surprise. "You came here? Oh, Joshua!"

He looked off into the distance. "Yeah. I exhausted myself and ended up sleeping in my car, right here."

Lillie's eyes glittered with tears. "I worried that it was the wrong thing to do...to give you that letter."

He nodded, still turned to the side. "I have to admit I was mad at you for awhile. You *did* dredge it all up again!"

Lillie searched his face, and when she saw the twinkle in his eyes, she knew he was teasing her. Drawing back, she punched him in the shoulder.

Joshua bent over, pretending to be in pain.

Lillie grinned. "Want me to punch you again, you faker?" She advanced on him laughing, fists up as if she was ready for a fight. When he yelped and jumped away, she turned and headed back to the car. "Come on, you! Let's go have a picnic!"

Safe in the car, they turned around and headed for the river. After a moment or two, Joshua cleared his throat. The levity had passed. "Lillie, it hasn't been easy, and now I can't stop all the feelings. So, I've been thinking about what you said...about going to see Abigail."

"Really?"

Joshua marveled at the way Lillie's face was transformed by her smile. She was so expressive, so beautiful, and he couldn't help but smile back at her.

"Yes, really. I have to admit it helps that she already knows what happened." He felt the old shame creep up on him. "And I feel like I'm going to break apart if I don't tell someone."

"I think you'd like her. I went to see her again the other day and I...told her about you." A look of hurt and suspicion sprang to his face and she instantly regretted having told him. She realized it was one of those moments when it would not be so easy to be honest, but she gathered courage and went on. "It's okay. Really. I needed to talk about...us."

They sat silent for a while, not looking at each other, just letting the world go by outside the car.

"Are you afraid?" asked Joshua.

"No. I just didn't plan on liking you!"

"I know. Me neither." They exchanged weak smiles.

"There's a lot of baggage," she said.

Joshua looked at her with boyish pleading, a touch of resignation in his voice. "Too much?"

"I'm willing to find out." Lillie paused. "Abigail gave me some really helpful advice."

"And...?"

"She said we both need to be willing to...how did she put it?" Lillie screwed up her mouth and wrinkles appeared on her forehead. "She said ...ask yourself if you care enough about him to...to wade through all the waters—muddy and clear, no...calm and troubled. Something like that. Then she told me to be true to myself and honest and patient with you."

Joshua thought about all she had said before responding. "I like that. Muddy and clear explains it, calm and troubled...yes, that too. I feel all of those things these days." He glanced at Lillie with questioning eyes. "So, she said for you to be patient with me and true to yourself at the same time?"

"Yes, and honest. I think we always have to be honest with each other."

They pulled into the parking lot and Joshua changed the subject. "Here we are."

Lillie looked around, noticing the surroundings for the first time since they'd left the scenic lookout—it was as though they had traveled in a private bubble. She looked back at Joshua and waited until he turned off the engine. "Can we do that, Joshua? Be honest with each other?"

"I'll try." He lowered his eyes to avoid looking at her.

"Not *try*, Joshua. Just *be* honest. I think that's the only way to navigate— that's word Abigail used! Navigate those waters. Will you promise me to always be honest with me?"

"Yes, Lillie, I will do my best, but I need you to be patient with me. I haven't done this before."

She chuckled at the odd mix of submission in his posture and rebellion in his eyes. "Okay! If you'll do your best to be honest, I'll do my best to be patient!"

He lifted his head and smiled. "It's a deal!"

She opened her door and jumped out. "Come on!" she yelled, retrieving the basket and jogging toward the water.

Lillie loved the river. Inhaling deeply, she picked up the scent of water and mud and fish. A whiff of pine and sun-baked grass drifted by as well. She plunked the picnic basket down in a mossy area, skipped away towards the river's edge, slipped off her sandals and stepped into the water, wiggling her toes in the sand underneath.

Then, rinsing her feet and stepping onto the grassy bank, she turned, with sandals in hand, to see Joshua spreading the blanket out on the ground. Joining him, she helped him spread the checkered tablecloth on top of it, and then the contents of the basket. Before long they were eating and playfully enjoying their surroundings.

Lillie had brought along her well-used field guides for birds and flowers. She had learned the identification process from the local nature center. When her father had seen her interest in nature as an adolescent, he'd taken her to summer programs at the center and it had become her pleasure.

She named all the birds that came into view and identified every flower and plant nearby. Joshua gently teased her and asked questions, just to keep her talking. He loved watching her face as she explained with knowledge what gave her such passion.

Lillie grabbed her binoculars and jumped up. "Oh, look! A pileated woodpecker!"

As she adjusted the field glasses, she slowly walked towards the tree that held the large black bird, with striking white markings on its wings and red on its crest, busy drilling the tree with its long, pointed bill.

"Joshua, come here. You have to look at this bird!" She whispered loudly.

Joshua watched from where he was for a moment and then got up to follow her into the trees.

"Here, *you* look," she whispered as Joshua came closer, extending the binoculars to him. The strap remained around her neck. He leaned in close, but was unable to see the bird. Instead, suddenly aware of the musky scent of her hair, he pulled away. The intimacy of the moment felt awkward.

"Did you see it?"

All he could do was give her a lopsided smile.

She persisted. "Well, did you?"

"No...I couldn't..." He stumbled over himself, unsure what to say.

"Here, take these, try again." Lillie removed the binoculars from around her neck and handed them to him. He took them and held them up to his eyes.

"Can you see him...in that tree...there?" Lillie pointed and Joshua tried to find it in the view of the binoculars. Suddenly a large bird came into focus.

"Oh, wow! It's huge!"

"Yeah, it's the biggest woodpecker—but it's not always easy to see."

"I guess the big ones hide," Joshua said, as he gave back the binoculars. "And the *best* ones."

"Why do the *best* ones hide?" he asked, oblivious to the double entendre.

Lillie gazed at him for a moment. "I don't know. You tell me."

Joshua blushed and then turned and walked back to the blanket. When she arrived behind him, he turned to her. "Maybe they don't want to be found."

When they'd eaten most of their lunch, Lillie encouraged Joshua to walk with her along the river, and he did, she in bare feet and him in his running shoes. They quietly followed the footpath by the water in single file, and Lillie was delighted to find that Joshua understood how to listen.

As they walked, they took in the iridescence of the water reflecting the sun and, as shadow covered its surface, it revealed abundant life underneath. They saw fish flashing in the light and disappearing into muddy clouds, and brilliant green reeds swaying and rippling, pulled into a dance in the current. They listened to the chickadees and titmice twitter and peep in the trees overhanging the water, and watched as purple martins swooped and dove overhead.

They came around a bend and Lillie held up her hand for Joshua to stop. A great blue heron stood stock still at the water's edge. They quietly observed as the tall bird thrust its head into the water with lightning speed and came up with a wriggling fish in its sword-like bill. After swallowing its catch whole, the heron lifted its feet, one at a time, and slowly moved on down the shallows.

When they started walking again, the heron startled and lifted its long body into flight with surprising grace and flew up river with slow, powerful beats of its large wings.

Lillie identified every flower as they went—tiny blue forget-me-nots low on the river bank, fragrant viny virgin's bower lacing itself into a net over tall riverbank growth, brilliant red cardinal flower shouting out its color higher up on the bank, thistle-like lavender bristle flowers of common burdock.

When they returned to their picnic spot, breathless from the sprint to the finish, it was immediately evident that they had had visitors. Their picnic food had been picked over and strewn about. Sandwich bags were chewed and had been carted off into the tall grass and bushes, carrot and celery sticks nibbled and scattered, and eggshells littered everywhere. The chocolate bar, which they had saved to eat upon their return, had a few chew marks on one corner. It had taken some effort for the offending creature to get through layers of paper and foil to the chocolate morsel inside.

Joshua and Lillie stood and laughed. Finding great humor in this turn of events and deciding that they'd eaten enough anyway, they sat down amongst the clutter of their picnic to share what remained of the chocolate, appreciating it all the more for having nearly lost it.

After cleaning up and packing away the dregs in the basket, they sat on the blanket in the afternoon sunlight, drinking the last of the wine. "Abigail said I could go with you the first time," Lillie said, breaking the silence. "Are you really interested in going to see her?"

Joshua reclined on his side, supporting his head on his palm. "I guess so. I told my mother I'd find a counselor this week. Is that what Abigail is?"

Lillie screwed up her face, thinking. "I don't know if that's what I'd call her, but that's what she does. I think she offers what you're looking for."

He flipped onto his back, resting his head on his hands, and looked at the sky. "When can we go?"

"Whenever you're ready."

Joshua closed his eyes. He dreaded having to face the details of his trauma, wishing to avoid the whole thing. But it was past that now.

Lillie watched him. "I'll warn you—she's a spiritual person and she does strange rituals."

"Like what?" Joshua asked lazily, his eyes still closed, the wine making him a little sleepy.

"Well...she prays, sings, and plays the drum...and she lights candles. There's an altar and she serves tea."

Opening his eyes and turning to face Lillie, Joshua raised one eyebrow for dramatic effect. "What are you dragging me into, Lillie Farmer?"

She laughed. "And then there's the fact that she talks funny! And she'll probably want your first born child as payment!"

It began to sprinkle and they snapped to attention. The weather was changing fast—dark clouds threatened overhead and it promised to rain harder any minute. They jumped up and quickly folded the blanket. Running for the car through pelting drops, they hurried to stow the picnic basket in the trunk and dove into the car just as the rain began to pour.

They sat in the car, two drowned rats, gasping, giggling and listening to the rain hammer on the roof. Seeing one another in this condition only added to their hilarity. Joshua turned the key in the ignition to start the car so they could get the heat going. Even on this warm summer day, being soaked caused them to shiver. On impulse, Joshua flipped on the radio and turned the volume all the way up. "I figured we needed more noise!" he yelled.

Lillie laughed heartily, throwing her head back, and the two delighted together in the joy of the moment. Their hearts were full.

After a bit, the rain eased up and the river of water rushing down the windshield turned to rivulets.

"Shall we go?" Joshua gasped, turning down the radio and still trying to catch his breath from laughing.

"Yeah," Lillie hiccupped back. "Let's go get dry and warm!" They became silent as Joshua pulled the car carefully through puddles of water and out of the park. Classical music played softly on the radio and the heater was beginning to warm them. Lost in thought, the music and the sounds of rain pattering on the roof accompanied the feelings playing out inside of them.

Lillie was happy. She liked what she knew so far of Joshua. He, on the other hand, was struggling with his feelings about the young woman sitting next to him—her loose, damp hair and the body beneath her wet clothing. Simultaneously, fear and pleasure sliced through him like a knife and left the sensation of fire burning in his loins. Self-conscious, he worried she would notice he was aroused.

He drove faster. All he wanted now was to go home, shower…and be alone. He had had a wonderful time with Lillie and he didn't want his confusion to ruin it.

Unaware of what was happening, Lillie picked up the conversation from earlier. "When do you want to go see Abigail?"

Joshua didn't answer.

"Joshua?"

He gave her a sideways glance with his eyes. She saw his jaw muscles working.

"Joshua, are you okay?"

He still couldn't look her in the eye. "Yup!"

"What's wrong? You're obviously not okay!"

After a long pause Joshua spoke quietly, still looking straight ahead at the road. "Lillie, I am…attracted to you." He swallowed and went on. "I get scared when I start to…respond…when I'm attracted…"

"Are you having memories of…when he…?"

"Yes, Lillie, I am!" A fierce and helpless look flashed in his eyes, and her face reflected fear at his anger. When he saw it, Joshua quickly interjected, "I'm sorry. I didn't mean to get angry. I just get so tangled up. And you turn me on!" When he finished, the air seemed to go out of him like a deflating balloon. Exhausted and embarrassed, he turned away from her.

Lillie didn't know what to do—she was both pleased and embarrassed by his words. She had suspected as much, but now he'd said it aloud, and she wasn't sure what to do or how to feel. "So what do we do now?" she said. "You're not the only one who is turned on!"

"Well, *I* need a cold shower!"

Lillie began to laugh. "I think it's funny that we're so tied up in knots because we're attracted to each other! I'm actually flattered, " she said softly.

"Good," he replied. "Because you are a beautiful woman…and I don't want to do anything to hurt you or rush you or scare you. Let's just take it slow, okay?" They were nearing Lillie's home.

"Okay. So when do you want to go see Abigail?"

Joshua slowed the car to a stop as he turned off the road. "How about Saturday? Does she see people on Saturdays?"

"I don't know," replied Lillie. "I'll call her. If Saturday doesn't work, how's Monday?"

"Yeah, that's good."

Joshua hesitated. "Can I see you on Saturday anyway?"

"Yes," Lillie said in a whisper. They had worked through their first storm and had made it safely to the other side.

Part Two

The Porch

22

bigail agreed to meet with Lillie and Joshua on Saturday at ten, so Lillie packed her backpack with a novel, a bag of snacks, a bottle of water, a sweater, binoculars and her two field guides—she planned on hiking around the lake while Joshua met with their healer.

At 9:30, Lillie pulled into the Crumley driveway, and Joshua came out the door with a sweater over his shoulder. He wore his regular uniform of T-shirt, jeans and running shoes.

As he climbed into the car, she looked at him with questioning eyes. "Are your ready for this?"

"I guess so." He paused. "Thanks for coming along."

"You're welcome," she said, as she started the car again.

They rode in silence for a minute, each considering the enormity of what they were headed into. "My mother would be glad that I'm doing this," Lillie finally said as she drove along the tree-lined roads. "Taking you to Abigail, I mean." She glanced over at Joshua and smiled. "But you're the one doing all the hard work."

He considered what she'd said for a moment. "You know, let's just turn the car around!"

"No, Joshua!" she said, with over-dramatized sternness, but then her voice softened. "It'll be okay."

"I hope to God you're right."

For a few moments, neither spoke again. Joshua looked out the window and Lillie kept her eyes on the road ahead.

"Speaking of God," she finally said, "I've been wanting to ask you… What happened to your faith? What do you believe, now, that is, after your experience…?"

Joshua continued staring out the window and Lillie tried again. "We grew up going to the same stupid little church, you know!"

He glanced back at her and nodded his head. "Yeah, I know."

"It's been so long since I went to church." She paused, trying to remember the last time she'd attended services of any kind. "I'm not even sure what I believe anymore."

"I sure as hell don't believe the crap I was fed by that bastard!"

Lillie thought for a moment. "Well, you don't need to worry about Abigail. What *she* does—the spiritual stuff—I find really kind of cool, refreshing, real...I don't know. You'll see."

Joshua shifted in his seat. "I haven't thought about anything religious or spiritual in...forever. Actually, I've just sort of existed." He looked at her, eyes glowing with intensity. "Until you came along, that is." Lillie reached out and gently touched his arm.

Soon they arrived at Abigail's forest parking area—the VW Beetle hadn't moved from the spot it had occupied before.

Joshua glanced around and shook his head in amazement. "She sure lives off the beaten path."

Lillie grabbed her backpack and led the way into the woods down the two-track, which was the width of a small car. Joshua caught up and walked along beside her. "What *is* this place?"

Lillie smiled dreamily. "Abigail lives in a cabin on Lake Osampi. This is where she does her work."

As they walked, Joshua became aware of all the smells of the forest: rotting leaves, pine, damp earth, and the fresh smell of water. When the two-track narrowed into a footpath, he felt flutters of nervousness rise in his stomach. When Abigail's cabin finally came into view, he felt as if he had swallowed a stone. More than anything, he wanted to turn and run, but taking a step in faith, he followed Lillie to the door.

Lillie turned and looked at him, searching his face again. "Are you ready?"

"Yup. Let's do this before I change my mind!" Before she could even knock, Abigail's voice was heard from inside, inviting them in.

It took a few minutes for Joshua's eyes to adjust, but soon he could see Abigail in front of them. She was shorter and rounder than he had imagined, and wore a long colorful dress forgiving of a voluptuous figure underneath.

Dark brown hair hung loose to her shoulders and she wore a beaded necklace with a large pendant—the figure of a woman made of silver.

But it was her face that caught his eye. It was radiant.

Abigail smiled at the two of them, and crow's feet appeared by her eyes. She gazed up at Joshua. "I am very glad to finally have thee in my home."

She reached for the young man's arm and led him gently to the porch, gesturing for Lillie to follow with a tray of tea and scones which she had set on the counter.

Lillie noticed that the porch was different from the last time she'd visited. The chairs and tables had been arranged so that three could now sit comfortably in a semicircle around the altar and face the lake at the same time. She smiled in appreciation—it was clear Abigail intended to include her in the ritual before sending her away so she and Joshua could talk privately.

Abigail motioned for Joshua to sit in the middle chair, from which the view of the lake was unobstructed. "I'm so glad Lillie has brought thee to me. I knew thee would find thy way here one day." Her smile was one of such compassion that although he was still adjusting to the unusualness of the place, the knot in his stomach began to dissolve. He nodded without speaking and Abigail continued.

"Lillie has likely told thee we do sacred ritual here." She glanced out toward the lake. "Nature has healing energy and each of us has the capacity to heal. What we seek to do here is combine our power and intentions with the power and intentions of the Divine Presence and the forces of nature to bring about transformative healing where it is needed." She paused to let Joshua absorb all she had said.

"Our rituals acknowledge and call upon the sacred, the spiritual, before we start our work." She paused again. "And at the end of our session, we take time to honor and thank the Divine Spirit before we return to our regular lives. I encourage thee to relax now and stay open and observant as we begin our ritual." Abigail stood, took up a smudge stick and lit it. As she used her hand to pull the smoke from the burning bundle over the three of them, a deep and resonating sound emerged from her throat. First a chant, it became a song.

Continuing to sing, she replaced and dowsed the smoking sage. Then, turning her face to the lake, she closed her eyes and gestured to Lillie and Joshua to stand with her.

"Oh Holy One, Great Creator of all life draw us now into thy presence and embrace. We bring to thee today thy special one, Joshua, who has been deeply wounded and who needs thy healing touch. With great courage he has come here. Oh Great Spirit, thee has drawn him here, and with him, his friend Lillie. We ask that thee help us as we all work in partnership to do this healing work. Bring release, closure and an end to the damage caused by past trauma. Bring forth thy power to guide, illuminate, clarify, cleanse and transform. We thank thee, Amen."

A loon's haunting call echoed across the lake and an eagle screeched in response. Shivers ran up and down Lillie's spine as Abigail gestured for them to be seated again.

"So, my dear child," she said to Joshua. "Lillie tells me that thee is a man of justice and has been all thy life."

He swallowed a piece of scone and sipped some tea to wash it down. "Yes, I suppose that's true."

"Tell me about thy work."

Joshua talked of assisting the county prosecutor in preparing cases for court. He described the function of his office—to defend victims of abuse and crimes of all kinds.

Abigail squinted at him. "What made thee choose to take on such a profession?"

Joshua shrugged his shoulders. "I guess I've always had a desire to defend the underdog."

"Was thy motivation to defend and protect the underdog heightened after thy experience at Hopeston Church?"

Joshua gulped. Here we go, he thought. "Yes..." he said, "it's like a fire that has roared within me ever since to burn away all offenders." He was stunned at the image he had conjured up, and assessed the accuracy of his statement even as he spoke the words.

"Ah," intoned Abigail. "It burns within thee still, this fire."

"Yes. It threatens to consume me at times. Other times it just fuels my work and keeps me going."

"Fueling fire is good. Consuming fire is *not* good," Abigail said.

Joshua nodded—simultaneously shaken and comforted by how quickly Abigail had homed in on the crux of the matter for him.

She turned slightly toward him. "Then what we want to do is get this internal flame under control so that it is helpful to thy passion and work for justice, but no longer forces thee to live in fear and isolation. So, tell me, how do we begin to dismantle the destructive force within thee?"

He thought for a minute. "I suppose I need to tell you my story."

"I agree," she said. "Does thee want Lillie to stay or to go?"

Joshua looked at Lillie, who had already set her empty teacup on the table and was starting to stand. He wasn't sure he wanted to be left alone with Abigail just yet, but he also knew he wasn't quite ready to speak of the details in front of Lillie. He was determined to get it over with but he wanted to protect her from the horror he had known. After a moment, he looked apologetically at her and said gently, "I need to do this alone."

She nodded and touched him gently on the shoulder. "I'll be with you," she whispered.

Abigail saw the tenderness pass between them and smiled. "When we are done, we will ring this bell. That way thee'll know when to return." She reached for a large cowbell lying next to her on the floor, and rang it a couple of times. "Take my canoe out onto the lake, if thee wants, and take the paddle with thee." She motioned to the corner where a single paddle stood.

Lillie smiled in thanks, retrieved her backpack and the paddle and departed quietly. Abigail watched until she saw Lillie appear at the water's edge and then turned her chair toward Joshua.

"I know this will be difficult, but I wonder if thee can tell me what happened to thee?"

He nodded. "I'll try."

"Start from the beginning. And take thy time."

Joshua settled himself and began to go back in his mind. At first it felt as though he were trying to pry open a rusty door inside himself and the hinges wouldn't give—then slowly, memories began to form and the stone in the pit of his stomach returned.

"We're Jewish and my mother wanted me to get religious training. But after my father died, she couldn't handle our religious traditions at home. The wind got knocked out of her, I guess." In his mind, he saw his mother, a decade younger.

"She found a pastor at the local church to teach me good religious values. She said the Christians had plenty to teach me." He shook his head again, and looked out at the lake. Catching sight of Lillie paddling out from shore, his look softened.

"So I started attending the Hopeston Church and I met Mrs. Farmer. She was my Sunday School teacher." A myriad of emotions registered on his face.

"In June after the seventh grade, she suggested I participate in the Summer Bible Series she and the pastor were leading." A slight smile came to his face and he snorted in subtle amusement. "Lillie was in my class. She and I were in school together, all the way through."

"So you two have known one another for many years."

Joshua nodded. "Yes. We didn't always like each other. I'm not sure she liked how close I was to her mother, but I've *always* been aware of Lillie."

He thought of Melodie for a moment. "Mrs. Farmer was very sweet, and friendly." His voice broke.

"Go on."

"I remember that she was a wonderful storyteller. I don't think the other kids, including Lillie, appreciated her teaching as much as I did…she was kind and gentle, open…and funny." He glanced down. "Though I was just a kid at the time, I think I felt the need to rescue her."

"What did she need rescuing from?"

"I don't know. That thought just came to me."

"Was she somehow unprotected, unguarded? Is that what thee means when thee says she was open?"

Joshua considered the question. "Yeah, I think so."

"Could it have been that same open, unprotected quality that drew a predator like Pastor Lane?"

Predator. Joshua had never thought of the word in reference to the pastor before, but he had certainly had experience with it in his work. Something clicked in his mind. "Yes, that's it," he said, nodding his head. "She was his prey."

"What does thee think about that?"

Joshua thought of what he'd learned on the job about predators and their prey, and began to apply it to his own situation. Things were suddenly crystal clear. "*That's* why he invited her to teach the Summer Bible Series in the first place. He was setting it up to get her alone!"

Abigail nodded slightly and offered a smile of approval.

Lillie paddled slowly on the lake. No matter what she was feeling, the unspoiled beauty of nature could always bring her back to center.

She was glad she had brought her guidebooks along—she had encountered many birds and plants she had never seen before—and was inspired once again by the connections between all living things and the mystery of life.

Lifting the paddle and laying it across the canoe, she reached for her backpack and dug for her binoculars. A light flashed at the water's edge and as she turned toward it, suddenly she was overwhelmed by the awareness of a presence—shining, loving, penetrating—that commanded her attention and left her full and breathless.

Almost as quickly as it came, it went away and in the aftermath of the moment she was filled with peace. Somehow she knew it involved Joshua—implicit in the peace was a promise…and a special responsibility. Filled with love for her newly-retrieved friend, she was reminded of the story in the Bible, when Zechariah, father of John the Baptist, was struck speechless by the astonishment he'd felt at the promise of God that his aging wife would conceive and bear a child. It was both mysterious and wonderful…and incredible.

Joshua was flooded with memories. It *does* make sense to re-examine all of this, he thought.

Abigail interrupted his brief reverie. "Why was it, does thee think, that thee became so close to Melodie Farmer?"

"Well," he replied, "I was never in a hurry to go home to an empty house and...mother. My mom wasn't there for me." He recalled Miriam's words of apology from days before: *"I was hiding away from life after your father died..."*

Joshua looked up at Abigail and she nodded, encouraging him to continue.

"Just like Mom, I was looking for something."

"What was thee looking for?"

"I don't know. I felt so alone."

She cocked her head. "What was missing in thy life at that point?"

"Parents."

"Okay. So what was thee looking for?"

"Someone to take their place."

Abigail waited as Joshua considered what he had said.

"Wow," he said, softly, realization dawning.

"Joshua, thee had an open hole, a gaping need left by parents who for one reason or another were not able to nurture or be present to thee. In early adolescence, a time when a child is especially in need of guidance and love, thee was looking for adults to fill that hole, that need." She stopped to let him think again. "Who did thee find to fill it?"

"Mrs. Farmer...and..." The silence was suddenly thick.

"And who?"

"Pastor..." Unable suddenly to call the minister the name by which he had always referred to him before, Joshua realized the word "pastor" suddenly no longer applied.

"Mrs. Farmer and Lane Richardson."

Joshua's mind reeled. He had latched onto Mrs. Farmer and the minister out of his own need for nurturing parental figures after the death of his father. Seeing that he was overwhelmed, Abigail gently took back control.

"Joshua, let's take this one step at a time."

"Okay."

"Thy mother was stricken with grief over the loss of her husband. This made her unavailable to thee at the time thee was also grieving over the loss of thy father."

Hot tears stung Joshua's eyes and he tried not to blink, so as to keep the tears from running down his cheeks. He fought as he had so often done to hide the intensity of his sorrow.

Abigail noted his struggle for composure. "Without placing blame, we see the circumstances of thy life left thee vulnerable."

At the word "vulnerable," he was unable to hold back any longer. The tears spilled down his face. Unresolved grief washed over him and he lowered his head into his hands and began to sob. He cried for his father, whom he hadn't allowed himself to miss in years. He cried for his mother, whom he hadn't been able to make feel better after his father's death. And then he cried for himself—the lonely, sad and needy boy he'd been. Emotionally alone, he'd been ripe for the picking.

Abigail hummed a lullaby deep in her throat and the comfort of the song gave him permission to weep. He sat for a long time, head between his knees and shoulders heaving, until the tears finally ceased.

When he looked up, he saw that Abigail had placed a box of tissues on the altar between them. He reached for one and their eyes met. "Thank you," he said, through the tissue.

She tipped her head and smiled warmly at him in response. They sat quietly, listening to the twitter and peep of small birds in the trees outside the porch. The lake shimmered in front of them. "Let's take a lunch break," Abigail said after a time. He nodded in agreement and she rose from her chair and headed into the cabin.

Joshua leaned back in his chair, and took a deep breath. Exhausted and hungry, he realized that in talking with Abigail he had worked much harder than he might have predicted, and he marveled at the way this odd woman had helped him navigate through the rough waters—her timing and responses exactly right.

But, as he thought about it more, he realized she had only provided the container—a safe place for him to tell the truth. With her guidance, he had figured out most of it himself.

Abigail called from the kitchen. "Shall we invite Lillie to join us?"

"Yeah!" Joshua responded, immediately warmed by the thought of the young woman out on the lake.

"Take the bell down to the shore, then, and let her know we're ready for her to return."

Glad for the opportunity to take a break from the porch, he stood and stretched, picked up the bell and headed through the kitchen to the outside door. Once on the ground, he was instantly aware of the warm moist air on his skin and the crunch of pine needles and dead leaves under his shoes. He saw the velvety moss that lined the path and ferns that stood as sentinels deeper in the woods. Rays from the sun, now high in the sky, slanted brightly through the trees and lined the forest floor. Usually numbed, his senses had come alive and he noticed the life around him as well.

He arrived at the small sandy beach below the place where Abigail kept her canoe and stood at the water's edge. Seeing a collection of Lillie's footprints in the sand, he looked out at the shining lake and searched for signs of the canoe. He rang the bell—tentatively at first, and then with strength—allowing it to clang loudly. Still acutely aware of his surroundings, he listened as the rings echoed over and over until their sounds faded. Nearby, birds and forest animals rustled in response, and cawing as they went, two crows flew noisily away.

Feeling the tightening of dried salt on his cheeks, he squatted at the lake's edge and washed his face with the clear water. Refreshed and cleansed, he dried his face with his sleeve and looked out over the lake, and then rang the bell again.

A giggle exploded nearby. "Okay! Okay! I hear it!"

Joshua looked in the direction from which the voice had come. Through the branches of an overhanging white pine, he spied Lillie quietly paddling the canoe toward him along the shore.

"You'll scare away all the water fowl with that thing," she said with mock irritation. Joshua grinned sheepishly in response.

Lillie pulled the water hard with her paddle so as to shove the bow of her boat onto the sandy shore. Once landed, she walked gingerly along the spine of the canoe, and finally stepped out onto the beach. "How'd it go?"

Joshua shook his head and smiled. "Abigail is amazing. You were right about her. Some things came clear."

He reached for her shoulder and placed his hand on it, and let it rest there for a while. "Abigail's making lunch for us now. I think we're going to do more after we've eaten. How was your time on the lake?"

Lillie's face shone. "Joshua, I saw three great blue herons out there! Two were fishing, one was flying overhead!"

"Maybe you'll get to see more." Joshua reflected her joy and this time led her on the way back to the cabin.

When they stepped onto the porch, they saw that lunch was ready and a table set. On wooden plates were slabs of sharp cheese and homemade wheat bread. In large mugs was hot bean soup. Glasses of cold spring water perspired on the tablecloth. They pulled up their chairs and dug in.

While all of them ate heartily, Abigail turned to Lillie. "Thee should tell us about thy time in the canoe."

Though not ready to talk fully about her experience on the lake, Lillie was delighted to be asked and recounted her sojourn paddling along the shoreline of the lake and the birds, fish, frogs, flowers and plants she had encountered. Abigail responded by telling of a number of mysterious and wonderful experiences she'd had with animals and waterfowl since she had lived on the shores of Lake Osampi.

"How did you end up living and doing your counseling here?" asked Joshua.

Abigail leaned back in her chair and took a deep breath. "My mother's people, the Osampi tribe, have lived on this land for centuries. This cabin is the last remaining structure of the original settlement. They were westernized by white settlers, but retained many of the old ways. My father was a Quaker who came to live among my mother's people to help them build a school."

She related how her father had fallen in love with her mother, a young Indian beauty, and had stayed to live within her tribe. After marrying, they had eventually moved and raised a family. Abigail and her four younger siblings had been schooled in the nearby Quaker community.

She told them how after high school, she had attended college and graduate school, and had studied a wide variety of subjects—anthropology, psychology, world religions and philosophy—but that it had been her mother's gifts in spiritual and medicinal wisdom and her father's spiritual training that had informed her. "My healing methods sprang from the wisdom I gained from them as well as from my formal education," she said.

She shared that although she had worked in the town for many years, people she worked with were either sent to her or they found her somehow.

She spoke of faith in the movements of the Spirit to bring clients to her porch.

When they were done, they all cleared the table, and then Lillie jogged quickly down the path back to the sandy beach and the waiting canoe. Joshua stood on the porch and watched until she pushed off from shore and paddled away. A halo of light hovered over her. My angel, he thought, as he turned and sat down again.

Abigail returned to the porch. Wiping her hands on her apron, she removed it and laid it aside. Once settled in her chair, she closed her eyes and sat in silence.

Joshua wasn't at all sure what to do, but finally closed his eyes as well and began to listen to the sounds of nature around them. The silence lasted for what seemed like half an hour—but however long it was, it was just long enough to bring him to a complete sense of calm.

Abigail cleared her throat. "What we just did was Quaker prayer. Silently, we wait on the guidance of the Spirit. I believe we're ready now. Let's go back to where thee was helping Mrs. Farmer clean up after Summer Bible lessons."

Nervousness crept back into Joshua's stomach. "I looked forward to helping her clean up. All the other kids generally scrammed out of there fast. So it gave me time alone with her." He swallowed hard. "Then one day…the pastor called her into his office. At first I was mad, because it left me alone to clean up without her, so I went over to the door to eavesdrop on what they were saying. I couldn't hear very well…but I caught a glimpse of them standing together…kissing.

"I couldn't believe it! I knew that she was married and that it was wrong to kiss another man when you're married. At first I blamed her—I thought she was the one who had started it…the kissing, I mean." He hung his head, feeling the weight of how wrong he had been. "After that day, I watched her very closely, and tried to stay close to her to keep her from going to him." Tears began to fall again and he reached for a tissue. "Then, the next thing I saw…was Mrs. Farmer with her blouse…"

Joshua looked pleadingly at Abigail. "I tried to get her not to go to him. I think by that time I had figured out that it was him who was making *her* do what they were doing, because I couldn't imagine Mrs. Farmer cheating on her husband."

He thought for a moment and then shook his head. "I guess the pastor wasn't married. I never really knew—he never talked about his private life."

Abigail nodded, encouraging him to continue.

"I thought about it a lot. I tried to figure out what to do. I sort of took it on as my job to save her." He shook his head again. "I know now, but I should have gone for help." He clenched his jaw and pounded the arm of his chair. "Why didn't I go for help, Abigail? Why didn't I go for help?" He looked up at her, stricken with grief. His expression was that of a young boy daring to hope he hadn't ruined something by his misbehavior. She smiled benevolently, responding to the child within him.

"Remember that thee was just a boy, Joshua. Thee wouldn't have known how best to handle it. It was not thy fault."

Tears spilled down his cheeks as he looked at her. Abigail leaned toward him. "Can thee go on?"

He nodded and grabbed another tissue to wipe his face.

"Then that awful day came." He closed his eyes, remembering. "I told her not to go when he called her. But she wouldn't listen to me!" Joshua leapt from his chair and began to pace back and forth. His arms were stiff at his sides, his hands clenched into fists.

"Why wouldn't she listen to me? I could have kept it from happening if she had just listened to me!"

Abigail sensed that it was as if what he saw in his mind's eye was happening in the present. "Joshua! That was a long time ago."

He turned to look at her with a wild look, almost as if he didn't know who she was. His face changed and he dropped heavily into his chair. "I tried to stop her!"

"Yes, Joshua, thee did. But adults make their own choices. Mrs. Farmer chose not to listen to thee. It is not thy fault!"

He sighed.

"Can thee go on?"

He nodded in response. "*That* day, I was ready. I was mad and I was going to burst in there and catch him red-handed and make him stop. Since she wouldn't listen to me, I tried to make *him* listen." His voice broke. "But that didn't work either."

He said the final sentence with such hopelessness that it struck Abigail hard, in the pit of her stomach. She waited, watching him closely.

"I pushed open the door and there they were. He had his hands all over her! The pastor didn't really seem surprised to see me there but a strange look was in his eyes. He came over to me, almost as if to invite me to join them!"

Abigail spoke calmly. "How did thee feel about that?"

"I was mad!"

"Anything else?"

"Confused...and scared. He locked the door! We were trapped!"

"Go on."

"I told him that what he was doing was wrong! And then his face completely changed."

"How did it change?"

"It was evil. He grabbed me by the neck and hurt me, and he started calling Mrs. Farmer names. I was terrified. He told me I was going to watch him teach her a lesson for being such a...sinful woman. He threw her on the floor...she was so afraid...I could see pure fear in her face...I felt so sorry for her."

Joshua squirmed in his seat. "And then he...he...pulled down my pants. He told me I would go to hell if I didn't do what he said, and I believed him." He slid down low in his chair. "He started touching me. I tried to pull away but he hurt me.

"I had never been...touched there...not by someone else. I couldn't help it." Joshua stopped.

Abigail leaned toward him. "Tell me what happened."

He hesitated, but finally went on. "It felt good...and my...it...had a mind of its own! There was nothing I could do to stop it!

"Once I was...aroused...he ordered me to stay where I was. I could tell that Mrs. Farmer was frightened but I could see in her eyes that she was also worried about me. She tried to move away at first, but he pinned her down. She begged him to leave us alone, to let us go."

He ground his palms into his eyes as if trying to erase the image in his mind. "And then he did it to her! As if it were a perfectly normal thing to do, the pastor raped Mrs. Farmer right there in front of me!"

Joshua sat motionless, eyes closed. "When he was finished with her, he told us both we were going to hell! He called her a whore…and he told me that I was beyond help. I wanted to kill him. But I was afraid and ashamed. I felt dirty and bad. I was such a bad boy."

"No, Joshua," Abigail said softly, "thee was not. It wasn't thy fault."

He opened his eyes and wheeled his head around. "BUT, ABIGAIL, I DIDN'T STOP IT!!"

"No, thee didn't," she said calmly, completely present with him in his pain. "But thee *couldn't* have. Thee was his prey as well."

He looked at her, blankly at first, and then slowly, the rage drained from his face.

"Thee was not a bad boy that day," said Abigail. "Thee was a needy, vulnerable boy, without proper parental attention and guidance, and thee thought it was thy job to rescue Mrs. Farmer. But it *wasn't* thy job. To rescue Mrs. Farmer…or…thy mother."

A look of surprise appeared on Joshua's face. "What does my mother have to do with it?"

Abigail smiled at him, compassion pouring from her eyes. "Thee said this morning that thee felt the need to rescue Mrs. Farmer. Why would thee think it was *thy* job to rescue her?"

He thought of both his mother and Mrs. Farmer and the truth began to dawn on him. "Because I had to rescue my mother after my father died." He wrapped his arms around himself and leaned forward in the chair.

Abigail nodded her head. "Precisely. Under other circumstances, this horrible, unfortunate thing wouldn't have happened to thee because thee wouldn't have been vulnerable and thee wouldn't have been there."

Joshua began to sob. Abigail waited for the convulsions to cease.

"But those *were* the circumstances, Joshua. None of them were ever in thy control nor were they thine *to* control. Thee is not to blame for any of it." She leaned forward to make eye contact with him. "Thee was a *good* boy, Joshua—a *very* good boy."

She settled back in her chair and looked out over the lake. "Mrs. Farmer was too naïve and confused to make wise choices. And the pastor was a dangerous man who was out of control. She *and* thee were victims of his evil, pure and simple."

A long time passed and finally Joshua spoke again, in a boy's small voice. "All these years, I've never told anyone! I thought I should have been able to stop it. I thought I'd failed her when I didn't. I thought I was as bad as him! But I wasn't, was I?"

"No," she said. "Thee wasn't."

Suddenly Joshua was on his feet. He punched his fists in the air. "It was him...it was *all* him. Well, FUCK HIM!" He screamed aloud, and his voice echoed through the forest around them.

After several moments, he dropped his hands to his sides and turned to Abigail. "Was Mrs. Farmer ever able to come to terms with all of this before she died?"

Abigail smiled at the young man's compassion, even for a woman now deceased. "I believe she did, Joshua. I'm not sure she was able to get it all out, but she came a long way." She motioned for him to sit down again, and suddenly exhausted, he complied.

Leaning forward, she took his hands into hers. "Why don't we stop here for today?" He nodded and she closed her eyes and prayed aloud. *"O Great Spirit, thank thee for this purging and clarifying session. Go with Joshua now as he lets it settle. Protect him and give him a healing rest. Thank thee for thy love."*

She sang a sad song to the woods and then looked with kindness at the young man across from her. "I want thee to go home now. Thee needs to process all of this. And talk about this session with trusted friends or family."

Joshua quietly nodded.

"Has thee told Lillie about this?" Abigail asked.

"No," he replied. "She knows what she knows because she read about it in her mother's diary."

"Yes, but in her diary, Melodie didn't include the part about what this predator did to thee. That's for thee to tell, and thee will need to tell it all—to Lillie—someday."

23

On the way home, Joshua dozed and Lillie listened to soft, classical music on the radio. When they pulled into his driveway, Lillie laid her hand on his shoulder, and gently shook him. "Wake up, sleepy head."

Joshua stirred, opened his eyes and looked at her, disoriented and innocent in his sleepiness. He stretched and yawned, and then realizing where he was, grabbed her hand. "Lillie, don't go yet. Will you come in, say hi to my Mom, have a Coke or something?"

"Yes. I'd like that. But then I think I should probably go, okay?"

"Okay." He relaxed, and a more confident look settled on his face. He let go of her hand and they emerged from the car.

As they stepped into the kitchen, Joshua and Lillie were met by the smell of something baking. Miriam bustled in and greeted them.

"Hello, Mrs. Crumley," Lillie said, offering her hand.

"Hello." They shook and smiled kindly to one another.

Joshua headed to the refrigerator. "Can we have something to drink?"

Miriam noticed his eyes were red and swollen. "Yes, dear. Would you like some iced tea?" She kicked into hostess mode, setting out glasses and something to eat, and Joshua led Lillie toward the table.

"I hope everything went well today," said Miriam.

Joshua glanced at Lillie. "Yes. It did."

Lillie suspected talking about what had happened would be difficult for him for a while, so she lightened the subject. "I spent time canoeing on the lake while Joshua had his sessions."

Miriam was confused. "Where *was* this? Who did you go to see?"

Joshua looked at Lillie, and she responded instead. "We went to see a counselor named Abigail that my family knows. She lives in the woods on Lake Osampi and conducts her sessions right there overlooking the lake."

A host of questions flooded Miriam's mind. "So your sessions...were helpful?" She looked from Joshua to Lillie and back.

"Yes," said Joshua. "She's actually quite amazing."

Miriam gazed at him. "Well, I'm glad."

Lillie jumped in. "Abigail has been very helpful to our family. I think she's already been helpful to Joshua."

"I'm glad Lillie was there," Joshua interjected.

Miriam observed the looks exchanged in front of her. "Son, you look pretty worn out. Maybe you should take a nap before supper."

They finished eating the snack and Lillie excused herself. "Thank you, Mrs. Crumley. That hit the spot."

Joshua watched as Lillie turned and walked toward the door. After the door closed softly behind her, he pushed his plate aside and laid his head down on the table, limp with exhaustion.

Miriam stood up and placed the remaining dishes in the sink. "Come on, hon, let me take you upstairs." Gently taking him by the shoulders, she nudged him to stand. Like an obedient little boy, he let his mother lead him to his bedroom, remove his shoes and tuck him in. He smiled slightly in thanks and laid his head on the pillow. Within minutes he was fast asleep.

Miriam stood at the door of her son's room and watched him for a moment. Understanding whatever it was he was struggling with would have to wait.

Martin sat on the porch smoking his pipe. Lillie's taking Joshua to see Abigail had proven to be an all-day affair and he had begun to be concerned, so he was relieved to see her car pull into the lane.

He knew something of the emotional strain involved in talking about the painful past, and suspecting his daughter was worn out, he had chicken, rice and vegetables in the crock-pot ready and waiting for her. She came through the screen door and slumped into the wicker chair beside him.

"Hi, Dad."

"Hello, sweetheart. How was your day?"

"It was good. Very hard for Joshua, I think, but good." Lillie leaned over and unlaced her hiking boots.

"Abigail is really good at what she does, Dad. I'm so glad Mother found her." They exchanged a look that held both grief and gratitude.

"I'm glad she could help Joshua too," Martin said softly.

"Yeah. He did a lot of crying and yelling—one time I could hear him all the way out on the lake. He seemed more peaceful at the end, though."

"You were out on the lake?"

Lillie's mood changed instantaneously. "Abigail let me use her canoe! I spent *hours* paddling around on the lake. I saw all kinds of waterfowl and identified several new flowers! I even took a short nap in the sun, just floating on the water. It was wonderful!"

Martin reflected the joy in her face. "That's my girl! You always have loved being steeped in nature."

"That's true, isn't it?"

"Yup."

"Do they *pay* people to do that? To be out in nature all day?"

"Why? Are you finding insurance boring?" He chuckled at the idea that it might be anything but.

"Yes, as a matter of fact, I am!"

"Well, then, you should look into the possibilities. There are conservationists around here—as a matter of fact, I believe Lake Osampi is historically a conservation area. There are burial mounds out there. I guess Native Americans lived there once."

"Abigail's ancestors! She told us her people have lived on that land for centuries. Her mother was a Native American and her father was a Quaker."

"Really?" Martin considered this interesting twist to Abigail's heritage. It answered some of his questions about her. "I bet she knows a *lot* about the area then." They sat quietly for a while.

"I had a pretty amazing experience out on the lake. It was like...I was...I felt I was in the presence of God."

"Hmmm." Martin took a puff on his pipe.

"I don't really know how to put it into words, Dad, but I felt a presence... there was a shining light...it was all inside of me. I felt like I was given a special promise and...a responsibility. I don't know what about exactly..."

Martin knew what his daughter meant. In his life, there had been quite a few significant moments of what he could only describe as holiness. They had given him strength and vision at crucial points in his life.

"I think it's about Joshua and me," continued Lillie.

Martin recalled the vision he'd had in his workshop, about Lillie and Joshua as the phoenix rose up to bring healing. He felt a flutter in his gut, a connection between the vision and Lillie's experience on the lake. "What do you mean?"

"Well," Lillie said, "I felt such a strong love for him. It filled me, as though it was given to me—not me making it up."

He thought of telling Lillie about his own vision, but decided there would be time for it later. He wasn't yet sure how he felt about his daughter in a serious relationship with Joshua Crumley. "Well, sweetheart, the power of God is an incredible thing. Be faithful to your own heart and I don't think you'll go wrong."

Lillie appreciated her father's counsel. She knew he was nervous about Joshua, so she was grateful for his understanding, and she realized she had never spoken of spiritual things with her father before. The realm of the spiritual was something she had shared only with her mother, back when they'd both believed in a hellfire and brimstone God who told you how to live, word for word, in the Holy Scriptures.

Lillie had missed reading the Bible. She had loved poring over it, and learning to follow its guidance—had once felt it was a collection of her own personal holy writings, precious and alive, given to her by God. After leaving the church, however, she had begun to question what she'd been taught and had pulled away from a literal view of the Bible. It had never been the same after that. She'd felt estranged from a good friend. But since she'd been home, that had begun to change.

"Thanks Dad," she said in the midst of her reflections. "I think I'm doing a pretty good job being true to myself...and setting limits with Joshua. Can you trust me about that?"

He smiled ruefully, humbled by her maturity. "Yes, sweetheart. I trust you." He thought of the phoenix and a calm assurance settled over him. "Hungry yet?"

24

Abigail was exhausted. It had been a draining, albeit successful, session with Joshua. Taking care of herself, she took a long drink of cold water, which she stored in used milk jugs she filled from a natural spring on her land, and then peeled and ate an orange. After washing her hands of juice, and tossing the peeling into her compost bucket, she crept behind the curtain and crawled into her bed. Indian quilts, hand-sewn by her mother, her aunts and her grandmother, offered a toasty warmth.

A twenty-minute nap was all she needed. Once rested, she donned her walking shoes and packed a hand-woven backpack with sacred objects and a bottle of water. Slinging the pack on her back, Abigail headed outside and walked down the path that led away from the cabin down to the shore and around to the other side of the lake. The events of this day required a special spot for her daily meditation.

A natural throne-like structure, an old stump covered with lush green moss, stood at the center of a small clearing ringed with trees. One side of the stump was missing, creating a perfect moss-covered backrest for her. Abigail reached into her backpack and placed a small braided rug on the damp moss, and sat down. Placing a colorful woven cloth on the rug next to her and a candle at its center, she created a simple altar. She took loose sage from a pouch to put in a tiny bowl for burning, and stuffed her pipe with tobacco.

Closing her eyes, she relaxed her body and focused on her breathing. Once she'd reached a state of peace, she opened her eyes, turned to the altar, and lit both the candle and the sage in its bowl. Holding the bowl in one palm, she pulled the fragrant smoke over herself with her other hand, chanting softly all the while. She lifted the bowl up to the sky, down to the earth and then turned slowly, facing for a moment in all four directions—east, south, west and then north.

When done, she set the smoldering bowl back on the altar and lit her pipe, an offering to the Great Spirit. Smoking contentedly, she leaned back and watched the lake in front of her. After a while she closed her eyes again, cradling the pipe in her hands. Thoughts flowed peacefully through her mind.

Soon, vibration caused Abigail's body to quiver. Her mind clear of thoughts, she felt surrounded by light. She listened for the wisdom of the spirits that offered her guidance and direction in her life and work.

Images appeared in her mind's eye, the first of Joshua and his mother talking and walking together. His father was there, and members of their extended family—some facing them with warm smiles and others rigid, backs turned.

Then came Lillie with a big heart, surrounded by angels, walking behind Joshua and his mother. A beaded necklace hung from her neck and her light brown hair was braided in two strands down her back. Clothed in a buckskin tunic, she was adorned by a solitary eagle feather, which stood up from the back of her head. A medicine bag hung from her belted waist.

Lillie's mother, Melodie, full of love and pride, led the group of angels that surrounded Lillie. Her father walked close behind with a tall man who looked a lot like Lillie. Another larger man with two young children, a boy and his younger sister, stood at the sidelines watching.

Abigail lifted her heart in prayer and felt energy and light surround the people in her vision. And then it faded and she slumped forward.

She sat quietly in her clearing for a long time, resting. When she opened them, her eyes alighted on a doe and her fawn taking a drink by the water's edge. Alerted to something, the doe bounded into the thicket, her fawn leaping after her.

Abigail packed her things and started back to her cabin. Dusk was beginning to fall when she opened her door and felt the welcome and familiarity of her tiny home. After preparing herself a simple meal and lighting the candles on the table on her porch, she fell asleep to the evening song of the nightingale. In her hands was a delicate teacup with hand-painted roses.

25

Joshua rose from his bed, still in his clothes, and padded downstairs in his stocking feet. Miriam was reading the newspaper in the living room and looked up to see him slump down in the armchair opposite her.

"Hello there," she said gently.

"Hi, Mom," Joshua responded, yawning.

"It's 2:30 in the afternoon—yesterday must have really taken it out of you."

"Wow, I guess so." He yawned and stretched. "I know you want to talk about it, Mom, but I need to wake up first. And besides that, I'm starved!"

"I could heat up your supper from last night or I could make you some breakfast. What would you like?"

He squinted at her as if the light was too bright. "Some of your special potato pancakes?"

"Okay." She smiled, pleased with his choice. "I'll make some up."

"I'm gonna go take a shower."

Miriam chuckled and watched him rise slowly and stretch high to the ceiling as if he were trying to touch it with his fingertips. As soon as he left the room, she busied herself in the kitchen. By the time he reemerged in faded jeans and a clean T-shirt, his newly washed hair standing out all over, she had set a plate of crisp, potato pancakes with applesauce and a mug of hot coffee on the table for him. She sat opposite him, holding her own refilled mug and watching while he inhaled his food like a hungry lion.

He ate a second helping and pushed back from the table satisfied. "Gosh, Mom, that was great!"

"I'm glad you liked it." Miriam wrapped her hands around her mug and looked down for a moment. "Josh?"

"What, Mom?"

"Will you please tell me what you are struggling with?"

Joshua sighed. Abigail had encouraged him to talk about his sessions, and Lillie had shared her advice from before. *Be true to yourself and honest and patient.*

He looked at the woman across the table from him—this was the mother he had needed so desperately as a teenager, the mother who had recently asked his forgiveness for her absence to him. He needed her once again, and, for the first time since his father's death, she was obviously trying to be there for him. Though he wanted to let her in on his private pain, he shuddered at the thought of talking about it with her. However, though he knew it would be difficult for both of them, he needed her support if he was to take the steps toward his own healing. Once the door was open, there would be no turning back.

He took a deep breath. "Mom, it goes back to Dad's death." Tears filled his mother's eyes, but she nodded at him to continue.

"Abigail helped me see that our grief when Dad died left us distant to one another and that left me vulnerable…" An apologetic look appeared on Miriam's face.

"It's okay, Mom. Abigail said it wasn't anyone's fault!" Miriam nodded sadly and he continued.

"I was kinda looking for substitute parents and that left me open to… abuse." He watched as redness rose up the length of his mother's neck, and he could hardly bear it. Tears came to him, too, and he reached across the table and gently took her small, aging hand. Miriam cleared her throat, which was thick with emotion. "What kind of abuse?"

"Sexual abuse, Mom." He said it and watched his mother's face crumble before him. She closed her eyes and began to weep and moan softly.

Joshua gripped both of her hands in his. "Mom, I need you to help me. I need *you* to be strong to help me face this!"

In her mind's eye, Miriam saw the young boy he had been, ripe in his pubescence, fatherless…motherless…vulnerable. Her heart broke, and pain coursed through her like a fierce and fiery wave, leaving her weak and breathless in its wake. Before her now, though, was her handsome, grown-up son, a successful professional dedicated to his work, and he was pleading with her for help. Gathering herself, she cleared her throat, and spoke in a hoarse whisper. "I'm here…Joshua…I'm here."

At her response, he closed his eyes and wept audibly, lowering his head to rest on the table, and she rose and walked around the table to her son. Standing beside him, she pulled him to her, and rocked him gently. Once his sobs ceased, she held him away, her hands on his broad shoulders and reached up to wipe his tears away.

"Honey, I am *so* sorry…" Her voice broke. "I have always loved you so much. My own grief got in the way—and I couldn't handle your pain and sorrow along with my own. But I see now that I must bear whatever pain there is—along with you—in order to help you, and I am ready now."

Joshua looked into the face of his mother's love and gently pulled away. "Mom, there's more to this story than I'm able to tell you just now. I'll need to tell you more as I work with Abigail, but right now there are some things I need to take care of first."

A worried look returned to Miriam's face. He placed his hand on her shoulder, speaking to the need he thought he saw. "Mom, I'm okay. I'll be back." She nodded, producing a weak smile, but her heart was raw.

Jumping in his car, Joshua headed for Lillie's house and, this time, drove all the way up the lane. He knocked on the back door.

When Martin finally came to the door, Joshua smiled nervously. "Hello, sir. Is Lillie here?"

"No, she's gone to Broadley to do some errands. But she should be back around four-thirty."

Disappointed, Joshua tried to figure out what to do next. He was embarrassed at his indecisiveness in front of Lillie's father.

Reading his discomfort, Martin offered help. "Would you like me to give her a message?"

"Yes, thank you…um…" he stuttered, "Please tell her I stopped by and would like for her to call me. Thank you." He lingered on the step.

Martin looked at his watch. "She should be back in less than an hour, Joshua. You could wait here for her. Besides, I could use your help."

Joshua's face lit up. "What do you need, sir?"

"Well, I could use some help cutting up a big tree that's down over there." He pointed toward the barn. "I'll cut it up with the chain saw if you'll haul the logs away and stack them by the woodpile."

Joshua thought for a moment. He had nothing else to do while he waited. "Sure, I'd be glad to!"

When Lillie drove up behind Joshua's car, she was both surprised and pleased that he had come to see her, and her heart raced as she carried the grocery bags to the house.

Wondering where he was, she heard the noise of the chain saw beyond the barn. She chuckled contentedly, guessing her father had invited Joshua to do hard labor in exchange for seeing his daughter. She stowed the bags in the kitchen, and strode swiftly back outside toward the barn, restraining herself from breaking into a run.

As she approached, Joshua caught sight of her and flashed a grin. She smiled back, suddenly shy. Joshua deposited a load near the pile and turned back to face her. Martin turned off the saw and the sudden silence rang out.

Lillie grinned mischievously at her father. "You must be desperate, Dad! Bringing in bums off the street to help you cut this thing up!"

Martin looked at Joshua and then back at Lillie, and winked at her. "He's not so bad. I don't think this one has ever stacked wood before, though."

Joshua saw the twinkle in Mr. Farmer's eye. He turned toward Lillie, lowering his head and clasping his hands in front of him. "Yes, Ma'am, thank you, Ma'am. If you'll feed me a meal and let me sleep in the barn tonight for my labor, I'll be on my way in the mornin' afore the sun comes up."

Without missing a beat, Lillie joined in the act. "Oh, no! You'll be invited into our home, young man. Come, you must be sweaty from all your workin'!"

They all laughed joyfully at the antics. Martin headed to the barn to put away the chain saw, giving the two a moment alone.

"So, what brings you over here, Joshua Crumley?" asked Lillie.

"Well, I hear tell there's a beautiful woman that lives here!"

Lillie laughed, throwing her head back. Her hair whisked like a horse's mane. "Well, I'll have to go look for her!"

Joshua crossed the distance between them in a few long strides and caught her by the hand. "It's you they sent me here to find, Lillie Farmer."

"Who's they, Joshua Crumley?" She stood very still, aware of his closeness and the flutter that had started in her stomach.

"They is me," he said, pointing to his heart. "We couldn't wait another minute to see you."

Lillie felt the tension building between them. She looked down at their clasped hands and said, "Who's we?"

He pulled her a little closer, and responded softly, "Me and my heart."

She looked up into his face, which was now very close to hers. His eyes held a soft intensity, a hopeful invitation. Locked in his gaze, she felt her body begin to tremble, and she feared her knees would buckle beneath her.

"Okay, so you *see* me." Though Joshua stood only inches from her, only their hands were touching. She wanted him to kiss her more than anything but she fought her own nervousness. "Did you and your heart wish to…" Her courage failed her again and she was silent, lowering her head to look down at their clasped hands again.

Joshua leaned his head beside hers and whispered in her ear. "Wish to what?"

She felt his breath hot on her hair, and the smell of him filled her nostrils. "Wish to…kiss…me?"

She felt him take her chin in his strong fingers and lift her face to his. Trembling, she felt the quiver in the pit of her stomach become stronger. Thinking she might have seen a slight frown on his face, she leaned back. Honesty and patience, she thought. "Joshua, if you're feeling uncomfortable…"

He answered her question by gently placing his lips on hers, and she melted at his touch. A shiver of pleasure flew through her, and she pressed her lips to his in response and closed her eyes. After a moment, he slowly pulled away.

She opened her eyes and looked into his. She saw there a mixture of pleasure, joy, fear…and a question. She smiled sweetly at him, took her free hand and wiped away the worry lines from his brow.

"Thank you," she said with her eyes. She took a step back and pulled him by the hand she still held in hers. "Come. You can help me cook!"

Joshua sat dazed at the kitchen table while Lillie unpacked the food from the grocery bags. She had captured his heart—there was no denying it. Their kiss had been a wonderful moment of tenderness between them, but best of all, he had felt no fear.

Lillie's Redemption

Coming in through the kitchen door, Martin interrupted Joshua's thoughts with a conspiratorial look, sneaked up behind Lillie at the counter and looked over her shoulder at the loot she was unpacking, sniffing as if hunting for scraps. Lillie swatted playfully at her father. "Go away, pest!"

Martin ducked and winked at Joshua.

"Joshua and I are going to make supper! You go away!"

"Ah-h-h!" her father exclaimed, duly impressed as he scuttled out of the room. "Call me when it's ready! I'll be lounging on the veranda."

A few hours later, the three were seated around the kitchen table enjoying a meal of vegetarian lasagna, garlic bread, salad and white wine. On reflection, none of them had been happier in a long time.

26

Miriam sat numbly at her kitchen table. She had wondered why Joshua had never brought home a girlfriend—she had even thought once that he might have been gay. He had always been very private about his social life so she had no way of knowing for sure. To know now that her son had been abused in some way certainly muddied the water.

Her imagination began to run wild—what had actually happened to him? Who had done it? What did Lillie Farmer have to do with it? She wondered desperately how she would be able to maintain support of her son when her heart was breaking and she felt her world crumbling around her.

Then it occurred to her that Joshua had somehow survived for years under the weight of the trauma, whatever it was—and if he could survive and now face it all over again in order to bring himself some relief, then she could too. Her husband came to mind and a stab of grief pierced her heart. She wished he were there to help her and sent up a prayer.

"Sam, we need you. Josh needs a father so much right now!" Tears flowed silently down her cheeks. "He needs me and I feel so weak! Please help me be strong. I will do my best to be both mother and father to him, please help me."

She thought, too, of her older sister and decided to call her. She had always been able to count on Rachel for support.

Miriam stood, shifting her weight back and forth, as she listened to the phone ring on the other end of the line.

"Hello?"

The sound of her sister's voice made her emotional all over again. "Hello... Rachel?"

"Hi, Sis! How are you?"

Miriam hesitated. "Well...I need..." Her voice caught in her throat.

"What is it, Sis?"

Miriam knew it would take courage to speak the truth but she wasn't sure what to say. It occurred to her suddenly too, that she hadn't asked Joshua's permission to tell anyone else, even his aunt. But she needed support and her older sister was the only living person in whom she could even imagine confiding.

"It's Josh...he's home for a while..."

"Yeah? Why? What's going on?"

"Well..." Her voice cracked.

"Miriam, what's wrong?"

"Rachel...he confided in me about some difficulties he had after Sam died..." She took a deep breath to stay calm. "He started seeing a...counselor this week."

"He did?"

"Yes. And it was his idea, too."

"Really." Rachel hesitated. "Are you saying he's having trouble, *now*, with Sam's death?"

"Well, trouble, yes. He's pretty upset." She moved on before she lost her nerve. "Rachel, I don't know how to tell you this because this is his private struggle. But he's made it clear that he needs my support."

"Wow! He's reaching out to you for help? That's new for him, isn't it?"

Miriam felt her throat constrict. "Yes. I thought he'd been so independent all these years. But...really, he's been alone. Now he needs me...and Rachel... he's in pain! It breaks my heart!" She sobbed once and then began to cry.

Her sister remained quiet, listening intently.

"I wasn't there for him when he lost his father. There were things...that he needed from me back then...but I wasn't able to deal with his pain along with my own!" She sobbed audibly, no longer able to hold back the force of her feelings.

"Miriam, you can't blame yourself for that. You did the best you could."

"But it wasn't good enough, Rachel! He was deeply hurt and had to carry it alone all these years!"

"What happened, Sis? What are you talking about?"

"He was sexually abused."

"Oh, my God! When?"

"I'm not sure. He hasn't told me all the details yet. He says he will as soon as he works with his counselor some more."

"Miriam, it's good that he's seeing a counselor now."

"Yes, but, Rachel, how could I have missed that? He's been carrying this all alone. What have I done to him?" She started to cry again. "What have I done to my boy?"

"Sis, you didn't know. We can't know everything that happens to our children."

"Yes, but I should have realized...his change...when he became mean and...reclusive. I should have recognized the signs, done something!"

"Perhaps you should have. But you didn't. There's no point in beating yourself up over it—you understand now and you can help him now."

"But Rachel, how could I be so oblivious? How?"

"Honey, you were grieving! You'd lost your husband! Mom was like that when Dad died. I remember it was like she was empty—she had nothing to give. I ended up stepping in to take care of you guys. She just couldn't be a mother to you for a while."

"How long did it go on?"

"Oh, I don't know...a year, maybe two. But Sis, everyone handles grief differently and you just were unable to see clearly. Don't blame yourself."

There was a long silence as Miriam considered what she'd said. Finally Rachel changed the subject. "Tell me about his counselor."

"She's a woman...that he seems to find very helpful." Miriam tried to express in her voice a confidence she did not feel.

"Good. So, as he works with her and is ready to share more with you, you'll be ready to support him."

"How? With Sam gone..." She cleared her throat. "How can I face this?"

"I know. Parenting requires more than we think we have to give sometimes. But you can do this, Sis. You have to. Josh needs you now."

Miriam sighed. "Of course! You're right. But will you let me call and talk to you now and then?"

"Sure."

"Thanks, Sis...you're a big help. I feel better already."

"Call me anytime...I'll just listen. I love you."

Miriam hung up the phone and went into the living room. It helped to talk about it, to have someone else carry the burden with her. Temporarily relieved, she sat down in a chair and laid her head back. Soon, she was snoring softly, exhausted from all the emotion of the day.

Samuel looked at her with eyes full of love. His face disappeared and then she saw herself standing in the middle of a dark room with a window up high where light poured in. She wanted to move towards the window but her feet appeared to be stuck in cement as if they were built right into the floor. She couldn't move but she wanted desperately to get to the light.

27

Violet stood, fuming, as she did the dishes. Her brother hadn't visited her father once in the two years since their mother's funeral, and he had suddenly appeared. But not when she and *her* family were there! He'd arranged to come when *Lillie* was there, without even considering her. She'd been left out again!

Kevin entered the kitchen and quietly approached his wife from behind. He encircled her with his arms and nuzzled her neck.

She pulled away. "What are you doing? I'm trying to get this place clean!"

"Mmmm." Kevin squeezed her tighter and nuzzled deeper.

"This place is a mess, Kevin," she said, pulling away from him again.

"I'll clean things up tomorrow while the kids are in school."

"You say that everyday."

"And everyday I clean up."

"Not enough, you don't!"

Kevin attempted to nuzzle her again. Violet snapped at him. "Get away!"

Standing back, he observed his wife. "What's got you all riled?"

"Nothing, I just hate it when this place is such a pig sty."

"It's no more a pig sty today than any other day, Vi."

"Well, it should never be a pig sty! You don't keep up with things around here. I have to do everything!"

"No you don't. Vi, stop a minute." He pulled her towards him away from the sink. "You know I do my share."

She looked away and he turned her face back to his. "Look at me. You know I do my share. You just think you have to come after me and do it again. But no one makes you do that." She turned, but he moved his head to keep her eyes on his. "You can relax, Violet Parks. It's okay. Things are okay."

He took her into his arms and held her against his large chest.

Tears welled in her eyes. "Well, why doesn't anybody listen to me?"

"Who's not listening to you?"

"My family."

"What has your family done?"

"They got together without me. Bruce came home to Dad's house, Kevin, and Lillie was there. Why didn't they ask *me*?" Violet was beginning to cry.

"Well, it's about time Bruce returned to your Dad's. How long's it been?"

"I don't know. I don't care. I wasn't there."

"Well, next time." Kevin pushed her gently out in front of him so he could wipe her face and kiss her forehead. "Don't let it get to you, Vi. There'll be another chance. Now, I gotta finish my article by ten. Why don't you finish up here and come read by me in my study. I'd love your company." He turned her gently around to the sink and kissed the back of her head before leaving the kitchen.

Violet returned to the dishes. It bothered her when people didn't do as they were told. Something was changing, and her control was slipping. Her usually cooperative father was focused on Lillie again—she had always gotten the lion's share of attention from their parents. She understood what Lillie was about—depression was an effective way to keep all of them hovering around her. With Mother gone, it had been all their father seemed concerned about— Lillie and her depression!

During their last visit, Martin had suggested she and Kevin take a few days for themselves and leave the kids in his care. She had appreciated the gesture, but Bruce's secret visit had erased all sense of his thoughtfulness. Still brooding, she thought about asking Bruce to come back so they could all be together, but she wanted to see if he would call her first—to apologize for hurting her feelings by leaving her out.

No one seemed to appreciate the sacrifices she made—caring for the house, taking the kids to soccer and ballet and piano lessons and boy scouts, making meals plus working full time. She never got a moment's rest and though she complained about it, no one appeared to care. Claiming he was writing a book while he worked out of a home office writing free-lance articles for national magazines, Kevin often retreated to his study. The house was never clean enough and Kevin just didn't see it. On top of that, Samantha, her youngest and she were always butting heads. Sassy was as strong-willed as Lillie. Her oldest, Ben, a quiet, studious boy and a deep thinker like his father, was beyond her comprehension—she was often frustrated with him too. He retreated into a book, much as Lillie had often done.

During their childhood years, Bruce and Lillie had become close to each other, but not to her—she had had nothing in common with them. As a result, self-pity and feelings of exclusion often flared up for Violet and the whole family suffered for it.

But this summer something had changed. Violet could feel the erosion of her influence. She enjoyed the power to make others scurry around but she had no idea that by doing it, she alienated the people she cared most about. The more she tried to control them, the further they slipped away from her.

28

After leaving Lillie and Martin and the delightful evening they had spent together, Joshua headed home relaxed and happy. He had forgotten what good companionship could be—Lillie's father was interesting and funny and Joshua liked him.

Feeling warm inside, he drove up to his mother's home. The house was dark, so he assumed his mother had already gone to bed. Still flying high from the evening, he looked in the refrigerator, poured himself a glass of milk and, wandered thoughtfully into the darkened living room. He sat in an armchair to think.

He was attracted to Lillie and glad to be near her. But although he felt warm and safe when he was with her, he was still vaguely uncomfortable. She had invited him to kiss her! What would that lead to? Did she like him?

A rustle came from the other side of the room, and Joshua focused on his surroundings. Staring into the darkness, his eyes still adjusting to the lack of light, he could make out the form of his mother in the chair across the room. The thought of the earlier conversation with his mother washed over him and he recalled the tears they had shed together. It made him sad that she hadn't been able to be there for him so many years before, but he was grateful that she would be there, this time, to share the burden.

He finished his milk, and after putting the empty glass away, he returned to the living room and quietly knelt by his mother's chair. It was his turn to take a sleepyhead to bed. "Mom?" he whispered, gently shaking her.

She stirred and moaned and then woke with a start. "Oh, Joshua...I guess I fell asleep."

"And it's time to sleep some more. Let's go to bed." He helped his mother from her chair and they climbed the stairs together.

That night, Joshua slept better than he'd slept in as long as he could remember. When he woke, the smell of brewing coffee filled his nostrils and he felt warm and content inside. Dozing off and on, he was conscious of his mother's movements across the hall, and heard her start the water for her bath. The next thing he knew there was a faint knocking downstairs on the kitchen door. He could hear the water still running, so he got up, pulled on a pair of pants, and went down to answer it.

Upon opening the door, he found Lillie grinning in the warm light of morning. She looked at him, chest exposed, and the warmth of embarrassment filled him head to toe. "What are you doing up so early?"

"Want to go out to breakfast with me?"

Joshua looked around outside to see if the rest of the world was awake, and then looked back at Lillie's upturned face, full of life and sparkle.

"How could I turn down an invitation like that?" His face broke into a grin. "Come in. I'll get dressed." Joshua bounded up the stairs, pulled on a T-shirt and socks and shoes, combed his hair, washed his face, brushed his teeth and sprayed cologne on his shirted chest in record time. Yelling to his mother that he was going out to breakfast, he jumped the last three steps on his way back downstairs, causing the house to shake.

Lillie turned to look at him as he entered the kitchen, and her face glowed with delight. Reveling in her attention, Joshua realized that he felt lucky for a change, for perhaps the first time in his life.

Chattering all the way, Lillie drove Joshua into town. "You know, people are going to talk when they see us together."

Joshua thought about it for a moment. "Does that bother you?"

"Nope. I rather like the idea of being the subject of town gossip!" Her grin was defiant—they were taking a big step, going public with their budding relationship.

Pulling up to the café, Lillie parked on the street in front. They entered and slid into a booth.

"Well, look who the cat dragged in!" said Betty, arriving with menus.

A knowing look was exchanged between them. Seeing a mischievous twinkle in Betty's eye, Joshua and Lillie smiled.

When she'd taken their drink order, Betty noticed that her friend, Debra Hundley, had come in and taken a seat at the counter.

Debra was a local writer who lived a very rough life. A woods woman who cut and chopped wood and heated her house with it, she lived alone. Having come to Hopeston after a bitter divorce fifteen years before, she had lived in the town as a recluse. The reddish-purple color of her nose and cheeks revealed a penchant for alcohol, and there was always a cigarette hanging from her lips. Both were in stark contrast to the strength of body and character suggested by her physical fitness and tough masculine dress.

Though she was known in the community as an intellectual—a writer—no one had ever seen one of her published works, but she was always working and seemed to have plenty of money to support her habits. When she was sober, she was an introvert and kept very quiet. But when she'd had too much to drink, she had a tendency to be friendly and outgoing. And she loved to gossip—many a personal tale had been heard and passed on by her in both Hopeston and Broadley.

Betty delighted in this fact. Having decided that she was entitled to information about the people of Hopeston, she felt a maternal possessiveness about "her people." When word had reached Betty from Bill Hadley that Lillie had come into town looking for Joshua Crumley, for instance, she had not been surprised. Now she could clearly see that something was going on between them.

Lillie was of special interest because Betty had often wondered what had happened to cause Melodie Farmer to abruptly leave Hopeston Church, after pouring so many years of her life into it. Too practical herself to be interested in what she considered the narrow-minded teachings of that local non-denominational church, Betty had never darkened its doors for Sunday worship. She did, however, understand the importance of religion in bringing people together and she had attended every funeral celebrated in the little church during the past 40 years.

So she had been to Melodie Farmer's funeral just two years before. She remembered that the new pastor had not known Melodie—and had said virtually nothing about her in the service. But the funeral, like all memorial gatherings, had given the townsfolk a place to gather and a chance to reach out to one another, facing together the issues of faith and struggle, of life and death.

Betty leaned with her elbows on the counter in front of Debra. She could see by the look in Debra's eyes that she had already been drinking, and it was a good bet she was in the mood to talk. "So, old gal, the usual?"

"Yup, Betty, old gal!" Debra grinned almost too widely and tossed her head as if to put an exclamation point on her order.

Betty smiled, and turned to pour a cup of coffee for someone else while she spoke. "Have ya heard how Delbert's doin' lately?"

Debra took out a cigarette and lit it, inhaling deeply before responding. "Yap, he's not doin' too well. They say he's dyin'!" Smoke trickled out of her nose and mouth.

"No! Really? This thing's big enough to kill 'im?"

"Poor guy can't fight it off any longer, I guess." Debra took another drag from her cigarette and then twirled it in the ashtray.

Betty submitted Debra's order, and started to prepare drinks. Depositing theirs with Lillie and Joshua as she made the rounds to check on her other customers, she cast a look back over her shoulder at the two young people. Lillie was energetically recounting something to Joshua and he was watching her face intently.

Betty was astonished. In all the years he had lived in Hopeston, she had never seen Joshua look like that before. He was happy and engaged—it made him strikingly handsome. As she continued to go about her business, she surveyed his physique and tried to remember what he did for a living. Was he a lawyer? Yes, that was it. Big city class, too.

The couple looked up at her to signal they were ready to order food, so she returned to them with her mind ready to memorize. "Whadda you kids want?" she asked.

Joshua placed his order and Lillie looked once more at the menu. "Okay, I'm ready..." she said. "I'll have a vegetarian omelet and home fries. No toast!"

Betty crossed the room to put in their order and leaned on the counter in front of Debra.

"See those kids?" she whispered, tipping her head toward Joshua and Lillie. With the looseness of drink, Debra turned to look in an obvious manner.

"Yeah, so?"

"Well, that's Joshua Crumley, Miriam's boy, and Lillie Farmer, Martin and Melodie's youngest."

"As I said, yeah, so?" Debra took another bite of her breakfast.

"Oh, for goodness sake, you're dense!" Betty exclaimed in exasperation. "They used to hate each other in high school! *Now* look at them—no don't look—just trust me. They're acting like lovebirds!"

"O-o-oh." Debra's voice rose and fell with a conspiratorial inflection. "I wonder what got them going?"

Betty thought out loud. "They both work and live in the city now, so I think they're just home for visits. And I heard Lillie came into Bill's store the other day, asking if Joshua was in town." She disappeared to bus some tables and tally up checks for customers preparing to leave.

Debra sat musing on the Crumley and Farmer families and tried to think of what she knew about them. By the time Betty returned, she was clearly pleased with herself, and looked like a cat who had just eaten a mouse. "Wasn't Melodie Farmer Joshua's Sunday School teacher back in the early eighties?"

Betty thought for a minute. "You know, I think you're right. In fact, I remember there was quite a fuss over the mess she left in the children's Summer Bible program when she suddenly dropped out of view." She paused. "I had forgotten all about that. It was all kinda weird, wasn't it?"

"Why was it that she left?" Debra asked.

"I don't know. I don't think anybody knows."

Debra pulled a couple of bills out of her wallet and left them on the counter, and then grabbed her cigarettes.

Betty winked at her. "I guess we'll just have to watch these two...and see what develops." Debra slid off the stool and walked out of the café with a wave.

An older couple, Jerry and Julia Bomont had been sitting in the booth closest to the counter. Because he was hard of hearing, Jerry had missed the hushed conversation between the waitress and her writer friend. But Julia's hearing was as sharp as her mind, and she had heard every word.

She waited until Debra cleared the café, and leaned closer to her husband. "That Lillie Farmer left the church at the same time her mother did, and it's shameful! If Melodie Farmer was such a wonderful Bible teacher, then why did she leave such chaos for poor Pastor Lane to deal with? Remember…he *told* us she tried to seduce him! She probably left in a huff when he put her in her place! There was never a kinder pastor than Reverend Lane Richardson!"

The old woman crouched even further in toward her husband. "And I'll bet Lillie is a loose woman just like her mother! Look over there, Jerry. Now she's pursuing that Joshua Crumley. He never did amount to anything. He was such a troubled boy…after he lost his father at such a young age."

She sipped her coffee. "And they're Jews! Don't belong here." She sat back, staring surreptitiously in Joshua and Lillie's direction. "Why would Lillie want a Jew anyway? I'll bet she's a loose woman, just like her mother, and will chase anything with pants on!"

Jerry Bomont was used to the vicious gossip of which his wife was capable, and was glad at times that he was hard of hearing. He nodded and grunted at strategic points in her monologue and kept eating his breakfast.

Meanwhile, oblivious to everything else around them in the café, Lillie and Joshua had truly begun to get to know each other. Delighted, they discovered that they were both avid readers, were athletic, loved music and, though different in family traditions, had similar notions about religion—all of which made for lively conversation.

Lillie liked to read novels, mostly historical fiction and books about nature and animals and real people in real places doing things that made a difference in the world. Joshua read newspapers on a daily basis, both the local Broadley Gazette and the New York Times, and subscribed to several magazines. He was into politics, judicial and legal matters, scientific journals and he, too, liked to read about what people were doing to make a difference in the world.

Joshua's personal fitness routine involved running on the treadmill and lifting weights at a local gym while Lillie preferred the outdoors. She hiked, canoed, backpacked, biked, skied, snow-shoed and played virtually any outdoor game. They both liked modern music, and some of the same bands, but their favorite music was classical.

And both had developed a pessimistic view of religion. Lillie had been raised with a combination of ideas—her mother's narrow, authoritative Christian faith, which gave her a sense of security early on, and her father's nature-focused, largely unspoken spirituality.

Joshua, on the other hand, had had, in his early youth, a devout Jewish father who had maintained the Hebrew traditions of the Sabbath and the celebration of holy days. This had not given Joshua a sense of community or belonging, as there were no other Jewish families in the area, but it had given him a strong sense of roots and tradition that provided structure to his life.

So, when after his father's death his mother hadn't had the stomach to continue the traditional Jewish religious practices and sent him to Hopeston Church, he had identified so thoroughly with the faith of his teacher, Lillie's mother, he had virtually renounced—or simply forgotten—his own Jewish heritage and had found a place to belong and a sense of community among the Christians. He told Lillie that when her mother had left the church and he'd felt unable to return, he'd lost any faith in religion, in the church and in God.

In general, however, Lillie and Joshua discovered they shared the basic values of decency and love and family taught by the Judeo-Christian culture. But neither was interested in attending an institutional church of any kind, much less the one that had been a source of so much pain to both of them. In the end, they admitted, though, that they were thirsty for a sense of connection and purpose in their lives, and as they learned more about each other, their thirst for spiritual nourishment grew as well.

Lillie laid her fork on the empty plate in front of her. "Do you want to hike up Monroe's Hill with me?"

Joshua found himself suddenly more than willing to do anything if it meant being with Lillie. "Yeah, sure," he said, light shining in his eyes.

29

From the café, Joshua and Lillie drove to the trail head and parked in the gravel parking lot. Lillie suggested they hike into the woods on a trail that led to the summit of a modest hill from which the view promised to be great. At the base, she said, could be seen the houses of many of the inhabitants of Hopeston. It would be a good hour's climb.

Warm with shafts of sunlight shining through the canopy of leaves far overhead, the forest hosted mosquitoes aplenty, forcing Lillie and Joshua into constant motion to avoid being eaten alive. Their swatting and waving of arms became humorous and started them giggling and running in spurts on their way up the hill. As they neared the top, Lillie leapt up on Joshua's back for a piggyback ride and he took off running with her.

Soon thoroughly out of breath from the exertion and laughter, they fell into a heap, gasping for breath. Tangled up with one another, they lay looking at the sky overhead until their heartbeats returned to normal. Suddenly aware of the warmth of Lillie's body next to his, Joshua abruptly pulled away and stood up, leaving Lillie lying on the ground.

"What are you doing?" she asked, her face contorted in confusion.

"I don't know," he said. "I don't know!" He pulled her to her feet.

"I don't know either!" she exclaimed. "Yesterday you kissed me. Now you can't stand to touch me?"

"I know. I'm sorry."

"What's going on?" Lillie tried to be kind, but failed at holding back the force of her frustration.

"I don't know, Lillie. I start to feel…fear…in my stomach. It happens all the time. When I get aroused, I feel not only pleasure, but…terror."

Her frustration melted away. "But you didn't feel that way yesterday when we kissed!" She stopped for a moment. "Or *did* you?"

"No, I didn't." He looked down thoughtfully and examined his shoe, like a little boy.

"Joshua, I love you. I won't hurt you!" As they rolled off her tongue, Lillie was shocked at her own words.

Joshua's head shot up. "Don't say that if you don't mean it!" All of a sudden, neither of them noticed the mosquitoes anymore.

"I didn't know I was going to say that..." She looked down and began to cry softly. "But I *do* mean it. I've been falling in love with you all along." Overcome with emotion, she closed her eyes.

Joshua reached out and touched her cheek with his hand. "Come here." he said softly. "You're covered with leaves."

He circled her, brushing her off and gently picking leaves from her hair. "Lillie, I love being with you. You make me feel so peaceful inside. But the peace goes away when I get a...hard-on." He paused, embarrassed. "I just don't want to feel pain and fear when I'm with you."

She turned around quickly and stood so close he could feel her breath on his face. "But Joshua, if we are gentle and help each other, don't you think we can overcome those feelings from the past?"

"I don't know...I've never tested it." He looked deeply into her eyes, as if searching her soul to be sure she was for real. "I've never had anyone who was able, or willing to work through this with me."

Lillie felt a sudden resolve she hadn't known she had, and spoke it aloud. "I am willing to work through anything with you, Joshua Crumley!"

He wanted to believe her more than anything he could think of. "Okay, so how do we begin?"

She lay her hand lightly on his chest. "Remember that whatever we do is ours and we can have our own feelings about it. I think as we learn to be close with each other we will be able to replace one set of bad experiences and feelings for other very different feelings—kindness, love, gentleness, joy."

Joshua placed a hand over hers, which still lay on his chest, and curled his fingers around them. "Okay. So, you promise you'll help me?"

"Yes. May I begin by kissing you?"

"Please," he said.

She reached her neck forward and found he was too far away. "I need your help here," she said, giggling.

151

Placing her hands on his shoulders and pulling him to her, she reached her face up to his. Gently, she placed her lips on his and pressed into their softness. A feeling of bliss flooded her. Opening her eyes, she pulled away from him just far enough to look into his, searching, and she found what she was looking for—desire in his eyes. Compelled to kiss him again, Lillie leaned into him, this time allowing her breasts to touch his chest, and she kissed him hard.

He lifted his right hand and took her into a one-armed embrace that pressed her body against his. She felt his physical response against her and tentatively offered her tongue. He willingly parted his lips in invitation.

Joshua focused his mind on Lillie, and the smell and feel of her. He explored her mouth and it became the whole world. Moaning softly, he released her mouth from his, and gazed at her face.

Lillie smiled. She too felt alive in a new way, enjoyed the feel of his arm holding her. She shivered as she felt his hand move up and gently cup her breast. She felt his touch, alive with desire.

He, in turn, watched as desire permeated her face as well. It pleased him, and he let his hands travel across her chest. Lightning charged through Lillie's body—she felt him continue to harden against her and wondered if they should stop—if she *could* stop. Laying her head on his chest, she breathed deeply.

Sensing her decision to slow what was happening, he held her with both arms gently against him, and they let their arousal slowly flow out of them until their breathing was normal again. The tension between them ebbed away and they relaxed, warmed by the desire that had filled them and the tenderness of their embrace. Joshua kissed the top of Lillie's head and spoke softly into her hair. "Should we go?"

Her face muffled in his chest, she replied. "Uh, huh. I think we'd better."

They climbed the rest of the way up the hill in silence, and in perfect cadence, walked as one synchronized body. Delighted, they began to smile and then giggle as their matching steps increased in speed.

Playfully, they raced the last yards to the summit outcropping and discovered they had the place to themselves. They stood together looking out over the view of forests, fields and homesteads below. Hopeston spread out beneath them, as if nature had loaned pockets of herself to the few, brave inhabitants of the small town.

Lillie was struck by the lives she knew were being lived in the valley. She had spent most of her young life there and now wondered, sadly, why she'd ever left it for the city so full of noise, chaos, and pollution, so disconnected from the natural world.

Joshua, on the other hand, looked out over the hometown of his childhood with mixed feelings. He had loved it, but he had been deeply wounded there. He had run away from the grief and pain that haunted him and thought he had successfully severed the tie that bound him to this place. At a great price, he had been forced to shut his heart down and close himself to the people he cared about—including his mother and Mrs. Farmer and…Lillie.

Joshua's heart felt suddenly raw and vulnerable. He staggered back, faint from the sensation of ground shifting beneath his feet. Lillie was immediately at his side holding his arm and looking into his face.

"Are you okay?"

"I'm a little light headed," he said. "It's all that kissing and stuff you make me do!" he teased.

She led him to a tree and helped him sit and lean against it for support. "I can stop anytime you want me to."

He laughed out loud at the challenge on her face.

"Really," she said, seriously. "Are you okay?"

"Yes, I'm just defenseless around you."

On impulse Lillie leaned forward and kissed him again. When she pulled away she saw joy and teasing in his eyes.

"There you go again, kissing me!"

"Well, if you weren't so incredibly handsome right here in front of me, I wouldn't have to!" She plopped down next to him against the tree and lifting his arm, he put it around her and pulled her close beside him.

Lillie closed her eyes. Heart full, silently she began to pray. *O God, thank you for this man! Please heal his wounds. Help him to forgive himself. Release him from the pain that haunts him! Use me as you will, God, to help him heal and blossom. He's so wonderful!*

She soon drifted off to sleep and Joshua sat calmly looking out over the valley. Feeling her warm weight against him, he breathed deeply and looked up at the trees swaying against the blue sky. He smiled, recalling Lillie's patient instruction about all the plant life—the ferns, wintergreen and wild lilies of the valley waving in the breeze on the ground around them. The name her mother had given her, he thought, had been well-chosen.

A lot had happened over the past several days—the conversation with his mother, the supper with Lillie and her father, stacking wood with Martin. He felt grateful for Abigail, and for Lillie's mother, too, who, though she had been wounded herself, had started the healing process for him with her letter. He was overcome with gratitude and humility.

Sunlight fell on a bright red cardinal in a tree close by, and Joshua watched, amazed at his beauty. Almost as if aware of Joshua's attention, the red bird turned to face him, and the two looked at each other for a long time. Joshua felt a strange sensation—blessed with the grace of presence, love flooded his heart. He'd been a stranger to the love of the people around him, and now he was choosing it. He no longer felt like the fearful, angry, wounded boy he had been, he was being transformed into an *innocent* boy—cared for, guided and bathed in love.

The cardinal took its flight, and Joshua, stunned by the power of the moment, looked at the woman in his arms. Was she too an envoy from God, this God that was blessing him? Was he being offered a great gift, the gift of Lillie and her love, at the same time that he was being offered the chance to heal from the pain of his past?

Is that how God works? Does God give priceless gifts that bring such joy and happiness in the same moment of challenge to step up and take on the hard task of healing?

He reached out to touch his finger lightly to Lillie's cheek and she opened her eyes and looked at him. "Lillie," he whispered, "thank you for loving me." He leaned down and kissed her tenderly on the lips.

The sun was now bright overhead, and the two walked hand in hand down the hill to the parking area. Lillie dropped Joshua off at home and headed for the farm. Both spent the rest of their day puttering around and thinking about their intimate exchange—secure in the burgeoning knowledge that they were loved.

That night, Lillie dreamed again.

The doe led her along the paths in the woods once again and as they went along she saw crushed flowers on either side of the path rising up and unfolding as air was being blown into them returning them to their original pristine state. She noticed it was her passing by each flower that caused this phenomenon.

She saw the clearing ahead, with the fire at its center and felt a strong pull to join the circle of people dancing around the leaping flames. As they whirred by in a blur she reached into the stream of passing dancers and grabbed a hold of a hand. Drawn into the dance and once she was moving along with the others in a smooth motion, she saw it was Joshua's hand she held.

Joshua also dreamed, but his would be a nightmare.

As adults, he and Lillie walked happily hand in hand to the church. Pastor Lane was waiting for them as they entered the church, and, scowling at Joshua, he began to chastise him for being with the Farmer girl, yelling that he was a sinner and that he would ruin Lillie like he had ruined her mother. Afraid, Joshua cowered in the corner, feeling like a thirteen-year-old boy again. He looked at Lillie and before his eyes, she turned into Mrs. Farmer. Then she was on the floor, half-naked, pinned down by the pastor who looked at him with an evil face and told him to violate her. Obediently, Joshua moved toward the pastor in fear. When he looked again, it was Lillie on the floor.

Joshua awoke in a sweat. The dull ache in his chest had returned. What had he been thinking? There was no way he could be sure of himself with Lillie. He should leave her alone for her own sake—for her safety.

He buried his head under the pillow and wept. He wept for the loss of the joy and happiness he had shared with Lillie. He wept because he was sure he would never be able to have a normal relationship with *any* woman. He wept in anger that what Lane Richardson had done to him still held power over him.

The sense of freedom and movement he had gained was gone—he was right back where he started. He would never be free of the pain, the fear, the anger and the isolation. Worst of all, he knew he had to tell Lillie all of what had happened, that he had been molested by the pastor and forced to watch as her mother had been brutally violated.

At noon Miriam knocked on Joshua's door to see if he was awake. Hearing no answer, she peered into the room. Joshua pulled back in fright, a wild look in his eyes.

"Oh, I'm sorry, dear. I didn't mean to startle you. Are you okay?"

Joshua stared at her, his look changing from fear to painful resignation, and her heart sank.

Miriam had seen this look before, but it had disappeared in the last few weeks. "What's wrong, Josh?" When he didn't answer, she said, "I'll see you downstairs, hon—I'm going to make you breakfast, so get up and come down, please."

Joshua lay in bed feeling miserable. He decided that when she knew the whole truth, Lillie would never love him—he would be doing her a favor if he left her alone and went back to his life in the city. He'd neglected his work anyway, the one thing that had given purpose and meaning to his life. She would be hurt, he knew—their time together on Monroe's Hill had meant a lot to both of them. He had wanted to believe it was possible to feel normal, to be in love with a woman like Lillie. But it was too good to be true.

Abigail's words drifted into his mind. It wasn't thy fault. Oh, how he wished he could believe her! But the nightmare was still vividly with him, and Lane's evil face displaced the voice of the kind healer.

Miriam called to tell him breakfast was ready, and he threw off the cover. He would pack and leave quickly before Lillie showed up or called, but first he would eat.

Once downstairs, Joshua sat and stared at the heaping plate of food. Not the least bit hungry, he pushed his chair back from the table, and Miriam placed her hand on his.

"What's wrong, son?"

"I don't feel good."

She felt his forehead. "Are you coming down with something?"

He waved her off angrily. "No!"

"Well, *something's* wrong! What happened yesterday? Where did you go?"

A myriad of emotions played across Joshua's face. Slumping forward, he laid his head on the table and wept. "I was with Lillie…we went for a walk…then I dreamed…Oh, Mom, I have terrible nightmares and this one was about Lillie!"

"What about her?"

"I was going to hurt her." Tears continued to stream down his face. "I don't deserve her, Mom!"

"Why not?"

"Because!"

Damn it, he thought. She may as well know. The dam broke within him and the words gushed out. "It was the pastor, Mom! Pastor Lane! He's the one who sexually abused me…"

Miriam reared back in horror. "What are you saying? In real life? Pastor Lane did this to you in real life?"

"Yes." He looked at his mother and knew the time had come, whether he wanted it or not. "Mom, I need to tell you what happened. But I want Lillie here."

"Do you want her here…now?"

"Yes, please…"

This was the answer, he thought, the only answer to breaking the cycle of secrecy and isolation that had trapped him for over a decade. Honesty and patience, as Lillie had said. It would start by his being honest with himself.

Fear began to subside and his courage returned. In an instant, he knew he loved Lillie, and he didn't want to lose her! He'd lost her once before, when they'd been in high school, because of the pastor and his unrelenting nightmares. He couldn't, wouldn't let it happen again. Telling his story would finally place the blame where it belonged. It would be hard—it would require a great deal of work to overcome his demons, but he could do it! There were people who loved him and would be there for him. His mother, once distant, was strong and helpful and he felt her love. He could hear her now, dialing the phone.

The hunger of his soul to be free matched the growling of his stomach, so he devoured what was in front of him, gaining strength to do what he'd needed to do for so long. The time was now.

Miriam took a deep breath when she heard the young woman's voice on the other end of the phone.

"Lillie, this is Miriam Crumley…Joshua asked me to call you…He is very upset and would like you to come over…Yes, right now…Thank you…Okay. Thank you, Lillie…" She returned to sit with Joshua as he ate. "She said to tell you she's on her way."

Mother and son remained silent, calm as if in the eye of a storm, both knowing that would all change when Lillie arrived.

When Joshua was done eating, he set down his fork and spoke to her gently. "Thanks, Mom, for the food. This isn't going to be easy. But I have to tell you what happened. We have to deal with this. I can't keep it bottled up anymore. It's like poison inside of me. I can't deal with this all alone."

Miriam nodded slightly and rose from the table, busying herself with the dishes.

30

When Lillie arrived at the door, it was Joshua who let her in. He took her by the hand and led her into the living room where the light was dim.

Joshua sat by Lillie on the couch, holding her hand. Miriam sat in an armchair opposite them.

His voice was steady but hoarse. "Lillie, I've decided I need to tell Mom, and you…" He gazed at her with a vulnerable look in his eyes. "All of what happened at the church."

Lillie nodded, and settled herself next to him.

"Mom, Lillie knows most of the story. She read about it in her mother's diary." He gave her a minute to let what he'd said sink in. "What happened involved Mrs. Farmer, too. Remember?"

Miriam nodded, tense from head to toe.

"I was helping her clean up after Bible School that summer, and…the pastor kept having her come to his office. I knew something wasn't right. And after a while, I figured it out. He was…seducing her." He watched his mother's face and felt Lillie's substantial presence next to him.

"I knew it was wrong, and then one day, I tried to stop him. I burst in on them, thinking I could catch them in the act and make him stop."

He shrugged. "I know now how foolish that was. But back then, I was just thirteen, and didn't know any better."

Miriam sat frozen.

"He grabbed me and…messed…with me and…" Joshua swallowed and looked at Lillie with fear in his eyes.

"I was scared…and confused. And then…when I was…he turned on Mrs. Farmer. He pinned her down on the floor. She begged for him to leave us alone, but he threatened us both and told us we were going to hell. And then he got himself ready." The two women gasped.

"She cried out to him to stop…but he didn't. And then he…I'm sorry, Lillie…he raped her, right there in front of me." A sob escaped and tears streamed down his cheeks. "When he was done, he left. But not before daring us to say anything to anyone. He told us that no one would believe our word over his, and I guess we both believed him."

Lillie was stunned, hesitating before she reached her arm through his and held on, and he looked at her, searching her face for clues to what she was thinking.

From across the space that separated them both in time and distance, Miriam finally spoke. "Oh, my God! I don't know what to say. I am so sorry—so sorry for all of it."

Joshua curled up into a ball on the couch, relieved to be done with the story and Miriam rose and went to him. Patting his shoulder and leaning down, she kissed his cheek and held him. She began to cry and heard Lillie weeping too. Reaching out her hand for the young woman, she drew her into the circle, and the three of them held each other for a long time. Joshua cried until he was limp with exhaustion and finally fell asleep with his head in Lillie's lap.

Miriam looked at the young woman sitting on her couch. "I am so sorry, Lillie! Your poor mother! No wonder Joshua worried about getting involved with you."

"I knew about Mother's rape, of course, but I didn't know…that the pastor molested Joshua and forced him to watch until now."

"Does your father know?"

Lillie nodded. "Yes, he knows about Mother. He read her diaries a few months ago. He needed to know what happened and then he had me come home to read for myself."

She stopped and wiped the tears from her face and stroked Joshua's hair. "But he doesn't know all that happened. With Joshua, I mean. In Mother's diary, she mentioned a letter to him that she never sent. It was still there."

"Is that why you wanted to meet with Joshua that first time?"

"Yes. I felt he needed to have it, but I didn't realize how much." Lillie sighed. "I think it's helped him, Mrs. Crumley. In the letter, Mother told him it wasn't his fault and that she didn't blame him for any of it. I didn't understand at first about why she felt the need to write it, but I certainly do now." Lillie looked down at Joshua, tears blurring her vision, and touched his sleeping head with her hand. "And on top of all that, I think I've fallen in love with your son."

Miriam looked at Lillie and then down at her boy, and laid her hand gently on his shoulder. "Then I'll leave him with you now, Lillie. I need to be alone for a while myself. I'll be upstairs if he asks for me."

31

B ruce had managed somehow, to put the news of his mother's rape out of his mind temporarily. He had returned to his life of high-powered finance, sports cars, parties with friends and attractive girls he didn't really like.

He earned a lot of money, so he had never lacked for funds, but he had felt unsettled after returning from the visit to his father's. Stuffing away his thoughts and feelings had been effective for a while, but in time, he could no longer contain the impact of what he had learned.

Unbidden, the image of his mother's rape, vivid with detail, floated across Bruce's mind. He knew he needed to talk to someone about what had happened and he wondered if his sister Violet knew.

In the last few years he'd avoided calling her because he never knew what sort of a mood she would be in, what kind of emotional junk she would try to unload. But now, he felt the need to connect with someone else in the family. She had been gone during most of those painful years too. On impulse, he picked up his phone.

Violet's husband's deep baritone voice came on the line. "Hello."

"Hey, Kevin. This is Bruce."

"Hey! How ya doing, brother?"

Bruce felt genuine affection for his brother-in-law and was always happy to talk to him. "I'm okay. Life's treatin' me well, I guess."

"Good! I hear you stopped by the farm."

"Yup. It had been a while. First time back since Mom died."

"You want to talk to your sister?"

"Yeah. Thanks."

Bruce waited, straining to hear the sounds in the background as Kevin went to get Violet. She finally arrived, talking as she approached the phone. Bruce shook his head—she was always telling people what to do.

"Bruce? Is that you?"

"Yeah. I thought I'd call to see how my big sister was doin'."

"Well, that's nice. I really appreciate it when you call me. It doesn't happen very often…"

"Yeah, I know," Bruce said, regretting already that he had placed the call. He took a deep breath. "I visited Dad recently."

"I heard." There was coldness in Violet's voice.

"We talked about Mom."

"You did?"

"Yeah. I need to ask you something. Do you remember anything changing about Mom the summer after I graduated from high school?"

"No, not really. I think I already had my apartment in Broadley by then. Why?"

"Well, it seems she was raped that summer."

Violet gasped. "What?"

"I guess you didn't know about it either."

"No! God, no!"

Bruce could tell she was crying. "I'm sorry to break this to you, Vi. I guess I just needed to know if I was the only one who didn't know what was going on back then."

"You and I had already moved out by that time."

"Yeah. Lillie hadn't though. She was only thirteen. I think she was hit pretty hard by the change in Mom after that."

"Change?"

"Yeah. Dad says they lost Mom *then*, that she was so crushed by everything that happened that it may have killed her in the end. Lillie thinks he may be right."

"Oh my God! I had no idea!" Violet thought for a moment, her mind reeling. "You know, I wondered why she moved out of their bedroom."

The siblings were silent for a moment. Bruce thought of the diaries, but decided not to tell his sister about them.

"What happened? Who did it?" The emotion had disappeared from Violet's voice.

"I don't know all the details. We need to hear them from Dad."

"I guess we should go there to talk about it, then. I had wanted for us to all be together, but not for something like this."

"Vi, I think this is what caused Lillie to get so depressed."

Lillie's depression had become one of those subjects not talked about when Violet was around because it had only triggered arguments. She abruptly changed the subject. "When can you go to Dad's?"

Bruce sighed. "Anytime. Just plan it and let me know. By the way, Lillie's still there, so maybe now would be a good time."

"Okay. I'll be in touch."

He heard a click and then a dial tone.

Part Three

The Church

32

The afternoon sun poured through the living room windows, and Joshua began to stir. Disoriented at first, he didn't know where he was, nor did he remember for a moment what had transpired an hour before.

He looked around sleepily. Lillie! Where was Lillie? Frightened for a moment, he calmed when he became aware of her arm over his waist and her warm body molded to his. She was still there.

Feeling her shallow breath on his neck, he lay in her embrace, paying attention to all of the sensations of her presence—how it felt to have her body against his, her warmth along his back, even his feet. As Lillie breathed, he could feel her breasts and the rhythmic movement of her belly against his back. He marveled at the simple intimacy of the moment—it made him feel safe and loved in a way he'd never experienced.

Lillie stirred and stretched, and then lifted her head to look at his face. "What are you thinking about?"

"I don't know. I've never done this before. Cuddling with anyone, I mean. I've tried, but I could never go through with it, because...well...no matter how hard I tried to keep it from happening, your mother and the pastor always came to mind, and I felt bad...dirty...evil, even. Sometimes I feel that way with you, but it's different somehow. I've never...felt so close to anyone like I feel with you!"

He turned and kissed her on the mouth very gently and then pulled back, looking into her eyes with tenderness. "I love you...Lillie. I don't want to mess it up. I don't want to hurt you."

"You're not messing it up," she said softly. "I love you." She smiled at him. "It's amazing to me that you don't know how wonderful you are."

Joshua nestled his face against her neck and breathed in the smell of her. They remained quiet like that for a long time.

Lillie spoke softly, "Joshua?"

"Yeah?"

She giggled. "Is your mother still here?"

He lifted his head and looked around. It hadn't occurred to him that anyone else even existed, let alone his own mother. They were in *her* house.

He sprang up, grabbed an afghan from a nearby chair, and jumped back on the couch with Lillie, pulling the afghan over them. He grinned at her as he snuggled down next to her. "I have no idea where my mother is! Do you?" he said, nuzzling her face with his lips.

Lillie giggled again. "After you went to sleep, she went upstairs to be alone…and then I fell asleep too."

Joshua slid a hand under her neck and wrapped his arms around her. With her head on his chest, they drifted back to sleep, this time in each other's embrace.

Long shadows stretched across Miriam's room. She lay still for a moment as the events earlier in the day returned to her mind. Thinking again of what she had learned about her son, tears welled once more in her already salt-swollen eyes.

Flooded with a sense of defeat, she recalled her son's honesty and determination not to be crushed by what he'd experienced. Strength began to seep back into her bones—this was his to work out, not hers. But she would be there to help him any way she could. One day at a time, she said to herself. This was an all too familiar refrain. She returned to a place of grief and loss, remembering her own devastation when Sam had died.

Pulling herself out of painful memories, Miriam went to the bathroom to wash her face and comb her hair. After straightening her bed and clothes, she made her way quietly down the stairs. Peeking into the living room she quickly took in the scene before her. Joshua and Lillie lay asleep on the couch mostly covered by the afghan her mother had made years ago. Feet protruded from one end.

She was too weary to even think about the relationship developing between Lillie and her son. She headed to make coffee, forgetting it was time to start making the evening meal until she stepped into the kitchen.

Sipping his afternoon tea at the kitchen table, Martin wondered where Lillie was and when she'd be home. She had left in a hurry after getting the phone call from Mrs. Crumley. All she had said, as she dashed out the door, leaving her lunch half-eaten, was that Joshua was upset and needed her.

What had he started? Would it have been better to leave the secret hidden? Somehow, though what he and Lillie had been through since reading the diary was painful, he knew that keeping it buried would have been worse. But he also knew they were headed into things no longer within their control.

Did Miriam Crumley now know? Had Joshua told her? What must she be feeling? Like him, she too had lost her spouse and was concerned about the wellbeing of a grown child. Martin had done the best he'd known how with Lillie and she seemed to be doing well. He knew she really liked Joshua— spending time with him was bringing out the best in her. He sighed with a mixture of resignation and release.

Bruce knew now what had happened to his mother, and his rage was still eating away at him. Violet knew nothing about any of it, as far as he knew. He grimaced at the thought—telling *her* wouldn't be easy.

The phone rang, interrupting his thoughts, and a man's voice barked into the phone. "I need to speak to Lillie Farmer!"

"She's not here at the moment. May I give her a message?"

"This is her boss. Have her call the office right away."

"Does she have your number?"

"I would hope so!" The man hung up.

Martin returned the receiver to its cradle on the wall and was writing a message for Lillie when the phone rang again.

"Dad?" It was Violet.

"Hi, sweetheart!" He tried to sound chipper.

"How are you and…Lillie doing?"

"Good."

"Dad?"

"What is it, Vi?"

"Bruce called me. We've decided we should come home for a visit… while Lillie is still there."

Martin stopped. Had Bruce told her? "Okay…That's fine, honey. When are you thinking?"

"How about this weekend? We'll come Friday evening…and stay the weekend if that's okay."

"That's fine. So, Bruce is coming too?"

"Yes. I'll call him to let him know this weekend works. Maybe the kids can share beds with him and Lillie and that way we can all fit. I'll bring some food." She paused. "We don't want to overburden you, Dad."

"What's on your mind, Vi?"

"Bruce was very upset when he called me. He was disturbed by something Lillie told him."

Here it comes, thought Martin.

"He said that Lillie told him Mom was…raped."

"Yes, honey, that's true."

"Oh my God, Dad! Why weren't we told? Bruce said it happened twelve years ago! Why weren't we told about this?"

Martin took a deep breath. "I understand you're upset now, Vi. But let's talk about it when you get here, face to face."

"Yes, let's! I need to be brought into this exclusive little circle, Dad! I should be allowed to know what happens too! How could you not tell me?"

"I'm sorry, honey. There will be plenty of time to talk about all of it when you come. I'll explain then. Call Bruce and make your plans." He paused. "We'll look for you Friday evening."

Lillie awoke. "I should go home."

Joshua murmured in agreement. Noises came from the kitchen, and he sat up. "Oh, shit! We'd better get up!"

Lillie laughed out loud. After straightening the living room, they headed into the kitchen. Miriam eyed them as they came in.

"I guess we were all pretty wiped out."

"Yeah," said Joshua, sleepily.

Lillie turned to Joshua and grabbed his hand. She turned back to Mrs. Crumley and smiled. "I'm so glad you called me."

Miriam turned away, a pang of longing stabbing at her heart. "Thank you, Lillie, for coming so quickly."

Joshua walked Lillie to her car and Miriam watched from the kitchen window as they kissed and hugged goodbye. A mixture of feelings threatened to overpower her—here was her son, in love, for the first time she could remember, with a girl intimately tied to a past of pain.

Lillie came through the kitchen door to find her father sitting at the table, lost in thought. "Dad?"

Martin turned to face her. "Hi, Lil."

She sensed fatigue in her father's voice and looked around the kitchen for evidence of why. She saw a message on the counter and picked it up.

"I see my boss called."

"Yup, seemed urgent."

"Did he say what it was about?"

"Nope. Sorry."

Lillie went to the phone and dialed. A minute later, she was back at the table, looking glum.

Martin shifted his attention to her. "What is it?"

"My boss said I have to be back at work tomorrow morning or I'll be fired."

"Didn't you take an unpaid leave?"

"Yes," she said. "I thought so. But he says he doesn't recall giving me leave and that I've already used up this year's vacation time."

"What will you do?"

"I don't know."

Martin tapped his fingers on the table. "I have some other news, too."

"What?"

"Your sister called. Bruce told her what happened to your mother. They're all coming here this weekend to hear the whole story. She's angry with me because she was the last to hear."

An ache formed in Lillie's chest. It was suddenly clear that she couldn't leave Joshua to return to work, nor could she leave her father in the midst of a maelstrom.

"Well, I guess I'm out of a job!"

Martin sighed. He'd known his athletic, nature-loving daughter was not designed to sit at a desk and work with numbers and paper all day. It had been only a matter of time until she figured that out for herself, he guessed. He also saw her wisdom in staying no matter what her job situation was.

The family was headed into a difficult time. As the information about Melodie and Lane Richardson became public knowledge, it would hit them hard and they would have to adjust. Bruce and Violet were in for strong feelings like those he and Lillie had experienced.

Martin looked at his daughter. "Does Mrs. Crumley know what happened?"

"Yes. That's what we were doing today. Joshua needed to tell her and he wanted my support."

"Good."

"Dad?"

"Yeah?"

"There's more to the story than you know."

"There is?" Martin's heart stopped.

She nodded and looked down "Joshua told us…that…" She hesitated.

"Told you what?"

"He was not only there…in the room…when Mother was raped. Pastor Lane did something to him…first…and then forced him to watch." She looked closely at her father's face.

Martin stared at her, frozen for a moment. Then he lowered his head and cursed out loud. "God damn you, bastard! Who else have you destroyed?"

Lillie waited a moment. "Dad, you're not angry at Joshua, are you?"

Martin looked away and shook his head. "No…Lillie. I don't know how I feel, exactly, but I'm not angry with Joshua. I can't help but wonder if things might have been different if he'd told somebody—if we could've helped your mother. But he was only, what, twelve or thirteen at the time?" He took a deep breath. "No, I'm not angry. But...I *do* wonder what your siblings will feel towards him."

At the thought, a look of concern crossed Lillie's face. "God, Dad, this is going to be one hell of a weekend!" She reached out for a hug and he pulled her into his arms. They held one another for a long time.

"I think I'm going to take a shower," she said finally, pulling away. With a weak smile, she turned and headed upstairs.

As he watched his daughter walk away from him, an image of Miriam Crumley floated across Martin's mind. He wondered if she felt as inadequate as he to deal with the tragedy they had both lived oblivious to. Perhaps it was time they talked—as the remaining heads of their families, maybe they could find comfort in that.

He roused himself to prepare a simple meal of soup and muffins for himself and Lillie. They would have tea in his wife's china cups.

"Miriam, this is Martin Farmer."

"Martin. Hello. What can I do for you?"

"I feel we should talk, you and I, considering all that has happened." He hoped to God Lillie was right that Miriam would know to what he was referring.

"Yes, maybe that would be helpful."

"Would you prefer I come to your house or you are more than welcome to come here. Wherever, I think we need privacy for this conversation."

"If you would come here...I would appreciate that. Thank you."

"May I come tomorrow perhaps?"

"Why don't you come for coffee in the morning. Ten o'clock?"

"That would be great. Thank you...I'll see you then."

Miriam came into the living room and sat down on the couch across from Joshua, who was reading the newspaper.

"I'm stunned. That was Lillie's father on the phone. He wants to get together with me, to talk about what happened to his wife…and you."

Joshua lowered the paper slowly. He felt a knot forming in the pit of his stomach. "You're not going to, are you?"

"Yes, I am," responded Miriam. "I think it's a good idea. This thing involves us both, after all."

"What do you mean? This is my pain, not yours."

"Son, this is larger than you…"

He threw the paper aside and got up from the armchair. "Okay, Mom. Do what you want!" He stomped out of the room, grabbed his keys and almost ran to his car. When he pulled out of the driveway, headed for the bar in Broadley, he spun away with such speed that gravel flew across the yard.

33

At ten o'clock sharp, Martin drove up to the Crumley house. As he approached the back door, Miriam opened it and greeted him. He stepped into a warm kitchen that smelled of coffee and something baking. The table was set with a vase of fresh-cut flowers—it reminded him of Melodie.

Miriam motioned for him to sit and brought a plate of freshly baked banana nut muffins and two mugs of hot coffee to the table. Once settled into her chair, Miriam looked expectantly at him, clearly waiting for him to begin.

"Our kids are spending a lot of time together," he said, clearing his throat.

"Yes," said Miriam, nodding her head in response.

"I've been getting to know your son. He helped me cut wood the other day, while we were waiting for Lillie. And then they cooked a wonderful meal..." He smiled, remembering.

"So...you are not...uncomfortable...with my son?"

"Miriam, we have a difficult situation here. To be honest, I'm not sure how I feel about him...that's why I appreciate the chance to get to know him."

"He told me what happened...just yesterday." Tears filled Miriam's eyes, but she maintained her composure. Martin nodded.

"I am not angry with your son...I know there was nothing he could have done...my wife certainly didn't blame him. I *am* a little concerned, though, about the complicated nature of Lillie's involvement with him."

"I know. I'm not sure what to think about it either. And they *are* getting very close."

"But," said Martin, "I know my Lillie, and I trust her. She seems happier than she's ever been."

Miriam couldn't help but smile at the cock-eyed look Martin gave her. "I trust Joshua, too, Mr. Farmer. He's never shown any sustained interest in a girl before this." She considered what she had seen in her son in the past few days. She had to admit it pleased her. "Come to think of it, I've never seen him so willing to communicate and deal with his feelings."

Martin paused. "So, perhaps this is a good thing. Their relationship."

Miriam sipped her coffee. "Joshua has made it clear that he needs my support, but it's his job to deal with his past."

"Yes, it's their life, but I'm concerned about what will happen as this story gets out."

"What do you mean?"

"Well," Martin sighed, "my other two children are coming home this weekend. They both know now that something happened to their mother and I owe it to them to tell the truth…the whole truth. But I'm concerned for your son, for both Joshua *and* Lillie."

Miriam considered what he was saying. She hadn't thought about Lillie's siblings. "How long have you known…about what happened?"

"Several months. I read about part of it in my wife's diary. Lillie told me the rest of the story yesterday."

"Why must Joshua's part be told?"

"Well, for one thing, if Lillie is serious about Joshua, her family deserves to know the truth about how he figures into what happened to my wife. I can only imagine the trouble down the road, otherwise. They're angry enough at me for not telling them what I knew about Melodie before."

"If Lillie and Joshua were not involved with one another then I could see not needing to mention his part…but it looks like they are." Martin looked at the food in front of him, took a sip of coffee and found it tepid. He bit into the muffin.

Miriam spoke almost in a whisper. "You believe honesty is the best way to handle this?"

He chewed and swallowed. "Yes I do, frankly. I've thought a lot about this. There is no easy, painless way to handle it, I'm afraid. We may as well get it out and be honest about it. I wish now I had told my children as soon as I knew."

Miriam looked pleadingly at him. "Do you think there is hope…for…peace?"

In that moment, Martin began to feel a kinship with the woman before him—they were somehow bound together because of the tragic events that had forever linked his wife and her son.

"Yes, I do have hope that we can all recover from this, at least in part, and find some peace." He didn't know how he knew it exactly, but he did. "And I think we will need each other in order to find it."

"It will help me if we keep in touch…and walk this carefully, one step at a time."

Martin nodded. "I'll begin by telling my children about it this weekend."

"I would ask that you ensure that they protect Joshua's privacy."

"Of course."

"That sounds good," Miriam said. "You know, Martin, I was feeling that I had no one I could talk to about this."

"I suppose that is one thing you and I offer each other—someone else who knows and who cares with equal force." Martin excused himself, thanking her and promising to keep in touch.

Joshua sat at the bar, drinking for the second night in a row. He'd hoped after their discussion the night before that his mother would honor his desire that she not talk to Mr. Farmer, but she hadn't.

Abigail's words came back to him: "It was not thy fault!" Even so, the need to escape and hide was strong in him. How he wanted to believe her! He was sick to death of turning it in on himself. When would he be ready to put the blame and guilt where it truly belonged?

When Joshua returned home, reeking of beer and cigarettes, Miriam called out to him. "Josh?"

"Yeah?"

"Are you okay?" She stood at the foot of the stairs.

"I just needed time to think."

"Mr. Farmer came because he's concerned about *you*."

"And why is that?" Joshua asked, turning and sitting down on the stair.

She tried to lay the news on him as gently as she could. "Lillie's siblings are coming home this weekend to hear the whole story about what happened to their mother."

"Shit!" He lowered his head into his hands.

"I know, son. But I am very grateful that Mr. Farmer is as sensitive as he is about this."

Joshua remained quiet, looking down at the stairs through his knees. His heart felt like stone.

Miriam continued. "We decided we needed to be honest and to keep in touch with each other so we can be careful."

Joshua pounded the banister with his fist. "I'm not ready for this Mom! I don't want people to know!"

"I understand that, son, but you said yourself that it had to stop being a secret and that you needed others to know too so they could help share the burden. You never know what allies you'll have!"

"Or *enemies*!"

"True, but we might as well weed them out now as later!"

34

everend Lane Richardson entered the office of Broadley Community Church, his congregation of eight years.

A large, handsome man in his late fifties with a full head of dark hair, his large hands were puffy, like his belly. He greeted his secretary, Judy, with a warm smile. "How are you this fine morning, my dear?"

Judy looked up from her typing and smiled. "Fine, Pastor. The ladies are already preparing the luncheon. And I have some things for you to look over. I'll bring them to you in a minute." She slid a pile of mail to him across an immaculate desk.

"Thanks, hon." He walked into his adjoining study riffling through the mail. Once he was settled behind his large oak desk, Judy came in to give him the final draft of a funeral program and the first draft of the bulletin for Sunday's worship.

After she had returned to her desk, an older woman came bustling into the outer office and uninvited, continued into the pastor's study. She stood waiting impatiently for him to notice her.

"What is it, Harriett?" he asked, looking up from his reading.

"Pastor, how do you want the tables arranged?" she asked, as if the weight of a decade teetered on her question.

"What's wrong with the usual arrangement?"

"Gertrude says we should put the buffet table up front instead of where it is, by the kitchen!" she exclaimed, bitterness coming untucked in her voice.

"That's fine, Harriett." He sighed, familiar with the frequent butting of heads between the two women. He was often called upon to make the final decision in trivial matters.

"But, Pastor, people will be confused! It will create chaos and back up the line! The food will get cold!"

"People will adjust, Harriett. You two work it out." He went back to reading his mail, dismissing her. Fuming, she turned and walked out.

Just then, graceful, well-dressed Rebecca Jones, with her perfectly coiffed long blonde hair, entered the office. "Is the pastor in?"

"Yes, Mrs. Jones, he's expecting you." Judy waved her hand for Rebecca to go in and heard the pastor's warm greeting as he shut the door behind her.

The secretary thought for a moment. How had the pastor fit in a counseling session when there was a funeral in a few short hours? Not my problem, she thought. She shrugged and went back to her work.

After an hour, Rebecca and the minister emerged from his study, exchanging gentle banter about her family. When she had gone, he turned and winked at Judy as he returned to his study.

35

"Hey, little sis! How ya doin'?" said Bruce when Lillie answered.

"Great, now that *you're* calling!"

He went straight to the point. "I don't know about this weekend, Lil. I think it's gonna be tough. Vi's pissed."

"That's what Dad said."

They both paused, thinking, and then Bruce changed the subject. "So, what have you been up to?"

Lillie reeled off a list of things. "Oh, picnics, cooking and hikes. I'm reading a great novel! Oh, and I got fired from my job the other day."

"Fired! Why?"

"I've been gone too long. I thought my boss had approved an unpaid leave of absence. But I guess not," she said. "I don't care, though. Insurance wasn't a good fit for me anyway. I was starting to hate it."

"Wow, Lil! So when will you start looking for another job?"

"I don't know. With all this family stuff going on, I think I need to stay here with Dad for a while."

A huge sense of relief came over her as she spoke the words—she had voiced out loud what she'd felt for days. She was enjoying life with her father—they were getting to know one another for the first time and she was in no hurry to interrupt the process.

"Oh...well...cool. Life is full of surprises."

"When are you getting here?"

"Around noon prob'ly."

"Good! See you then!"

Anxious to be with Joshua before the weekend began, Lillie called and asked him over. She was waiting for him on the porch when he arrived.

Bounding down the steps to meet him as he got out of his car, she threw her arms around his neck, nearly knocking him over.

"How are you?" she asked, after settling down a bit.

A shadow crossed his face.

"Fine. I'm fine."

She took him by the hand and led him onto the porch. They remained silent for a while, soaking in the warm breeze and the smell of sun-baked meadow grass. Finally Lillie said what she had on her mind. "You know, my family is coming tomorrow for the weekend."

Joshua was oddly quiet, so she continued. "They want to know what happened to Mother."

Still no response from Joshua. She reached out and touched his arm.

"I think we'll have to tell them everything, Joshua," she said softly. "Are you going to be okay with that?"

He slowly removed his arm from Lillie. "What does it matter whether I'm okay with it? You're going to do it anyway!"

"They have a right to know what happened to our mother!"

"What, so they can hate me?"

"They're not going to hate you!"

"How can you be sure of that, Lillie?"

"*I* don't hate you! My *father* doesn't hate you!"

"But everyone is not *like* you."

Lillie watched as the sadness returned to Joshua's eyes. Neither knew what to say next—they had not argued before and it felt like hell.

"I know you're afraid," she said. "But I just don't think there's any way to avoid telling *some* people."

"Yeah, well, I thought I could expect a little more understanding from you. But it's obvious you've already made up your mind." He paused for a moment. "What do you think it feels like, Lillie, to have people find out you gawked as someone...someone you loved...was raped and you did nothing? It was better just to keep this whole damn thing hidden! I mean, look what you've done by opening up this goddamn can of worms!"

"What? Bringing things out into the open so we can all get rid of this poison? So we can all try to heal from this? That was *wrong*?"

"Whatever happened to patience?" he said, teeth clenched.

"Whatever happened to HONESTY?"

Shocked at the animosity that had risen between them, they both sat staring across the meadow.

"Do what you want, Lillie. Have it your way. I don't care," said Joshua finally, in a small, defeated voice. The strength he had felt when he'd arrived had been sucked out of him. He stood and started down the porch steps. "Have your weekend. Tell them whatever you want to and we'll see how much they'll want me around." He turned and strode away. Lillie was dumbfounded.

Joshua's heart began to shut down as he drove away. Why had he said anything? He knew in his gut that it had to be told...*all* of it. He'd been impotent to act as a 13-year-old, but he wasn't 13 anymore. Why was it so hard? It frightened him that he and Lillie had argued—she was his only true friend. Then again, he thought, maybe it was letting her into his heart in the first place that had weakened him. He had been fine before all of this. Hadn't needed anyone. What was he doing with her anyway? What was he thinking, falling in love with her?

Shame washed over him. It was clear what he needed to do—shut everyone out of his heart. It was too hard, too painful, too exhausting to care about people or even to care about his own feelings. He stopped the car and leapt out, kicking the hard surface of the dirt road with his foot. He picked up a handful of pebbles and flung them into the field as hard as he could.

"Why, God? Why did you do this to me?" he yelled. "How could you allow this? Lane Richardson was *your* man! What the hell were you thinking?" Stripped of all walls, all pretences, Joshua stood naked before God.

"You have so thoroughly destroyed me that I can't live a normal life! I can't love like everyone else! I want to love but you have so fucked with me that...I can only crawl back to my cave and..." And leave Lillie and her family alone.

Resignation cloaked him. That's what I have to do, he thought, for their sakes. I'll leave them alone. Falling to his knees on the hard-packed dirt, he began to sob. "Okay God! Okay! I get it! You win! I'll leave her alone."

Kneeling there, in the middle of the road, he was overwhelmed by his grief and he wept until there was nothing left but emptiness. He returned to his car. His decision was made—he would leave Hopeston for the last time—and return to the life he had made for himself in the city…alone.

Numb after their confrontation, Lillie headed into the woods to walk off her frustration. Not having seen the side of Joshua he'd displayed since high school, she was shocked at how childish, how selfish, how unreasonable he seemed. Her siblings had a right to know what happened to their mother! He had to accept the fact that his story would have to be told because it wasn't just his story! Her mother had been brutally betrayed, viciously raped that day, and people needed to know. Joshua's part in it was an unfortunate thing, but he couldn't keep others from learning the truth just because he wasn't okay with it! Anger boiled up in her. She walked hard and fast to keep it from boiling over. Who did he think he was?

A pang of guilt sliced through her. Who did she think *she* was? Joshua was in pain! The incident had deeply wounded him. And he had trusted her with so much. Why now, then, had he stopped trusting her?

They both knew the truth—that she had no idea how her siblings would react, but couldn't he trust that she would still love him no matter what they felt or did? And then she knew the answer.

No, he couldn't.

Stock still on the path, the breeze blowing her hair, she saw it clearly. Joshua was afraid—of losing her. It would take time for him to sort out what had happened to him, to understand what he needed to do, to gain the courage to take the steps toward healing—it had taken her years to work through her own depression.

Oh, God, she thought. Of course! He'd asked her where her patience was. It was all moving too fast for him.

Lillie began to walk again, this time less agitated than before. There would be many storms ahead, and if she wanted to be with him, she would have to weather those storms as well.

Then, again, she thought, there were other men out there. Now that she had experienced love with one man, she knew she could have it again. Did she want to be with him that much?

A small voice within her spoke.

The answer was yes. Tears filled Lillie's eyes and her heart filled with warmth. She was willing to go through anything—any storm—with Joshua Crumley. Flooded with peace, the red hot coals of anger, guilt and pity she had felt moments earlier burned away.

But he would have to be patient with her. Right now she had to focus on her family.

36

Saturday morning finally came and the Farmer family settled nervously on the porch. Bruce draped himself on the railing, leaning against a post with his long legs stretched out in front of him, while Violet sat primly in a chair, back straight and lips pursed. Kevin took his place in a chair in the corner of the porch where he could keep an eye on his wife and the whole proceeding. Martin and Lillie sat in wicker chairs side by side in the middle.

Martin had arranged with a neighbor who had children, and horses, to take Sassy and Ben for the day. Violet had argued with him about having made the arrangement without consulting her, but in the end had agreed, relieved to have them gone. For once she had to admit her father was right, something she hated to do.

Martin cleared his throat and began. "After your mother died and we lost her for good…" He coughed again to subdue rising emotion. "I realized how much I had missed her…for so long."

All of his children listened intently, watching his face as it registered a host of feelings—sorrow, disappointment, shame.

"I couldn't tell you when it happened…but she slipped away from me. I dearly loved your mother…in the early years, things were good between us. It seemed kind of sudden…like she just shut down. After that I felt locked out of her life altogether.

"I tried to get her to talk to me, to tell me what was wrong," Martin continued. "I encouraged her to get counseling so she could talk about whatever it was, since she refused to tell me. But the more I tried to reach her the more she pulled away." He shifted in his chair and looked off toward the meadow.

"Finally I gave up. I didn't want to push her away entirely. I guess I let her have it her way, just so I could have her near me…even though there was nothing left to share…nothing meaningful…" He looked around at each of his children in turn.

"So, when I finally did lose her...for good...when she died...I was reminded of all the good times and I grieved hard.

"After a few months, I felt the need to know what had happened to cause this sudden shut down in your mother...and I knew she had always kept a diary..."

Violet gasped, realizing what was coming. "How could you, Dad? That was her private property! She told me that so many times!"

"I know, Vi. But she was gone...released, and she didn't need them anymore. Frankly, because of what we once had together, I felt she would have wanted me to know."

"I can't believe you did that!"

"There was another reason, Violet." A force seemed to come from deep within him. "Lillie was severely depressed again. I knew then that there was a link between the moment your mother left us the first time and Lillie's depression."

"Oh please! Here we go again! It's always about Lillie!"

Bruce glared at his sister. "Violet, shut up and listen to what Dad has to say!" She sank back in her chair, arms tightly crossed.

Martin went on. "Anyway, when Lillie's depression dipped down so dark and low again after your mother died, I thought that finding out what had happened to her might help me help Lillie."

Violet hissed. "Everything is *still* about Lillie."

Martin was livid, but controlled. "Violet, when I see my child close to suicide, yes, it's important to focus on her in order to help her get better. I had already lost one of my precious ones...I was not going to lose another one of you. So, I read your mother's diaries—all of them—and I discovered finally, in the twenty-fifth one, why she had shut herself away from the world, away from all of us."

The whole family now listening intently, he continued with renewed energy. He told of the pastor's invitation to Melodie to lead the Summer Bible Series, his implication to her that she was an unfit wife with respect to her husband's needs, and his offer to teach her to be more responsive. He spoke of the trust she had had in the pastor and the ease with which he'd used that trust to seduce her.

Martin glanced at Lillie. He would be careful with the next part. "But there's more. There was a boy, about Lillie's age, who attended the series, a boy your mother took a special liking to, who figured out what the pastor was doing and tried to stop him."

"Who was that?" demanded Violet.

Lillie's heart sank. She had hoped that they could keep Joshua's name out of it. Martin looked at her and his eyes told her he was sorry.

"His name was Joshua. Joshua Crumley." The name meant nothing to Violet. Bruce, on the other hand, felt a tingle of recognition.

Martin looked directly at Violet and intentionally repeated himself. "Joshua wanted to stop the pastor from taking advantage of your mother. So, one day he burst in on them…your mother and the pastor…in his office."

"But Reverend Richardson…" Martin said, naming the man for the first time, "would not be stopped, and turned on Joshua too. He molested him in front of your mother…"

He let what he'd said settle in—it was clear that his two older children were having a hard time absorbing it all.

"And then made him watch as he violated your mother."

Everyone was mute.

Bruce finally spoke. "Whatever happened to the boy? Did he tell anyone?"

Martin glanced at Lillie—it was time for her to take over the telling.

She cleared her throat, and tried to calm her now racing heart. "No, Bruce, he didn't. He couldn't. But he grew up to become a lawyer. He works for the prosecutor's office in the city and puts predators like the pastor away."

Violet's eyes narrowed. "How do you know this?"

"Because I went to school with him, and…I've recently had a chance to get to know him again."

Violet was furious. "Why would you do that?"

"Why wouldn't I? Mother never blamed him for what happened. He was molested by the pastor, too! He was just trying to protect Mother and he ended up being hurt as well!"

"And how do you know that?"

"Because Mother wrote Joshua a letter that said so! She never sent it. It was still in her diary."

Violet jumped up from her chair, livid. "What? So *you've* read Mom's diaries too?"

Martin had seen and heard enough. "Violet, sit down and be quiet for once!" Completely unprepared for such an authoritative tone from her father, Violet obeyed without thinking.

"Let me explain, please," said Martin. "Your mother met a woman, a counselor, after this happened, who suggested she use her diary in order to write it all down as a part of her healing, and she suggested she write a letter to Joshua too. When I read the diary entries and began to understand what had taken place, I wondered if knowing what had happened would help Lillie."

Violet smirked at her father. "So you decided that Lillie was the only one who needed to be let into Mom's private world? What about *me*? What if *I* needed to know what was going on inside of her?"

A deep voice came from the corner. "Vi, this isn't about you." Violet's husband, Kevin, who'd been quietly observing all that was happening came and knelt by her chair. "It's okay. Martin agrees that we all needed to know. That's why we're here, now."

Violet sputtered and started to speak again but Kevin stopped her. "Violet, let it be. We are here to focus on your mother and what happened to her." His voice was calm, as though he were talking with a child.

Recalling her argument with Joshua the night before, Lillie was suddenly afraid, because of the way Violet had responded, that he'd been right about her family, but pushed on with raw courage on behalf of the young man she had fallen in love with.

"Joshua is a...close friend."

"What do you mean, Lil?" Bruce asked.

"We're dating."

"You're what?!" Violet was on her feet again. "You stupid girl! How could you? How can you stand to be near him?"

"God, Vi! You don't listen, do you?" Lillie challenged her, angry enough now to move mountains. "HE TRIED TO PROTECT MOTHER!"

Violet responded in kind. "NO, LILLIE, HE STOOD BY AND DID NOTHING AS OUR MOTHER WAS RAPED AND HE TOLD NO ONE! HE MAY AS WELL HAVE RAPED HER HIMSELF!"

Lillie ran from the porch, taking the steps in a single leap, and disappeared into the woods.

"Is it true, Dad?" Bruce asked.

"What? That Lillie and Joshua are dating? Yes, I think it is."

Violet was barely able to speak through her anger. "How could you let such a thing happen? You *are* her father, aren't you?"

Martin glared at his older daughter. "Yes, Violet, I *am*. And I'll thank you to leave it up to me as to how I do my job."

"Well, I can tell you that I don't want to ever see him on this land or in this house!"

"The last time I looked, this was *my* land and *my* house, and *I* will be the one to decide who comes here and who does not!"

Suddenly feeling very old, Martin stood and turned toward the door. "We'll have lunch in an hour. If anyone wants to help me prepare it, I'd be glad for the help."

37

Joshua brought his things downstairs. He stuck his head into the living room where his mother sat reading the newspaper. "I'm heading back to work, Mom. I need to get back—it's been long enough."

His mother heard the deadness in his voice and sat up. "Are you sure?"

He forced a smile. "Yup! They're depending on me."

"Okay, well…call me. And, son, I hope you know you can come home anytime." There was still so much unsaid.

"Yeah, I know. Thanks. But I don't think I'll be home for a while."

"Why, Josh? What happened?"

"Nothing. If Lillie tries to get hold of me, just tell her to leave me alone."

"What happened with you and Lillie?"

"Just tell her. Bye, Mom."

Miriam followed him into the kitchen. "At least let me hug you goodbye." He allowed her to embrace him, though he kept his arms stiffly by his side.

Lillie ran until she was breathless, finally crumpling to the ground. She lay in the dirt long after her tears had stopped—she had had no idea that her sister hated her so. Thoughts of Joshua flooded over her—she wanted to be with him, in his arms. Wiping her face, she got up, brushed herself off and headed back down the path. That's what she would do—she would go to him.

Martin now inside, Bruce jumped off the porch and went for a walk in the meadow, leaving Violet and Kevin sitting alone. Numb, Violet couldn't reach her sorrow about what had happened to her mother. Grief was an emotion she had long since learned to stuff and ignore, masking it with hurt and anger.

The whole family had turned against her, she thought. And not only that, they had turned their backs and allowed Lillie to become involved with Joshua Crumley, leaving her the lone defender of her mother's honor against this pastor…and the boy who had as good as helped him violate her. If her father wouldn't stop this travesty from happening, she would.

Violet turned to her husband. "Hon, we forgot some things for supper tonight. I think I'll use this break and run into town to the grocery store. I'll be back in a jiffy."

Kevin accepted it all with relief. His wife could be exhausting and he often needed time alone to counterbalance her effect on him. He nodded to her and settled down for a nap in his chair. Violet drove into town and went straight to the phone booth at the back of the grocery store parking lot. Finding the Crumley's number in the phone book, she dialed it.

"Hello?"

"Hello, this is Violet Parks. I am Lillie Farmer's older sister."

"Yes, Violet, I know who you are."

"I would like to speak with Joshua."

"He's not here at the moment. But I would be glad to give him a message."

"Mrs. Crumley, your son needs to leave my sister alone and *never* set foot on our land or in our house ever again!"

Shocked by Violet's words, Miriam started to respond but chose rather to end the conversation.

Hearing the dial tone, Violet returned the receiver to its cradle and strode across the lot. Having accomplished her mission, she went into the grocery store and bought a few essentials to cover her clandestine deed.

Lillie emerged from the woods. The porch was empty, except for Kevin, whom she heard snoring from a distance, so she went around back and crept in the kitchen door. Tiptoeing up the stairs, she retrieved her purse and put on a pair of sandals. She grabbed a sweater and quietly retraced her steps.

Climbing into her car, she drove down the lane, sighing with relief when she came to the dirt road, out of sight of the house.

As she pulled into the Crumley's drive, she noticed that Joshua's car was gone and she felt in her gut that something was wrong. She knocked on the door and Miriam answered, greeting her with a coolness Lillie hadn't seen for a while.

"Lillie."

"Mrs. Crumley, is Joshua here?"

"No, he went back to the city." Seeing the obvious look of confusion on Lillie's face, she turned and motioned for Lillie to join her. She waited until Lillie had taken a seat at the table. "He told me he had to get back to work."

"He didn't tell me goodbye." Lillie was on the point of tears.

"He was upset when he left. Did something happen between you?"

"Yeah. We had an argument."

"Well, that explains his message. He said to tell you to leave him alone." Lillie gritted her teeth. "So…he's run away!"

"Run away from what?"

"From *me*, from *love*…"

"Or from dealing with your family's reaction to what happened?"

"I guess you're right," Lillie said, with apology in her eyes.

"Do you blame him?"

Lillie shook her head. "No, not really. But he won't give them a chance… he doesn't trust me." Remembering Violet's angry outburst, she'd begun to wonder if he should.

"Given what we now know, Lillie, maybe he has difficulty trusting."

"I'm sure you're right, Mrs. Crumley. *Please* tell me where he lives. I need to talk to him!"

Miriam reached for a pad and pen to write down her son's address and phone number. "I will, Lillie, but before I do, I think you should know that your sister called here just a while ago."

"My sister? What did she want?"

"She told me to tell Joshua to leave you alone—that he was no longer welcome on your land or in your house."

Lillie closed her eyes and lowered her head into her hands. "I don't care what my sister says or thinks…" She looked up. "I love Joshua and he will always be welcome in our home!"

She smiled through tears. "Mrs. Crumley, I would do anything for your son. I've never felt this way about anyone before in my life!"

Miriam saw the sincerity and fierceness of love in Lillie's eyes and smiled. "I think you're right that Josh has run away. And just maybe he needs you to run after him."

38

Joshua heard a knock on his door. Moving quickly to his bedroom, he pulled on a pair of jeans. After a minute or so had passed, the knock came again with insistence. He took time to put on a T-shirt and then opened the door. There on his step stood Lillie. His eyes momentarily lit up when he saw her, and then clouded over.

"Don't you look at me that way, Joshua Crumley!"

Joshua tried to appear nonchalant. "What are you doing here?"

Lillie ignored him. "May I come in?" He reluctantly moved aside and allowed her to enter. His apartment was messy, which was uncharacteristic of him, but Lillie didn't notice. Once inside, she swung around to face him.

"You ran away! You didn't say goodbye!" She screeched at him with frustration in her voice.

"It's for your own good, Lillie."

"What's for my own good?"

"You don't need me messing up your life."

"And how exactly are you messing up my life, other than telling me you love me and then taking off without a word?"

Lillie stood before him, beautiful in her anger. He looked away to keep his composure. "I will always be a reminder of the pain...I carry it in me all the time. You'll never be free from it if you're with me."

"Look at me, Joshua!"

He obeyed Lillie's command, his eyes pleading with her to just go and leave him alone.

"Joshua. I love you *just as you are*! I *know* what happened! I *know* you struggle every day with the pain of it and I love you *anyway*!"

"How *could* you?"

"I don't know, exactly. I just know the day you met with Abigail, when I was out on the lake, something happened—I was filled with peace and a strong love for you. God was there, I'm sure of it.

"I was given a promise and a kind of responsibility...and somehow it involved my love for you. And ever since then I have been totally open to you and willing to let you into my soul, to touch me, to *love* me, as I know you do!" Tears welled up in her eyes.

Joshua wanted to take her into his arms but he couldn't. He turned away instead. "But I can't do that...I'm not..."

"Joshua," she pleaded, "don't pull away from me. Please trust me, trust what we have together. I *love* you."

"Oh, God! Lillie Farmer, how am I ever going to be able to resist you?"

Approaching him slowly from behind, she put her arms around him, pressed her nose against him and breathed in his scent. He batted at her arms, which only made her laugh. Finally, he whirled around, freeing himself. "It's not funny! I'm trying to keep you out of my heart here!"

"How's it going?" She giggled at the effort he was making to hide his feelings.

In spite of himself, he began to laugh, too. "Not very well! You're a pest!"

"I know," she said, reaching to grab him again. Eluding her, he ran through the apartment and she chased after him. They ran into the kitchen, back through the living room and into his bedroom. Joshua leapt onto his bed, turning to face her, and Lillie leapt up right after him. A wrestling match ensued and they rolled around on the bed, until Joshua suddenly found himself sitting on top of Lillie, pinning her arms above her head.

Fear surged through him. An image flashed in his mind...an image of the pastor on top of Melodie, holding her arms just as he was now doing to Lillie. In confusion and dismay, he started to roll over and away from her, when suddenly she giggled. "Now that I've got you where I want you, Joshua Crumley, what are you going to do to me?" she said with a beguiling smile.

Everything changed in an instant. Releasing Lillie's arms, Joshua leaned forward and gently kissed her nose, her forehead, her chin, and then her lips. She took his face in her hands and smiled at him lovingly. "It's gonna be okay, Joshua. I promise. I'll be with you as long as it takes."

His arousal mounting quickly, he pulled her to him, and kissed her with a new hunger. She moaned as he lifted her shirt and began to stroke her soft skin underneath. He marveled at the fact that he felt no fear, no shame, no despair.

Lillie opened her eyes and looked at him. "You don't *act* like someone who doesn't want to be involved."

Joshua feigned ignorance of their earlier conversation."Who says I don't want to be involved?"

Aroused by his closeness and his strength, she pulled his head down to her again and whispered into his ear, "Prove it to me."

He hesitated. And then his resolve to resist her crumbled altogether. The light returned to his eyes and Lillie saw there the intensity of his desire. He leaned down and licked her lips with the tip of his tongue. She parted them and he kissed her hard. He raised up again to look at her. "How's that?"

She shook her head, smiling. "Not convincing enough."

"Oh, you want more, do you?" With her arms still above her head, he put his hands on her breasts and her nipples hardened under his touch. He smiled and she delighted in his pleasure. "I think you may regret coming here all by yourself, little girl, by the time I'm through with you."

"Are you trying to scare me?"

He stopped cold. "No, Lillie, never!" He slid off her and lay on his side, still pressing up against her.

"Joshua, it's okay. We were teasing. I'm fine. Please...don't stop."

He leaned over to kiss her again. In response, she explored his mouth with her tongue, loving the intimacy of the exchange. He slid his hand under her shirt again, found her hardened nipple and touched it with his thumb. Lightning flashed through her and she gasped.

He delighted in the way she responded to his touch. He moved his head down to her breast and nibbled through the shirt and bra. Then he traveled over to her other breast waiting for his touch.

She pushed up towards him in her arousal and then reached down and pulled up her shirt to reveal her bra. When Joshua helped her pull her shirt completely over her head, and began to touch her again, she moaned slightly and reached down to uncover one of her breasts, letting it fall free, full and inviting. Cupping it in his hands, he suckled on her nipple, and felt himself grow erect. Again, he noticed he felt no fear, no pain—just pleasure—and marveled at the miracle of it. Lillie pulled her other breast free so that both were exposed to his touch.

"Oh, Lillie! You are *so* beautiful!" said Joshua, who had moved to straddle her again. He leaned down and buried his face in her soft, full breasts as she held them close. She smiled and felt the warmth of pleasure all through her body as he continued to move from one nipple to the other.

"Joshua?"

"Hmmm?"

"There's another place…"

He looked at her with fire in his eyes and reaching down, unzipped her shorts and pulled them off. Sitting up, he looked down at her now completely naked body, at the smoothness of her curves and the patch of light brown hair between her legs. He put his hand on it and felt its softness. Searching with his fingers, he found the point of her pleasure. Lillie gasped and he felt his penis rise and pulse, pushing to be free. His mouth still on her naked breasts, he began to stimulate her in both places at once.

She raised her body up to meet him, her arousal growing more intense. Suddenly a burst of pleasure spread through her like fire and she shuddered in climax until it began to ebb away. Warmth and total relaxation spread through her body. Opening her eyes, she gazed at him with love and desire. "Will you take off your shirt?" He returned her gaze and pulled his shirt up and over his head.

She looked at the muscles in his chest and arms and exclaimed, "Joshua, *you* are so beautiful!" He smiled shyly back at her as he raised up and removed his jeans. For a moment, he hesitated, his erect penis standing in full view. Lillie reached to pull him down on top of her.

Suddenly, the image of Melodie watching as the pastor stimulated him flashed through his mind, and a surge of nausea washed over him.

"Are you okay?" Lillie whispered.

"Yeah, I just want you to hold me for a minute." Lillie put her arms around him as he relaxed his body, his full weight on top of her.

After a moment, Joshua raised his head. "Would you mind if I…entered you?" His eyes spoke of fear, humility and hope.

"Mind? Please do!"

He looked at her, searching for reassurance. "It doesn't bother you…that I…?" His look was heartbreakingly vulnerable and she responded.

"Joshua, I love you. Nothing can change that now. And, quite frankly," she said with a lopsided grin, "I'd rather deal with this later."

With that, he lowered his head and buried his face in her warm breasts. Lillie kissed his head and stroked his hair. "In case you're wondering, I'm on the pill," she whispered.

Smoothly and gracefully, he raised himself up, and Lillie opened her legs and lifted her hips to receive him. He slipped his hard shaft into her warm wetness, filling her suddenly and completely. She pushed up to meet him, and felt her pleasure rising again. At first he slowly slid in and out of her and then began to plunge more swiftly until finally he shuddered wildly. Moaning and gasping, he pushed convulsively into her.

Their pleasure reached its peak simultaneously and then it was done. With him still inside of her, Lillie lay warm and satisfied. Tears trickled down the sides of her face, wetting her hair and the bed beneath her. She was astonished at the power and depth of their feelings for one another, and the fact that Joshua had wanted—no *needed*—her permission to make love to her. The kindness of the gesture to her and its redemption for him moved Lillie all the more. There would be no turning back this time.

Entwined in each other's arms, Joshua and Lillie awoke to the late afternoon sun, which cast a soft light over the room. Rolling up onto his side, Joshua propped his head on his hand and gazed into Lillie's eyes, amazed at what had happened between them. He opened his mouth to speak, and then thought for a moment about how to say what he wanted to say.

"I've never felt like this—so close to anyone like I feel with you! My feelings for you made it so I could enjoy your beautiful body…without worrying that I was hurting you, without feeling evil." He looked into her eyes with tenderness and leaned down to kiss her gently on the lips.

"I was afraid, but only for a moment. And then I knew I wouldn't hurt you because I love you." He smiled brilliantly, realizing from the look on Lillie's face that it was a sacred moment for both of them. He said it again. "I love you, Lillie Farmer!"

Tears began to trickle from the corners of her eyes, and Joshua leaned down to kiss them away. "Because I love you, I felt only pleasure—no fear, no memories. I didn't think..." he said, his voice breaking just a little, "... even once." Tears began to slide down his cheeks, and he wanted to tell her everything.

"Lillie, I've never had sex with anyone...until now. I couldn't." He watched closely for her response. She watched as his sorrow was replaced first by a humble expression, and then with a look of joyful realization.

"But, now, with you...I have." He lowered his head and nuzzled her.

Lillie reached up and gently ran her fingers through his hair. "Joshua," she said mischievously, "can I ask you something?"

"Sure." He raised up, momentarily apprehensive about what she was going to say.

"If you've never..." she said, choosing her words carefully, "...done what you just did with me...then how did you know what to do. I mean...how did you know how to do it so...well?"

Joshua breathed a sigh of relief and then turned to lie on his back next to her, arms behind his head. "I don't know. I guess I've learned a few things... watching videos..."

Lillie's eyebrows shot up and she stifled a giggle. "Wow! I'd like to see *those* videos!"

Joshua shook his head. "No, you wouldn't! What we had is much better than any of that stuff! And besides, there's more that I'm going to show you *right now,*" he said, turning to pull her close.

It was clear to both of them that something of major consequence had happened to Joshua Crumley. With Lillie, he had finally been able to show a woman how he felt about her, to release his fear—the fear that had kept him isolated and lonely for so long. He was flooded with gratitude for the beautiful woman next to him—the soft, warm, and oh-so-real woman who loved him too.

39

iolet returned to her father's house. The men of the family were gathered in the kitchen, preparing food. Kevin and Martin stood at the counter cutting cheese for sandwiches and stirring soup. Bruce sat at the kitchen table slicing vegetables. Martin looked up as Violet entered with her bag of groceries. "Where've you been?"

"I went to buy food, Dad. I knew you were out of things."

Martin looked at her with a puzzled expression. As she unloaded the bags, he took a mental inventory. There were eggs, bread, milk, oranges and butter, all items of which he had plenty. He started to comment, but thought better of it.

Violet folded the empty bag. "Where's Lillie?"

Bruce answered, his voice filled with irritation. "No one knows."

"She's not back yet?"

"Nope."

The silence was thick in the room. Violet poured herself some lemonade and left the men to their cooking. As she made her way out to the porch, Bruce and Martin exchanged looks.

"Where do you suppose she is?" asked Kevin.

"Do you think she's still out there in the woods?" Bruce asked, still looking at his father.

Martin responded to his real question. "I don't know. Maybe someone ought to go after her." Bruce stood, as if on cue, and headed out the back door. Violet watched from the porch as he disappeared into the trees.

Once the soup was simmering, Martin headed for the porch. Kevin went out the back way to give him time alone with his daughter. Martin sat down and lit his pipe, and after taking a puff or two, spoke to Violet.

"Honey, your desire to punish your sister is clouding your vision. It seems to me that you didn't come to hear what happened to your mother—instead, you came looking for something else to blame Lillie for."

Violet avoided his gaze. "Well, she's behaving like a spoiled brat. She always gets her way in everything!"

"Who's acting like a child now?"

"You wouldn't have told me *anything* if I hadn't planned this visit. You didn't offer to let *me* read mother's diaries!"

Martin took a deep breath. "I admit, Violet, I have not handled this perfectly. But I fear there is no perfect way to tell any of your children their mother was raped...by her trusted minister."

He paused and looked at his daughter, pleading with her to hear what he was saying. "Joshua was as much a victim in this as your mother was. It was the *minister* who did it.

"You are blaming the wrong people, Vi. Lillie has helped all of us, including Joshua, heal from this trauma. She took your mother's letter to Joshua so he could find relief from a sense of guilt. The boy has carried this painful experience all alone for all these years. And, without thinking, you lashed out at the two of them. Lillie didn't have to be open with us about her relationship with Joshua. But she was, because she thought she owed us that."

Violet said nothing.

"Whatever it is that eats away at you so that you can see Lillie only through eyes of jealousy—whatever it is, I want you to work it out. Twice, Lillie has come dangerously close to taking her own life and you have never once shown even the slightest concern. It's time you grew up and became the sister she needs."

He stood up and walked down the steps and towards the woods, where he met Bruce returning. When Violet heard her father and brother discussing her sister, she felt suddenly embarrassed—she was jealous of their legitimate concern for Lillie. Perhaps her father was right.

Martin jogged back to the house with his son on his heels and went directly to the phone.

"Where you calling, Dad?" asked Bruce.

"The Crumleys. She may have gone to be with Joshua."

Martin dialed the phone. After a few rings, Miriam answered. "Hello, Martin. I seem to be hearing from your whole family today."

"So Lillie is there?"

"She *was*, but not now. She's gone to the city—after Joshua."

Martin was relieved to hear that Lillie was safe, but confused. "You've heard from other members of my family?"

"Yes. Your daughter Violet called here as well, quite angry. She wanted to talk to Joshua, but since he wasn't here, she told me what was on her mind."

"And what *was* that, if I may ask?"

"She said she wanted him to leave Lillie alone and that he wasn't welcome in your home."

Martin paused to compose himself. "Miriam, I'm sorry you had to experience the worst of my older daughter. This has been a hard day for my family, as you can imagine, but there is no excuse for Violet's behavior. Please accept my apology."

Miriam was civil but frank. "I have no reason to doubt your kind concern for Joshua and I believe Lillie also has his best interest in mind. But please ensure that Violet directs her anger elsewhere. My son has enough of his own issues to deal with right now."

"I will do that." Martin paused. "Did Lillie say when she was coming back?"

"No. All I know is she went to find Joshua at his apartment in the city. Would you like his phone number?"

"Yes, thank you." He wrote down the number and stuck the folded note in his pocket, and then headed out to the porch, where Bruce and Kevin were sitting with Violet, who had obviously been crying.

Martin sat down, exhausted by the myriad of emotions they'd experienced during the day, and took a moment to calm himself. "Violet, you didn't go shopping for groceries. You went and called the Crumleys."

"Joshua wasn't there," she said weakly, not refuting the truth of what he said.

"No, luckily he wasn't. But his mother certainly was."

"I just want him to leave us alone."

"He *has* been leaving us alone. All these years! He didn't come here on his own—it was Lillie's effort to bring him peace of mind that got him, and them, involved. He's done this family no harm."

Violet began to cry.

Martin's anger began to dissolve at her anguish, but he remained firm. "I want you to call Mrs. Crumley and apologize to her."

A long silence ensued.

"We found Lillie, by the way," said Bruce.

"Where?" responded Violet.

"She drove to the city. She's with Joshua right now."

Joshua lay quietly enjoying the smoothness and warmth of Lillie's body. He slid his arm under her and pulled her closer to him. She opened an eye and peered at him. "We're official now, you know."

He nuzzled the nape of her neck. "Official what?"

"Lovers. And I hope we're going to make a habit of this."

"I guess you're right. You just happen to be the most gorgeous woman around."

Lillie rolled over onto her back and looked into Joshua's face. "Really?"

"Yes, really!" He raised up on his elbows and looked at her, a mixture of joy and amazement on his face. "Lillie, this is a first!"

"A first?"

"Yeah. You're the first woman I've ever brought to my bed."

"I'm not sure that's exactly how I'd put it. You didn't exactly do the bringing." She raised an eyebrow and smiled. He leaned down and kissed her gently on her mouth. Both felt the enormity of his confession.

"Thanks," he said simply.

"What, for chasing you down?"

"For everything." He lay back down beside her. "How did it go today, by the way? With your family, I mean."

Lillie shook her head. "Honestly? Terribly!"

He blanched, seeing her expression change so dramatically. "Do I want to know?"

Lillie saw the vulnerability in his eyes, but elected to be honest. "Joshua, I'm going to tell you so there won't be any surprises, okay?"

"Okay."

"Violet lost it. She's mad at you and she's mad at me for dating you."

He sat up for a moment. "What did I tell you?"

"Joshua, you can't let Violet get to you. She's been angry with me for a long time and she takes it out on anyone connected to me." Lillie scooted closer and began to gently stroke his muscular chest. "I think she just needs time to let it all sink in. Besides, I love you, boy, and we're not going to let my stupid big sister bother us."

They lay together for a little while longer and then Lillie got up to take a shower. While he waited for her to get ready, Joshua tidied up his apartment.

As she stood in the hot water, Lillie felt beautiful—a first for her as well. She felt sexy and feminine, curvaceous and real. Never before had a man told her these things about herself and Joshua had given her a gift by showing her his passion for her body, for her soul. She was a woman—a beautiful woman. It felt good to be loved and to be *in* love.

Joshua yelled over the sound of the water. "Hey, you want to go out? To my favorite bar?"

Lillie yelled back. "Sure do!"

As they entered the bar Lillie noticed people looking at them. They settled themselves at a table, an unusual seating arrangement for Joshua, a fact that did not go unnoticed by the regulars. A slim waitress came to the table. With a smirk on her face, she looked first at Joshua and then at Lillie as if she were examining a specimen in a laboratory. Once she'd gone to place their order, Lillie leaned in close to Joshua across the small round table and whispered, "People are acting weird!"

Joshua broke out into a hearty chuckle. "They're not used to seeing me with anyone I care about."

"They can tell?"

"Oh, yeah. They can tell."

The waitress arrived with their food and, as soon as she left, they both dug in heartily. After a few moments of clanking utensils, Joshua laid down his fork. "I used to think you couldn't know God if you didn't go to church…and I think I felt banished from God when the pastor did what he did to me. I could never go to church again after that. He was God's man, after all…"

There was a long pause and Lillie waited, not wanting to interrupt his train of thought. He rewarded her. "Do you think God brought us together?"

She nodded and beamed at him. "You know, I feel freer to be me now that I don't go to church anymore. Since I read my mother's diary and got together with you…I feel closer to God than I ever have before."

"Yeah, me too. You and Abigail…what *is* it about her and all her rituals?" Joshua asked, chuckling.

"I don't really know…but it just seems real and simple. Like all you really need is to ask and pray and be quiet and God will be there."

"So, how does the church screw up so badly? How can a pastor do that in a church?" Suddenly it occurred to Joshua that he could never have had this discussion with anyone else. Still warm from their lovemaking, he felt somehow shielded from the horror of the subject matter and its effect on him.

Lillie pondered for quite a while before answering. "Maybe it's the people. Maybe they have an attitude about sex and how you can't talk about it. Maybe it's going on in the shadows all the time, behind closed doors…where stuff like that happens and no one wants to look at it, no one wants to know it's happening."

Joshua shook his head. "People are so two-faced, so shallow. All they care about is that it *looks* good—the church, I mean—not whether it *is* good. People want to be seen as being good Christians, but churches aren't always good places! You *expect* them to be and you expect the people in them to be good—truly good—but they're not!"

He kept talking as though years of pondering had found expression, as if he had been imprisoned in his head for a long time. "I suppose people are taught to fear and pretend they don't see it when it comes to sex and power and authority. In order to fit in, I mean, to find their place."

Lillie chimed in. "So the church ends up being a place that teaches people to cover up for abusers like the pastor."

Joshua thought about what she'd said, and then asked her a question that had been on his mind from the beginning. "Do you think there have been other victims?"

"Oh, my God," she said. "Maybe so. What if there *are!*"

Joshua dabbed at his mouth with his napkin. "I'll bet there are, Lillie, and you should know something. I've decided to go after Lane Richardson."

"Really?"

"Yeah. It's time to stop punishing myself for what happened and make him face up to what he's done…especially if there are others. Will you help me?"

Lillie smirked at him. "What do *you* think?"

40

Lane hastily gathered his papers and stuffed them into his briefcase. He left his office and told Judy he was going on home visits with members of the congregation. She nodded and smiled without interrupting the flow of her typing.

The pastor exited the church, got into his car and headed quickly across town, straight to the home of Rebecca Jones, the woman who had come to his office for counseling. He pulled into her driveway, parked the car and nearly ran to her door. Within moments, Rebecca answered his knock.

Her face was tear-streaked and she held a crumpled tissue in her fist, which she used repeatedly to dab her swollen eyes and nose between sniffles. The pastor removed his suit coat, hung it over the railing to the stairs, and put an arm around her as he guided her into her living room. He sat her on the couch with him and bending his head to look down into her face, he spoke gently to her. "Tell me what happened. You sounded very upset on the phone."

She started to sob and a fresh batch of tears began to flow. It took her a while before she could answer him. "My sister's son…" She sobbed and then tried to go on. "He was in an…accident!"

The pastor moved closer, rubbing her back and shoulders. "What kind of accident?"

She wiped her eyes and composed herself. "A car accident, Pastor…he's in critical condition!"

"There, there," said Lane, stroking her hair.

The amount of physical attention the pastor was showing seemed a little too much for the situation, but Rebecca told herself it was just his way of demonstrating support. "He was driving down by the river and took a curve too fast. His car slid off the road and crashed into a tree!"

The pastor took her by the chin and turned her face to his. "It's okay, Rebecca. God will make him well." Then he leaned forward and kissed her on the forehead.

She submitted to him. Though she still felt uncomfortable, she decided not to complain about his methods—the pastor had helped her so much since the devastation of her divorce, she hated to rebuff him.

"Where did they take him? What hospital?" he asked.

She inched away from him. "He's at Broadley General." She took a few jagged breaths. "My sister and I are very close and my nephew is special to me."

The pastor wrapped his arm around her and hugged her tightly. "And I bet you wish you had someone to lean on during this crisis."

"Yes, that is so helpful."

"Well, I'm here for you—I'll stand in for your husband." He leaned over and kissed her on the mouth.

Rebecca was shocked. He held her tightly, and she tried to push him away. "Oh, no..."

"It's okay, Rebecca," said the pastor. "When a woman loses her man it helps when another steps in." With that he slipped his hand into her blouse.

Rebecca tensed, and panic rose in her belly. "What are you doing?"

"Don't be upset, Rebecca. I'm comforting you. I know what kind of comfort you need." He pushed her down onto the couch and pressed the weight of his body on top of her. A button on her blouse popped off as he groped her.

She struggled but he held her fast. Terror coursed through her as she wiggled fiercely. "Please, Pastor..." she begged, "no...don't...please..."

"If you'll just relax, Rebecca, no one will get hurt." He leaned down and pressed his mouth on hers, forcing his tongue into her mouth.

Suddenly she was unable to breathe. Frightened and enraged, she felt a burst of energy fill her and she kicked and wiggled free of him. He lunged for her, missing her by inches as she dashed around the couch. She ran down the hall and into her bathroom, slamming the door behind her and with fumbling fingers, managed to lock it. Shaking and crying, she screamed through the door. "Get out of here! Leave my house! Get out! Get out!"

The pastor got up from the couch and straightened himself. He checked his appearance in the hall mirror and used his hand to comb his hair into place. Then he put his suit coat back on and went to the bathroom door.

"Calm down, Rebecca. Nothing happened. I was just comforting you like a husband would do. I'll come and visit you again later."

It would be an hour before Rebecca felt safe enough to come out into her own house.

🌸

Bruce wasn't sure what to think of all that had happened. Needing time alone to process it and find an outlet for the rage he felt, he went behind the barn and began to chop wood. Placing a log on its end, he took up the axe, and positioning his feet, swung down with such force that the wood split open before him. Horrified that his mother's minister had so thoroughly violated her trust and that he had forced a young boy to witness his evil act, he wielded the axe and swung again. He was beginning to think that his mother had been so completely devastated by the betrayal and brutality of the minister's behavior that it had probably killed her in the end.

He lined up four more logs and attacked them one after the other, sweat pouring from his face. As he continued to swing the axe, he saw clearly how Lillie, too, had been deeply wounded—by the neglect and quite unintentional abandonment of her mother. He saw how it had caused her to become depressed. He saw that his absence from home at the time had spared him the devastating effects that his younger sister had experienced, and he was left with a mixture of gratitude and guilt.

He stood still for a moment, and the image of his mother's face as he remembered her in his childhood formed in his mind. He missed her suddenly in a way that he hadn't since her death—a sharp piercing of his heart took his breath away. In that moment, he knew he would have done anything to bring his beloved mother back. Swiping his forehead with his forearm, he resumed his fierce chopping, and let his thoughts flow once again.

What puzzled him was the behavior of his sisters—how Violet had focused her anger on the wrong person, lashing out at Lillie and calling the Crumleys, burdening them with her hateful words, whatever they had been. He appreciated her anger and her protectiveness of the family, and it crossed his mind that, though her feelings were wrongly directed, if she ever got it straight, his older sister would be a formidable force to be reckoned with.

His own anger began to ebb and he stopped for a rest. His chest heaved and his heart raced from both the physical exertion and the intensity of his emotion. He pulled off his shirt, now soaked with sweat and dropped it on the ground.

He had been impressed with his father, too—his ability to gently but firmly confront Violet. His chopping slowed, becoming less ferocious than before.

Was his younger sister emotionally attached out of a desire to rescue Joshua? If so, it could only end in her getting hurt. He was puzzled about how emotional his sisters were, and yet it was obvious he had very strong feelings himself. Bruce kicked at a log that had rolled onto his toe.

The truth was that he wanted to find that minister and wring his neck. He wanted to slap Violet into awareness of what she was doing and he wanted to stand guard, barring the way from any intrusion, in order to protect Lillie from further hurt. Raw warrior bravery pulsed in his chest as he lodged the axe in one of the uncut logs and picked up an armload of firewood.

As he stacked the firewood against the barn, it occurred to him that their father was aware of Lillie's involvement with Joshua and yet seemed to be okay with it. If he was okay with their being in a relationship, then why shouldn't he and Violet give them their blessings too?

He wiped his face with the back of his large, grimy hand and stood for a moment. His chest heaving from the exertion, he wanted to meet Joshua himself, to get to know him before deciding how he felt about his being in Lillie's life.

Lillie had made wise choices in the past—he knew she had turned men down before due to their less than honorable intentions. But in this case, she hadn't. She had, instead, embraced a relationship with Joshua. Maybe this guy was different.

Bruce now knew that as a boy Joshua had tried to protect a woman from abuse and injustice, at what had turned out to be a great personal price. Since then, he had become a lawyer and worked in a prosecutor's office—where he could fight for justice on behalf of victims.

Lifting his face to the sunlit sky and closing his eyes, he breathed deeply, and understood what he had to do. As long as his little sister was involved, he would develop a working relationship with Joshua. He would do what he could to support Violet to re-direct her feelings and actions in a good way. And he would be available to his father, whom he respected now more than ever before.

Finished with stacking, he scooped up his sweat-soaked shirt and walked back toward the house. It was time to stop distancing himself from them. His family needed him, and he would stay in touch and make himself available. To honor his mother, he would come home, to the home of his own heart.

41

Violet sat crying on the porch. Deeply troubled, she couldn't get her mind around the idea of what her mother's minister had done, and her feelings threatened to take her down. Part of her wanted to grab her children and head home to get away from it all. But another part of her wanted to stick it out and try to fix things.

She stowed her tissue away, oblivious to the shimmering beauty of the meadow in front of her. Recalling her father's demand that she make amends with Joshua's mother, she wondered if calling Mrs. Crumley would get Lillie to come home, but she wasn't sure she could make the call.

Bothered by the thought of Joshua, she was even more repulsed by the thought of Lillie with him. No matter how she looked at it, she considered him an accessory to the crime. When she thought of him, the mental pictures of her mother's rape came unbidden, and acid rose in her throat.

She thought perhaps if she cooked a big meal for her family things would be better. Swallowing several times in an effort to settle her stomach, she stood and went into the kitchen. She opened the refrigerator and began pulling food out and placing it on the counter.

Bruce wiped his feet and came in the back door, making his way to the sink to get a glass of cold tap water. Violet stood at the sink, chopping vegetables.

He leaned over her shoulder. "Whatcha cookin'?"

"Vegetable lasagna. I thought we could all use something good to eat."

"Lillie back yet?"

"Not that I know of. Can we call her and get her to come home?"

"Dad got the number at Joshua's. Maybe we should."

"She should be here with us, not with him!"

"Okay, I'll go see what Dad thinks." Bruce dashed to the basement for a fresh T-shirt and pulled it over his head. He looked on the porch and out in the meadow to see if he could catch a glimpse of his father, and when no sign of him appeared, he ran upstairs and found Martin sound asleep on his bed.

A quick scan of the room told Bruce his father had emptied his pockets on his dresser. Spying a small folded piece of paper, he took it and quietly left the room. Quietly walking back downstairs, he took the phone into the hall and dialed the number, but there was no answer, so he stuffed the number into his own pocket and headed back to the kitchen to see if he could help Violet with dinner.

Lillie and Joshua finished their meal and walked back, in the balmy evening air, to Joshua's apartment. They stopped on the street outside and Lillie drew him into a hug.

"I'd better go. By now they're probably wondering where I am."

"Yeah, I suppose." Joshua held her close to him, pressing his body against hers. An electrical pulse ran through them, and Joshua basked in the wonderful feel of her, solid and real, in his arms.

"Are *you* coming back?"

He considered it for a moment. "No." He couldn't say why, exactly, but he wasn't ready to return to Hopeston. "But that shouldn't keep you away."

"Can I call you?"

"Yes! Please." He looked into her eyes.

"Did you like my visit?" she asked, grinning up at him.

"Uh, huh."

Lillie shook herself out of the trance. "Then wish me well. I'm going to face my big, bad sister!"

Joshua remained silent but held on to her tightly. He smiled slightly as he watched Lillie's face.

"Let me send you off properly, then." Taking her chin in his hand, he lifted her face to meet his. He kissed her gently on the lips, backed away, and looked at her with shining eyes. He bent down to kiss her again, more passionately this time.

She moaned softly and he released her lips from his. "Official lover!" she said with a deep chuckle, and pulled away from him.

Joshua watched as the taillights of her car disappeared from sight, and with an unfamiliar peacefulness, he turned towards his apartment. In a few strides, he reached the stone steps to his building.

As he came through the door to his apartment, he heard the phone ringing. Leaving his keys swinging in the lock, he sprinted to answer it.

"Is this Joshua?"

"Yes." Joshua answered, feeling his guard go up.

"This is Bruce—Lillie's brother."

"Oh. Hi."

"Is Lillie there? We don't know where she is. She took off this mornin' and hasn't come back yet."

"She was, but she just left to go back to Hopeston. It'll take her about two hours to get there."

"I know." Bruce hesitated. "It seems my little sister likes you, man."

Surprised at Lillie's brother's directness, Joshua acknowledged the statement, but didn't respond. He wasn't going to stick his neck out until he knew where Bruce was headed.

"I'd like a chance ta get ta know ya myself if I could…since she's my little sister and all."

Joshua took a deep breath. "You drink beer?"

"Yeah, man!"

"Well, we could meet at Flanigan's in Broadley in a day or two."

"I was thinkin' more like tonight."

Joshua suddenly knew that despite the fact he'd told Lillie he wasn't coming home, he would have to head back into the heat of the situation. Her whole family needed to know what kind of person he was—his work would have to wait. He would call his boss and ask for a leave of absence.

"Okay. Tell me when. I'll be there."

"How 'bout eight?"

"Sounds good."

Bruce was optimistic—he had reached out to Joshua and found Lillie at the same time. As he entered the kitchen, Violet looked up at him expectantly. Martin sipped his after-dinner coffee and looked out the window. Kevin sat quietly next to his wife.

"Well? Did you find her?" asked Violet.

"Yup. She's on her way home right now from Joshua's place in the city."

Violet rolled her eyes and said nothing. The others remained silent too.

Lillie pulled into the driveway. Though she wasn't looking forward to seeing Violet again, she was ready for her, having had plenty of time to prepare on the way home. She had even more confidence after having spent such an incredible afternoon with Joshua.

Bruce was first to see her pull in and was out the back door in a flash. He opened his long arms and took her into a big bear hug, squeezing a bit too hard, as he was prone to do.

"We were worried 'bout ya, Lil." He loosened his embrace, but kept her in his arms.

"I know. I'm sorry. I just couldn't take another minute of it."

"You went to Joshua's." Lillie pulled away and looked questioningly into his face.

"Yeah! I called him."

"When?"

"Just after you left to come home."

"Really."

"By the way, I'm gonna meet 'im at the bar in about forty-five minutes."

Lillie frowned, confused. "He said he wasn't coming back."

"Well, I told 'im I wanted to see 'im tonight, and he agreed. Said it was no problem."

Lillie had to admit she was pleased, but curious. "Why do you want to see him?"

"Cause I gotta make sure he's a good guy, Lil. That kinda stuff, what the minister did, can screw people up. I gotta make sure he's not gonna dump his stuff on you."

Lillie smiled at her protective older brother. He wasn't the best at talking about his feelings, but she knew he was wise and had a good heart. She also knew, in her gut, that he and Joshua would hit it off just fine.

She beamed at her tall blonde brother and hugged him tight. "Okay! But say hi to him for me!"

Bruce put his arm around her shoulders. "C'mon, Lil, the others wanna see ya too." They walked into the house together.

Violet stood in the kitchen waiting for Lillie. Martin leaned with his back against the counter, his arms crossed over his chest. Kevin was nowhere to be seen. As Lillie entered the kitchen, with Bruce right behind her, she felt a rise in the tension in the room. No one wanted to speak first. Lillie took the lead.

"Sorry I didn't let you know I would be gone so long, Dad."

He gave her a nod and a slight smile.

The sisters made eye contact, and Violet spoke first. "Why did you have to run off?"

"Why? You don't know?"

"No, Lillie, I don't, or I wouldn't have asked, now would I?"

"Well, Vi," Lillie retorted, matching her sarcastic tone, "let me tell you why. I got tired of your anger and your blame being dumped on me."

It occurred to Lillie that Violet was doing just what Bruce had said he wanted to make sure Joshua didn't do—dumping her "stuff" on her.

Violet smirked. "Well, that's no way to handle it...by running away!"

"I didn't run away. Sometimes removing myself from you when you are so totally unreasonable, is the *only* way to handle it!"

Kevin appeared from somewhere in the house and stood quietly listening.

"Well, I was upset!" Violet retorted.

"Yes, but you attack us when you're upset. We're all upset about what happened to Mother but we need to help each other, not attack each other!"

"Okay, okay! I'm sorry! But how can you be with that...J-Joshua boy?" Violet was barely able to utter his name.

"I don't know, except that he's a true gentleman and he's wonderful to me. He's the first man I've ever felt comfortable letting into my life like this!" Emotional, Lillie held herself in check. She didn't want to break down in front of the whole family, Violet especially.

"But how could you? Of all people! After what happened!"

"I didn't *do* this on purpose! All I know is that I don't blame him. Reading the letter Mother wrote him was helpful. *She* wanted him to feel free of blame and guilt. My anger is focused on the pastor, not on Joshua Crumley!" There was a long and pregnant silence and, for a moment, no one dared to breathe.

Violet's voice softened. "So, reading Mom's diary was helpful?"

"Yes, it was. I'm so glad Dad let me read it. It's very clear that Mother struggled to make sense of things in her life after that. I guess that's what each of us has to do." As Lillie spoke, she realized what a role model her mother had actually been for all of them.

Violet looked at her father with pleading eyes and he nodded.

"Vi, you may read the diary. The others I will keep private between her and me, but you may *all* read the one Lillie has. I think it would help you." He looked over at Bruce as well, who blinked and shook his head.

Violet turned back to Lillie and spoke with a manufactured warmth. "I'm just trying to protect you."

"Yeah? Well you stink at it!" Lillie said, breaking into a chuckle. "And calling Mrs. Crumley with an ultimatum wasn't a good way to go about it!"

Violet flushed red with embarrassment.

Martin watched as his youngest daughter stood up to her overbearing older sister with strength, grace and wisdom. He saw how much the past few weeks had changed her and he felt both pride and relief. At the same time, he looked at his oldest child and saw what he thought was a slow melting taking place. With time she would work through this, too.

"Okay," said Violet, "so I stink at it! At least I care."

"And I'm glad you do!" Lillie moved towards Violet hoping for a hug, but Violet put up a hand to stop her.

"One more thing."

"What?"

"Did you really try to…kill yourself?"

This very subtle look in Violet's eyes was new. Lillie thought she saw fear and sadness there. "Yes, I did. My depression took me to a very dark and helpless place a couple of times. The pain and the fear were so great, I wanted it to stop and I tried to make it stop." She paused, amazed now that she had ever wanted to end her own life. "I'm sure glad I failed."

"Me too!" said Violet with a sob. She welcomed Lillie into her arms and they hugged, long and hard.

The men in the room all realized they'd been holding their breath, and sighed in unison. The tension was gone.

Bruce announced he was off to Broadley to meet Joshua.

Martin raised an eyebrow. "You are?"

"Yup. We're gonna meet at Flanigan's for a beer."

"Well, good for you, son."

Bruce smiled at his father, then waved at them all and departed.

Violet watched him leave. Though no one noticed, hardness had returned to her eyes.

42

When Joshua hit the city limits of Broadley, he headed straight to Flanigan's, arriving fifteen minutes early. It gave him a feeling of control to be settled ahead of time.

He remembered Bruce vaguely from his growing-up years as one of the "big kids," but had no real idea what he looked like now. He ordered a beer and smoked a cigarette to calm his nerves while he waited.

At ten past eight, a tall guy with broad shoulders and curly blonde hair entered the bar clearly looking for someone. Joshua raised a finger to identify himself.

Having pictured Joshua in his mind as the scrawny, pimple-faced boy he had been in school, Bruce was surprised to find this tall, grown man in front of him. He approached him with a smile.

"Joshua?" He slapped him good-naturedly on the shoulder in greeting.

"Bruce." Joshua nodded and stuck out his hand. They shook and sized each other up. Bruce sat on the bar stool next to Joshua and looked at the Heineken he was drinking, then turned to the approaching bartender and nodded in his direction. "I'll have what he's drinkin'!"

He turned back to Joshua. "So, you're a lawyer."

"Yup, a year since the bars."

"Why a lawyer?"

"Always had a thing for justice…law just made sense."

"Lillie says you work in a prosecutor's office."

"Uh, huh." Joshua took a swig of his beer.

They continued drinking in silence for a few moments until Joshua put out his cigarette and ordered another beer. "You're worried about Lillie being hooked up with me."

"Should I be?"

"I can't tell you about the future. But I can tell you that I care about her. I'd leave her in an instant…if I thought I was doing her any harm."

Joshua took out another cigarette and tapped it nervously on the counter. He offered Bruce one and he took it. They smoked quietly together.

Finally Bruce spoke again. "Lillie's my fav'rit. She's pretty special."

"Yes…she is."

"And she does seem happier than I've ever seen her."

The hint of a smile appeared on Joshua's face.

"Why do you think that is?" asked Bruce.

Joshua waited. He didn't want to screw it up by saying something stupid. "I don't know, maybe you should ask her."

"Well," Bruce went on, "She's never been interested in a guy like this before…she even said that this evening."

Joshua looked at him and Bruce caught a glimpse of hope in his eyes.

"I think she really likes you, man!" He held the younger man's eyes with his own. "So you'd better be worth it!"

Joshua looked away at the liquor bottles on the shelf behind the bar and took another swig of beer. They smoked and drank in silence for a while.

Bruce ordered another beer, swallowed half the contents and set it down. "Pretty awful…what happened…you and my mom and that bastard!"

Joshua felt the muscles tighten around his heart. He remained silent, not sure he could speak without showing emotion.

"They said you tried to stop 'im."

"Yeah…and a lot of good it did." He paused for a long time. "I was just a kid, but I liked your mother. A lot."

"So ya figured out what the bastard was doin'."

"Yeah, I thought I could stop him, but there's no stopping someone like that. I know that now. But back then, I thought I could save her." Joshua gripped the bottle in his hand.

"Are you puttin' Lillie in my mom's place? Trying to save her too?"

After a long silence, Joshua replied, as honestly as he could. "I see a little of your mother in Lillie. But she's so much her own person, there's no seeing her as anyone but Lillie. And as to saving…I don't know what you call it, but we're kind of saving each other."

He turned to face Bruce and look him in the eye. "I've never loved a woman before…I think it does something to you…saves your soul or something…"

Bruce saw a helpless look of love in Joshua's eyes and suddenly felt envy grow within his own heart. He had never truly loved a woman, either, and he was beginning to think maybe Joshua was right. It might be a powerful enough thing—loving a woman —to save a man's soul.

He slapped Joshua on the back again and smiled broadly.

Joshua stuck out his hand. "I'll do my best to be nothing but good to her," he said. "I promise you that."

43

L illie sat on the porch in the dimming light listening to the evening sounds of sparrows twittering in the meadow and the breeze gently moving through leaves in the trees, wondering if she was ready to pass her mother's diary on to Violet. The door opened and her father came out to join her.

"Dad…"

Martin looked at his daughter as he settled himself in his favorite chair.

"What, Lil?"

"Do you think there are other victims?"

Martin thought for a while. "You know, I think I recall reading something about that in your mother's diary." He mused for a moment. "Yes, I'm sure I did."

"Tell me."

"Well…it was after she had been working with Abigail for some time. Let's see…" He took a few puffs on his pipe while he thought, and then pointed it at her. "I think a woman called her, out of the blue. I can't remember the details." He went back to smoking his pipe. "Why?"

"Joshua and I were talking about it today." She paused, hesitant to tell her father they had decided to confront the pastor.

"Go get the diary and I'll see if I can find that entry."

Lillie got up and went inside to retrieve the diary. She could hear Kevin and Violet talking in the kitchen. Stepping quietly so they wouldn't hear her and interrupt what she and her father were doing, she quickly returned to the porch and, plunking down in her chair, handed the diary to Martin.

He held it for a long moment and closed his eyes. Then he opened his eyes and started slowly flipping through it. He stopped, read silently in a few places, repeating this until he seemed to come to something.

"Here it is."

"Read it out loud," Lillie said.

October 10, 1985

I received a very strange phone call today. She wouldn't give me her name at first but just said, 'I know what you've been through.' I asked her what she meant and she said, 'About Pastor Lane. I know what happened.'

I found her very mysterious and it frightened me a little. Then she said, 'He did it to me too. I left the church afterwards and I can't ever go back.' I asked her why she called me to tell me this and she said she had never told anyone what had happened to her and that she needed to tell someone. When she heard I had left the church suddenly after helping him with SBS she knew it must have happened to me too. Then she said she had heard a rumor that I had seduced the pastor and was 'kicked out of the church.' That was when she knew for sure. The same thing had happened to her.

Can you imagine? Me seduce him! Me kicked out of the church! I was astonished. It helped a little to know that Joshua and I weren't the only ones. But it also made me angry and sick to think that he had hurt others too. I told Abigail about this later and she wondered how many others there are. I can't stomach it to look for them. I just can't think about it. But I do think it might be helpful for Joshua to know.

Martin looked up at Lillie with tears in his eyes. "I had forgotten she wrote that, Lil. She never stopped worrying about Joshua. You'll have to share this with him."

Crying softly, Lillie sniffed and nodded. Martin returned to the diary.

She told me more. Apparently the pastor had been using SBS as a way to isolate one teacher at a time to molest and abuse. He had done this for years. She said she had looked into it and found that most of the teachers that worked with him in the summers had stopped coming to church afterwards and people never saw them again. Her year was 1980. She finally abandoned her teaching before the summer was over because of what he was doing. According to her there may be half a dozen other victims. I was the first she had gotten up the courage to contact.

Martin stopped. His face was white with shock. "Good God! How did I miss all that before?"

"You were focused only on Mother. Is there more?"

Martin handed Lillie the diary. She picked up where he left off.

She finally told me her name. Elizabeth Hallman. She is married, has a daughter and lives in Broadley. She thanked me for listening. I was able to tell her she was right about the pastor molesting me too. I didn't go into detail though and I didn't tell her about Joshua. We've never spoken since. I guess I'm glad she called. I have no idea what to do with what she told me. Mostly I just don't want to think about any of it. It makes me feel a little guilty, but I can't.

Lillie and Martin heard a car pulling in the driveway and a distinctive little girl voice. Lillie shut the diary and turned to her father. "Thanks, Dad! Joshua and I plan to go after Lane Richardson." She watched his face as the anger was replaced by sadness.

He smiled weakly. "I wondered if it would ever come to that."

Lillie patted the diary. "This will be helpful. Perhaps Elizabeth would be willing to help us, and maybe some of the other victims."

"Honey, this won't be a pleasant task you two embark on. You need to be ready for a fight, I'm afraid. Are you really prepared for that?"

"We can't not do it, Dad," she said. "Joshua's finally ready to stop punishing himself for what happened and wants Lane to pay for what he's done. That's good, I think. It's a healthy direction to go in."

Martin pressed his lips together. "I hate to say it, but I think you may be right."

Sassy burst through the screen door. "There you are! Grampa! Aunt Lillie! We rode horses all day! I can ride one all by myself! You should see me, I'm really good!"

She stood holding on to the arm of Martin's wicker chair jumping in place on the balls of her feet. Her hair flew in all directions and her face, her hands and knees were smudged with dirt. A triumphant grin spread across her face.

Martin and Lillie smiled and congratulated Sassy in turn. Allowing his granddaughter to drag him by the hand, Martin got up and followed Sassy inside, while Lillie went upstairs and quickly stowed the diary in its drawer. She wasn't done with it just yet.

44

Bruce pulled into the lane and cut his engine to keep the noise of his car from waking the household. As he entered the kitchen, he saw that no one was up, so he headed upstairs on tiptoe to see if Lillie was still awake. Opening her door, he peered into the darkness and ventured into the room. Moving slowly and feeling his way to the bed, he found it with the tip of his boot.

As his eyes adjusted, he was able to make out two forms in the bed—a small one and a large one. Guessing that Sassy was sleeping in Lillie's bed with her, he turned to leave.

"Bruce, is that you?" Lillie's voice was clear but soft.

He knelt down beside the bed and put his hand on her arm. "Yeah."

She smelled beer and cigarettes on his breath. "How was it?"

Lillie could see Bruce's white teeth shining and she smiled back.

"He's a good guy, Lil," he said. "I like him. He said to say hi and asked you to call him."

"He's staying in Hopeston?"

"Yup. But I don't think he feels comfortable calling here right now."

"Thanks," said Lillie, nodding. "Bruce, you should go to bed."

"Yeah! G'night. Love ya, sis!"

"I love you too!"

Bruce stood and walked unsteadily out of the room. Lillie heard the clunk of his boots on the stairs as he made his way to his room in the basement. As she drifted back to sleep, she hoped he would notice Ben in his bed before he lay down.

✿

Joshua drove carefully home. He crept quietly into the house so as not to wake his mother—he had not called to let her know he was coming home again. As he undressed, he was surprised to feel no desire for sexual release, having experienced such total satisfaction with Lillie earlier in the day. He was warmed at the thought of their playful fighting, cuddling, sleeping naked together, their intense pleasure and heart to heart conversation. Never before had he known the joy of deep companionship and the intimacy of mutual pleasuring that loving another could offer. He sent Lillie a silent message of love and gratitude.

The thought of Bruce brought hope to his heart as well. Recalling his mother's words about sorting the "allies from the enemies" as the story of his abuse came out, he realized Bruce was an ally. He had openly shared elements of his story with Bruce and had not been rejected or judged. It was yet to be seen on which side Lillie's sister Violet would fall but for now he felt at peace.

His thoughts turned to their decision to go after the man who had started it all, and he wondered again if there were other victims. He looked forward to talking more with Lillie in the morning—there was much to do.

Pulling up the cover, he lay in a relaxed state of contentedness for the first time in as long as he could remember and dropped off to sleep.

Lillie couldn't quite make out the cause of the wiggling in her dream. Then she heard voices. "Aunt Lillie! Wake up Aunt Lillie!" The fog of sleep lifted as her niece jiggled her and whispered her awake.

"Aunt Lillie, I rode a horse all by myself! I want to go horseback riding again today!" Sassy was no longer whispering.

Lillie spoke through sleep-encrusted lips. "I think you're going home today, Sas."

"No! I want to ride the horse!" The authoritative tone in Sassy's voice sounded a lot like her mother.

"Well, go see what your Mom and Dad say."

Sassy slipped out of bed and ran, barefooted, out of the room and down the hall to the room where her mother and father slept in Violet's narrow childhood bed. To Lillie's astonishment, Sassy succeeded in waking the entire household as she screamed and yelled her displeasure at learning they were going home.

Lillie jumped into the shower. As she emerged steamy and clean, the smells of bacon, sautéing onions and coffee called to her from downstairs. Even Bruce, looking very rumpled and sleepy, was up, sitting at the kitchen table and staring into the mug of coffee in front of him. Next to Bruce sat Ben, a miniature copy of his uncle, with the exception that he had hot chocolate in his mug.

Grandpa and Sassy were chefs again while Violet, dressed in her robe and slippers, set the table and poured coffee. Kevin was already outside rearranging the car, readying it for their trip home. Other than Lillie, he was the only one who had gotten dressed.

Breakfast turned into a lively affair. Scrambled eggs, home fried potatoes with onions, crisp bacon, wheat toast with butter and jam and cold orange juice were passed around the table more than once, and coffee was poured several more times as well.

Martin smiled. The Farmer family was finally all together for the first time since Melodie's death. He felt his wife's presence in the room. Content to have his children and grandchildren all around him, he was in no hurry to change it.

He looked at each of the faces of his family members. Bruce was animated and teasing, now that he was awake. Ben was giggling as Bruce tickled him and ruffled his hair. Kevin now stood leaning against the counter, mug in his hand, watching and adding his two cents, now and then, in his deep, calm voice.

Sassy, uncharacteristically quiet, sat on her mother's lap, watching the silliness of her brother and uncle across the table, while Violet absentmindedly stroked her hair. She, too, sat quietly taking in their conversation for a moment before interrupting Lillie and Bruce's light banter. "Ben, tell us about your adventure yesterday."

Sassy wiggled in her mother's lap. Violet held her close and spoke softly into her ear, asking her to let her brother talk. Sassy slid off her mother's lap and went with arms raised to her father, who lifted her up and held her quietly while Ben told the family about feeding and rubbing down the horses at the Sampson ranch. Martin's friend, Jed Sampson, who taught horseback riding lessons, had been thrilled to take Ben and Sassy under his wing for the day.

Ben told how they had started riding around a fenced-in riding ring to learn how to handle their horses and then after a few hours and a lunch break, had gone on a trail ride all afternoon. Sassy piped up at this point to say she had gotten to ride her own horse.

Ben scowled at her and went on, relating that they had ridden with the Sampson family, which included four children ranging in age from younger than Sassy's seven years to older than Ben's ten.

After patient instruction during the morning, Ben and Sassy had been deemed ready for a long trail ride, an experience they alone shared.

It was clear that it had created a bond between them, something new and wonderful. A clue to the existence of this new bond was Sassy's willingness to let Ben tell the story.

For reasons that go deep in the heart of a sister who admires her older brother, Sassy watched Ben from her father's arms. Ben included Sassy in his story, referring to her part in it and even looking at her when he did so. Though he, instead of she, was in the center of everyone's attention for a change, Sassy saw the joy and confidence in her brother's face and somehow knew that her silence was allowing it to happen.

Kevin kissed his daughter's silky head, her hair tangled from sleep, while Ben told every detail of the day, the memories coming alive in his mind, animating his face and eyes. Bruce laid a large hand on his nephew's thin shoulder, while memories of his own childhood played out on his own face.

Lillie watched this young older brother and his lively but patient little sister and in her mind, saw herself and Bruce at about that age, innocent, free and happy. A sudden wave of sadness stung her nose and eyes—those days of free innocence and togetherness had passed—now they had to grab fleeting moments at family gatherings that were too short and too soon gone.

She glanced over at her sister, whose eyes shone with pride and love for her firstborn child, so often overshadowed in his shyness by his younger sister. Lillie felt a pang in her chest to think of how she might have grabbed attention Violet had needed and was overcome with apology.

Violet sensed Lillie's eyes on her and looked up. They exchanged shy smiles and a moment of recognition passed between them—the love they shared as sisters, strong even through all the falling outs and fights and jealousies, even through their strong disagreements and recent estrangement. Lillie saw a humble rawness pass over Violet's face, and felt she'd seen into her soul for a shining moment.

Violet saw the sadness in her sister's eyes. She realized that she had always wanted her little sister to be happy but her jealousy had obscured her awareness. Her tears matched the glisten of Lillie's.

Then, as if by mutual consent, they returned their attention to Ben.

"And when we got back to the barn, Mr. Sampson told us we were good horseback riders! Didn't he, Sassy?" Ben said, looking up at his little sister triumphantly. She nodded silently and laid her head back on Kevin's chest.

"They said we could come back any time. Mom, can we? Go again sometime?" Ben asked.

His petition seemed to bring Sassy out of her quiet, watchful mood and before Violet could answer she had slithered free from her father and climbed back onto her mother's lap, facing her. Placing her hands on Violet's cheeks, Sassy pulled her to attention and said with all the seriousness she could muster, "Don't say no, Mother. Ben and I need this."

Violet smiled at her earnest little daughter and everyone laughed—even Ben—knowing that Sassy had spoken the truth of it. The healing energy in the room was akin to the blessing of a full moon at night in the woods—the truth that unharnessed light penetrates even the darkest of places.

45

As the Parks family headed out the back door, Lillie grabbed the phone and disappeared quickly into the dim of the hallway.

"Hello Mrs. Crumley, is Joshua there?"

"Well, no, Lillie, didn't you go see him in the city?"

"Yes, but he came back last night."

"He did?" Lillie could hear Miriam's heavier breathing, as she walked with the phone.

"Well, what do you know? Yes, I guess he did. I see his car out there. Let me see, I suppose he's asleep."

Lillie grinned to herself. Joshua must have crept into bed late, just as Bruce had and not told his mother he was home. "Can you have him call me when he wakes up?"

"Yes, I will."

After hanging up Lillie headed outside to see Violet and her family off. Kevin had finished packing the car and stood waiting patiently as Violet tried to corral their children in the yard. Martin and Bruce looked on.

As Lillie came down the steps, Violet looked up. Glancing back at her children, she turned and approached Lillie. Lillie's gut wrenched at the expression on her face.

"Lillie, I'm sorry but I really think you should reconsider your relationship with Joshua."

Lillie looked away in frustration.

"I know you think I'm just being a bossy big sister trying to meddle..." Violet went on, "But I think you both will find..."

"Violet, you don't know!"

"Won't you even consider it, for the rest of us?" She choked on her words and Lillie saw tears come into her eyes.

"You don't know Joshua. You haven't even met him yet."

"Lillie...I can't."

"Bruce met him. I think you'll like him, too. You just need time."

"God, Lillie, you're impossible!" Violet turned away in frustration. "Come on kids!"

"Get in the car." Kevin's deep voice boomed in echo to his wife's direction.

Violet turned back. Her father, brother and sister stood in a row. Each came forward to hug her goodbye. Lillie hung back, waiting to be last.

Lillie whispered in Violet's ear as they hugged. "It'll be okay, you'll see."

Violet gazed at Lillie once they'd released one another. "I'm not sure how to get my mind around all of this."

"I think it'll help you to read Mother's diary. I'll get it to you when I'm done with it."

"No, Lillie. I'm not ready." Violet looked down at the ground. "Keep it. I'll read it later…" They squeezed hands and Violet turned to go.

"Bye!" Sassy ran up to hug each one of them just as her mother had done.

"G'bye Sas'!" Bruce lifted her way up high, and she squealed with delight.

Ben waved and smiled at them as he climbed into his side of the car. He seemed different somehow—a little more grown up.

Lillie knelt down and hugged her niece. "I'll miss you!"

Sassy kissed her sloppily and then ran to the car giggling.

Martin and Bruce and Lillie stood and watched as the car disappeared down the lane, then silently turned to walk single file back into the house.

The phone rang as they entered the kitchen. Martin answered it.

"Hi, Joshua," he said in response to the caller. Lillie turned to look at her father, who was winking at her.

"Yes, just a minute." He held the receiver out to her, its long coiled cord dangling.

She took it and stretched the cord into the hallway.

"Hello there."

"Hello." Joshua's voice sounded sleepy.

"Did you just wake up?"

"Yup."

"How come you didn't tell your mother you were coming home last night?"

"Dunno. No time."

"Your poor mother! She didn't even know you were home when I called." Lillie chuckled.

"I know." A comfortable silence rested between them.

"I love you." Lillie said, heart full.

"Hmmm."

"Are you falling asleep?"

"Nope…just…taking it in …slow."

"You sound awfully sleepy to me."

"Lillie…can you come over here…talk to me here?"

She thought about it for a moment. "On one condition."

"What?" He said after a long pause.

"That you stay sleepy. You're awfully cute."

"Hmmm."

"That's the deal!"

"See what…I can…do." Joshua yawned into the phone.

"Okay. I'll be over in a bit."

"Okay. Bye."

Lillie returned to the kitchen and sat with her brother and father at the table. They saw the glow in her face and the gleam in her eye and exchanged a knowing look between them. Soon they were all grinning.

Blushing, Lillie changed the subject. "How long are you staying, Bruce?"

"Till Sunday evening. Why?"

"I thought we could have Sunday dinner together, here, with Joshua!" She spoke with an enthusiasm neither Bruce nor Martin could resist.

"Sounds good," Martin said.

Bruce just smiled at his little sister.

"Okay, good!" Lillie said, leaping up and going for her purse. "I'm going to Joshua's. See you two later!"

She ran out the front door and down the porch steps.

"She's really happy." Bruce said to his father as they heard the car start.

"Sure is," agreed Martin, with a light smile and a far away look in his eye.

233

Lillie bounded up the steps to the Crumley's kitchen door and knocked vigorously. Miriam came to the door wiping her hands on her apron.

Miriam greeted her warmly. "Hi, Lillie. Come in."

"Good morning, Mrs. Crumley," she said, breathing in the aroma of cinnamon and pineapple.

"Joshua's still in bed."

"Can I go up?"

"Yes…I guess so."

Lillie nodded her head slightly in thanks as she headed quickly for the stairs. Joshua's bedroom door was ajar, and from the hall she could see him lying in bed, his head partially buried under his pillow.

Approaching the bed slowly, Lillie dropped her purse silently to the floor and slipped off her sandals. She looked down at him for a long moment, watching him breathe. Unable to resist her newfound need to touch him, she lowered her head and gently kissed the back of his neck.

"Hmm."

"Hi, there," she said softly, kneeling at the side of the bed.

"Hi." A muffled voice drifted from under the pillow.

"You went back to sleep." She leaned over and laid her arms over his.

"Uh, huh." He turned over, looked at her through one eye, and closed it again, "It's too early. Too bright…"

"Oh no, it's not. You just stayed out too late last night with my brother."

Lillie laid her head on his chest. Joshua put his arms on her back and gently pulled her close. They remained that way for a few peaceful moments, silently listening to each other's heartbeats, feeling the rise and fall of each other's breathing.

"Are you going to get up, or am I going to fall asleep with you?"

"Both." He said yawning and stretching. "Sleep first."

"You have to move over then," she said, getting up and pushing gently on his side. He rolled towards the center of the bed and she climbed onto the bed and lay down, spooning behind him. She put her arm over him and snuggled close. They lay quietly breathing in unison for some time. Soon Joshua was softly snoring. Before long she too dozed off.

When she woke she realized that in his sleep Joshua had taken her hand and pressed it close to his chest. She jiggled him a little with her body. His breathing altered only slightly, so she jiggled him again. This time the snoring stopped.

"Hey, sleepy head," Lillie whispered, remembering Sassy's efforts to awaken her that very morning.

"You're a pest!" He turned around, grabbed her and pulled her against him. Lillie yelped playfully. "Help, help…"

Joshua loosened his hold and Lillie slid onto her side, supporting her head on her hand.

"How was your time with Bruce last night?"

Joshua turned his rumpled head to look at her. "Cool…really cool. He had some good questions."

"Yeah? Like what?"

Joshua rubbed his face and thought for a moment. "He wanted to know if I was mistaking you for your mother."

The thought had never occurred to Lillie. "And what did you tell him?"

"I told him you are such a wild and crazy pest that I couldn't mistake you for anyone." He grinned and Lillie dug her fingers into his ribs. Joshua curled up instinctively to protect his ribs and belly.

"You didn't!" Lillie challenged as she dug deeper.

"I did…I did…well, maybe not exactly in those…WORDS…" He gasped for breath, his eyes twinkling. Lillie pulled her hand away and let him continue.

"I told him you're too much your own person to mistake you for your mother."

"Am I?" At that, Lillie suddenly felt vulnerable.

He pinned her hands to the bed to keep her from jabbing him again. "Who else do you know that attacks sleeping men in their beds?"

"That's sleeping, HALF-NAKED men!" she exclaimed, grinning, and Joshua smiled back.

"Okay," she continued, "so I may be a bit wild…but I'm not crazy!"

Joshua saw a flicker of something other than humor pass through her eyes. Releasing her hands, he reached out to her and pulled her close to his side. All need for his own self-protection melted away.

"He wondered if I was trying to save *you*..." he said gently.

Lillie buried her head in his chest.

"But I told him," he said, pressing his cheek against the top of her head, "that we're saving each other..."

She remained silent.

"It's the love, Lillie."

Lillie raised her head. "That saves us?"

"Yeah..." he said quietly. "You are loving me back to life, Lillie Farmer." He looked at her with such tenderness that her heart threatened to break wide open.

Savoring his words, Lillie snuggled her head back into the place just below his shoulder and held him close. "You're loving me back to life too." Joshua leaned his head against hers and they held each other, feeling the power and fullness of their love.

"You're not crazy, Lillie. But you are *always* surprising me...and I *like* that."

"I've been surprising myself lately," she said, thinking of Violet and their interactions during the past few days. She was reminded of the conversation she'd had with her father about the diary. "Oh! Joshua!"

"What?"

"Dad remembered that Mother received a call from another victim."

Joshua's head jerked forward, the last of his sleepiness disappearing in an instant. He lifted himself to his elbows. "He did?"

"Yup. Mother wrote about it. We found it and read it together."

"Tell me."

"I have it written down." Lillie looked at her purse on the floor, but not wanting to leave him, she tried to recall the details. "A woman named..." She searched her memory. "Elizabeth something. She lives in Broadley now."

Joshua's eyes opened wide as he considered the news. He had many questions but didn't know where to begin.

Lillie smiled softly. "And Joshua, my father wanted me to tell you..."

Joshua looked at her expectantly.

"...that Mother never stopped worrying about you. She thought you would be helped to know that you and she were not the only ones."

Lillie saw the same mixture of feelings in Joshua's face that her mother had described—relief, anger and pain.

"Do you know what happened to Elizabeth?" he asked.

She reached out and put her hand on his knee, which was still covered by the sheet. "Yeah. Are you ready to hear it?"

"I guess so. I always assumed that it was just us." In that moment, he felt a familiar bond with Mrs. Farmer. It was an odd feeling, both comforting and disturbing. Lillie watched him closely.

He exhaled and turned back to her. "Lillie, I've spent all these years feeling so alone, feeling that no one could possibly understand that I don't really know how to feel…" His voice broke.

They sat in silence for a few moments, and then Lillie watched as Joshua climbed out of bed and pulled on his jeans. He grabbed a T-shirt out of a drawer and, making his way barefooted and bare-chested back to the bed, slipped it over his head and shoulders. He sat down on the floor and leaned against the wall for support. "Okay, tell me," he said.

Lillie glanced at her notes. "Elizabeth was the Summer Bible Series teacher in the summer of nineteen eighty." She watched as Joshua's mind worked to put things together. "He called her into his office for personal Bible instruction lessons," she said, making quotation marks in the air with her fingers. "Apparently she quit her teaching mid-summer after he molested her."

Joshua was wide-eyed. "How did she know to call your mother?"

"Apparently she figured out that Mother had gone through the same thing."

"Was she raped?"

Lillie speculated. "I don't think so. She may have gotten out before it got to that. But I don't really know."

"How do you think she figured out about your mother?"

"I guess she saw the pattern." Lillie felt pressure from Joshua—as if he were cross-examining her. "I think she said that other SBS teachers had gone through the same thing…all of them just left the church and never came back, like Mother."

Joshua hit the bed hard with his fist. Rage flashed in his eyes. "How many?"

"I don't know, Joshua!"

He leapt up and began to pace the room. "I'm sorry, Lillie, I'm just really angry right now and I want to know…" He came to her and knelt beside the bed, taking her hands in his. "I *need* to know as much as I can—what else he's done and who else he's hurt."

He swallowed hard. "Did she…Elizabeth…know about me?"

Lillie squeezed his hands. "I don't think so. Mother wrote that she didn't tell her about you." She paused for a moment. "I think she was very protective of you…always."

In that moment all the feelings that Joshua had ever felt for Melodie Farmer came flooding back to him. He laid his head on Lillie's lap and began to cry silently. She gently stroked his head, combing her fingers through his hair.

As he wept, Bruce's question came back to him. *Was* he trying to put Lillie in her mother's place in his heart? It frightened him to think he might be doing just that. He felt a surge of the old need, the need to run away and leave Lillie so as not to draw her into this sickness of his. Feelings of disgust came over him and his weeping turned into sobs. Lillie leaned down and held him as his shoulders shook with it. Wrapping his arms around her hips, he clung to her.

But he cried not just for himself—he cried for the pain of the other victims, Elizabeth and all the other SBS teachers. He cried for the gentle woman he had loved and sought to protect, the one who had wanted to protect him even though she could never face him. That her gentle concern for him had survived the trauma was incredible. Guilt flooded him because he had tried to exorcise her from his mind during the years—to remove the demon of the fear he had seen in her eyes as she lay pinned to the floor that day.

He began to sort out in his mind his feelings for Lillie and those he still had for her mother. When he thought of Mrs. Farmer he felt longing, sadness and guilt. When he thought of Lillie, he felt comfort, pleasure, joy and peace. Relief spread through him and he began to chuckle.

"What's so funny?" Lillie asked.

He heard the smile in the lilt of her voice and his heart filled with love for her. Raising himself up to match her height, he looked directly into her eyes.

"You are, and I love it. It saves me…"

46

Violet couldn't wait to go to church on Sunday, which was odd, considering she'd never felt that way before. Deeply troubled by the news about her mother, she couldn't shake the images evoked in her mind's eye. And she was afraid for Lillie—it wasn't good to let Joshua anywhere near any member of her family. Nothing good could come of a relationship with a man who had stood by and watched the rape of a woman, no matter what the circumstances.

She felt guilty for not having called to apologize to Mrs. Crumley, but she still couldn't bring herself to make the call and it haunted her. Her father's words stuck in her mind. She had begun to see her own jealousy for the first time and realized she had no control over it. In fact, it often reared its ugly head, even with Kevin at times.

Violet felt in need of the forgiveness and guidance of God. And she knew of no other way to access God than by going to church. She had never felt the need for church growing up. As a very capable, self-sufficient person, church hadn't been necessary for her.

But, for the kids, she and Kevin had started attending in the last year, and now, all of a sudden, it was necessary for her. She would reach out for help in the only way she knew how.

Sunday morning rolled around and Violet woke the kids and helped them pick out appropriate clothes for church. Ben dragged his feet all morning, which irritated her, but Sassy was excited and willingly donned the summer dress and white sandals her mother had laid out for her. Seeing her friends in Sunday school was always fun.

As long as it made her happy, Kevin was willing to do anything Violet wanted. He had watched her struggle since they'd returned from the family gathering at her father's house. At night in bed, he had held her close while she

239

cried and he saw the urgency in her face now as they prepared for church. He hoped she would receive what she was looking for.

Arriving in the church parking lot, along with other churchgoers, they got out of their car and walked together past bulging flowerbeds and freshly manicured grass to the double front doors of the church. Violet checked and adjusted her children's hair and clothing and "spit polished" their cheeks.

Other mothers did the same, smiling apologetically at one another for not having better-looking children, while the fathers followed behind, hoping not to be drawn into this ritual of poking and prodding, remembering when it had been done to them as boys.

As they entered the church, the smell of clean linoleum, candle wax and ladies' perfume met them. Once inside the foyer, they listened as the organist, playing the prelude in the sanctuary, called worshippers to their pews.

The Parks family made their way to the entrance of the sanctuary and marched single file halfway down the aisle and side-stepped into the wooden pew. Sassy observed the organist as she played with her back to the congregation, managing the large double keyboard and huge foot pedals. The choir, dressed in long robes with shiny scarves hanging down, filed in from a side door and settled in seats beyond the organ and Jesus' Table. In Sunday School, she had been told that the table up front belonged to Jesus and from it he served a meal of bread and juice.

How would Jesus serve his meal? Sassy was impatient—she hadn't seen him serve a meal yet. This morning, as on other Sundays, there was a huge goblet under a white cloth and next to it a large silver plate piled high with something under another white cloth. That must be it, thought Sassy.

More and more people entered the sanctuary, whispering and sitting, slowly filling the pews. Then, when the minister entered from a side door on the opposite side from the choir and took a seat behind the pulpit, a hush came over the place.

Sassy was still watching the fanfare and wondering what was happening. Why did the minister hide down low where no one could see him? All of a sudden, the organ music stopped, and the clatter of whispers and shuffling of feet quieted. In the expectant silence, the minister rose up from behind the pulpit, almost like a ghost, and began to speak.

Sassy's attention quickly moved to people around her. Old Mrs. Dumpler, two rows up, had bad breath and a wart on her chin with bristles coming out of it. Sassy always tried to avoid her as she would take your face and pull you close so she could see you and then you got a full blast of her breath. She kissed you with her wet lips, too.

The Saxton twins, a row up on the far right, were whispering and giggling, heads together. Sassy wished she had a sister to giggle with too.

Across the aisle Sassy caught sight of Jacob Forby, sitting with his family. He was wearing a navy blue coat and red tie. He was one of her friends from Sunday School, so leaning over her mother's lap, she hissed to get his attention.

Violet patted Sassy's hand to quiet her. But since Jacob hadn't looked at her, Sassy hissed again, more loudly this time. Just as Jacob turned to look, Violet lowered her head to talk to Sassy and blocked her view. Frustrated, Sassy pushed her mother's head out of the way. Violet responded by grabbing Sassy's arm. Sassy squealed in pain.

Before long the children started getting up and filing out of the sanctuary for Sunday school, and Sassy wondered who'd given the magic signal to release them. Even so, she excitedly waved goodbye to her parents and followed Ben.

Violet sighed with relief when her daughter had gone. Now she could pay attention and listen for the comforting words she sought. After the Bible verse was read aloud the choir stood as one, and sang a beautiful anthem. Violet felt the tension leave her body.

After a short prayer the minister began his sermon in a warm voice.

"The passage just read to you about the woman caught in adultery shows a very important difference between a typical human response to this woman's sexual sin and the response of Jesus Christ. Those angry men stood in judgment around her, ready to throw stones of punishment for her transgression. But Jesus points out to her accusers that they are in no position to cast stones of judgment at her. Jesus' righteous challenge is enough to convict them of their own failings and they back off.

"How often do we stand ready to throw stones of judgment at others for their sins when we ourselves are no better?

"Jesus then turns his full attention on the woman. He doesn't look at her or even speak to her at first but his presence and his love is already at work in her, burning away

her sin. He issues her a challenge to 'go and sin no more' and we see her transformed by his challenge. But there are two things we must recognize here.

"First, without the love of Jesus, the challenge of Jesus would not have brought about the forgiveness that changed the woman. Clearly we must love one another first and foremost if we hope to help one another change. We only earn the right to issue a challenge to another if we have first loved them. Do you see the difference between the aggressive and violent nature of loveless judgment and the challenge that comes with compassion, which reaches, as you can see in this woman's case, to the very heart of a person?

"Secondly, let us not leave this story thinking that it is only the woman with her sexual sin that receives the challenge to change her ways. The retreating stone throwers are also being challenged. All of us are being issued the compassionate challenge of God to leave our sinful ways of the past behind us and to become like Jesus in our behavior towards others."

Violet felt the sermon was being preached specifically for her and the words pierced her heart. No longer hearing the minister's voice, she saw herself throwing painful stones at Joshua and his mother, and she was filled with guilt.

Then she saw herself as the woman on the ground with the word "Jealousy" written across the back of her robe. She saw Jesus gently offering her a hand. As he touched her, she felt a cleansing power surge through her body, ridding her of all sin, and leaving her pure and innocent, obliterating the word on her back. Jesus encouraged her to go to Joshua and his mother, who were crouching together in the dirt, to help lift them up, so they too could hold their heads up high. "Love them first and foremost," the minister had said.

Forgiveness is what changed the woman. She was to forgive and to love Joshua. Wasn't that what Lillie was doing?

Violet knew in that moment that she too could have her burden lifted by her loving Savior. He was already sending her out to love and thus to help heal others, beginning with Joshua. Tears came to Violet's eyes as she let the words of the minister wash over her like fresh, cleansing water. As he concluded his sermon, Violet looked around as if seeing with new eyes. Retrieving a tissue from her purse, Violet wiped her eyes and blew her nose. Noticing her husband watching her, she smiled shyly. He took her hand in his large one and held it gently.

The minister now stood behind the altar preparing to serve communion to the congregation. Violet had always taken communion with an intellectual understanding of what it meant. Partaking symbolically of the body and blood of Jesus Christ in the form of the elements of bread and wine, or in this case, grape juice, was meant to symbolize the way we dwell in Jesus and he dwells in us.

As the congregation lined up to file down the center aisle to be served, Violet's heart led her and she stood and walked. Approaching the minister, who stood in front of the altar holding the cup of juice and the loaf of bread, she felt her heart open.

Looking into her eyes as if able to read her thoughts, the minister said, "This is the body of Christ, broken for you, Violet." He smiled slightly, holding her gaze with kindness.

Suddenly it was Jesus who stood in front of her, hands outstretched to offer Himself to her. She reached out and saw the minister, again, as she ripped a piece free from the loaf. Tears stung her eyes again. *She was ripping the flesh of Jesus.*

"Violet, this is the blood of Christ, shed for you." The words filled her with the very lifeblood of Jesus. Heart overflowing, she nearly buckled at the knees. Kevin reached out and took hold of her arm. The minister flashed an understanding smile as he offered her the cup. After dipping her bread into it, she was compelled to close her eyes before placing it in her mouth.

Again she saw Jesus standing in front of her, His heart pumping His blood into hers. He embraced her and held her as she wept for a lifetime of pain. Rooted where she stood until her tears subsided and Jesus released her, she watched as He smiled into her eyes and His love reached all the way into her soul, flooding her with light.

Violet and Kevin made their way back to the pew. He knew intuitively that Violet had received what she was looking for and though he didn't understand what had happened, it gladdened his heart. He placed his hand on Violet's back as they entered their pew and once seated, put his arm around her shoulders and pulled her close to his side. When the organ postlude began to play, he sensed that Violet was in no hurry to leave. A peaceful aura came over them as they let the sanctuary empty around them. The minister noticed them and smiled.

After several moments of silence, they heard the pitter-patter of running feet and Sassy appeared at their pew.

"C'mon, Mom and Dad! The cookies are almost all gone!" Her eager little face shone. Violet reached out a hand past Kevin and caressed her daughter's rosy cheek. Sassy saw the tear-streaked glow on her mother's face and quickly scooted down the pew.

"What's the matter, Mom?"

Sassy placed her little hands softly on her mother's chest, and looked deeply into her eyes.

Violet answered without hesitation. "I met with Jesus, Sas!"

Sassy whipped her head around and looked at Jesus' Table and saw that it was empty. "Did he serve you his meal of bread and juice?"

Violet smiled and her eyes filled with fresh tears. She reached out to take Sassy onto her lap for a hug.

"Yes, sweety. He did."

Just then Ben arrived at the pew holding a stack of napkin-wrapped freshly-baked chocolate chip cookies. He found his family hugging and looked questioningly at his father, who beckoned for him to join them. Placing the cookies carefully down on the cushioned seat, he slid towards them. Sassy reached out, encircling his neck with her arm and Kevin put his free hand on Ben's back. Violet smiled as she looked at her children with new understanding. Love overflowed and spilled down.

"Ben, Jesus was here! He served Mom and Dad his meal!" Sassy exclaimed, releasing him and pointing to the altar. Ben looked at the altar and then at his mother with a wrinkled nose and brow, too old to believe such nonsense.

His mother rescued him from having to respond to his sister's comment. "It looks like you've brought us a feast, Ben."

He smiled sheepishly. "Yup! These are the last four!" He turned, unwrapped the cookies, and distributed them to his family, looking like a minister distributing the body of Christ.

In a close huddle they ate, delighting in this second generous meal: the love of family, the thoughtful act of a child, the wisdom and spiritual insight of the youngest, the reality of mystery and the way it touches the human heart so powerfully.

Joshua and Lillie drove to Lillie's house with a bag of groceries they had purchased to cook Sunday dinner. As they pulled in the lane they could hear the chain saw roaring behind the barn. Exchanging a smile, Lillie took the groceries into the house to put them away while Joshua headed out to help at the woodcutting site.

Bruce looked up in greeting and turned back to his sawing. Martin welcomed Joshua with a smile and headed to the woodpile with an armful of logs. Loading up himself, Joshua quickly fit into their rhythm like a third cog in a well-greased machine.

All were silent as Kevin drove the family home from church. Uncharacteristically calm in the back seat, the children were aware that something special had happened to their mother. It continued as she prepared Sunday dinner, as if she were floating on a cloud of peacefulness.

Once, coming through the kitchen, Kevin had even caught her humming to herself while she stared out the window, a grater in one hand and a carrot in the other. Smiling to himself, he left her alone and carried on with his Sunday chores.

Sassy's screech in the living room and Ben's quiet voice in response, so like his father's, made Violet think of Lillie and Bruce when they were young. She felt the sting of jealousy, and then, in an instant, it dissipated like a soap bubble that pops on landing.

Violet gasped at the incredible sense of relief she felt. Tears flooded her eyes and gratitude drenched her heart. She felt like falling to her knees but instead stood motionless, and a little wobbly, sensing the presence of God.

Have I been healed? she asked silently. Have you taken away my jealousy? A wordless answer saturated her being. "You have been cleansed. But you must work to make it a reality in your life."

In the next moment, she felt the challenge of Christ followed by an overpowering sense of love. "Love them first." The minister's words came back to her. "Challenge with compassion," not "loveless judgment." The words rang like church bells in her mind.

Looking around to see if anyone else had heard the ringing of bells, Violet realized she was being drawn into yet another mystical encounter with her Savior. It came through loud and clear that she was to call Joshua's mother and make her apology.

Shame covered her like a shroud. And then, as though a divine hand had been placed on her shoulder, she felt relieved of her burden. Deeply humbled, she knew in that moment she was finally ready to make the call.

47

L illie and Joshua arrived at the wooded parking area and pulled in beside Abigail's old car. Their windows open, they could hear the forest sounds and smell its fragrances. They stayed in the car for a few quiet moments after Joshua turned off the engine. Without saying a word, Joshua reached over and put his hand gently on Lillie's shoulder.

"You ready?" she asked.

"Yeah," he said. "It's so different this time. I'm actually looking forward to it."

Lillie smiled, thinking of all that had happened since they had last been at Abigail's. They had become lovers for one thing, and she wondered if Abigail would be able to tell.

They made their way up the path and entered the cabin through the open kitchen door. Abigail greeted them with warm embraces. The smell of blueberry scones wafted in the air.

Joshua looked around to see what Abigail's home looked like. He had been unobservant of his surroundings the first time he had been there. A wood stove stood against the far wall of the main room, flanked by a neat pile of kindling and another pile of logs that waited for colder weather. The walls of the room were lined with bookshelves filled with books of every imaginable shape and size, except for the wall facing north, which was mostly one large window.

Two old armchairs on either side of a coffee table sat in the center of a large coil rug on the floor, creating a tiny living room area in front of the wood stove. It was well lit by natural light from the window.

The kitchen, on the other end of the room, consisted of a shallow alcove with a small table in the middle, hugged by a motley crew of ladder-backed chairs. A wooden bowl of fruit decorated its center and a stained glass lamp hung above it. A narrow counter was attached to the wall, with a sink, a small refrigerator and a tiny ancient stove nestled in between. There were shelves above the counter where dishes, a basket of cutlery and a collection of mugs rubbed shoulders with spices, honey and salt and pepper. The teacup and saucer Lillie had given Abigail was placed carefully in the center of the middle shelf, a treasure in its place of honor.

A curtain of faded calico hung in the doorway to what Joshua assumed were Abigail's private sleeping quarters. Near this doorway was another curtain pulled aside to reveal pantry shelves filled with jars of home-canned peaches, tomatoes and beans, paper goods and other household items. Against the wall by the door was a stack of wooden crates with oranges, potatoes and bags and bottles to be recycled.

In the far northeast corner of the main room stood a desk and chair with a phone, a lamp, writing materials and a stack of magazines on top. Abigail's lifestyle is very simple, tidy and organized, he thought. Her needs are not many.

Abigail sensed something different about Lillie and Joshua. They seemed more peaceful and more connected to each other. She could tell that Joshua had come a long way in his healing since she'd seen him last. Lillie looked content—a glow emanated from her.

Abigail had seen something special about Lillie the first time she met her. This new light that surrounded her and filled her aura was no surprise. Together she and Joshua contained an energy that was powerful and strong. She smiled as she watched them take in their surroundings.

"You have a wonderful home, Abigail."

"Thank thee dear. I like it. It suits me just fine."

"You live very simply," Joshua said.

"That's intentional, my boy. I do not need much and I choose to live in tune with Mother Earth as much as possible."

Joshua and Lillie looked at each other. Abigail saw the silent communication that passed between them. She recognized the deep silent conversation of two souls who have shared their hearts and mingled their bodies in the intimacy of love. It delighted her to see this wonder before her.

"Come," she said, beckoning them to help her bring the tea out to the porch. Lillie took up the tray with the teapot in its cozy and teacups; Joshua took the tray with a plate full of hot scones.

Abigail led the way, her long purple dress swishing and sweeping the floor in front of them. Once settled around the altar, they entered into silence.

The forest, as usual, teemed with sounds. A blue jay squawked overhead as it flew by and two mourning doves rose in flight in response, the characteristic whistle of their wings identifying them.

Lillie breathed in the pine-scented air. She had come to love this place with its aroma of damp earth and the hint of lake water.

Joshua felt the tension begin to drain from his body as he took in the peacefulness of their surroundings. He hadn't expected to feel tense but he was reminded of his first sessions on the porch with Abigail. Some of the anxiety still lingered, and he reached out and took Lillie's hand into his for comfort. She smiled without looking at him, and gently squeezed his hand. They closed their eyes as a current of intimacy ran through them.

Abigail began to intone a song and play her drum in the way that had become familiar to Lillie and Joshua. A soothing vibration began to envelop them. The song and the drumming filled their ears and their hearts and it seemed to fill the whole world. After a while Lillie experienced a sensation of flying and could see the lake below as if she were up above it looking down. Joshua saw a light and felt warmth enter his entire body. They remained suspended in vibrational energy until Abigail became silent. Slowly their consciousness returned to the here and now of the forest and the porch and the altar in front of them. Abigail voiced a prayer.

"Holy Mother of the Universe and of all the Earth, we thank thee for the many blessings thee gives to us and pours over us like fresh water. Thee has given us the Love that heals and we are caught up in it. Thee has chosen to bring us together in this place for a mighty purpose. This is both a blessing and a responsibility. We are aware that we need thee and we need one another in order to fulfill this purpose. Speak to us so we might know our purpose and see clearly the path that leads to its fulfillment. Draw us close to thee, O Holy One. We are thine. Alleluia, Amen."

Joshua squeezed Lillie's hand and let it go. Lillie opened her eyes and the three of them looked at one another. Mystery hung over them. Abigail passed out teacups filled with aromatic tea and a plate of hot buttery scones.

"So, tell me how you've been, you two." She peered, with great interest, over her teacup at them. Lillie and Joshua exchanged glances and smiled.

Joshua spoke first. "Well, I guess you can say we know each other better than we did the last time you saw us."

"I'd say so!" Abigail exclaimed.

Lillie knew there wasn't a gesture or an expression on their faces that Abigail didn't see and read the meaning of.

"We've become pretty close, actually." Lillie said. She blushed.

Abigail felt within her a resounding affirmation of this news—as though a band of angels encircled her heart, applauding. Her eyes twinkled with joy. "I'm glad."

She paused and then turned to Joshua. "Has thee been able to continue to tell thy story?"

"Yes. I told my mother…with Lillie's help." He looked at Lillie with affection.

Abigail nodded slightly. A question appeared in her eyes.

Joshua nodded. "Yes, Lillie knows the whole story now. And I was able to talk a little bit with Lillie's brother…"

"My father and I told my brother and sister what happened to mother… and to Joshua." Lillie interjected.

Abigail looked at Lillie. "So thy family knows about Joshua's part in what happened?"

"Yes, and telling them was difficult."

"It's been hard for me to have people find out what happened." Joshua admitted. "I'm used to keeping it all to myself."

Abigail smiled with compassion. "And does thee find it helpful to no longer carry this burden alone?"

"Yes, I do."

"Good, I'm glad! Does the fire within still consume?"

He reflected on the answer to her question for a moment. "Not as much. But it does seem to flare up from time to time." He reached out an upturned hand to Lillie in invitation and she placed her hand in his.

"Tell me about the flare ups," Abigail said. Lillie looked up at Joshua and he gave her a sheepish look in response. She took away her hand and lifted a scone to her mouth for a bite.

Joshua turned back to Abigail, who was watching closely. "I have nightmares about the abuse…and negative thoughts…and then I start to feel it's better for others if I just go away and leave them alone."

He looked at Lillie. "I become afraid of people knowing what happened. Then I run away and try to hide."

"Thee tries to go back into isolation?" Abigail asked.

Joshua nodded.

Lillie took a sip of tea and looked up at Abigail, eyes twinkling. "And I don't let him," she said into her teacup.

Abigail smiled approvingly and turned her attention to Joshua. "So the consuming fire creates nightmares and negative thoughts?"

"It's like I have two personalities. One that's in pain, is irrational and afraid, always afraid. And one that is learning to trust."

"And how does that feel?"

"Like I am coming back to life…after a long absence. Like I'm stepping out of the pain." Tears welled up in his eyes.

A long silence passed before Abigail continued.

"So, the pain and the fear fuel the fire that threatens to consume and control thee?"

"Yes, I guess so."

"And thee reacts by running and isolating thyself?"

Joshua nodded silently.

"Is thee able to escape the pain and the fear by running and hiding?"

"No." Joshua said. "They follow me. They hunt me down."

"So, how is thee able to get away from them?"

Joshua looked down in shame. "Well, I used to make it go away by drinking."

"So thee numbed thy feelings."

"Yes, I guess I did."

"And now?"

"Now, if I face it and talk about it, it goes away, mostly." He came to a full realization of the truth of what he was saying as he said it out loud. He was amazed and his expression showed it.

"Thee is learning to heal thyself, my boy!" Abigail said with delight. "Through facing the pain and the fear, and the nightmares and the negative thoughts they create, and through talking to people about that, and by letting thyself be supported and loved, which builds self-esteem, confidence, courage and strength, thee is then able to experience relief from the pain and the fear. Is that right?"

Joshua nodded and Abigail smiled in response.

"And look how far it has brought thee." She looked back and forth between the two of them before settling on Joshua again. "Now, how is thy *mother* handling it?"

"Well, I think. She's been pretty incredible about being supportive and helpful." Joshua said. "We've even had a few good cries together."

"Good." Abigail said approvingly. She took a sip of tea and looked out at the lake for a minute. Joshua was content to sit and reflect for a time.

Abigail turned her attention on Lillie, clearly done with Joshua for the moment. "And Lillie, how is *thy* family handling this?"

"It's been hard, but my brother got together with Joshua…to check him out, I guess. He wanted to be sure Joshua wasn't going to dump his issues on me. He likes Joshua and things are good between them and they're good between my Dad and Joshua too. It's my sister, Violet, that's having the hardest time." Lillie stopped for a moment. "It's been very upsetting for her to hear about what happened to Mother."

"What was thy sister's response?" Abigail asked, curious, recalling her vision. Violet hadn't been there.

"She glossed right over the part about the minister at first," Lillie said. "So when I told them that I'm dating Joshua, she went nuts and blamed it all on him." Lillie looked out over the lake and sighed deeply, seeking strength. "Her anger towards me came out full force."

"Why does thee suppose she's angry with thee?"

"She thinks I'm stupid to be dating Joshua after what happened!"

Abigail waited, listening.

"She thinks I'm being selfish. She doesn't want Joshua in our lives, even though he makes me happy." Lillie looked at Joshua to see how he was taking this. He smiled at her but his eyes held sadness in them.

252

Abigail noticed Joshua's expression too. "So she's angry at thee because thee loves Joshua instead of blaming him?" This was the first mention of the word "love" in reference to their relationship and Abigail used it intentionally.

"Maybe," said Lillie, confused. It was the first time the thought had arisen and it sounded ludicrous.

Abigail saw Lillie's need for help in sorting out what she had suggested. "Does thee suppose Violet is misplacing her anger and that it's not thee she's angry with at all?"

"I suppose," answered Lillie. "But why does she take it out on me and Joshua?"

"Well, let's see if we can figure out what she's really mad about and at whom she's really angry."

Lillie nodded and Abigail continued. "What does thee suppose she's feeling in relation to thy mother?"

"Sorrow? She misses her?" Lillie said, wondering.

"Yes, and what else, now that she's learned what happened to her?"

"Anger," said Lillie.

"Okay, so what is Violet angry about?"

"About the abuse Mother received?" Lillie said.

"Yes." Abigail paused before going on. "Thee said Violet was sad and misses your mother. Why?"

"Because she's dead," Lillie said, feeling it was rather obvious.

"And that means she's no longer available to Violet, right?" Abigail asked.

"Right."

"Now when does thee think Violet first felt your mother was not available to her?" Abigail's eyes were twinkling at Lillie. She was enjoying setting the stage for inner learning.

Lillie began to see where Abigail was heading. "When she was raped and retreated into herself."

"Yes, and was there perhaps another reason she may have felt abandoned by her *before* that summer?"

Lillie thought for a long time, but her mind was blank.

Abigail planted a new seed. "Is it possible that Violet felt she lost her mother's attention to some degree when thee was born, Lillie?"

"Oh my God, is *that* why she's so jealous of me?" Lillie had never thought of that before. "I think it might fit."

"If Violet felt misplaced by a new baby sister," Abigail said, "and felt a distance grow between her and her mother when she was still young herself, she might have taken it out on thee. Then as her mother continued to pull away at the time of the rape and then finally by dying, it would be only natural for Violet to continue to take her hurt and sorrow out on thee."

"But why?" Lillie asked.

"Because she doesn't realize she's doing it. It's what she's always done. So, when the news of your mother's rape came to her awareness the other day, all her feelings came bubbling up and, in typical fashion, she focused her anger and blame on thee."

"Are you saying that when I said I was dating Joshua she blamed *both of us* for all of this?"

"Yes, I think so. When thee indicated thee was, in effect, siding with one of your mother's abusers, thee became an abuser in Violet's mind as well. She feels better when she can align herself with your mother and make thee the enemy. It makes her feel closer to her mother and less powerless if she can fight her abuser."

"So that's why she was so angry about Joshua being in our lives, and why she called his mother." The puzzle was coming together in Lillie's mind.

Joshua suddenly came to life. "She called my mom?"

Lillie nodded in his direction. "Yes. She was very angry."

She turned back to Abigail. "But why doesn't she place the blame on Pastor Lane? *He's* Mother's abuser!"

"Well, because she's developed a pattern of reacting and misplacing her anger. Thee said she didn't hear the part about the minister at first. A denial mechanism kicks in for her—she *couldn't* hear that part. And it may be some time before she is able to place the anger where it belongs."

Joshua spoke again, softly. "It's like how I misplaced the anger and blame on myself all these years, instead of on Lane Richardson, where it belongs."

"Yes, exactly!" Abigail grinned at both of them. "That's when the healing begins—when a person stops stuffing and misplacing their true feelings and starts facing the truth and dealing with it appropriately."

"Okay, but how do we deal with Violet in the meantime?" Lillie was exasperated. "It could take her forever to figure this out and stop taking it out on us!"

"Ah…that's the thing to *learn* in life, isn't it?" Abigail said with a twinkle in her eye. "How not to take on another person's emotional issues."

"What do you mean?" Lillie asked.

"Practice not taking it personally. You both know she's misplacing her feelings of anger and blame onto you, and you know you don't deserve it. Right?" Abigail eyed them closely.

"Right!" exclaimed Joshua, turning to Lillie. "We're not to blame for the abuse or for Violet's loss of your mother's attention." His eyes shone at her.

Lillie felt the force of his words and realized that he had truly arrived at a place where he believed he was not to blame for the abuse. That was significant. He had, not so long ago, blamed himself and considered himself to be as good as a rapist. It was clear that he had arrived at an important point in his healing. "Don't let her bother you," he said. "It's *her* issue. If you don't react, if you don't engage with her, she will eventually take her anger elsewhere. She seeks a reaction that justifies her anger."

"So I guess we all have healing work to do." said Lillie.

"And only Violet can do hers," Abigail affirmed. "But in the meantime, thee can deflect her attacks rather than absorb them as thee's done in the past."

"Can we help her to heal?" Lillie asked.

"Yes, by not taking the bait and getting caught in her issues, thee will be helping her."

"Oh." Lillie and Joshua sat in silence and took this new information to heart.

Abigail waited as the two young people in front of her processed all she had said. When she saw Joshua look at Lillie and then expectantly toward her, she spoke again."There is something else on your minds."

"Yes." Joshua said. "We have discovered there is at least one other victim of Lane's abuse, maybe more."

Abigail held her teacup close. She was not at all surprised to hear this news.

"And we've decided to contact her."

Abigail waited again.

"And to go after Lane," he added.

It was Lillie's turn. "We wanted to discuss it all with you first."

Abigail looked out at the lake for some time before answering. Finally, she turned and looked each of them in the eye. "You are taking on a very difficult task. It will be painful and discouraging and even dangerous at times. You must be sure to have good support and to prepare yourselves for a battle."

"I do this for a living." Joshua spoke as if to assure Abigail he was ready.

"Yes, but this is thy own abuser and thy own pain, Joshua. It will affect thee personally more than thee realizes. As a professional, I presume thee is trained to keep from becoming personally involved in thy cases? Well, in this one, thee won't be able to do that."

Abigail remained silent for a long time. "But..." she said, "it is the right thing to do."

Part Four

The Funeral

48

ildred Brown hung up the phone. She had expected the call for days. In charge of the luncheons for funerals at the Hopeston church, it was her job to buy the food and gather the ladies from the church who would help cook and serve the luncheon. She was good at finding bargains and at calculating how much to buy and prepare for crowds of various sizes.

She picked up the phone and immediately dialed Louise Cardwell, her right hand helper...and sometimes rival. They had worked together for years, arguing their way through many luncheons, but Mildred depended on Louise—they were true partners when it came to these events. Both of them were now widows and their partnership gave them each a sense of purpose.

"Louise?" Mildred spoke into the receiver.

Louise dispensed of the normal social chatter. "Is it Delbert?"

"Yes. He died last night."

"Well, well. Bless his heart. It's been a long struggle, poor man. May he rest in peace."

"Yes, it's a good thing. His family has been waiting a long time. So," she continued, "we must plan."

"Yes."

"This will be a big one. Delbert was well known from his years as the city clerk. We may have to put tables out in the hall."

"I wonder what they'll do?" Louise was still thinking only of Delbert's passing.

Mildred ignored Louise. "We'll use the special menu to make it festive. Everyone in town will come, you know."

"Do you think Pastor Terry can *do* this funeral? He didn't know Delbert, did he?"

Mildred stopped. Louise was right—it had been Pastor Lane who knew Delbert the best. They had been good friends and worked together on many projects at the church and in town.

"But would Pastor Terry let Pastor Lane do it?" Mildred asked, now joining Louise in her train of thought.

"I don't know."

"Well, let's get planning. We'll see what happens. I'll mention it to Marie and she can talk to the pastor." Mildred was anxious to get to work.

"Okay."

"I'll call you later today, once I've got the details."

Terry Bunker was the second minister Hopeston Church had had since Lane Richardson's moving on. A kindly, retired minister had stepped in while they searched for a replacement.

It had been difficult to replace Rev. Richardson. He had had a generous, friendly way about him that made his congregants feel special. His sermons were well delivered teachings that made the Bible real and he had a way of applying it to everyday life.

In contrast, Terry was young and inexperienced. His sermons were lively and fun but lacked the scholarly knowledge of his predecessor. His enthusiasm and willingness to learn and try new things was admirable—the younger folks in the congregation seemed to like him and easily embraced his new ideas.

But the older members, for the most part, were finding it harder and harder to handle the changes their new pastor was bringing into the life and worship services of their church. Mildred tolerated him but had not been convinced that he was the right minister for their church. She missed Pastor Lane and probably would forever. In her mind no one could compare, and Terry had picked up on that. There was a subtle tension between them because of it.

The change Mildred disliked the most was the way he served communion. He made it clear that passing trays of little cups of juice and tiny cubes of postage-stamp-sized bread through the pews was not to him a sufficient honoring of the Lord's Supper, insisting instead on serving each congregant at the altar rail. He preferred them to break off a piece of the loaf of bread he held and then dip it into a communal cup of dark red grape juice. He said the sharing of one loaf and one cup symbolized being one with Jesus and with one another in community and was the *proper* way to re-enact the original meal of Jesus and his disciples in the upper room.

She had also heard him say, many times, that women disciples were present in the upper room for the Last Supper, even though the Bible didn't say so. Mildred felt it was wrong of him to take poetic license with the Word of God and with the traditions of her church.

Marie Calsik unlocked the church office door and turned on the lights. She looked inside the pastor's study to see that it was tidy. The Nelson family was coming in an hour to meet with Terry and plan Delbert's funeral.

The Nelsons were a prominent family in Hopeston and they would want the best funeral that the small church could manage. Delbert was survived by his wife, five children, and eight grandchildren. Two of his children still lived in Hopeston and were members of the church. Marie knew this would be a challenge for Terry and that he would welcome her support.

By the time the pastor arrived, Marie had arranged the chairs in a circle and there was fresh coffee in an insulated carafe with cups and cream and sugar on a tray on a table at the center of the circle.

"Thanks, Marie." He smiled at her when he glanced into his study. In his mid-thirties, he was of medium height, with a slight build, and his mouse-brown hair had begun to thin. His outdated wire-rimmed glasses sat on a sharp nose that was a little large for his otherwise well-proportioned face, but his understated dress did not obscure the light of intelligence and interest in his eyes.

Marie nodded in acknowledgement and went on with her work.

The pastor rubbed his forehead to banish a steadily developing headache. He had only done a handful of funerals and felt unsure if he could carry this one off to the expectations of all involved. He checked his notes, put his pad and pen on the table and opened a cabinet in his office to retrieve a couple of Bibles and hymnals.

Terry had visited Delbert during his illness and had stayed in touch with his wife and two of his daughters. But when Delbert's death had come they had not called for him. Instead he had heard of his death from another member of the congregation. Sitting in one of the chairs, he bowed his head and prayed. *"Help me Lord, to do justice to this well-loved man, to work well with his family and to remain calm."*

As he finished the prayer, he heard the sounds of Delbert's family arriving in the lobby. Taking a deep breath, he rose to his feet and went out to greet them.

"Hello Mrs. Nelson." The pastor thrust out his hand.

Pamela Nelson neither looked at him nor gave him her hand.

"I'm sorry for your loss, Pamela." She tipped her head in response.

He turned to the others in the room. "Welcome. We'll meet in my study, here." He gestured to the open door, hanging back to follow the group to the waiting circle of chairs.

Once everyone was seated he offered coffee and except for one of Delbert's children, there were no takers. He could feel the tension in the room—there was more to this than grief and sorrow.

"I'm glad you're all here. For those of you I haven't met, I'm Pastor Terry Bunker." He took a breath in an attempt to relieve his nervousness. "Would you mind sharing your names with me before we begin?"

Reluctantly, the family members shared their names, Pastor Terry nodding and smiling at each one and gesturing in recognition to Susan and Mary Anne, who were members of the Hopeston congregation.

"Let me share my condolences with you for your loss. I know Delbert struggled for a long time so this must be a time of mixed feelings for you, knowing he is free from his suffering even as you grieve his loss." There were grunts of acknowledgment and some tears. A heaviness filled the room.

Pastor Terry felt unsure of how well the meeting was going but tried to remain confident. "We are here to plan his funeral. Maybe we can talk now about what you want included in the service." He waited with paper and pen poised.

No one said a word for a long time. Mary Anne broke the silence by saying that her father loved music and that there should be beautiful music in the service. Pastor Terry breathed a sigh of relief at having some place to start.

"What sort of music did your father like?"

Susan answered his question. "Classical. Chopin, Beethoven, Mozart, stuff like that."

"Any particular pieces?" The family members began to relax as they thought of their father's interest in music. A couple of others reached for coffee.

Susan turned to Mrs. Nelson, who had remained silent with eyes cast down. "Mom, what was that violin piece Dad loved so much?"

Glancing up at her daughter, Pamela responded and then looked down again. "Mendelssohn's Violin Concerto."

"Could we have that in the service?" asked Mary Anne, looking at Terry.

He nodded. "We can certainly look into the possibilities. Our organist also plays the piano and sings as a soloist. Other than that we could use a recording."

Their discussion of music went on for a while and the pastor began to relax as well. They chose the Twenty-Third Psalm and Ecclesiastes 3:4-8 as Biblical passages. They settled on the date and time for the funeral and then turned to the discussion of eulogies.

"Is there someone in the family who would like to do the eulogy?"

Susan turned to her brother, "I think you should do it, Fred, you're the oldest. Plus, I get too emotional…"

"Me, too," said Mary Anne. Fred said nothing.

Susan jumped in again. "We can all give you our thoughts to add to what you say."

"Yes," said the pastor. "Any of you can write down what you'd like said and perhaps Fred, you can be the one to read it." Another long silence followed.

Tugging at his tie, Fred Nelson looked at his mother and sighed. "I suppose I could do it."

Pamela patted him on the arm. "Thank you, honey. That would mean a lot to me *and* your father."

Terry waited for a moment and then pressed on. "Is there anything else you would like included in the service?"

Everyone looked at Mrs. Nelson. She lowered her gaze to the table, lips pursed. Phillip, who had said nothing cleared his throat. "Come on, Mom, you'd best spit it out."

Nodding, Pamela took a deep breath and looked the pastor in the eye. "We would like Reverend Lane Richardson to do the funeral."

Terry felt as though he had been struck in the chest. He tried to hide his feelings of surprise and hurt, and looked down at his notes to collect himself.

Susan, seeing the pastor's response, explained. "Dad and Pastor Lane were very close. He knew Dad really well."

"He was there when Dad died," interjected Julia.

This news was another punch in the stomach to Terry. They had called a former minister instead of him to come in Delbert's final hours. Pastoral care was *his* job and they hadn't given him a chance to do it. If they had allowed him to be the one to be there with them at their father's deathbed, they might not be asking for someone else to do his funeral now.

"Well..." he began and words failed him. He cleared his throat. "We have a policy..."

Julia defended the family's wishes. "You didn't know our father!"

Again, this struck a nerve. Terry had visited Delbert Nelson on several occasions over the many months he had been pastor of Hopeston Church. They had had meaningful conversations before Delbert had declined to the point he'd no longer able been able to converse, and Terry felt he had appreciated their moments together. He had done his best work with this widely loved, dying man—coming many times just to sit by his side in prayer. Terry tried again to shrug off his hurt pride, as Pamela spoke again.

"It would mean a lot to me. I always thought it would be Pastor Lane who would do his funeral."

"No offense, Pastor Terry, but we all really love Pastor Lane." Mary Anne chimed in, a mixture of apology and defiance showing in her face. "It would just be more meaningful to us if we could have *him* do it."

Terry knew Mary Anne was trying to be helpful but she was rubbing salt in a tender wound—reminding him that he just didn't compare to the previous pastor. He had worked hard to make this his church and to establish his own connections with the congregation, and though he hadn't even met the man, he felt undermined by Lane Richardson. His connection to many at Hopeston Church, and in the community as well, was so strong that Terry wasn't sure he would ever break through. Defeated, he rose from his seat.

"If you'll excuse me for a minute…" He left the study, closing the door carefully behind him.

This is not about me, he reminded himself as he walked the dark halls of the church. These people are grieving and they want what will be most helpful to them. It's not about who should be the officiating minister—this is about relationships of support and love and the deep connections that are built over time. It is those types of relationships that are a deep comfort to people in their grief.

Marie approached him in the dim light of the hallway. "Pastor…are you okay?"

"The Nelsons want Lane Richardson to do the funeral."

Marie was silent. She too had heard an awful lot about the former pastor after coming to work at the church. She had met him only once herself.

"You can invite him to *join* you in officiating at the funeral. It's church policy. He could do a second eulogy."

"Yeah, maybe." Terry walked back down the hall with Marie keeping pace at his side. As they came through the lobby he turned and smiled at her.

"Thank you." He breathed in deeply and opened the door to his study again.

The family quieted as he entered and watched him as he sat down.

"Our policy allows for the current pastor to invite past ministers to participate in funeral services," he said.

The family exchanged looks between them. After a period of silence Fred spoke. "We think this should be done as our mother wishes."

Terry reiterated the policy. "I would be happy to have Reverend Richardson participate in the service."

The meeting had come to an end. Julia and Mary Anne rose and helped their mother to her feet. The rest of the family rose in silence and left the pastor's study without a word or a nod to the pastor.

Terry closed his study door and collapsed into his chair. Was he being self-centered and insensitive to a family in pain? He had struck a compromise—met them halfway—and offered an appropriate solution. Convinced he had done the best thing for all concerned, he turned his attention to writing the announcement for the newspaper.

"Funeral Service for Delbert W. Nelson, 75, Hopeston City Clerk from 1972 to 1992, held at Hopeston Church on Saturday, August 14, 1995 at 11:00 a.m., luncheon to follow. Reverend Terrance Bunker officiating. Delbert is survived by his wife, Pamela G. Baker Nelson, their five children: Frederick (Rosalyn) Nelson, of Tipsley, Susan (Robert) Appleton, of Hopeston, Mary Anne (James) Hodge, of Hopeston, Phillip (Sally) Nelson, of Grand Hedge, Julia (Thomas) Mannington, of Portsmouth, California, and their eight grandchildren. Donations may be made to Hopeston Church."

Pastor Terry emerged from his study and handed the announcement to Marie. "Would you get this to the newspaper so it goes out in the morning edition?"

Marie looked up at him and smiled. "You know, if you were to let this family replace you like that, many other families might want the same thing. As much as they wanted their way, you did the right thing."

"I think so too. Thank you for your help. I guess I wasn't prepared for that. It's hard sometimes when people's emotions are involved to set reasonable boundaries."

Marie nodded in response.

Word spread quickly through Hopeston that Delbert Nelson had died. As soon as the morning paper arrived on their doorsteps, plans to attend began.

Betty Juniper, owner of the café, spoke with each of her customers about Delbert's death and made sure they knew about the funeral. She exchanged stories about him with townsfolk as the day went on. Some people even came to the café just for that purpose.

Every member of the Nelson family acquired celebrity status as they went about town preparing for the funeral. People gave them space and respected their need for privacy for the most part.

Pamela had generally been a very gracious woman who volunteered actively in local causes. She and Delbert had always loved the little church and were at the center of the core of folks who had faithfully attended and kept things going through the years. They had been very close to Pastor Lane during the fifteen years he had pastored the church and they had been welcoming to the new minister as well. Pastor Lane and Delbert Nelson had often teamed up in doing things for the community, and would always be linked together in the minds of the Hopeston residents.

Marie answered the phone and recognized Julia Bomont's voice on the other end of the line. She steeled herself for she suspected what was coming.

"What is this I hear about Pastor Terry refusing to let Pastor Lane do Delbert's funeral?"

Marie took a deep breath and paused before responding. "I'm not sure what you have heard, Julia."

"Well, the Nelson family is very upset with Pastor Terry over this!"

Marie shook her head. She was very familiar with Julia's rantings and tendency to get her nose into everyone else's business and to put her spin on things, often distorting reality. Marie had also learned to stay out of the traps Julia wished to draw her into. "I believe the funeral plans are between the Nelson family and their pastor, Julia."

"Well, Pamela is hurt by the pastor's refusal to honor her wishes. Is that what a pastor should be doing, Marie, at a time like this? Hurting a grieving widow?"

"As I said," Marie responded, trying to keep her voice calm, "the pastor will work this out directly with the family. Thank you for your concern, Julia. Goodbye." She hung up before Julia could say another word.

Marie was sure this was going to be a tough day. Sure enough, the phone rang again. To her relief it was Mildred Brown calling about luncheon details. Marie fielded questions all day long about details for the funeral while she and Pastor Terry worked on the bulletin for the service. People wanted to make donations. Flowers would be delivered. The funeral home would take care of the casket and the ushering during the service. The organist was given the music requested to practice and she was asked to locate certain recordings of chosen pieces. The church's sound operator called back.

Pastor Terry dreaded making the call to Pastor Lane. In a quiet moment, he stuck his head out the door. "Marie, do you think the family will be okay with Reverend Richardson only doing a eulogy?"

"I don't know. Maybe you should call Pamela to make sure."

"I was afraid you would say that." They both chuckled at the ridiculousness of the situation and then Marie heard him pick up the phone and dial. As Pamela answered, Terry shut the door.

"Mrs. Nelson, this is Pastor Terry. I wanted to go over specifics with you concerning the funeral."

"Yes." Her voice was flat.

"Regarding the role of Reverend Richardson...I think it would be appropriate for him to say some words, a sort of eulogy for your husband. Does that sound good to you?"

"That'll be fine." There continued to be no feeling in her voice.

"Okay then," Terry said. "I will give him a call and let him know. Is there anything else we should discuss?"

"No. Thank you." A click sounded in his ear.

49

Miriam sat at her kitchen table with the newspaper spread out in front of her. Just as Joshua wandered in to get a cup of coffee, she noticed the announcement.

"Oh, Josh...Delbert Nelson died!"

Joshua leaned against the counter. "Really? When? How?"

"Yesterday. It doesn't say what he died of, but I heard he had cancer. I think he had suffered for a long time."

Miriam looked back at the paper. "It says here that the funeral is Saturday."

"Where?"

"At Hopeston Church." Miriam looked up at Joshua.

His eyes clouded over. "Will you go?"

Miriam paused. "Yes, I think so. I liked Delbert a lot. He did a lot for Hopeston at very crucial points in the life of this community."

Joshua stepped behind his mother and read the announcement over her shoulder. "Do you know Reverend Bunker?"

"No. I think he's fairly new."

Joshua had not been back inside the church since the day of his abuse, but he too had liked Delbert Nelson and his family. He wanted to go to the funeral but he felt uneasy about it, and then he thought of Lillie. If she was going, then he would too.

***

Lillie picked up the newspaper and took it out onto the porch with her. Martin, as usual, was already sitting out in the cool morning air. When she came upon it, she read the announcement of Delbert Nelson's funeral out loud to her father.

"Did you know he'd died?

Martin shook his head. "No. I knew he was dying, though."

268

"I think I'd like to go to the funeral."

"Yeah?" Martin glanced at his daughter in surprise.

"Yeah." Lillie looked out over the meadow and thought about what it would be like to step inside the church again.

The phone rang and she went inside to answer it. It was Joshua.

"Did you see Delbert Nelson died?"

"Yeah, just read about it."

"Are you gonna go?"

"I was thinking about it."

Joshua was silent for a moment. "Well, that settles it then. I decided if you were going, I'd go too, as long as I can go with you."

"Are you sure?"

"I don't know. It might be a good time for me to go back. Abigail would probably say it would bring closure or something!" He chuckled, thinking of the healer sitting on her porch.

"Maybe so. Not going would certainly mean we were giving Lane Richardson and his abuse too much power. We should go to support the Nelsons, at least."

"Yeah, I agree." Joshua said. "And as long as we're together, I think I'll be okay."

50

Terry Bunker dialed the phone and listened as it rang, heart pounding.

A deep male voice answered. "Hello?"

"Reverend Richardson?"

"Yes, this is Pastor Lane."

"Hello, Pastor. This is Pastor Terry Bunker of Hopeston Church."

"Well, hello there. How's it going at my favorite church?"

"Fine, thanks."

"Well, good! I'm glad. What can I do for you, Terry?"

"Well, as you know, Delbert Nelson has passed away and we are planning his funeral. I would like to invite you to do a eulogy. In addition to the eulogy his eldest son will do, that is."

"How nice."

"The family would like you to participate in the service."

Pastor Lane smirked. Pamela had already told him that she wanted him to officiate. "Are you sure that's what the family said?"

Terry chose his words with care. "That is what we are asking of you."

"I see." The irritation in the pastor's voice was evident. "Well, of course...I will prepare my comments... Delbert and I were very close...as I'm sure you have heard. I have a lot of material."

"Yes, I've heard, and I'm sure the words you share will be very meaningful to everyone there."

After apprising Lane of the date and time, Terry politely ended the conversation. As he laid the receiver back in its cradle, he crumpled his notes into a ball and threw them against the wall.

Lane slammed down the phone. The congregation he now served in Broadley hadn't been nearly as forthcoming with their affection towards him and he had been looking forward to being in the pulpit once again at the Hopeston Church—he had counted on officiating Delbert Nelson's funeral. But the new pastor had gotten in the way.

He thought carefully about what could be done. He'd been surprised at the strength of Terry's resolve in standing firm in the face of Pamela and her family, but it only fueled his drive to challenge the younger man. He picked up the phone and dialed an old friend.

51

Violet walked through the doors of the Presbyterian church. Because it was now a weekday, the large building was silent and empty. Following the carpeted hallway, she found the office with ease, entered, closing the door quietly behind her, as though conscious of the sacred work being done there.

The secretary looked up and smiled. "Mrs. Parks?"

Violet nodded and smiled back, glad to be anticipated.

"The pastor is ready for you. You may go right in." The secretary gestured towards the door to the pastor's study with her long fingers. Violet noticed that her nails were painted bright red to match her lipstick.

Gingerly opening the door, Violet let herself in and was greeted by Pastor Douglas' warm smile. He pushed his chair away from his desk and stood, stepping around it to offer his hand.

"Welcome, Mrs. Parks. Please, sit down." He released her hand and gestured to two chairs with a small coffee table between them. Violet sat in the far chair.

"I'm glad you called, Mrs. Parks. Would you like me to leave the door open?"

"No, I prefer privacy. Thank you."

Closing the door, the pastor settled in the chair across from her. "What's on your mind? You said you needed to talk."

"Yes," Violet said, her nerves jangling. "Last Sunday...I was deeply moved by your sermon...and by communion." She stopped, unsure of how to continue.

"I saw that."

"You saw?" Violet said, astonished that he had noticed her.

"Yes. It seemed to me that something profound was happening for you during worship."

"Profound." Violet thought about his choice of words. "Yes, Pastor, it was certainly that!"

"Would you like to tell me about it?"

"Well…" She sorted her thoughts. "I think I experienced healing…and a challenge…" She hesitated, suddenly feeling that having come to see the pastor was ridiculous and that he would never be able to understand.

"You preached about not judging others but loving them first before challenging them to change."

"Did I?" The minister chuckled softly.

"Yes. I felt you were speaking directly to me, as if you knew what I had been going through."

"That's the work of the Holy Spirit." The pastor spoke with modesty and conviction. "Please, go on."

"I felt the presence of Christ. In fact…I *saw* Him…" Violet hesitated, watching the pastor's face.

He nodded, encouraging her to continue.

"Jesus told me I am to love and forgive someone." She stopped, feeling emotion rise within her. "I also felt forgiven. You see, I've been jealous of my younger sister for a long time."

The pastor acknowledged what she had said but remained silent.

Violet began to feel even more foolish. "Does that sound strange to you? That I saw Christ?"

The look in the pastor's eyes changed. They took on a new depth and seriousness that shone intensely. "No, not at all. It's not strange to have a vision of Jesus. Perhaps a little unusual…but certainly not unheard of."

Feeling encouraged, Violet continued. "I could relate to both sides of the Bible story you talked about—the sinful woman in the sand *and* the stone throwers. I have been an accuser *and* I have been held captive in my own sin, my jealousy. I feel Jesus has forgiven me, given me the chance to…" She choked back tears. The pastor reached for a box of tissues, pushed it gently towards her on the table between them and waited patiently for her to go on.

Violet composed herself. "Pastor Douglas, He's given me the chance to heal." She took a deep breath. "It seems my own healing will come as I take steps to love and forgive others."

She looked at the preacher. He smiled at her and she saw the kindness had returned to his eyes. But there was something new there, too. Respect.

"Mrs. Parks, that sounds like Jesus to *me*. I believe He wants us each to heal and that is his way: to bring about our healing as we seek to help others heal."

"Yes, that's the message I received." Violet felt suddenly lighter.

"Good," said the pastor. "So, how will you go about doing that? Healing others, I mean?" His tone suggested that he genuinely hoped to learn something new.

"Well...there's my sister and her...boyfriend." The word "boyfriend" stuck in her throat but she made herself say it anyway.

"You said you've been jealous of your sister."

"All her life, I think."

"Can you tell me why?"

"I don't know, really. I guess I've been blaming Lillie all these years for..." Violet broke off and thought carefully about what she was saying. "For taking my mother from me." She looked to him for help in understanding what she had just said.

"You think you've been blaming your sister, Lillie, all these years, for losing your mother?"

"Yes. I think so."

"So, you feel you lost your mother when your sister was born?"

Violet began to cry and took a fresh tissue to wipe away her tears. "It was like she didn't have enough to give us both the attention we needed so Lillie got it all!" She sobbed once and then swallowed hard, wiping her eyes, desperately trying to keep her emotions under control.

"It's okay," said the pastor. "It's best to let it out."

Violet's resolve to hold back her tears crumbled. The floodgates opened and she began to cry in earnest. The walls she had kept so carefully in place through the years burst apart, no longer able to hold back the force of a river of emotion.

By the time her tears stopped, it felt to Violet that she had cried for an hour. When she looked up, she saw the pastor quietly watching her with a gentle smile.

"I guess I've found out what it is..." Violet finally said, her breath catching in her throat, "...I need healing for."

The pastor nodded in agreement. After another moment of silence he spoke. "You said your own healing would come as..."

Violet finished the sentence. "As I take steps to love and forgive others." She smiled weakly.

"So what *are* those steps?" he asked.

"Well, I need to treat her boyfriend with love and not judgment, for one thing. And I need to call his mother and apologize."

She reflected on what she'd said. "And maybe I need to apologize to Lillie too."

Pastor Douglas watched her closely, fascinated with the spirit in the room. "That sounds like a good place to start to me."

Violet reached for the pile of crumpled tissues on the table in front of her. The pastor signaled her to leave them. "That's fine. I'll take care of it."

Pastor Douglas rose and put his hand out to shake hers. "Blessings, Mrs. Parks. I'm glad you came today."

"Me, too," Violet replied. She made her way out of the pastor's study past the secretary, who acknowledged her with a smile and a slight nod.

Once out in the bright sunshine again, Violet stopped and took a deep breath of the pungent summer air. Now mid-August, the days were already cooler and clear of the haze of humidity. As she looked around at the plants and lawn surrounding the church and up at the cloudless blue sky, she couldn't help noticing how sharp and beautiful everything was. She too was sharp and beautiful, and she knew now just what to do.

52

"Marie, this is Mike Johnston."

"Hi, Mike. What can I do for you?"

"Is Pastor Terry available? I'd like to speak with him, if I may." Chairman of the board of the church, Mike was being unusually polite, and Marie felt a flutter in her stomach. She knew from his tone that something was up.

"I'm sorry, but he's on the other line at the moment. Can I have him call you back?"

"Well, maybe you can help me try to straighten things out here."

Marie wondered to what he was referring. "I'll see what I can do." she said.

"I understand Pamela Nelson has requested that Pastor Terry step aside to allow their good family friend and our long time pastor, Reverend Lane Richardson to perform the funeral service for her husband."

Marie listened with a sinking feeling. Someone had put Mike up to this. She suddenly regretted having offered to help.

"I think this is something you need to discuss with the pastor," she said. Feeling cowardice grow within her for passing this off for the pastor to deal with alone, she added, "He is going by church policy, Mike, by inviting Reverend Richardson to join him in the service."

"Well, I'm not sure that policy need apply in this case." Marie could feel herself getting angry, so she spoke her mind. "You don't think others will request the same thing after they see the Nelsons get this special treatment?"

Mike was quiet.

Just then Pastor Terry came out of his office and stood waiting at Marie's desk. She rolled her eyes and pointed to the phone.

Mike spoke again. "Marie, I wonder if it is worth making the Nelsons and the entire community angry just because Pastor Terry has to follow church policy?"

Pastor Terry watched in fascination as she responded. "Since when do we make decisions in this church based on how angry people get?"

He raised his eyebrows and smiled, giving her a thumbs-up sign. Mike sputtered on the other end of the line. "Well...Marie...I don't think..."

"No...you *aren't* thinking! This is a policy your board has worked hard to put into place...and you would discard it just because people would get *angry*?" Marie was on a roll. "Lots of people are still close to Reverend Richardson but that doesn't mean we should rob our pastor of his job, does it?"

"No, I suppose not. You've got a point. You say Pastor Terry has invited Pastor Lane to participate in the service?"

"Yes, Mike, he has. He'll be doing an additional eulogy."

"Well, that will be just fine, then."

"Yes, Mike, I believe it's an appropriate way to honor Pamela's wish and to honor the work of our pastor at the same time."

"Okay then, Marie. I guess that takes care of it."

When his secretary hung up the phone, Terry looked at her with new respect. "Wow! You sure took care of that!"

The door opened and Mildred Brown bustled into the office, carrying two bulging plastic bags, which she plunked heavily to the floor. "I think we're all set for the luncheon."

The pastor looked at her with stronger kindness in his expression than Marie had ever seen him muster for Mildred before. "Good," he said. "We have enough tables and chairs for everyone?"

"Yes, I think so. We'll set some up in the hall. We're set for a hundred and fifty people!" Pastor Terry nodded his head, indicating his approval.

"I hear Pastor Lane is doing the funeral."

Pastor Terry and Marie exchanged glances. She nodded slightly in his direction. It was his turn to handle the situation.

With an almost imperceptible smile, he responded, "No, Mildred. *I* am officiating the funeral. But we have invited Pastor Lane to offer some words in the service."

Mildred looked astonished. "That's not what I heard!"

The pastor asked calmly, "What did you hear and from whom, may I ask?"

"Well...the ladies said that Pamela wanted Pastor Lane to do the funeral."

Pastor Terry responded calmly, realizing for the first time he no longer felt hurt or attacked. "Why would *he* do the funeral, Mildred? He doesn't work here."

"They were close friends! He was Delbert's pastor all those years!"

"Yes, but he is no longer Delbert's pastor. Reverend Richardson gave that up when he left this church."

Mildred pressed her lips together.

"Is there anything else we should discuss?" asked the pastor, looking her directly in the eye. Mildred looked at both of them with narrowed eyes and then picked up her bags and left the office in a huff.

The pastor waited until Mildred was well out of earshot and then quietly shut the office door. Unable to contain his amusement any longer, he snorted and Marie burst out laughing. "I guess she'll go tell 'the ladies'!"

"Yup, probably the best way to get the accurate word out to this congregation," the pastor said, chuckling.

"To the whole town!" Marie said.

Once they'd settled down, Pastor Terry looked at his secretary. "Do you think that's the end of it?"

"I sure hope so!" said Marie, "But I'm afraid it's just the beginning."

"Well, one thing is clear."

"What's that?"

"We make a good team!"

From the moment he woke, Joshua's mood changed almost hourly. He thought several times of backing out, wondering if it would be a good thing given the strong emotional and physical reactions he was having. But each time he was tempted to run and hide, he remembered Abigail's words: "Stand and face the pain and fear, and thee'll experience relief."

This was the simple formula that would help him. She had reminded him that there would be bumps along the way but that he would experience the pain and the fear less and less often. He would go to the funeral no matter how severely "the fire raged within him, threatening to consume." Though every fiber of his being sometimes suggested the opposite, he now believed confronting his past was the only way to move beyond it.

Miriam, in turn, was worried about her own anger, but, like her son, she was determined to handle it. Martin focused his attention on Joshua and on his daughter.

Lillie was confused and overwhelmed. Feeling weak as well, she would cling to Joshua as much as he would to her. Good memories of church flooded her mind—memories of the friends and their parents who had been so nice to her as a girl, memories of the times she spent with her mother in the church and the closeness it created between them, memories of the pastor with his warm, friendly voice and affectionate manner.

But all of those memories had been displaced by the outrage she felt at her mother's violation. When she visualized the rape in her mind, it sent her to a dark place indeed. She hoped that going to the church now would help to rid her of her rage.

Miriam and Martin had decided to accompany their children to the church and sit as a unit. They stood quietly in Miriam's kitchen, waiting until it was time to go.

"I'm grateful we're going to this funeral together," Miriam said.

"Me too!" said Lillie.

Joshua looked at her with amusement and affection in his eyes. There was a side of Lillie that always reminded him of a little girl, uninhibited and always ready to break the rules of etiquette in order to say or do what was really important to her. He had been too ready to hide behind proper etiquette all these years so as not to be discovered, but Lillie was incapable of hiding, and he found it wonderfully refreshing. *And* he realized, that since meeting Lillie, he'd begun to do the same. "I have to admit," Joshua said, "I feel quite nervous about this."

Martin was glad for his honesty. "Yes, but it feels right to be going."

The others agreed in unison.

Just as Miriam was about to say something to the group, the phone rang. The others were silent as she answered it.

"Mrs. Crumley?"

"Yes."

"This is Violet, Lillie's older sister."

"Violet?" Miriam turned and looked at the others, raising her eyebrows in surprise.

"I'm calling to apologize to you, Mrs. Crumley. When I called before I was angry. In shock, I think."

Miriam waited.

Violet went bravely on. "I have a tendency to lash out when I'm angry and hurt. I'm afraid I was blaming Joshua for what happened to my mother, and I see now that he is not to blame. I would like to ask you to forgive me."

Filled with emotion, Miriam was unable to respond at first. She was loathe to indicate it to Violet but she knew the woman on the phone was anxious for a response, so Miriam sniffled to let her know she was still there. "Violet. I can see that you understand. I believe you're sorry, and I…forgive you."

The others in the room listened with amazement at the conversation unfolding before them.

"Thank you Mrs. Crumley!" Violet felt her knees almost give way under her.

"Thank *you*, Violet."

Miriam slowly put the receiver back in its wall cradle and turned to look at the three faces waiting expectantly to hear what had happened. Lillie asked the question everyone was thinking. "That was *our* Violet?"

"Yes," said Miriam, sitting down and gathering her thoughts, "that was Violet!" She relayed the conversation word for word.

Martin smiled slightly. "Well, I'd say that's pretty good timing."

All of them felt it—Violet had quite "accidentally" given them the gift of her support just when they needed it.

Joshua took Lillie's hand in his. He was relieved, as he had unconsciously waited for the final door to Lillie's family to open to him. There were now no remaining barriers.

"Well," said Martin, "are we ready to face this now?"

"Yup!" said Joshua. "Let's do it!"

53

Rev. Bunker had talked to a host of people in his effort to gather information and anecdotes in order to make his remarks at Delbert's funeral a good reflection of the man he had been. He had worked to make his words personal and inspirational, and had assisted the church organist in gathering all of the musical pieces the Nelsons had requested.

The tables in the fellowship hall were set with white linens, fresh cut flowers, fine china, newly polished silverware, colored cloth napkins and long tapered candles. Mildred and her ladies had prepared a delicious luncheon of manicotti, garlic bread, a mixed green and walnut salad and baked apple cobbler with vanilla ice cream for dessert. Coffee and lemonade were in abundance. This would be a feast to celebrate Delbert's life and the ladies of the church bustled about the kitchen poised to bring the food out at just the right moment.

The men from the Broadley Funeral Home arrived with Delbert's body in a shiny black casket draped with an arrangement of fresh roses and baby's breath.

When Rev. Richardson arrived, Terry greeted him with kindness and ushered him into his study to dress in his robe and to wait for his entrance into the sanctuary.

Cars quickly filled the parking lot. When the lot was full, they spilled out onto the grass and up and down the street in front of the church. The whole town had shown up dressed in its best finery.

Betty Juniper, dressed patriotically in a blue skirt, white blouse and red cardigan sweater, greeted a number of people in the parking lot as she made her way to the front door of the church. She saw Debra Hundley, in her slightly rumpled navy blue pantsuit, coming down the sidewalk. The two women greeted one another warmly and continued into the church together.

Families with children in tow, couples, both young and old, people who had worked with Delbert at the clerk's office, and faithful church members arrived in a continuous stream. Businesses closed for the funeral—the town of Hopeston was fully focused on the life and death of Delbert Nelson.

Lillie held Joshua's hand as they walked bravely up to the church and through its big front doors. Martin and Miriam followed close behind. They entered the lobby to the sound of the organ playing softly and the mixed aroma of flowers, food, women's perfume, clean-scrubbed surfaces and old leather. The smells brought back a flood of childhood memories for the two young people.

Flickering candles beckoned from the sanctuary. The Nelson family stood at the entrance, greeting people quietly, sharing hugs and tears. As mourners entered, they hushed, honoring the sacredness of the place.

Lillie felt the muscles tighten in Joshua's arm. She looked at his face and saw there the clouded look he had long employed to hide his feelings and thoughts from others. She understood his need to retreat within himself today.

He sensed Lillie looking at him and turned his head in response. As quickly as he had turned, however, he looked away, knowing that if he looked at her face too long, he would not be able to keep his composure.

Miriam was conscious of Joshua's expression and body language as well. Tense herself, she felt a heightened protectiveness for her son and wore her mother-bear instinct like a cloak.

Martin took in his surroundings in a detached way. His mind was focused on understanding what it was about this little church that his wife had loved so much.

As they were ushered down the aisle, and people recognized them, hushed whispers were heard—that Lillie and Joshua were holding hands, that Martin was in church for the first time in who knew when, that Miriam Crumley had come in with the Farmers. Led to a vacant pew near the front, they were all glad to get settled. Martin sat on one end next to Lillie, who sat next to Joshua with his mother on the other side of him, as they had planned. After a few moments, the foursome began to relax and sat listening to the unusually powerful organ music vibrating through the sanctuary.

Lillie glanced around. The beauty of this simple sanctuary where she had worshipped as a child was still in evidence. She felt the presence of her mother so palpably it was as if she were sitting right next to her in the pew. Lillie closed her eyes, took Joshua's hand into her lap and covered it with her other hand.

Joshua looked at Lillie and saw tears leak from her closed eyelids. He gently squeezed her hand and she opened her eyes and looked into his. They were each glad the other one was there to hold onto.

The Bomonts followed soon behind, Julia making her usual grand entrance, and were seated across the aisle from Miriam. Julia looked haughtily over at the four for a long time before turning to her husband and whispering loudly into his deaf ear.

Mike Johnston and his wife Penelope were seated nearby as well, along with Audrey Powers, the postmistress, and her husband Richard, Bill Hadley, the grocer, and his wife Henrietta. One familiar face after another filled the sanctuary around them.

Lillie felt warmed by the sense of community until she caught a hard look from Barbara Stacey, the mother of one of Lillie's best friends from church as a young girl. Her friendship with Nelly had ended abruptly when she had stopped coming to church. Why she had suddenly refused to hang out with her anymore was still a mystery.

Joshua stared straight ahead, looking at no one, though it was clear that many in the church saw him. Some were surprised to see him in church. Some noted how mature and handsome he had become, remembering him as a mop-headed, needy boy who was always underfoot. Others were astonished to see the Farmers and Crumleys together. There was something curiously compelling about the four of them sitting quietly together.

The single violin of Mendelssohn's Violin Concerto was heard and the procession began. The casket was wheeled in by two men, and followed by Pamela Nelson and the long line of her children and grandchildren. They were seated in the front two rows while the closed casket, buried under its mound of fresh flowers, was carefully placed in front of the altar.

The music played, swelling and flowing, filling the sanctuary, and then as it came to an end, a door in the front of the sanctuary opened and Pastor Terry Bunker appeared in a black robe and purple stole. Taking his place behind the pulpit, he looked out over the sanctuary jammed with people.

As he stood there he felt his heart open and the words that came from his mouth in greeting were inspired and compassionate. Offering a prayer, he felt the presence of the Holy Spirit enter and uphold him as he guided the gathered people through the elements of the worship service. Music soothed and people cried. Scripture put words to the truth and quality of Delbert's faith and God's love.

The pastor carefully unfolded the life of Delbert Nelson, lived so totally in the love and service of God. He told funny stories that reflected Delbert's humor and serious ones about his acts of kindness and generosity, while the congregation responded with laughter and tears. He demonstrated how God was at work through Delbert and then touched gently on the invitation God makes to all people, to come into the life of Christ and an eternity lived in God's presence. There was hardly a dry eye in the sanctuary when he was done. His sermon had hit the mark.

When he was finished, he stepped back to welcome his predecessor, who had entered the sanctuary and stepped up to the pulpit. There were exclamations of surprised recognition and adoration from the congregation at the appearance of their beloved shepherd.

Lillie, who had missed the entrance, felt Joshua's whole body tense beside her and heard a gasp escape from Miriam's lips. Looking up to see what had happened, she instantly knew. It was Pastor Lane.

Joshua felt as though his soul had turned to ice. His heart fluttered, threatening to quit its beating, and he could hardly breathe. More than anything he wanted to bolt from the church, but instead gripped Lillie's hand tighter and tighter until she wiggled her fingers. He relaxed his hold slightly, but didn't turn his head or move a muscle.

Joshua tried to make his eyes unseeing without closing them, but blurring his vision was not enough to keep him from seeing the shape of the man who had ruined his life. The cock of his head, the tip of his shoulders, even the shape of his nose were etched in Joshua's memory.

Lane greeted the crowd warmly, looking out over them as though they were still his flock. He spoke with honeyed words. "You are my favorite church. Of all that I have served over the years, you are special to me."

It suddenly seemed to Joshua that he and Lane Richardson were the only people in the sanctuary, and a dialogue between them began in Joshua's mind.

"What are you doing here?" sneered the pastor, locking eyes with Joshua.

"I'm a man now. I go where I want."

"You're not a man." The pastor laughed sarcastically. "You're just a worthless boy! You'll never be a man!" The pastor's voice rang in Joshua's head.

"No, Lane, you're wrong. You were wrong ten years ago and you are wrong now!" Strength began to return to him like the slow thaw of ice.

Just then Pastor Lane's voice broke through and Joshua was back in the filled sanctuary. He looked at the man before him unfolding a litany of sentimental reminiscences about Delbert as they had lived out a deep friendship and a partnership as pastor and chairman of the board of the church in the years when he had been their minister.

Joshua slowly rose to his feet and stood tall and straight and looked directly into the eyes of the pastor who now looked down at him. Their eyes locked. Lillie watched as a string of expressions played across the pastor's face—a surprised questioning, irritation, and then recognition. Stumbling over his words, Lane finally stopped talking—Joshua seemed to freeze his gaze and silence his tongue.

With everyone in the sanctuary staring at him, Joshua moved past his mother to the aisle. The pastor tried to proceed with the eulogy as if nothing unusual were happening, but whispering began to flutter through the crowd like leaves gently lifted from the ground by a breeze.

Slowly and deliberately, Joshua turned for the doors and with a straight back and his head held high, walked out of the sanctuary. Amidst stunned disbelief of those watching, he opened the doors quietly and with grace, and disappeared into the bowels of the church. Lane searched his notes and faltered, his confidence gone. Suddenly he felt old and weak.

Lillie looked at her father and then at Miriam before rising as well. Their faces reflected understanding and humility—they knew that what Joshua had done had required great courage and clear purpose of heart. Gleaning strength from Joshua's lead, Lillie too walked out of the church, looking people she knew in the eye as she made her way toward the doors.

The energy in the sanctuary had shifted. Pamela Nelson and her family had felt it. Others moved in their seats in uncomfortable response to what they considered the humiliation of their speaker and the discourtesy of the two young people who had just removed themselves.

Julia Bomont was seething. How dare Lillie Farmer, the seductress's daughter, be so rude? What did this Jew boy think he was doing disrupting such a sacred moment? Others throughout the sanctuary were obviously angry as well.

But one face in the crowd reflected a different sentiment—a woman in the back, a woman Terry had noticed during his sermon. After watching Joshua and Lillie leave, she seemed to sit straighter in her pew.

When Lane finally pulled himself together and concluded his eulogy, he said an elaborate, lengthy and sentimental prayer that was not a part of the order of worship. Pastor Terry hid his irritation at the intrusion, and rose to welcome Delbert's oldest son to the lectern.

Emerging from the church, Lillie made a beeline to Joshua, who now was pacing in the parking lot, and took him into her embrace from behind. Rigid in her arms, he was unable to return her affection.

When she saw the outer doors open and people begin to come out, Lillie released her arms from around his waist. "They're done, I think," she said.

Joshua's eyes blazed. When Martin and Miriam finally appeared at the door, he grabbed Lillie's hand and pulled her with him toward the car. "Let's get out of here!"

By the time they reached the sedan, their parents had also arrived. No one said a word as they got in the car, and Martin pulled quickly out of the parking lot. The group remained quiet until they reached the end of the street.

Miriam turned around to face the two young adults, trying to hide the hint of laughter in her eyes. "Well, you two sure created a stir!"

Joshua shook his head as if trying to understand. "What the hell was *he* doing there?"

His mother responded. "From what I overheard, the Nelsons wanted him there."

Martin snorted. "Well, I don't believe the Nelsons will be inviting *us* over for dinner anytime soon." The other occupants of the car exploded in laughter and the sweetness of relief washed over them all.

Joshua's heart began, finally, to slow down and resume a normal beat. "I couldn't stay there a second longer!" he said, shaking his head.

"Me neither!" said Lillie.

"I wanted to leave too," said Miriam.

"Yup. Me too." Martin made it unanimous.

54

Inside the church, people were abuzz about what had happened. Pastor Terry stood at the door of the sanctuary and greeted people as they made their way to the fellowship hall for food.

Pastor Lane disappeared into the pastor's study to compose himself. He had seen that unfortunate Jewish boy, now grown up, stand in calm defiance right there in front of the entire town of Hopeston. How dare he do such a thing! Only vaguely able to recall what had transpired between him and the boy, he put it out of his mind and justified his own indignation. He wondered what he had done to deserve such disrespect.

He knew himself to be a gifted man of the people, a clergyman of great wisdom and compassion—someone who had spent his entire career helping people. Perhaps there had been a few moments of personal indulgence here and there in his life, but nothing that compared with the endless hours of sacrifice and service he had poured himself into for so many years. He had given his life to others.

Perhaps his passion for people had caused him to cross a line once in a while but he felt forgiven by God, who had charged him with this work. He knew he was more righteous than most and excused himself for an occasional indiscretion. He was a man of the present and prided himself in being able to stay focused rather than dwell on the past.

Bolstered by his indignation, he regained his composure. What the boy, and the Farmer girl after him, had done was inexcusable and he intended to make that known. He disrobed, straightened his tie, put on his sport coat and went out to mingle with the people who loved him so thoroughly. He knew he would be welcome at the Nelson's table.

As the luncheon progressed and people visited with each other the attitude about what Joshua and Lillie had done grew into greater proportions. The overriding opinion was that the two young people had deeply insulted the grieving Nelson family and had thus committed a grave offense.

People spoke sympathetically to Pastor Lane about it, making apology for the way he'd been treated. He accepted their words with practiced humility, allowing them to fall over one another to try and make him feel better. People gushed about his eulogy and thanked him for taking time away from his busy life to come and bless them with his words, his presence and his prayer.

Meanwhile, Pastor Terry also received many genuinely grateful comments about the service as a whole and his part in it. Over all, the people said, it had been a successful service that met the town's need to encounter God, and it helped them remember, grieve and let go of Delbert Nelson. Except for the young couple's interruption, it had been a perfect funeral.

Pastor Terry felt it was the best he had ever done in officiating at a funeral. He felt happy and found it easy, now that it was over, to observe the congregation from a place of detachment. But something was definitely up, and he wanted to know just who those young people were.

Martin drove straight to the Crumley home and pulled in the driveway. He turned off the ignition and swiveled around to face the others. "Despite our humor, I'm afraid your actions today disturbed a hornet's nest. There will likely be consequences."

Joshua looked at him and considered what Martin said, the lawyer rising up within him. "I didn't mean to offend anyone. But something in me had to take a stand. There are other victims! Something has to be done! That was a moment, a moment for action."

Miriam spoke softly. "So, we must simply prepare ourselves."

"People were pretty angry coming out of that funeral," responded Martin. "You may have pissed off the entire town of Hopeston. By offending the Nelsons you may have offended everyone."

Lillie was taken aback. "No matter what, the truth must be told!"

Miriam and Joshua climbed from the car and then she turned and stuck her head back in. "I have an idea. Why don't you both come back for supper this evening? I need a nap first, but we should put our heads together and make a plan."

55

Furious, Barbara Stacey and her husband sat at a cloth-covered table with others, eating apple cobbler and ice cream. A loyal supporter and friend of Pastor Lane's, Barbara had worked closely with him on the Sunday school program and had taught the confirmation class when her Nelly had been involved. She had always *liked* the pastor but had developed an even deeper devotion to him during those years. He had done more to boost her self-esteem as they had worked together, more than anyone had ever done, including her husband of thirty years.

When Melodie Farmer had suddenly left the church, she'd left the Summer Bible Series in shambles, and the pastor had asked Barbara to help him. He had confided to her that Melodie had tried to seduce him and that when he had gently refused her advances she had walked out.

The closeness that Barbara had felt with the pastor increased as she had consoled him and worked with him to teach the remaining sessions that summer.

Furious with Melodie for her inexcusable behavior, Barbara felt completely justified in telling others what she had done. She had forbidden her daughter, Nelly, from ever having contact with Lillie again. And now Lillie had rudely interrupted Lane's eulogy during a *funeral*, of all things, showing her venomous attitude and inexcusable disrespect. It had taken ten years, but Lillie had proven her right.

As Barbara and her husband readied to leave, she made her way over to the pastor. "Lane, it is *so* good to see you. Thank you for your eloquent words today!"

"Barbara! You're welcome. It's good to see you." He reached out to shake her husband's hand. "Hello, Ralph, how are you, sir?"

Seeking to direct the pastor's attention back on herself, Barbara plunged ahead. "I am so sorry for the rude interruption of that Farmer girl and her apparent boyfriend!"

Pastor Lane assumed a wounded look. "Well, thank you."

"I could wring their necks! What unconscionable behavior! If only there were something I could do!"

"Now Barbara, we must remember who is *Christian* here." Though his expression was one of innocence, he gave her a knowing look.

He pounded Ralph on the shoulder and grabbed Barbara's hand, patting it affectionately. "Good to see you Barbara…Ralph. Thank you for coming."

Julia Bomont fumed. A group of older ladies who had loved Pastor Lane sat around her.

"Something must be done! We can't just let them waltz in here and treat him like that and get away with it!"

"What, though? What can be done?" asked one of the ladies.

"Should this be brought to the church board for them to handle?" asked another.

"Of course it should!" Julia was ready to get moving.

Another of the ladies piped up. "You know, it's widely known that the girl's mother was a seductress when she was here."

Julia responded with feigned outrage. "Yes! She had nothing but disrespect for our poor Pastor Lane!"

"She was forced out of the church for that, I heard." said another lady.

Julia was smug. "That's right, and her daughter seems not to have fallen far from the tree."

Pamela Nelson stood talking to Pastor Lane. Struggling to put on her coat, she shook her head sadly. "I'm so sorry, Lane, for what happened."

"Don't bother yourself about it, Pamela, it was nothing to me. Let's just focus on Delbert." He reached out to help her with the coat.

"Why would they do such a thing?"

"I don't know," replied the pastor, patting her on the shoulder.

"I wish it hadn't happened, but otherwise, I was very pleased with the service." Pamela said.

Pastor Lane gently rubbed her back. "Yes, I think it was what Delbert would have wanted."

Tears flooded Pamela's eyes. "Thank you for being here, Lane."

"Of course! I wouldn't have missed it. I'm just glad that young minister of yours let me come!"

Pamela felt a rush of irritation come over her again as she remembered Pastor Terry's refusal to honor her wish, but she was too exhausted to think about anything else but the loss of her husband. She needed to go home, so she headed towards her gathering family.

Once outside the church, the woman Pastor Terry had seen in the back stopped to speak to two women talking animatedly in the parking lot. "By any chance, can you tell me who the young couple was that had walked out during the service?"

"The girl was Lillie Farmer," said one. "She used to attend with her mother, but they stopped coming a long time ago. And the boy was…" She turned to her friend.

"Joshua something. Crumley, I think. They're Jews. I guess it's not surprising."

The woman thanked her informants and left, smiling sardonically to herself about Christian values.

Mike Johnston drove his wife and himself home, ranting all the way. "Why in the world would Joshua Crumley and Lillie Farmer walk out like that?"

His wife Penelope shook her head. "I don't know. It seemed very deliberate, though."

Mike struggled to make sense of it. "Weren't Lillie and Joshua involved in church as youngsters?"

Penelope shrugged her shoulders, but nodded her head at the same time. "I think so."

"I seem to remember that Mrs. Farmer was a devoted and hard working church member years ago."

"Yes, she taught Sunday School and the Summer Bible Series. You had to be special to be asked to teach that with the pastor. She and the pastor worked well together, I think."

"So, what's this about? Why would they *do* this?"

"I don't know, Mike. It's really strange."

"Well, I intend to get to the bottom of it. I can't have people offending faithful parishioners like the Nelsons."

"Yes, why would you come to a funeral if you intended to walk out?"

"Maybe that's it—maybe they *intended* to walk out…"

"People only do that if they have a cause. What could possibly be theirs?"

"I don't know, Penelope, but I'm going to find out," Mike said. "And I'm going to start by calling Martin Farmer."

After making a salad for Joshua and herself, Miriam fell asleep in an armchair in the living room. Joshua sat reading the newspaper, listening to his mother's soft snoring. He'd been unable to go to sleep and found the need to distract himself until Lillie and Martin returned.

Though it upset him to think about it, he *did* need to talk about what had happened. He recognized the wisdom of his mother's idea to talk as a foursome.

At the Farmer house, lunch consisted of soup and bread. Once the dishes were put away, Martin went to his workshop to putter around for awhile. Lillie lay down on her bed with the intention of reading a novel, but was fast asleep within moments.

The afternoon waned and Lillie and Martin appeared at the Crumley's door with a salad and apple pie. A chicken and rice casserole, still in the oven, smelled wonderful. The table was set beautifully—Joshua was busy with a corkscrew.

"I thought we might all need a little vino for our nerves," he said in a jovial tone as Lillie and her father entered the kitchen. Taking a glass each, they sat and sipped on their wine as the aroma from the oven enveloped them like a warm blanket.

Martin took charge. "Well...how about we take a look at the damages?"

Joshua watched as his mother brought out a pad of paper and a pen for notes. The idea of approaching what had happened from a logical point of view appealed to the attorney in him. "I'm sure people will misunderstand and be offended by what Lillie and I did."

"Indeed."

Lillie sat for a moment. "Like who, though...especially, I mean."

"Well, the Nelsons, of course," said Miriam as she wrote the word "Nelson" on the pad.

"And anyone who is close friends with the Nelsons," added Lillie.

Martin chuckled nervously. "That's just about everyone in Hopeston." He paused. "What about Lane?"

Lillie laughed sarcastically. "I *hope* he was offended...that was the point!"

"Put that down, mother." Joshua said, looking pointedly at her pad.

"And everyone who is close to *him*." Martin said.

"Well that covers everyone!" said Joshua, brushing his hands together in a gesture that indicated their job was done. They sat in silence for a while.

"Josh, you said people would *mis*understand," said Miriam finally. "But what if they *understood*..."

Lillie frowned. "Do you think anyone has a clue about what happened to my mother and...?"

"Well, weren't there people who used to know and love your mother, people who were close to her back when she was active in the church?" Miriam asked.

"Yes," answered Martin, on Lillie's behalf, his anger appearing from nowhere. "But none of them ever reached out to her after she left."

"That doesn't mean they didn't *know* something," offered Joshua, applying his prosecutor's knowledge and experience to the situation. "In fact, when people *do* know things like that they are often more likely to remain silent and pull away from a victim."

They sat in silence absorbing what he'd said.

Lillie sat up. "Somebody *must* know *something!*"

"Okay then, who?" Joshua asked.

Martin began to wrack his brain for information on whom his wife had been close to at the church before the summer she'd been raped.

Between them, he and Joshua and Lillie slowly pieced together a list of the names of people with whom Melodie had worked and socialized. They made special note of those who had afterward made it known that they disliked Lillie or her mother.

"Who was on the board at the time?" Miriam asked. "Doesn't the board concern itself with members who stop attending church?" No one remembered who had been on the board but they agreed they could locate the records that would tell them.

Joshua looked away for a moment and then turned back to the table. "What exactly are we doing here?"

His mother offered an answer. "Preparing ourselves for attack?"

Martin nodded. "Going on the offensive."

"Starting an investigation!" Lillie exclaimed.

"However we describe it, today was the last straw. We're starting an effort to go after Lane Richardson," said Joshua. "The question is are we ready for this? All of us?"

They sat again in silence, and then Miriam looked at her son. "We have no other choice."

"She's right, Joshua." Martin leaned back in his chair.

Miriam rose to retrieve the casserole from the oven, and once spoonfuls of the delicious food arrived on their plates, the foursome ate their supper with a heightened awareness. They had walked through a door together into a new stage of their lives. It was time to prepare for battle.

When the meal was finished, Joshua and Lillie cleared the dishes, giving them all room to work.

"So," Martin said, leaning on one elbow, "do we tell people what happened?"

Lillie shrugged her shoulders. "Abigail says to be honest."

"The truth shall set you free." Joshua recited a Bible passage he remembered from childhood.

"Yes, no more lies and secrets!" Lillie responded, reaching to touch him on the arm.

"So what shall we *tell* people? I think we should be together on this." Joshua's mother entered the conversation.

Martin thought for a moment. "Well, first, people are going to want to know why you two walked out."

Miriam shook her head. "This is going to be hard! I'm not sure this community is ready to hear about this."

"No, but they have to! It's time they woke up to the truth!" Lillie was adamant.

"Don't forget that some already know," Martin said.

Joshua, who'd been pacing the floor, turned to the group. "How about simply saying that Lane betrayed and violated members of the Farmer and Crumley families?"

Miriam nodded. "That will get people thinking and wondering, anyway."

"Yeah," said Martin. "We want to get people talking among themselves about what they know, what they've kept secret all these years."

The phone rang. All four of them froze. Miriam got up slowly from the table, and after letting the phone ring a few times, answered it.

"Hello. Is this the Crumley residence?"

"Yes."

"I'd like to speak to Joshua Crumley if he's there."

"May I ask who's calling?"

"This is Heidi Spellworth. I used to go to Hopeston Church."

"Just a moment, please." Miriam shrugged her shoulders and handed the phone to Joshua.

"Hello, this is Joshua." A flutter of nerves started in his stomach.

"Joshua, my name is Heidi Spellworth. I was at the funeral today. I saw you and Lillie Farmer walk out, and I just wanted to say I'm really glad you did."

Joshua was speechless. "You are?"

"Yes. I wish I could have done it myself."

Eyes wide, Joshua glanced at the others in the room. "Do you know *why* we did it?"

"Oh-h-h, yes!"

"It was that clear, huh?"

"To me it was. I doubt it was to most of the people there."

"Why was it so clear to you?" Joshua spoke cautiously, sensing he was walking on tender territory.

"I couldn't stand it when that man got up to speak. I hate him!"

"Were you...violated by him, too?"

"Yes, I was."

He repeated himself. "You were a victim too?"

"Yes." She responded without hesitation.

Suddenly, the little boy in Joshua rose up and he felt small and defenseless. His mother took the phone, as he slid to the floor and sat leaning against the kitchen cupboard, and put it to her ear.

"Ms. Spellworth?" Miriam said to the woman on the phone.

"Yes, I'm here. Please call me Heidi."

"This is Joshua's mother, Miriam. He's feeling emotional right now."

"I understand," she replied. "Boy, do I understand."

"May we have your phone number? I know Joshua would like to talk to you again." Joshua gave her several strong nods.

"Of course. Joshua may call me anytime."

"Thank you, Heidi," said Miriam scribbling the number on her pad. "Thank you so much for calling. We really appreciate it."

"She was *there*?" Lillie was incredulous.

Joshua nodded. "Yeah, she saw it all, and said she wished she could have walked out too!"

"Well, there's at least *one* person who didn't misunderstand or get offended!"

Joshua looked pleadingly at his mother. "How many are there going to be, Mom?"

Miriam responded with all the honesty she could offer her son. "I don't know honey, but we have to be ready to receive them, however many there are. She needs you as much as you need her."

Joshua heard Abigail in his head, asking him if it was helpful to share his burden with others. The answer was yes.

"Okay," he said, getting up from the floor and taking his place at the table again. "That's two victims we know of."

"Elizabeth and Heidi," said Lillie.

"Elizabeth *Hallman*," added Martin, for Miriam's benefit.

"And Heidi Spellworth," she responded, as she wrote their names on a new page.

"There are two more," said Joshua.

When all looked at him with a questioning expression, he smiled. There was a new conviction in his demeanor.

"Melodie Farmer and Joshua Crumley."

After a moment or two of reflection, Lillie spoke again. "We should try to get hold of Elizabeth as soon as possible."

"Yeah, and we should get together…" said Joshua.

"Abigail encouraged us to tell our stories, to share them." As she spoke, Lillie realized she had included herself in the list. It was evident to the others as well, who were looking at her now.

"I'm a victim too—a second generation victim!"

"Yes! Absolutely!" Martin nodded.

56

When they were done, Lillie and Joshua decided to go out for a drink and Martin returned home. When he arrived there, he saw the light blinking on his answering machine and discovered a phone message from Mike Johnston. He prepared himself and then returned the call.

"Mike, this is Martin Farmer."

"Hello, Martin. Thanks for calling me back."

"What's up?"

"Well, as the chairman of the board of Hopeston Church I feel I should ask you why Joshua and your daughter left the funeral service today in such a manner."

"Well, Mike, they felt the need to make a statement."

"Why? About what?"

"About Pastor Lane's presence at the funeral. Over ten years ago, he severely betrayed and violated both the Farmer and the Crumley families." Martin was suddenly grateful for the prearranged language.

Mike paused on the other end of the line. "What do you mean?"

Martin told him about the abuse, and that his wife had been raped.

Mike was stunned. "My God, Martin, why didn't you say something?"

Martin waited to gain control over his mounting emotion. "I just learned the truth about it myself a few months ago."

"How?"

"Melodie kept a diary. She wrote about it in detail."

"Okay. So what does Joshua have to do with it? Why did he leave?"

"She wrote about him too. She wasn't the only one violated that day."

Mike was reeling. "Melodie never *said* anything about this?"

"No. She was traumatized, Mike. She died without ever talking about it."

After a long silence, Mike finally spoke again. "Martin, please forgive me but, how do you know she didn't make this up or exaggerate what happened? Pastor Lane is a very friendly, affectionate guy—perhaps she misunderstood."

299

Martin fought to contain his anger before responding. "No, Mike. She *didn't* misunderstand. My wife would not have written anything that didn't actually happen." He paused. "Plus, Joshua's account matches hers exactly."

"I'm sorry, Martin, but this is hard to believe."

"I know."

"Why would Pastor Lane do such a thing?"

"I don't know, Mike. But I think you need to know that Melodie and Joshua aren't the only victims. There are others."

"What do you mean?" Mike still couldn't believe what he was hearing.

"There are other people the pastor abused."

"And how do you know *that?*"

"Melodie got a call from one of them not long after she left the church. She described it in her diary. And another victim called Joshua this afternoon after the funeral."

"Really? Oh my God!"

"She called to tell Joshua she was glad he did what he did today."

"My God, what are we going to do?" Mike spoke mostly to himself.

"I don't know, Mike," responded Martin, "but the truth must come out. The guy's got a serious problem and he might abuse again."

"I just can't believe this."

"I know it's hard to believe, but it has had devastating effects..." Martin thought of Lillie's fight with depression. "...on more than just the victims themselves."

Mike sighed into the phone. "Martin, I need some time to think about this. Thank you for your time."

Martin's heart sank. He was not at all convinced that Mike believed him. And if that was true of Mike, who was one of the most reasonable men he knew, then how would *unreasonable* people react?

Carrying a basket of laundry, Penelope wandered into the room. Mike sat staring off into the distance.

"What is it?" she asked.

"I just talked with Martin Farmer."

"And?" Penelope sat down next to him and pulled out a shirt to fold.

"And he says…" Mike stopped.

"Says what?"

Mike opened his mouth to speak and nothing came out at first, so he tried again. "He says Pastor Lane…*sexually abused* his wife years ago."

Penelope's eyes popped open. "What? Oh, my God! That can't be!"

"Yeah, I know," Mike said. "I can't imagine Pastor Lane doing something like that! But Martin claims there's a *record* of it and that there are other victims…"

"My God, Mike, what is he saying?!"

"I know! What are we going to do? The town will be buzzing about this before you know it!"

"What if it's not true?"

"What if it *is*?"

"Either way, what a mess!"

Mike stood and began to pace. "Yeah, what a mess!"

"What can *you* do about it, Mike? Let's think about this. Need you do anything? I mean, the pastor's not at our church anymore."

"True, but what if it *is* true and he does it again? Now we know. If we do or say nothing…oh my God, Penelope!"

Mike slumped down into his chair again. "I guess we should check it out."

"I don't know, hon. Do we want to get involved? Why not leave this up to Martin and Mrs. Crumley. They were there today when the kids walked out—let *them* deal with the aftermath."

"Okay. But what about Pastor Lane? Shouldn't somebody talk with him—check it out, warn him?"

Penelope thought for some time before responding. "I suppose if you were in his shoes you would appreciate knowing, being prepared to respond to the accusation."

"You think I should call him?"

"Yes, I guess you should."

Mike immediately went for the phone, picked it up and dialed the pastor's number. Penelope sat quietly listening.

Recognizing the voice on the other end of the phone, Lane leaned back in his chair. "Mike! How are you, my friend?"

"Not so good."

"Why, what's up, guy?"

"I just got off the phone with Martin Farmer. I called him about the funeral today." Mike cleared his throat.

"And what did he have to say about it?" asked Lane. Something about Mike's tone caused him to be defensive.

"Martin says the reason those kids walked out today was because... he says, that years ago...you...well...abused his wife."

"Well, I'll be damned! I thought that was taken care of long ago."

"What?"

"Mike, perhaps I should have told more than just the board at the time but I thought asking her to leave the church would take care of it."

"What do you mean, Pastor?"

"I guess there's nothing to do except say it, Mike. Melodie Farmer had a crush on me and she tried to seduce me. I guess she misunderstood my friendly manner. That's a problem I have, people sometimes misunderstanding my manner." Lane laughed uncomfortably. "So, when she wouldn't take no for an answer, I had to ask her to leave the church."

Mike was confused. "Are you saying Melodie Farmer tried to take advantage of *you?*"

"Yes, Mike, I am. She was very insistent."

"*Melodie Farmer?* I would never have guessed." Mike tried to picture the sweet woman he remembered coming on to the pastor. Or being inappropriate in *any* way, for that matter.

"I know it sounds crazy, but people like that are very good at keeping their real natures hidden."

Lane's comment found a place in Mike's gut and lodged itself there. When he didn't immediately respond, Lane spoke again.

"This is a terrible accusation!"

"Yes, Pastor, if, as you say, it was Melodie and not you who did something inappropriate, then it is..."

"Slander! That's what this is! You don't believe I would do anything like that, do you?"

"Well, no. I was quite shocked to hear Martin even suggest it." Mike was starting to feel nauseous.

"Of course you were, because it's preposterous!" Lane held the receiver away from him and looked at it in disbelief before returning it to his ear. "Farmer claims his wife *told* him this?"

"No. She apparently wrote about it in her diary."

"In her diary? He believes the vengeful words of a rejected, unhappy housewife written in her private diary?"

"Yes, he does," Mike responded. "Martin said she could never have told him any other way. He said that she also wrote about Joshua Crumley and claims you abused him too."

The pastor snorted. "Joshua Crumley was a needy, fatherless boy who was very attached to Melodie. Maybe he was jealous and made up stories. Who knows what Melodie told him? The nerve of these people!"

Mike thought for a moment. "It *was* inconsiderate of them to do it at Delbert's funeral."

"Inconsiderate? That's an understatement. It was the most disrespectful thing I've ever seen! Not only was it a show of disrespect to me, but to the Nelson family...to all of Hopeston, for that matter! And now Martin has the audacity to accuse me? Some sort of action must be taken, Mike. Really!"

"I agree, Pastor, but what do you suggest I do?"

"Well, as sad as it sounds, I guess the truth must be told. I didn't want to expose Melodie's indiscretions. That's why I've kept quiet about it all these years, but I see now that we must before this gets out of control."

Mike was incredulous. "So, you want to tell people what Melodie Farmer did?"

"Why yes, I do! If they're going to spread vicious rumors about me and tarnish my good name, I'd say so!" The pastor was yelling, so loud that Penelope heard his voice from the other room and stuck her head around the corner.

Mike saw her and grimaced. "Hold on, Pastor, calm down."

"It's hard to stay calm when people are spreading lies about me!"

"I understand. But let's not get carried away here. Let's think about this. So far, we don't know who has heard this accusation—all that's happened so far is two kids walked out of a funeral."

"Yes, but how did you hear about it?"

"I called Martin myself to find out why they did it."

"Exactly! And he didn't hesitate to tell you his vicious lies, did he?"

"No, he didn't."

"So everyone who does as you did will hear the same thing."

Mike sighed. "I guess. Maybe I should ask Martin to stop."

"Oh, yeah! He'll stop just because we ask him to!" Sarcasm rolled off the pastor's tongue. "No, Mike, I may have to take him to court for slander!"

"Well, Pastor, why don't you let me try talking to him first? Will you let me do that?"

"I guess you can try. It would be best if nobody else hears this."

Lane hung up the phone. It was obvious that he had to stop Martin. He poured himself a glass of wine to settle his nerves, picked up the phone again and dialed the Staceys' number.

"Hello, Ralph. It was great to see you and the missus at the funeral today."

"Yes, Pastor, it was good to see you too."

"Is Barbara there? I have something I'd like to pass by her, if I may." Minutes went by while Ralph got his wife to come to the phone, and nervousness grew in Lane's gut. Finally, a female voice came on the line.

"Pastor?"

"Hello, Barbara. Do you have a minute?"

"Yes, yes, always, for you!"

"Do you remember what you said today at the luncheon about wishing there was something you could do about what Lillie Farmer and Joshua Crumley did?

"Yes, of course!"

"Well, there may be. Apparently Martin Farmer is spreading rumors about me."

57

"Mrs. Hallman, this is Lillie Farmer, Melodie Farmer's daughter. From Hopeston?"

Elizabeth struggled to control a sudden rush of emotion. "Yes, Lillie…" she said, her voice thin.

"I don't know exactly how to say this, but…I think you called my mother several years ago to let her know…"

Elizabeth finished the sentence. "I called her to tell her that I knew what *he* did to her and she never called me back."

Lillie winced, hearing the hurt in Elizabeth's voice. "I know. She couldn't."

Silence ensued. "How *is* your mother?" asked Elizabeth finally.

"She's gone. She died two years ago."

"Oh, God. Really? I'm so sorry, Lillie."

"Thank you. I found out about what happened to her only a few weeks ago. She couldn't bring herself to tell anyone except her counselor, but she wrote about it in her diary. And she wrote about your call too."

"Really?"

"Yes." Lillie paused for a moment and then returned to the reason for her call. "Mrs. Hallman…"

"Please call me Elizabeth."

"Elizabeth, there are other victims."

"I know," she replied. "I looked into it after it happened to me."

"Did you ever contact any of them?"

"No, I couldn't get up the nerve. After I called your mother and didn't hear from her again I just gave up. I had to leave it alone. I guess I've been trying to pretend ever since that it never happened."

"We would like to get together with you."

"Who's we?"

"Joshua, who is another victim, and me. We are calling all the others that we know of. We think it would be helpful if we all talked."

"I don't know."

"Elizabeth, Joshua and I have been learning that it helps to talk about it… support from other people who understand helps too!"

"When? And where?"

"We thought we could meet at Joshua's house in Hopeston."

"How many others have you contacted?"

"You are the first. But we plan to invite a woman who called Joshua just the other day." Lillie would release no other names until she had been given permission to do so.

"Oh, well, I suppose I could come. Once, anyway." A short silence ensued. "Do you want the names I have?"

"Please!"

Elizabeth was uplifted by this young woman's energy and openness, but suspicious at the same time. "Why are you doing this now?"

"Well, we think it's time to hold the pastor accountable for his behavior—after all, he may still be abusing."

"Tell me when, Lillie. I'll come."

Heidi Spellworth was next on the list. Joshua was anxious to speak to her again, but his stomach was nothing but nerves as he dialed the phone. Heidi answered and he pushed himself to speak.

"Heidi, this is Joshua Crumley."

"Oh, Joshua, thanks for calling back so soon."

"I'm sorry about earlier."

"No, it's okay. I understand. It has a way of taking you down at unexpected moments. I know."

"Thanks." He paused. "Heidi…we're not the only ones. There are several of the pastor's victims out there."

Heidi began to cry and Joshua hurried to show his support. "I know. It's hard to deal with alone and I think we should get together to tell our stories. Will you join us?"

"Oh, God! Anytime, Joshua! Anywhere! Just let me know."

58

J ulia Bomont had prepared a luncheon at her home for the ladies' circle from church. They were gathered around the table, twittering—the invitation was unexpected. Julia rarely entertained anymore.

Once a prayer had been said and the serving dishes had been passed, Julia cleared her throat to speak. "Ladies, here we are after the funeral of our dear friend and beloved city clerk, Delbert Nelson."

"Yes! And wasn't it wonderful to have Pastor Lane do the eulogy!" said one of the ladies. Agreement was murmured all around.

"But what a shame his eulogy was so rudely interrupted!" Ann was a lady whose shaky voice and diminutive size indicated her advanced age.

"It was more than a shame!" said Julia, a hint of a smile on her face. She was glad Ann had wasted no time in bringing up the very subject she had invited them there to discuss. "It was a grave offense that must not be tolerated!"

"Well, and it gets worse," said Judith, a close friend of Barbara Stacey and youngest member of the circle.

"What?" said her hostess. "Judith, do tell!"

Judith, looking like the Cheshire cat, waited until she had the complete attention of all the ladies before she began to share the latest gossip. "Apparently Lillie's father, Martin Farmer, is spreading rumors..." She paused for effect. "...that Pastor Lane had sex with Melodie Farmer." Gasps of horror erupted around the table.

"And..." she continued, "he claims the pastor abused Joshua Crumley too!"

"This is, of course, absolutely ridiculous!" said Julia. "Nothing but the pathetic rantings of a jealous and lonely widower! It's well known that Melodie Farmer tried to seduce our good Pastor Lane years ago and he had the sense about him to set her straight. It seems clear enough that her family is trying to get revenge."

Ann spoke again. "Perhaps, Julia, but that's an awfully strong statement!"

Julia was indignant. "Well, that Martin Farmer's obviously a vicious, angry man!"

The ladies had quietly eaten for a while when a lady named Faith laid down her spoon and sat back. "Well, I *know* Martin Farmer is not a Christian. I'm not sure he's *ever* come to church."

"Not until his wife's funeral." The sarcasm with which Julia spoke was thick.

Letty Wilkerson, a shy, slight woman known for being a bit slow, piped up. "*I've* seen other non-believers show up for funerals and never attend worship."

"But he just sat there and allowed his daughter to leave like..." said Ann.

Julia growled. "I'd say it was evidence of the lack of proper discipline in that home!"

Another of the women joined the conversation. "Didn't I hear that the girl was depressed for a long time?"

"Well, yes, you would be too if the Lord was not taught to you and instilled in your heart and mind as He ought to be." Julia said.

"I think she was close to suicide at one time, poor girl."

Judith watched with amusement at the response to the news she had brought. "I feel sorry for anyone who has parents who lead them astray."

"What about the boy?" asked Letty.

"Oh, that pathetic little Jew? His mother's just another lonely and misguided widow." One or two of the ladies winced at Julia's blatant bigotry and she wheeled around to face them.

"What? You're horrified that I say 'Jew'? Well, it *was* the Jews, you know, who crucified our Lord! No good can come from a Jew!"

"*Jesus* was a Jew, Julia." Judith said, obviously struck by the irony of Julia's comment.

Julia glared back at her. "Jesus was smart enough to start a new religion. He didn't even claim his own blood relatives. Is that not an indication of a desire to leave the Jewish ways behind?"

Ann looked around the room. "Why did the Crumleys come here anyway? They're the only Jews for miles around."

"Who in heaven knows!" exclaimed Julia. "But it's obviously time they were encouraged to move on."

She stared at the disbelief on the faces before her. "What *is* it, ladies? Don't you have the sense to know when a troublemaker should be asked to leave? The pastor did with Melodie! I think we could all learn a thing or two from his example." She rose slowly with great dignity and began to move away from the table, calling over her shoulder, she said, "Ladies, let's retire to the sitting room for coffee."

Obediently they rose and followed their hostess like sheep following a shepherd. She had them right where she wanted them.

59

Mike thought long and hard about how best to approach Martin, and finally decided a visit in person was called for. Giving the incident a few days to quiet down, Mike headed out to the Farmer residence in his sedan.

As he neared the end of the long driveway, he saw Martin sitting on his porch. Parking his car, he walked up to the porch through the sun-hot, freshly cut grass.

"Martin," he said, tipping his head. "May I join you?"

"By all means, come on up." Martin gestured to the chair beside him and tamped his pipe.

Mike settled into a comfortable wicker chair. "Martin, I've thought about what you said, and I spoke with Pastor Lane about it." He paused. "What you claim is inflammatory, Martin. I don't have any way of knowing whether it happened or not. But I *do* know that Pastor Lane has been a faithful servant to many, many good people for a long time and this could ruin him. I'm not sure you want to be responsible for that."

Martin puffed on his pipe and looked out over the meadow, listening without comment.

"I'm asking you to please not share this information with anyone," continued Mike. "No disrespect intended and God bless her, but your wife is gone. If this is true, it can't hurt her anymore. But this could hurt the pastor. Can we just leave it alone? I think it would be best for everyone. Don't you?"

Martin could almost taste the heat that seeped up his neck and marched across his face, but he remained quiet for a moment, clenching and unclenching his jaw.

"Mike…how long have you been married?"

"Forty-five years."

"Would you say Penelope is the most precious person in the world to you?"

"Of course, Martin. But what does *my* wife have to do with this?"

"Well, I'll tell you," he paused. "How do you think you'd feel if Penelope were lured, unsuspecting, into a trap laid by a man she trusted with her life and her *soul* and was then brutally raped by him on the floor of his office?" He turned and looked piercingly at Mike. "Exactly how would you feel about that?

"How would you feel if you did your best to help Penelope get the poison out of her—to rid herself of whatever it was that caused her to get so completely lost within herself that you could no longer reach her? How would you feel, even after that, if she was never able to speak a word of it to you?

"How would you feel if your daughter slipped into the hellish fire of depression because of your wife's departure from life and you thought you'd lost her too? Would *you* be able to remain silent and pretend that it never happened…to save that man's reputation or his career? Would you even care?"

After a long silent moment, Mike responded. "No, Martin, I don't think I could."

"I didn't think so." Without saying goodbye, Martin stood and went into his house, closing the door behind him.

Mike sat stunned. After a minute or two, when it was apparent Martin would not return, he headed for his car. Lillie drove up, and he lowered the window, waved to her and then drove away.

As soon as Mike's car disappeared around the corner, Lillie ran into the house. Her father was sitting at the kitchen table.

"I saw Mr. Johnston leaving. Why was *he* here?"

Martin turned to face his daughter. She could see him slowly make the journey back from wherever he had been.

"Hi, sweetheart." He paused for a moment, shaking his head. "Mike came to tell me to keep my mouth shut. He doesn't think I should ruin the good pastor's reputation by telling people he raped my wife!"

"How does he know?" she asked.

"I told him. He called me a couple days ago to talk about the two of you leaving the funeral."

"And now that he knows, he wants you to keep quiet about it?"

"Yes. And apparently he told Lane Richardson what I said."

"Oh, *really*." The hair stood up on the back of Lillie's neck. "Dad, this makes me nervous."

Martin reached for his daughter's hand and held it firmly in his. "We've overturned a can of angry worms, my dear. People won't be happy having this intrude upon their lives."

"Well, they'll just have to be unhappy, I guess. The sooner we gather our group of victims together, the better," Lillie said, drawing strength from her father. "Joshua and I talked and we've decided on a date for the first meeting."

"When is it?"

"Thursday at Joshua's. And Dad," she said, "Elizabeth Hallman and Heidi Spellworth have both agreed to come."

When Mike Johnston reached his home, he went straight to his garage and started up his riding mower. After an hour of riding and thinking, he went in the house to find his wife. Finding her in the kitchen rolling dough, he took her by the shoulders and turned her around to face him, and then he hugged her tight.

Penelope leaned back from her husband's shoulder and looked at his face inquisitively. "What is it, Mike? What happened?"

But Mike couldn't respond—he had no words to express his confusion. He released her from his embrace, kissed her softly on the cheek, and returned to his mowing.

Miriam made her way through the aisles of the Hopeston grocery store. As she headed down the cereal aisle, she encountered two women, one of whom was Julia Bomont. Because of previous experiences, she had learned to stay clear of Julia, and turned to go down a different aisle, but she heard her name called, and looked up to see Julia speeding towards her.

"Hello, Miriam." Julia spat the words in false friendliness.

"Julia." Miriam nodded in acknowledgment.

Turning to the woman with her, Julia said, "Faith, do you suppose they have enough kosher food in this little store for our Miriam?"

"I wouldn't think so," Faith answered, as if following a script.

Julia continued her bigoted barrage. "Really, Miriam you should go shop where they cater to the needs of your people."

"This store is just fine, thank you."

"Oh no! You shouldn't settle for this little town. We Christians have nothing to offer you, here. Surely it is unsatisfying."

"You needn't concern yourself, Julia." Miriam turned to go, but Julia grabbed her arm.

"No, Miriam, I'm not sure you understand me. We have *nothing* to offer you here." Julia's eyes flashed like those of a lioness ready to spring.

Blood rushed to Miriam's face and she slowly extricated her arm from Julia's grasp. Staring as straight as bullets into the older woman's eyes, she remained silent in anticipation of what Julia would say next. She would not be disappointed.

"After that pretty performance your son made the other day, it is clear that you are unsatisfied here in Hopeston. We encourage you to find a more appropriate place to settle, don't we, Faith?" Julia said without taking her eyes off Miriam's face.

Miriam's growing anger emboldened her. "Julia Bomont, be assured that no threat of yours will ever determine my choices or decisions. Now, if you will excuse me..."

Julia moved to block her way. "No, Miriam! You will *not* behave as if you are free to make choices that offend the good Christian people of this town! What your son did at Delbert's funeral is unforgivable and quite frankly, the last straw. We have put up with you people and your little problems long enough. I think I can speak for the people of this entire town when I say we are more than ready for you to move on." The full force of Julia's venom showed itself. Even Faith seemed to cringe beside her.

Miriam pulled raw strength from within and stood her ground. She forced herself to maintain steady eye contact. "I don't believe you can speak for the entire town, Julia. And if you don't get out of my way and let me do my shopping, I will call upon the law enforcement of this town to remove you."

Julia smirked and stepped aside, leaving Miriam room to barely squeeze through. "Come Faith, we don't want to get in the way of this Jesus Killer. That wouldn't be turning the other cheek as our Lord taught us."

Miriam felt the blow of Julia's words as if they were fists pummeling her body but with great determination she pushed her cart past the two women and made her way to the end of the aisle.

When she reached the cash register, Bill Hadley was his usual kind self. His warmth restored a small sense within her heart that the world was okay. She gladly took in this comfort and headed out of the store. Once in the parking lot, Miriam breathed a prayer.

60

Joshua and Lillie worked together to tidy his mother's living room for the group meeting. Miriam baked cookies and set the coffee brewing.

Lillie felt nervous and hopeful. Joshua, on the other hand, was battling old feelings of fear and the need to isolate himself. He'd asked Lillie several times if she thought getting the group together was really a good idea. Lillie's response had been that Abigail would be very proud of them.

"God, I wish Abigail were *here!*" Joshua exclaimed. He sat down on the couch to rest for a moment.

Lillie sat on the coffee table, facing him. Putting her hands on his knees, she tried to reassure him. "Joshua, this'll be good! We need each other now that people are starting to attack us."

He closed his eyes and put his hands on top of hers as if to gather strength from her. "I know," he said, weariness evident in his voice. Then he opened his eyes and looked into hers. "Hey, maybe we should just go see Abigail instead. I bet she needs some of Mom's cookies."

Lillie's expression was a mixture of love and exasperation with his diversionary tactics. "Let's go see her *after* tonight so we can tell her about our meeting."

"Okay." Joshua surrendered, reflecting her smile back to her.

"We can still take her some of your mother's cookies," Lillie added.

An hour later Lillie greeted a tall, well-dressed, middle-aged woman at the kitchen door. The woman hesitated for a moment, and then offered her hand. "I'm Elizabeth."

"I'm Lillie. Welcome. Please come in." Lillie smiled warmly, attempting to put Elizabeth at ease. She ushered her into the kitchen where she introduced Joshua and his mother.

Miriam encouraged them all to make themselves comfortable in the living room. As she brought in a tray with fresh baked cookies, the doorbell rang. Lillie went to answer the door.

A large young woman stood on the steps.

"Heidi?"

"Yes."

"Welcome, I'm Lillie."

Once settled in the soft cushions of chairs and couch, they introduced themselves again and ate refreshments without much in the way of social chatter. A silence stretched out for a few uncomfortable moments before Lillie took the initiative to begin.

"Thank you for coming today. I know this isn't easy, but Joshua and I believe it will be helpful for us to share our experiences and knowledge."

Lillie told the two women how she had discovered the truth of her mother's abuse by reading the diary, about its devastating effects on her family and about her own history of depression.

She revealed that she had learned about Joshua from the diary and had found the letter, and how it had brought them together. She shared, also, that Elizabeth had called Melodie shortly after the rape, which Elizabeth corroborated, and she recited the details of Joshua and her abrupt departure from Delbert's funeral. Heidi nodded to substantiate the story.

With a slightly guarded look, Joshua took his turn and explained how he had helped Lillie's mother with the SBS program at the Hopeston church as a thirteen year old, and how his attempt to stop the pastor had caught him ruthlessly in the man's abuse. Both Elizabeth and Heidi cried silently as Joshua told his story.

Feeling the relief of safe disclosure loosening him up, Joshua talked about his years of isolation and pain, and how Lillie had interrupted them with the delivery of Mrs. Farmer's letter. He spoke of their visits with Abigail and the healing he was finally beginning to experience.

Heidi volunteered to go next. "Well, in the summer of 1985, two years after you guys, Pastor Lane invited *me* to teach the SBS program with him. I was delighted and honored! He complimented me for my exemplary teaching skills, just as he did your mother, Lillie, and gave me special care and tutoring.

"But after a while, this special care developed into inappropriate touching, and finally he sexually molested me. I don't know how I got the courage, but I finally just stopped going one day."

As tears flowed freely, Heidi spoke of feeling deep shame for having felt pride and pleasure in her abilities, and in the pastor's attention.

"I've been haunted by self-hatred because I couldn't believe how stupid I was. It's taken years of therapy to repair my sense of self, my ability to trust and to understand the full effect of the betrayal of trust on my life. I went to Delbert's funeral in an attempt to face old demons as part of my recovery. And believe me, I was as shocked as you two were to see him there!"

Turning to Joshua, she said with all the genuineness she could muster, "I don't know if you have any idea what you did for me by standing up and walking out of that funeral! You gave me a new desire to conquer this, to finally overcome the damage he did to me. Thank you.

"You too, Lillie," she said, concluding. "I hope you never regret what you did that day, no matter what happens!"

"I wish I'd been there!" Elizabeth said softly.

Lillie turned to her. "You *were* there!"

"What do you mean?"

Joshua answered her. "You were there with me. When Lillie found out you had contacted her mother, it changed this whole episode from something I had suffered alone into something bigger. It turned into a bigger cause instead of just my own sordid past. I'm an attorney—just knowing there were others to defend gave me strength and courage."

"Wow." Fresh tears brightened Elizabeth's eyes. She wiped them away and began to talk. "Ever since my call to your mother, Lillie, I've felt so alone. After finally making a connection with her and then hearing nothing, well, I hit a brick wall. Even though I *knew* there were others I didn't know how to get to them, so I gave up." The floodgate opened and she sobbed out loud. Once she'd composed herself, she continued.

"My story is a lot like Heidi's and Melodie's. The pastor asked me to teach SBS with him and then he abused me.

"I got away too, but it was too late. I've spent the last fifteen years trying to put it behind me. I've tried to pretend my life was normal but I've felt the pain every single day."

Elizabeth shared about her investigation of other SBS teachers after hearing about Mrs. Farmer's disappearance from the church. Joshua closed his eyes, trying to contain the anger boiling within him. The similarity of their experiences with Mrs. Farmer's was uncanny.

As they continued to talk, it became painfully clear that Lane Richardson was a dangerous predator who had chosen the most vulnerable women in his congregation and with shrewd calculation, groomed his victims through flattery, special attention, and skillful words and actions.

The pattern Elizabeth had thought she'd uncovered had been confirmed. The pastor had used the SBS program to supply himself with victims. She reached into her purse and brought out the list of names she'd told Lillie about.

Joshua listened carefully to what each of the women had said and then spoke of his work with the prosecutor, his passion for justice and his own avoidance of intimacy through an obsession with work.

Heidi looked at him with warmth and admiration. "Here you are, Joshua, for the second time, standing up to the man! Only this time he won't get away with it!"

61

Early the next morning, Lillie and Joshua found their way up the path to Abigail's cabin. They bore gifts for her: a batch of Miriam's homemade chocolate chip cookies, still warm from the oven with a note from Joshua's mother, a large box of matches, a package of small white candles, a bag of sweet smelling apples, a pad of lined paper, and two boxes of green tea.

They knocked on her door and when no answer came, they opened it hesitantly and peered into darkness. Entering the kitchen, they called out Abigail's name. Still no answer—there was nothing but stillness. They laid their gifts on the kitchen table and, with eyes still adjusting, began to investigate her diminutive home for clues.

There were signs of Abigail everywhere—her quilt and pillow rumpled on her bed, an open book and her glasses on the table beside her chair on the porch, her slippers set side by side, in place of her boots, at the door. But there was no Abigail and, thankfully, no sign of foul play. They decided to look around outside.

Making their way down the path to the lake, they emerged onto her tiny beach. There were no footprints in the sand, and the canoe napped face down where it lay. Joshua squatted at the water's edge, remembering his first time there. He was conscious of having journeyed far since that memorable day of tears and rage.

That day he had passed through his first emotional storm, the outpouring of the deeply buried emotional material that had bogged him down and held him captive for so long. He understood what Elizabeth and Heidi had both gone through and what they needed now.

He realized he felt lighter—each time he'd taken a stand or made a step towards his own recovery it had been as if another weight had been lifted from his soul. He yearned for the two women to experience this same growing relief and wholeness.

Joshua turned to find Lillie sitting quietly on the beach with her head cocked. She placed her index finger to her lips to silence him, and he froze where he stood. They could hear the tinny echo of a woodpecker resounded through the trees. Lillie beamed at him when it was done and beckoned him to come to her. She explained, in a hushed whisper, that the repeating call of the large pileated woodpecker was an alarm call indicating the presence of an intruder. They sat motionless, hardly breathing and listened as the huge red-crested bird, similar to the one they'd seen on their picnic, made drumming sounds on a tree nearby.

Then the sound of scuffling could be heard. They strained their ears and eyes in search of its origin. The sounds of many small forest creatures foraging were heard but to Lillie's well-trained ear, another more rhythmic rustling was discernible as a backdrop.

Joshua frowned in his effort to hear what Lillie's face told him she heard and then she pointed, beaming, at a flash of red and then brown, and they watched as Abigail trudged up the path along the lake that headed up to the cabin. Just as they looked at one another with relief, the woodpecker called again—this time a little further away. Abigail stopped in her tracks. They felt her eyes on them and shivered.

"Hello-o-o?"

"Abigail, it's us, Lillie and Joshua."

"Oh! Come on up, let's have tea!" She started up the path again.

When they came in the door they found Abigail stowing candles and matches and humming happily. Three of the cookies they had brought her were on a plate and the intermittent hiss of water from the teakettle greeted them like a song.

Warmth flooded Lillie's heart. She felt at home here in this simple cabin and forest home more than just about anywhere. Joshua moved forward to quietly take the tray from Abigail and Lillie pitched in to ready their cups for tea.

"We wondered what had happened to you," said Lillie as she watched Abigail light her lanterns.

"I was on my morning walk."

"You go every morning?"

Abigail nodded mysteriously. "Yes."

Lillie looked at her and caught a glimpse of glory shining from her eyes. A sense of awe settled over her like mist, and she shivered for the second time that morning.

Once settled on the porch with cups of the steaming green tea and cookies, the three of them basked in the beauty of the morning and one another's company. Abigail looked at Joshua with delight.

"Thy mother makes delicious cookies!"

He smiled, seeing that their gifts had been received with joy.

Lillie munched on a cookie. "Abigail, where do you go for your morning walks?"

The older woman looked out over the forest before them and mused as though she were communicating with a loved one. The two young people watched her and waited.

"I go to the Death Tree and the Sacred Clearing…I meditate…the spirits come to me…" A look of pain crossed her face for a brief moment and then she smiled a distant, longing smile. "I need that every day."

"What is the Death Tree?"

The pain on Abigail's face returned. She looked deeply into the eyes of her young companions. "My brother hung himself on it," she said.

"He struggled with being half Indian, half white," she continued, looking out over the lake. "All of us did. But none like him. He never belonged in either world—no matter what he did or where he lived, he felt like an outsider.

"Over time, he became brittle with bitterness. Couldn't stand his own skin. For a while he lived among the Quakers—my father's people—but they weren't warlike enough for his warrior spirit." She paused to let the memories flow before starting again.

"Then he lived among my mother's people, but he was uncomfortable with their dances and sacred rituals. He was never able to find his own way there, and he resisted the spiritual traditions of our tribe. So, he fled from them on the eve of his Vision Quest. He said he didn't believe in that hogwash."

Abigail chuckled to herself. "I think the truth was that he was really afraid of meeting himself out there in the wilderness."

She paused again and looked at her two young friends, now spellbound. "He wandered for years, searching for something, doing odd jobs and never putting down roots. Joined the American Indian Movement and ended up caught up in the 1973 stand-off at Wounded Knee. But when that ended, it was as if he wanted another battle to fight."

Abigail sipped her tea. "I still remember the evening he came home. It was out of the blue—we hadn't seen him for a while. I saw what I thought was hope in his eyes that night. But it wasn't. He'd already begun to feel the peace his decision to let go had brought him. That night he went off into the woods and we never saw him again.

"A couple days later my little sister came screaming hysterically up the path. She had found him." Abigail gestured in the direction from which she'd come. "Hanging from a tree near our ancestral burial grounds. In the end, I guess, he decided who he was."

Neither Lillie nor Joshua made a sound.

"We all went to get him, and lowered his body together. We buried him in the Indian tradition, alongside his ancestors. We tended the ceremonial fire in the sacred clearing for three days, taking turns singing his death song and drumming and dancing." Tears now flowed freely down her face.

"Afterwards, our mother stayed for a week under the tree. We brought her food and blankets, but she fasted and shivered and moaned, grieving for him. At the end of five days she came home.

"After that, she went each morning, at dawn, to sit under the tree. That's why we named it the Death Tree. It seemed to free her from her grief so that she could be present for the rest of us."

Abigail reached into her sleeve and pulled out a handkerchief. "I came to understand and appreciate her ritual, and as she aged, I began to do it in her place. Now, it gives me release as well." She wiped her face and returned the handkerchief to her sleeve and gazed at the lake for a long time. The rest of her story would wait.

"But that's not the reason you came today," she said, changing the subject. "I sense a decision needs to be made."

Joshua smiled in amazement. "You're right—we need your help." His expression changed, paralleling the shift in his mood. "A lot has happened since we saw you last…"

Lillie put her hand on his arm. "Maybe we should start with the funeral."

Abigail raised her eyebrows. "What funeral?" Lillie and Joshua exchanged glances and Joshua launched into the story.

"A man who was probably the best-loved city clerk Hopeston has ever had died after a long struggle with cancer, and the whole town turned out for his funeral last week. People were devoted to him, including my parents. He did a lot of good for our community. Anyway, Lillie and I decided to go, but it meant we would have to go to Hopeston Church, where all of this began…" Joshua paused, pain registering on his face.

"Lillie's father and my mother went with us and we all sat together. It was going pretty well, although being there brought back all kinds of memories and feelings, when all of a sudden…" He paused and looked at Lillie and then back at Abigail. "…we realized Lane Richardson was there! He'd been invited by the Nelson family to participate in the funeral."

Lillie jumped in. "It was really hard to be there as it was, but when it turned out *he* was there it became intolerable. We both ended up walking out, right in the middle of his remarks. It created quite a stir!"

"I suppose so."

Joshua picked up where Lillie had left off. "So, we talked—Mom and Lillie's dad and Lillie and I—about what to do. We feel like we're preparing for a battle."

"The townsfolk are angry about our walk-out." Lillie interjected, shifting in her seat. "We apparently couldn't have insulted a more beloved family than the Nelsons."

Abigail nodded. "Go on," she said.

Joshua complied. "As it turns out, though, another victim of the pastor—a woman named Heidi—was there too and saw us walk out."

"How do you know?" asked Abigail.

"She called me later that day and said she was glad we had done it. After talking it over with our parents, we called and asked her if she would come to the house and meet with us."

Lillie stepped in again. "And I called Elizabeth…you know, the woman my mother said called her…and invited her too. And they both agreed."

Her face revealing nothing, Abigail sought to clarify what she was hearing. "So you gathered as a group after that to share your stories?"

"Yes."

Abigail looked out over the lake. "What is your goal in having these gatherings?"

"We want to reach out to all those who have been victimized by the pastor."

"Why?"

"I don't know. I guess so none of us has to feel so alone. For support."

She pressed him. "Anything else?"

"We want to see if others are interested in going after the man for what he's done!" Joshua said, exasperated.

Abigail just smiled.

"What?" Joshua gripped the edge of his chair.

"Is this truly about justice...or is there revenge in thy heart?"

Her question pierced him. Was it revenge? Did he want to make Lane Richardson suffer like he had suffered every day all these years? Did he want to gather support from as many others as possible who knew his pain and felt like he did? Did he want to lead a murderous gang and descend upon the worm of a man that was responsible for all this pain, all this damage? Did he want to kill the man, to rub him off the face of the earth so no one would even recall his having lived or breathed or moved about? He glanced down, searching his heart for the truth.

Yes, he had to admit that a part of him wanted all of these things. But the rest of him didn't. He felt nauseous at the realization that he was capable of such rage, of desiring such violence against another. He swallowed as if to push it down and away. And, as he did so, he knew he would not be able to rid himself of it alone.

At the same time, he was confused. The anger that filled him also fueled him with the energy to fight. He had spent years hiding and running, and now, through his anger, he was ready finally to face his attacker. But the truth was that he didn't *want* to let go of his anger, his eagerness to avenge the victims of the one enemy he had in life.

He could feel the war within his own soul and was shaken. Abigail was right. He wanted both justice *and* revenge! He lowered his head before answering, but he spoke honestly. "Yes, Abigail, there is revenge in my heart."

She responded with tenderness. "And will that accomplish what thy heart truly desires?"

Joshua thought of the consequences of revenge. He saw a vision of a bleeding, humiliated man running through alleyways of darkness and halls of lonely desperation feeling the essence of himself dripping away, destroyed by blood-thirsty pursuers.

No. This wasn't what his heart desired. His thoughts had been the fantasies of a wounded child. He groaned and pounded the arm of his chair.

"I don't know what my heart wants! I just want this to stop!"

"Ahh…" Abigail responded, her eyes never leaving Joshua's.

"Isn't it okay for me to want to fight for justice?" There was a fierce desperation in his voice.

"Is that what the fight in thee now is truly after?"

Joshua stared at her, defiant. And then, his bravado deflated, he bowed his head in submission to her wisdom.

"No, it wants revenge." His voice was so soft that Abigail heard him more with her heart than with her ears. She leaned back in her chair and glanced out over the lake again.

"So, thee tells me these gatherings are to reach out to one another to offer support. But they are also intended to allow the venting of an anger that fuels a desire for revenge."

Joshua thought for a moment and then nodded. "Yes."

"And what will happen if you take your vengeful anger beyond the walls of these gatherings?"

"Carnage."

"Yes," said Abigail. "I'm afraid it might. But the venting of anger within the safe presence of others who understand and will keep it from leaking out, is the very medicine you all need in order to move on."

The light of her argument began to seep into his mind. "So we need to get this out of us and let it go before we can head towards justice?"

"I think so. Doesn't thee?"

"Will I lose my momentum if I lose my anger?"

"That thee will have to find out for thyself, my dear. But, Joshua, I truly doubt thee'll ever lose the fire that fuels thy passion for justice."

Abigail smiled and Joshua was quiet. She waited a minute, and then looked at Lillie. "How about thee? Does thee hold fear in thy heart, Lillie?"

Lillie shared Joshua's amazement at Abigail's ability to pierce through to the core of their emotions. "Yes, I'm afraid. I'm afraid we won't be able to handle all that we have inside us when it comes gushing out."

Abigail sipped more tea. "People are comforted by rules, by expected routines. Perhaps there ought to be some structure or rules to these gatherings.

"For example, why not start and end with prayer? Prayer for help and healing and safety in your sharing?"

Lillie suddenly saw how simple it was. Recalling all of their sessions with Abigail, ideas began to blossom within her, like flowers opening to the sunlight. She thought of how Abigail had always provided a safe and structured environment with tea and goodies, with ritual and prayer, with the beauty of nature, and the presence of God.

Joshua saw the look of revelation cross Lillie's face and he knew then they had gotten what they came for. "Thank you, Abigail," he said softly. "Once again you have helped us."

Lillie spoke in a soft voice. "Abigail, will you show us the Death Tree and the Sacred Clearing?"

The older woman felt the strength of the younger woman's curiosity and the intensity of her interest. "Yes my dear, that would be very fitting, I think."

After clearing away the dishes, Lillie and Joshua followed Abigail in single file down the soft earthen trail between ferns and sun dappled trees, while birds and animals made their noises all around. After a twenty minute walk, they came to a large maple tree with sheltering branches. A natural clearing had long since formed around its roots. The sun sparkled brightly as the tree's leaves moved in a gentle breeze dance, and seemed to whisper a message.

Lillie shivered. Feeling a mysterious presence, she was compelled to lower herself to her knees. Abigail stepped to the side and gently took Joshua by the arm. An energy seemed to emanate from the tree, and a voice came to Lillie's mind. "Hello, my child."

She looked up to see if Abigail had spoken and found she was alone. She closed her eyes again, and as she placed her hands palms down on the forest floor, the voice came again.

326

"I have waited for you to come."

"Who *are* you?" Lillie asked silently within her heart.

"I am the great, great grandmother tree."

Lillie's eyes flew open. The large, old tree in front of her was as solid and stationary as it had been at first. She looked up into its branches.

"Yes, that's right, I am speaking to you, child."

"Are you the Death Tree?" Lillie asked.

"Death is a part of all life."

Flooded with awe, tears choked Lillie as she saw the image of the great, great grandmother tree gently guiding Abigail's brother Tom from the pain of his life. Within her she knew, in that moment, that it is in the midst of death that peace comes.

She slumped down onto the damp earth. "Why did he struggle so?" she asked in her heart.

"Some of my children do."

62

Rebecca Jones stood waiting in line at the Broadley Bank. Since the trauma of the pastor's visit to her house, she had become fearful and timid. She seldom greeted people she knew as readily anymore. Lost in thought, she looked up to find herself face to face with Jocelyn Cherry, a friend from church whom she hadn't seen in a number of weeks, because she'd found herself unable to go to services.

Although she didn't feel like interacting with Jocelyn, Rebecca put on a good face. Jocelyn chatted away about her children, recipes she'd tried recently and her husband's business trip to India, things Rebecca was able to feign interest in.

"Did you hear what happened to Pastor Lane in Hopeston last week?" Seeing renewed interest in Rebecca's eyes, Jocelyn continued without waiting for a response. "He was giving the eulogy at the funeral of a friend, a member of the Hopeston congregation, I guess, and someone got up and just walked out right in the middle of it!"

"No, I hadn't heard," Rebecca said.

"Yeah, some young man. They say he had a bone to pick with the pastor."

"What sort of bone?"

"I don't know but they say he did it on purpose, just to humiliate him! Can you imagine?"

Yes, I can, thought Rebecca. "Do you know who the young man was?"

"Jason, Jordan…Jacob…something like that. I'm not sure. I know it starts with a J and his last name starts with a C, I think." She shook her head. "Young people these days are so disrespectful!"

"Oh, I know. What they'll do!" Rebecca paused so as not to raise Jocelyn's suspicions. "Isn't Hopeston where Pastor Lane used to be the minister? Before coming to Broadley?"

"Yes, I think so. He was there for years, I guess. The man who died was well known, apparently. The church was packed."

"Was the man who walked out a member of the church?"

"I'm not sure," Jocelyn said, her voice drifting off, interest waning. She turned to greet another friend who had entered the bank.

Rebecca took the opportunity to excuse herself and left the bank in a hurry, leaving the transactions for which she had come uncompleted. On the way home she thought hard about who she knew in Hopeston. Through a few phone calls and a little investigation she not only got the name of the young man who had walked out but also that of his girlfriend.

It took Rebecca a couple of days to get up the nerve to call the Crumley residence but she finally picked up the phone. She waited nervously as the ringing began. A woman's voice came on the line. "Hello?"

"Hello. Is this the home of Joshua Crumley?"

"Yes, it is. May I help you?" Miriam had begun to get used to calls for her son from women she didn't know.

"May I speak to him, please?'

"He's not here right now, but I'm his mother. Is there something on your mind?"

"Yes, there is." Rebecca swallowed hard, her voice now shaking. "I attend the church where Reverend Richardson is now serving as minister—Broadley Community Church—and I heard that Joshua walked out of a funeral the other day...at Hopeston Church...and I'd like to know why."

Miriam thought of the statement they had all agreed would be a standard response. "I'm Miriam. May I ask your name?"

"Rebecca."

"Rebecca, the pastor betrayed and violated my family and the family of my son's friend, Lillie Farmer."

Rebecca was speechless. She had wanted it not to be true, but at the same time, she'd desperately hoped there was someone she could talk to about what the pastor had done to her.

"Miriam, I too was...as you said...violated and betrayed by the pastor."

Miriam shook her head. How many victims were there?

"Rebecca, Joshua and Lillie are quietly making contact with people who have been through what you've been through and planning a meeting. Maybe you'd like to come." Miriam reached for the pad of notes she'd been keeping.

Rebecca felt faint. "There's a group? Who attends this group?"

"Well, so far there are four others. You'll make five if you come too." Miriam spoke with warmth in her voice—she was proud of the work her son and Lillie were doing.

"These people have all been violated by Pastor…Lane?"

"Yes."

Rebecca shrieked into the phone. "Oh my God! He's sick! Oh my God!" She took a breath and then composed herself before speaking again. "I'd like to talk with Joshua first, if you don't mind."

"Of course. Should I have him call you?"

"No. I'll call back. When will he be home?"

"Later this evening, I'm sure. Just for your information, the next support group gathering is next Thursday, here at our house, at seven o'clock. Call back tonight, if you can."

"Okay. Thank you. Thank you so much!"

Miriam hung up the phone and walked into her kitchen, where she stood for a long time, looking through the window at the newly turned soil and her tender plantings. She was astonished by the light and beauty of her garden in contrast to the darkness of what had been going on around them. Now there was a victim from his current church!

She turned away and sat down at her kitchen table, and finished writing a note to Joshua. If it had not been before, it was clear now—Lane Richardson would not stop on his own.

63

The next thing Lillie knew, Abigail had taken her arm and was gently helping her up. Once on her feet, she felt Joshua take her other arm and together, he and Abigail guided her a short distance from the Death Tree to a sun-filled clearing with a huge fire ring at its center.

Still supported, she gazed woozily out over the clearing and felt in her bones that they were in a sacred place.

Joshua watched Lillie's face intently. When she had knelt before the Death Tree he had seen something happen to her, and he knew that Abigail had seen it too.

"These are the sacred ceremonial grounds of my people," Abigail said. "Sacred rituals have been performed and enacted here for centuries. The energy is very powerful."

She led them around the wide ring of stones at the center of the clearing to a small, sturdy lean-to made of logs that included a bench. Once seated, a stunningly beautiful vista of the lake was theirs.

Abigail sighed, drinking in the aura of the spot. "It was here that my parents spent their wedding night," she said dreamily.

"My mother struggled some too with which world to live in. As a girl living amongst her own people here on this land," she said, sweeping her hand across the scene before them, "she knew nothing other than the Indian way of life—simple, land-centered living with gardens and hunting providing most of their food. They fished the pond all year round!" Abigail beamed at them like a little girl delighted with herself, and gestured at the lake glistening in front of them.

"She ran barefooted through these woods and knew every animal and bird. She helped grind the corn for the ceremonial meal and tan the hides for the ceremonial clothing her mother and aunts made for the tribe. Her whole extended family was here. She was steeped in the traditional dances, rituals and spiritual practices of her people.

"As a young woman, though, she became restless. Her father had acquired a radio. The outside world both called to her and began to encroach on the life of the village. More and more white people showed up looking to buy land on the lake. My grandfather was a wise leader. He knew we should protect the land and not sell it, but he also knew he needed help to do it legally—in the white man's way." She glanced at Joshua.

"So he sought help from a group of Quakers he knew who had settled just north of here. They were the only white people he trusted—their ways were similar in some ways to those of the tribe and he knew they would understand their needs and values. In the end it was my *father*, Henry Stewart, who came to live with my mother's people, and help the Osampis develop a trust for their land. He was twenty-one years old when he came, a young Quaker boy, really. He helped them establish a school so the Indian children could learn how to communicate with those of the white world who were coming closer and closer all the time.

"My father moved onto the land and lived by himself in a tent in the woods but he participated in every aspect of life here, and my mother fell in love with him. He was a simple, honest man who loved the land and understood the heart of her people.

"I think she felt somehow, too, that he was her way to escape. So, she waited until he fell in love with her." Abigail's eyes twinkled with delight. "My mother was lovely—with doe-colored skin and fawn-like eyes. She wore her jet-black hair in a long braid down her back. Father quickly became entranced by her grace and her ability to glide swiftly and silently through the woods. They began to take long walks into the forest together and she taught him many things.

"Henry, my father, worked during the day on the things he'd come to do: build the one-room school house, stock it with books and desks and supplies, have meetings with lawyers…but in the evenings he ran through the moon-filled woods with my mother. They would strip off their clothes and swim in the dark lake, or go for canoe paddles in the moonlight. And finally, in the way of Indians, my mother came to him at night in his tent and made love to him, claiming him as her own. My mother and father were married around the ceremonial fire in the Sacred Clearing."

332

Abigail smiled. "To my core, I am a Quaker. Those were my first roots. I learned, as a small child, to sit in silent worship, waiting for the Spirit to speak within my soul. As a community, we sought the guidance of the Spirit of Christ for our lives and then obediently followed that guidance without hesitation. So, it was among the Quakers that I learned to allow the Divine Spirit to speak to me and guide me in all things. To me, life lived in such a way is as natural as breathing air.

"When my mother's father, the chief, died, she told my father she wanted to move back. Henry Stewart was always a kind man of great compassion and sensitivity. He knew Mother's soul and loved her deeply. He had watched her grow in longing for her home over the years and so he was prepared for her request to return.

"I remember loving it *and* finding it very strange to leave our house and farm and our Quaker community to come here to this cabin, and live with the relatives I thought I knew and had visited regularly. I was homesick for the Quakers—but also in heaven, because I had the opportunity to live deeply into the lifestyle of my mother's world and apply the things she had taught me. At the same time, I was well educated. I loved school, so after we returned to this land, I walked to the bus stop, a mile out of the woods every morning and eventually graduated from high school. Once I was done, I went to college and on to graduate school.

She paused for a moment, looking at her young friends. "I also spent *my* wedding night here." She smiled and then sadness settled.

"My husband Luke was a beautiful soul. I'll never forget when I first saw him. He was surrounded by celestial light and angelic bodies. It was the first time I'd ever seen such a thing."

She turned to Lillie. "Thee has heavenly beings all brightly lit around thee too." Lillie took this in with reverence of heart.

"It was a balmy spring evening and everyone was out on the green. Luke was standing under a tree on the campus of my graduate school and there he was, shining like a beacon. I was helplessly drawn to him like a moth to the light.

"As casually as I could, I introduced myself. We became fast friends when we found we were both graduate students of the human sciences. I was a sociology and religion student and he was in psychology."

333

A sweet smile softly touched her lips as she gazed out over the clearing and the lake beyond. Turning to them, as if she had just remembered they were there, she said, "Luke was my one true love. He loved the mixture in my heritage and cherished his visits with both sides of my family. He especially loved it here." Tears sparkled at the corners of her eyes in concert with the bejeweled lake in front of them.

Lillie was mesmerized. "What did he do? What was he like?"

Abigail sighed. "He was a psychologist, in town, and saw clients while I worked for a local social services agency that assisted poor families in the county. Believe me, I may have had the ability to see visions and spirits and perform sacred ritual and do healing work, but Luke was the spiritual one. He didn't even try. He was naturally humble, clear, simple and deeply connected with the spirits. He understood people intuitively and had a wonderful touch in his work with them."

She paused, looking down at her hands, which were folded in her lap. "He was a quiet man but very funny, mostly with me. His was a private humor." She chuckled to herself.

"It was Luke that told me I was a gifted healer." Her voice fell away. "But I didn't believe it until after he died."

Just then a pileated woodpecker squawked and flew across the clearing. Abigail watched it as it landed in a tall dead tree close by. Lillie wondered for a moment if the bird was Luke come to comfort Abigail.

"Cancer..." she said, responding to the question on Joshua's face. "It went into his bones and then into his brain. It took him quickly."

Abigail remained silent for a while. She finally turned and looked straight at Lillie and Joshua. "It is my destiny to carry on the healing work of my people right here in this place, and to be the caretaker of the tribal land trust." She rose and walked to the fire ring and lowered herself down to a squat.

Lillie and Joshua remained in the lean-to, giving her space. They watched as she pulled from her pocket a small, heavily beaded, leather pouch and took from it a pinch of something. She placed it in a pile on the stone in front of her, lit it and began to chant.

Getting a whiff of tobacco, Lillie felt the energy of the clearing. It was as if it were crowded with a host of others they could not see. It wrapped and enveloped her like an embrace, and she had an overwhelming sense that she was home. She took Joshua's hand and squeezed it gently, then leaned her head against his shoulder.

They sat quietly together in the glory of the small lean-to, bathed in light in the sunlit clearing. The hammer of the woodpecker's drum matched the chant of the woman before them. They were honored—Abigail had drawn them into her private world, into the sacred place of the heart and into a universe of meaning.

After making her offering, Abigail returned the elements to their pouch, stowed it in her pocket and stood. She lifted her face and arms to the sky and stood there in silent thanksgiving before moving away from the ring of stones and ambling down the path towards her cabin.

The two in the lean-to watched her go. Finally Joshua turned to Lillie. "What happened back at the Death Tree?"

Lillie looked up at him. "You promise not to laugh?"

"Yes, I promise," he said gently. After seeing how seriously Abigail had taken all of what had happened he had no intention of doing anything different himself.

"Okay, then. The tree...spoke to me."

Joshua's eyebrows lifted in surprise but he remained silent and encouraged her to go on.

"I felt an amazing vibration and it resonated in my heart. Then I heard...a voice...inside of me."

"What did it say?"

"It said, 'I am the Great, Great Grandmother Tree.'"

Lillie looked down again. "And we talked about Tom hanging himself. She said she'd been waiting for me!"

Joshua looked out at the gleaming lake and let what she'd said sink in. He had to admit it was all a bit eerie.

"I have a strong feeling that I'm at home here...like I've been here before." Lillie stood up and started to move out of the lean-to.

Joshua rose quickly and took hold of her arm, pulling her gently to him.

"Lillie, I know you shine, like Abigail said. You are special! There *is* something about you—I've sensed it since you first came to me at the bar in

Broadley." He looked down at her glowing face, and then leaned down and kissed her softly on the lips. "I think Abigail is training you."

She pushed away from him so she could see his face. "What do you mean?"

"I don't really know. It just seems like she recognizes something in you. Do you think we would be here…" he gestured towards the clearing, "…if it weren't for you?"

"What about *you*, Joshua? I first came to see Abigail because of you! I think she wants us *both* to see and experience these sacred places."

"I think so too, but she's teaching me to see how special you are."

Lillie thought about what he'd said and realized it was true. Abigail *was* teaching them both, but differently.

They had found their way to Abigail and Lillie had asked the questions, but Abigail had willingly opened doors, and taken them into her centuries-old sacred world. Suddenly, Lillie pulled away from Joshua now and looked out over the clearing.

"Do you suppose Abigail…"

Joshua gently finished her thought. "…has known all along?"

"Yes…" Lillie whirled around, "but known what?"

"That you would seek to learn, to know…"

Lillie pulled closer again, her face alight with excitement.

"Do you think she's teaching me to be a…?"

"Yes, I do," he said, interrupting her.

Lillie turned and ran around the fire ring, flinging her arms to the sky and leaping through the air.

Joshua laughed heartily.

"Come, Joshua, dance with me!"

Abandoning all sense of propriety, he did.

Soon Lillie veered off down the wide path to the lake and ran, with Joshua close behind. When they reached the shore they stood looking at each other with heaving lungs, and bent over, hands on knees, to catch their breath. Laughter and breathlessness rolled into one.

After much gasping and hilarity, Lillie began to strip off her clothes and Joshua stared with curious delight. "Let's go swimming!" she said, standing before him.

Joshua, modest from years of carefully guarded privacy, looked anxiously around but when he saw Lillie there in her glorious nakedness, he could resist no longer. She reached for his hand and they walked to the shore and pranced together into the chilly water, whooping and splashing. The water felt wonderful on their sun-warmed skin.

When they were spent, they waded into the shallow water at the edge of the lake and embraced.

"Lillie, I love you." Joshua said, his voice rough with emotion and physical exertion.

She smiled up at him, her eyes filled with the light of joy.

Though refreshed after their swim by a warm lunch at Abigail's, they returned to Joshua's house still chilled. Lillie borrowed sweatpants and a large T-shirt and trotted upstairs for a hot shower. Miriam poured hot chocolate for herself and her son and sat down at the table with him. "You're wet."

"Yeah. We went swimming in Abigail's lake."

"Did she like the cookies?"

"Yes, very much."

"What did she say about the support group?"

"She says support is good but that our anger needs to be focused on justice, not revenge."

Miriam paused for a moment. "Josh you seem to have a special role in this as the only male victim."

"I know."

"How do you feel about that?"

"Oh, I don't know. Fine, I guess. I'm just glad to have people who understand." He had come to assume that the pastor was in the habit of abusing women and that he had simply gotten in the way. He had begun to wonder if his confrontation had caused the incident with Melodie Farmer to escalate, angering the pastor and making him take it out on both of them more fiercely than he had intended. An image came to him of a predator that had sneaked up on his prey, and just at the moment of capture, he'd been interrupted and pushed into a fierce "killing" spree. Rather than lose his prey, he'd struck twice, paralyzing his challenger.

Joshua shivered and tried to shake off the image. "I think I offer something different from my experience in the prosecutor's office and because I'm a man. I hope it's a comfort to the others."

That explanation made him feel better. The group viewed him as a front guard—his walking out of the funeral had been done on their behalf as well as his own, and they knew it.

In turn, Joshua felt the backing of these women as though they were fellow warriors in the trench. He had come out of hiding and found his voice and a new courage that fueled his determination to finally fight for justice.

Lillie bounced in, freshly showered, and Miriam rose to pour her a mug of hot chocolate as well. Lillie took it and joined them at the table, perching on the chair Indian-style.

Miriam smiled. "Joshua says Abigail gave you suggestions about the group meetings."

"Yeah, she was really helpful. She said people like structure and she suggested we pray together." Lillie took a tentative sip of her hot beverage, glad for the warmth. "And we've decided to send out invitations that outline the evening, so they know what to expect before they arrive."

"Well, you'll need to send out one more." said Miriam, now looking at Joshua. "You got a phone call while you were at Abigail's."

Joshua cocked his head. "From who?"

"A woman named Rebecca."

A long, rigid silence ensued as they all looked at one another.

"Another one?" Joshua asked softly.

"I'm afraid so."

"Really? How did she know to call me?"

Miriam shrugged her shoulders. "I don't know, but the word seems to be getting out about you walking out on the pastor. She's apparently a member of his current church in Broadley."

"Wow. So the news has spread even further."

"She plans to call you back this evening. She seemed very nervous. I invited her to come to the group meeting next week, but she wanted to talk to you first."

Joshua looked at Lillie. "I guess we should stick around so we'll get her call." The emotional highs and lows of the day had exhausted Joshua and Lillie. They wandered off to the living room to cuddle on the couch while Miriam put away the dishes and headed out to plant more tulip bulbs.

The afternoon sun was beginning to set, and back in the kitchen, Miriam heard stirrings in the living room. Joshua wandered blindly into the kitchen, rubbing his eyes. With his hair flattened on one side, he slumped into a chair.

Miriam stroked his hair, repairing its shape, and squeezed his shoulder. "Want some coffee?"

"Yeah."

Miriam took a coffee filter out of its box in the cupboard and turned to fill the pot with water from the sink.

"Mom?"

"Yeah, son?"

"I think Abigail sees something special in Lillie."

"Like what?"

"That she emanates a special light...has a special way..."

"I've noticed." Miriam started the coffeemaker and turned around.

"You have?"

Miriam stood against the counter facing her son, arms crossed over her chest. "She has a natural way with people...understands what they need."

"I think so too. I think Abigail intends to help Lillie develop her abilities."

"What sort of abilities?" Miriam asked, wiping her hands on a dishcloth.

"Healing abilities...spiritual abilities."

Miriam busied herself with making a salad while she listened to him.

"I knew she was special...even back in high school." He looked up at his mother as though this were a new idea to him. "And when I saw her that first night in Broadley, she had a special glow."

Miriam stopped her chopping and turned, knife in hand, to smile at her son, and the phone rang. As if by agreement, Miriam took the phone from its cradle and handed it directly to Joshua.

"Hello. Is this Joshua Crumley?"

"Yes, this is Joshua." He nodded at his mother's waiting face. As they both had suspected, it was Rebecca.

"Joshua, I heard about what you did…at the Hopeston church…at the funeral."

"That's what my mother told me."

"I'm glad, I think. But I'd like to know why."

"It was a protest. Lane Richardson doesn't deserve to stand in front of people acting as though he is a man of righteousness." He paused. "I couldn't stay there. I was compelled to stand and face him and walk out on him."

Wrapped in the afghan, Lillie wandered sleepily into the kitchen just as Joshua hung up the phone.

"Was that the lady who called earlier?" A hand escaped from beneath the afghan as she yawned.

"Yup," said Joshua. "And she agreed to come to the meeting."

64

earing about the Crumley-Farmer attendance at Delbert Nelson's funeral, Violet found it to be an interesting coincidence that she had called Mrs. Crumley to apologize that same day. And then to learn that Lane Richardson had been there, and that Joshua and Lillie had walked out on the man in the middle of his eulogy, was another thing yet again. Their actions had set off a ripple through the town of Hopeston, and Violet was secretly proud of them.

For the first time since she'd learned what had happened that summer, Violet realized that she respected Joshua. She hoped that her apology had helped him as he, and Lillie, had gathered the courage to enter the lion's den. It had been a humbling experience for her to call Mrs. Crumley, but she realized that her discomfort could not have compared with what it must have been like for Joshua to go back to the site of his horror.

Violet reflected on the support she received from her husband. He looked out for her unconditionally and had always been there as a solid foundation for her to rely on. Violet now saw that Lillie was doing the same thing for Joshua, and it made her smile to think of her little sister finally finding love.

She knew now that Lillie had struggled with relationships, that her sister's life had been disrupted by depression and she hadn't been able to live alone for long because of it. But Lillie glowed these days, and was staunchly devoted to Joshua.

It was odd, she thought, but Violet wanted to meet this young man for herself. She marveled at the change in her heart—she had changed in the space of a moment from wanting Joshua Crumley nowhere near her family to genuinely looking forward to knowing him.

What kind of man was he? He had responded to Lillie's love and friendship and allowed her and her family into his heart—quite an accomplishment for someone who had been withdrawn for so long. Even in the face of her own despicable behavior, Joshua had not lashed out at her. She ached at the thought of the hurt and loneliness he'd experienced by keeping to himself all these years, and felt glad he now had such a lively and loving woman in his life.

And then there was Lillie.

Violet was overcome with affection for her little sister. How could she have been so jealous and unavailable to her during the darkest times of her life? Violet realized that her own anger and jealousy of Lillie might have actually made her depression worse. Had she been secretly glad for that?

Violet fell to her knees, and began to pray. *"Oh God, please forgive me for my selfish arrogance and my cruel blindness. Help me release Lillie of the blame. Let me face my sorrow regarding Mom and stop putting that on anyone else. Oh God, I'm so sorry I blamed Joshua! Give him strength to face his deepest pain."*

As she stayed still for several moments, she sensed that the hand of Christ was upon her, healing her, and she knew then that her prayers had been answered. The lump in her throat disappeared and she was flooded with peace.

"Thank you, Jesus," she whispered, rose up and began to dance, all by herself in her kitchen. "What can I do to continue this journey?"

And then the answer came. She would have Joshua and Lillie over for dinner!

Kevin vacuumed the living room while the Parks kids scurried around picking up their toys. He had learned long before to make cleaning up a game, threatening that the vacuum would "devour" any toys it found out of place.

Ben, whose tiny Lego pieces were scattered across the carpet, lay on the floor sweeping madly with his arms to collect them, while Sassy squealed and ran screaming to her bedroom to deposit an armload of her toys before dashing back for more. Kevin and the vacuum were one, a merciless toy-eating-monster that not only ate children's toys but had been known to consume a whole child who fell in the demon's path. The final product of all their fun was a clean living room…and a happy family.

Sassy was particularly excited because Aunt Lillie and her new boyfriend were coming for dinner. She had decided to dress up for the occasion and had informed her mother that she would need no help in picking out her clothes.

Ben, on the other hand, was trying, unsuccessfully, to act nonchalant. Instead, he puttered endlessly in his room, repositioning his favorite objects so they could be better viewed.

He set his stuffed raccoon, which he and his father had found dead on the roadside and carefully taken to the taxidermist, in a prominent place on the top of the bookshelf. He dusted off his globe and straightened the area around his partially-constructed Lego Empire State Building. He even dusted off the books in his bookcases. Climbing onto the bunk bed his father had built for him, he smoothed his Star Wars comforter.

While all of the shenanigans had been happening in another part of the house, Violet had spent all afternoon preparing a special meal. Like her children, she wanted to please her sister and Joshua. She had decided to use her fine china and a salad of baby spinach, cheddar cheese, pine nuts and green onions already sat in the refrigerator plated and ready. She had baked a chicken with cornmeal stuffing, steamed broccoli and red-skinned potatoes, and for desert she would serve pineapple sherbet and coffee. They would drink ice water with lemon slices and the kids' favorite, sparkling grape juice in wine glasses.

Violet had trained her children to serve guests in their home, even with the best china, and they were excited. The doorbell rang and Sassy ran from her room to answer the door, dressed in her favorite pink party dress, red tights, a yellow cape with florescent pink sequins, and a tiara with white fluff and fake diamonds. Her feet were stuffed into turquoise high-heeled flip-flops, which made her toes resemble cherry tomatoes.

Violet stifled a laugh while her husband smiled broadly in anticipation of Lillie's response. They exchanged glances as Sassy slowed to walk, like a queen, on her way to the door.

Lillie and Joshua stood nervously on the doorstep waiting for the door to open. She glanced at him and whispered, "Are you okay?" He was about to answer, when the door opened with a flourish. There stood a diminutive and garish fairy queen in all her glory.

Sassy regarded her guests for a moment, demonstrating her haughtiest look, and then broke out into a high-pitched scream. "They're here!"

Lillie bowed like a good subject. "May we come in, Queen Sassafras?"

Squealing with delight, Sassy dove at her aunt's mid-section, hugging her fiercely. Then, extricating herself, she stood in front of Joshua and inspected him with a scowl.

Joshua squinted at her with a serious expression of his own, and then lowered himself to one knee and bowed his head. "Your Highness, Sir Joshua at your service."

Sassy tapped his head with the tip of her finger and the house exploded into laughter. Hugs were exchanged all around and introductions were made.

Violet was profoundly affected by the beauty of the young man Lillie had brought into her home. Though tall, his back was straight and he exuded a quiet poise. His dark hair and deep brown eyes were striking.

But by far the most appealing thing about him was that there was no trace of arrogance in him at all. He was humble and unassuming, and clearly intelligent. An easy intimacy existed between him and her sister—as the evening progressed, Violet saw the little looks, the small touches, the way they listened intently when the other spoke and laughed at one another's humor.

Though he'd been anxious before they'd arrived, Joshua was comfortable with the Parks family right from the start. Thanks to his masterful handling of Sassy's queenly test, the children loved him immediately and he had endeared himself, in that moment, to their parents as well.

Once they were seated at the table, which was fully set and ready with white linen tablecloth, fresh cut flowers and candles in silver candlesticks, the children carefully served the salad plates and then sat with the adults. Violet said a short prayer of thanksgiving and they began to eat.

After a few moments of awkwardness, Lillie turned to her sister. "Thanks for having us over," she said.

"It's the least we could do," Violet responded. "Besides, we needed to meet Joshua." She looked from Lillie to Joshua and back again.

Joshua smiled and took a bite.

Kevin, cued by the silence that ensued, stepped in. "Tell us about your work, Joshua."

Joshua laid down his fork and straightened in his chair. "I work in the prosecutor's office in Telmond County. My job is to prepare for the cases that go to trial."

"Like what?" asked Ben, who was all ears. An avid reader, he had recently discovered courtroom stories and was excited to find that Aunt Lillie's boyfriend was a lawyer who tried cases in real life.

"Well…" Joshua said, taking up his linen napkin to wipe his mouth. "We take the side of the victims of crimes of violence and abuse." He cleared his throat—the adults at the table understood the significance of his words. "We try to make sure they are protected and vindicated…um…supported. We do our best to send criminals to jail." Joshua worked at putting his thoughts into ten-year old language.

"What sort of cases?' asked Kevin.

"Murder, robbery, domestic violence, all kinds of abuse. Rape." The vibration in the room was raised to a new level when he uttered the last word.

"So you go after the bad guys!" Ben said, eyes shining. Everyone smiled at his exuberance, which offered relief from the sudden unspoken tension in the room.

"Yup, you got it," said Joshua, nodding and smiling at Ben.

Ben looked at his father. "I want to do that when I grow up!"

Kevin looked at his son with a passion, and reflected back to him a gentle challenge to do just that—to follow his true dreams and make them happen. The rest of the group missed the exchange, but Joshua caught it and smiled inwardly, recognizing that both Kevin and Ben were deep-thinking introverts like himself.

Violet turned to Lillie. "And what about you? I hear you're not doing insurance anymore."

Lillie's first impulse was to be defensive, but she took the question at face value. "That's right. I got fired for spending too much time here, away from my job. Makes sense, I guess. They can't exactly run a business without employees."

"Why didn't you go back and save your job?"

Hearing no criticism in Violet's voice, Lillie shrugged her shoulders. "I don't know what to say except that I felt a strong need to stay here. After learning what happened to Mother, dealing with that became a priority. Plus, I didn't want to leave…him." She smiled and poked Joshua in the ribs.

Joshua pretended that she'd delivered a blow that nearly knocked him out of his seat. "And I'm *so-o-o* glad!"

Everyone laughed.

"So, Lillie, what will you do for work now?" Kevin asked when everyone settled down.

"I'm considering land conservancy. I really never liked insurance, you know, being in an office all day."

"What does that involve?" asked Violet.

"Traipsing around outside and working to protect the land and wildlife habitats, I guess. For instance, Abigail needs a land advocate in place before she dies."

Sassy, who had been uncharacteristically quiet, piped up. "Who's Abigail, Aunt Lillie?"

"She is a woman who helps people get better from bad experiences."

"Does she work with Joshua in the prostitute's office?"

The table exploded with laughter, and Ben slumped out of his chair and rolled around on the floor, repeating what Sassy had said, over and over. "The prostitute's office…"

"No, Sassy," said Lillie, coughing to clear her giggles away. "Not the *prostitute's* office. The *prosecutor's* office." More laughter was heard and the "queen" crossed her arms and began to pout.

Lillie tried again, looking hopefully at Sassy. "Abigail works alone out of her house in the woods. She does counseling, to help people talk about their problems."

"Oh." Sassy said. She thought for a long time while everyone watched her. "So, I could go talk to her about *my* problem?" Sassy swept her arm broadly in an arc to encompass the entire room.

"Yes, Sas, you could go talk to her about us laughing at you! I'm sure she'd be very helpful."

"Good!!"

When the room had returned to normal, Violet asked the children to clear the salad plates and bring in the main course. As they moved around the table, she turned to Joshua. "Do you have siblings?"

"Nope. I'm it."

Ben shook his head. "You mean you don't have any little sisters always saying stupid things and bugging you?"

Joshua smiled at Ben and looked sideways at his sister. "That's right, Ben, I have no little sisters to bug me. But I'd love to have a sister as funny and smart and beautiful as Sassy!"

At that, Sassy began to parade around like a peacock, high on her flip-flop-cherry-tomato toes, flourishing her tiara feathers. The adults all smiled at Ben, who groaned and disappeared into the kitchen.

65

A
t seven o'clock, a gathering of women sat with Joshua and Lillie in the
Crumley living room. Heidi Spellworth was there and glad to be back.
Elizabeth Hallman had not yet come and it was suspected that she wouldn't
join them—the last gathering had been very hard on her emotionally. Their
discussions had stirred up a host of unresolved feelings and she was taking
care of herself by staying away until she was stronger.

Two new women were there, supplied from Elizabeth's list: Ruth Turner
and Gail Ligatho. A third had called at the last minute to say she would be
unable to make it, but hoped to attend the next time. There was no sign of
Rebecca Jones.

Lillie opened the meeting with prayer, asking for blessings and healing for
each individual and protection for them as a group. She introduced herself
and explained why she was there for the newcomers.

Ruth Turner was a quiet, older woman with short, tightly-curled, graying
hair. Neatly dressed in a light blue cotton dress with tiny purple flowers and a
white cardigan sweater, she wore stockings and low white pumps. She sat on
the couch with her legs crossed at the ankles, cupping her coffee mug in her
lap. She spoke very softly.

"I'm Ruth. I knew the pastor years ago, when he was young."

Next Heidi spoke. "This is my second time here and I am very glad to be
back. It felt good to learn that I'm not alone, that others understand. I was
abused by the pastor during the summer of 1985."

Then came Gail's turn. A big-boned, slightly overweight woman, she
wore new jeans and a tight-fitting scoop-necked top that emphasized her large
bosom. She seemed more relaxed than Ruth, but there was still an undercurrent
of nervous tension in her voice.

"Hello, everyone. Thank you for inviting me."

The doorbell rang and Joshua rose quietly and left the room. Lillie
prompted Gail to continue and she nodded her head.

348

"I worked for the pastor at the Hopeston church as his secretary, and I'm afraid I allowed him to ruin my life. He seemed such a wonderful, friendly, warm person, and he always took such an interest in me. We became very close and before I knew it we were…having an affair."

She reached up to wipe tears from her face. "It ruined my marriage. I became obsessed with him and it took me a long time to wake up to what was happening. By that time, I had lost my husband and custody of my two children."

The group turned to see Joshua return with a tall, glamorous woman in a suit and heels and long blonde hair curled at the ends. They made room for her to sit and then quieted to focus on Gail again, who had stopped to blow her nose.

"I have had to fight hard to get visitation rights with my children and to rebuild my life. It finally became clear to me that the pastor had a problem and that he was going from one woman to another."

She cleared her throat and regained her normal tone. "There was a pattern to his behavior—just as he was getting tired of the woman he was with, he would already be grooming the next one. I watched it happen. I put the pieces together. I could see it happening before my very eyes.

"Somehow I finally got the courage to get him out of my life. He'd become an addiction. I've spent years now trying to recover from it."

Lillie thanked her for sharing and then directed their attention to the woman who had come in with Joshua and he introduced her.

"This is Rebecca."

Everyone nodded and smiled in acknowledgment.

"We're glad you've come, Rebecca," said Lillie.

There was such fear in Rebecca's eyes that Lillie almost decided not to ask her to participate, but then she began to speak.

"I have to say it scares me to be here. I almost didn't come. But I think it will do me some good to talk about it, especially with people who've been through something similar. Can I be sure what I say here won't go anywhere?"

Joshua spoke in response. "Good point. Yes, one of our cardinal rules is that everything said during our gatherings is confidential."

Lillie agreed. "Yes, that's really important or else we won't be able to trust each other. Can we all reaffirm that?" Everyone responded with nods and exclamations of "yes" and "of course."

Lillie looked back at Rebecca. "Will you share with us what happened to you?"

"Everyone else has done this?" Rebecca asked, still decidedly uncomfortable.

"Yes," Lillie said. "All except Joshua. We haven't gotten to him yet."

Joshua looked at Rebecca. "Would you like me to go first?"

"No, I'll go." She took a deep breath and began. "I used to attend Broadley Community Church, where he serves currently. I was separated from my husband and went to the pastor for counseling. It was very helpful, as my divorce proceeded and then became final, to have someone supportive to talk to. He's a very good counselor."

Other heads in the circle nodded in agreement with what she'd said, which seemed to give her courage to continue.

"I trusted him totally and told him everything. All my secrets." Her eyes began to water and she looked around the circle at the others.

"Then I got news—just this month—that my nephew had been injured in a car accident and I was devastated. He was in critical condition and we didn't know if he would live. I called the pastor and asked him to come over and he did..." She stopped, struggling with her emotion and trying desperately not to cry.

Heidi spoke softly to her. "Rebecca, it's okay to cry here. You can let it out. It feels much better than keeping it all bottled up inside."

"Yup, that's why we're here, to let it all out, so we don't have to carry it alone anymore," Lillie said softly, handing her the box of tissues. Rebecca took it and shook her head, indicating that she couldn't continue. Lillie thanked her for sharing and turned the attention on Joshua.

"Well," he said, "I'm Joshua. Other than the first time, when we met with Heidi and Elizabeth, I've never been in a group like this before and certainly not with just women." He smiled brilliantly at them and they all giggled.

"As far as we know, I'm the only male the pastor has abused. It was an accident of timing in a way, but its result was equally devastating to me."

As Joshua told his story the women listened intently. Gasps escaped and tears fell as they heard the details and empathized with his anger and fear, the pain and the isolation of a boy hurt and a young man trying to live. Once he was done, there was a stunned silence in the room.

Having listened quietly to everything the others had said, Ruth cleared her throat. Her voice was so soft they had to strain to hear her words.

"I was a lifetime member of the first church the pastor served, Newbery Community Church. He came to us straight out of seminary—young, twenty-five years old, and full of energy and ideas. He brought such life to our congregation." She stopped and blew her nose.

"I couldn't help myself. I was so drawn to him. I had never met anyone like him before, so I volunteered to help him with one of his projects not too long after he arrived. We worked closely together and he was so attentive and friendly..." She dabbed at the corners of her eyes with the tissue and glanced up quickly.

"I'd never *been* with a man. I'm an old maid, I guess you'd say." She lowered her gaze, again. "So when he began to take an interest in me, I was in heaven. I thought he loved me. He even told me so. One day he said he wanted to marry me." She swallowed hard.

"I was overjoyed. The age difference was rather a lot, but I didn't care. He didn't seem to care either. I was totally carried away by his love.

"Then one evening we went to his apartment to talk about it, about getting married..." She pushed on with a husky voice.

"He was so sweet to me. That is, until he shut the door to his apartment..."

She paused. "He changed, his face changed, he was evil. He forced me to the floor, right there in his living room and he..." Ruth lowered her voice to a near inaudible whisper. "...had his way with me..."

Everyone froze, their own memories flashing through their minds.

Ruth continued, tears now sliding down her cheeks. "Once he was done, he left me there on the floor and went to his kitchen to get a drink, just like nothing had happened.

"I was so frightened. All I wanted to do was get away but I didn't know what to do or how to get away. So, I curled up in a ball and lay there trying to pretend I didn't exist, until finally he yelled at me to get out of his apartment."

Everyone in the room was in tears.

"So, I got dressed and left as quickly as I could before he changed his mind. It was dark, and I walked all the way home, across town. I was in shock—afraid he would come after me." Tears continued to flow down her cheeks. "I don't know to this day how I got home."

Ruth took a moment to recompose and then finished her story. "I didn't go out of my house for a week after that. I still don't go out much. I never heard from him again and I never could go back to the church. People who knew me from my childhood at that church tried to get me to come back, but I never could. I never told anyone what happened. I've been without a church ever since." She looked shyly at Joshua and fell silent.

Rebecca, who had listened intently as each of the others had spoken, shook her head in disgust at what she had heard.

"I suppose I should be grateful. He never got a chance to rape me." She looked at Ruth. "I am so sorry he did that to you. I was fortunate enough to have escaped. I ran, and he grabbed at me, but I got away and locked myself in my bathroom, and yelled at him to leave until he did.

"He had put his hands on me, had held me down and fondled me and when I said no, he wouldn't stop!" Her disgust transformed into rage as she spoke.

"He kept reassuring me everything was okay. God, I can still hear his voice! It makes me sick just to think about it!"

When all had shared their stories, something magical had happened. It felt safe and hope filled the space. They talked and comforted each other and promised to come back.

When the evening was over, Joshua took a tall glass of water with ice out onto the kitchen steps and sat down to smoke a cigarette.

Lillie stood with Heidi, who was the last to leave, at her car. When they were done talking, she hugged the heavy-set woman, and held the door as Heidi lowered herself into her shiny compact car. Watching as the car pulled away, Lillie reflected on the events of the evening. She turned to see Joshua sitting on the steps, and she smiled at him.

She was beginning to hate seeing these women leave after group gatherings. They were becoming fast friends, bonded by the traumatic events of their lives and the trust that develops between those who share their pain and struggle with one another. She had come to feel protective of them, too, as if they had somehow been placed under her care.

She sat on the step below Joshua and wiggled back to lean against him. He set his glass aside and stroked her hair. They sat quietly for a long time, savoring the closeness between them.

As the sun went down, the yard was left in shadow. A slight breeze cooled their skin and brought with it the fragrance of roses from Miriam's garden. Locusts and crickets sang loudly and filled the air with vibration. Lillie looked over at the flowers.

"Your Mom is really going to town on her garden."

"Yeah. She hasn't worked on that for years." Joshua responded, suddenly struck by the fact.

"You think it has anything to do with what's going on?"

"Like what?"

"Well, you opening up and talking to her, the walk-out, the support group, going to see Abigail…me?" Lillie grinned at the last. She lifted her chin and tipped her head back to look up at him.

He smiled and thought a moment before bending down to kiss her upturned forehead. "Yeah. Maybe she has more of a purpose, or maybe it's nervous energy. I'm not sure which. Whatever it is, I think it's good."

A few cars drove by on the street and a dog barked somewhere in the neighborhood.

"Pretty amazing group this evening. I'm proud of everyone for sharing like that!" said Lillie.

"Hmmm."

"It's unbelievable what that man has done," Lillie said. She turned to face him. "How can someone do all that and never seem to show any remorse? I just don't get it! How is that possible?"

He reached down and gently touched her cheek with his finger and smiled, the look of love in his eyes. "I don't know, my nature child, but you make up for people like that. You were amazing this evening."

"So were you," she responded. "When you told your story, I think it helped the others open up—Ruth in particular, and certainly Rebecca."

"I guess we make a good team."

"Yeah, I think so too." She paused for a moment. "Do you think Elizabeth will ever come back?"

"I don't know. But I think we should encourage her to. These women need each other."

"How about you? Do *you* need them?"

Joshua was thoughtful for a long time, looking off across the yard. "Yes...I do," he said finally.

"They give me solid ground under my feet...a place to feel known and be seen. They care and I need that." He looked down at Lillie and smiled, taking her by the shoulders. "But mostly, I need you, Lillie Farmer. You fill my soul and help me know myself. You've given me a reason to live, beyond my work, for the first time. I don't even think about my work when I'm with you."

His eyes glistened as he looked deeply into her radiant eyes. "I love you."

Lillie stood up and pulled him forward to her. "I love *you*!"

Then she pushed him back. "How about we go get a burger and a beer? I'm hungry as a bear after all that sharing!"

Joshua grinned at her and leaned forward, pecking her hard on the lips. She plopped in his lap and kissed him soundly. "None of that pecking stuff, Joshua Crumley."

He took her face in his hands and brought it to him and kissed her again very gently, long and sweet.

"Better?" he asked, eyes twinkling as she melted like jelly in his arms.

She broke away from him and ran, laughing, to the car.

Part Five

The River

66

enelope Johnston made her way up the neatly manicured front walk of Dorothy Banks' home.

For days, Penelope had kept herself busy to distract her thoughts, but in idle moments, the idea that Pastor Lane, a man she highly respected, loved and admired, might have done this awful thing to Melodie Farmer was all she could think about.

Penelope had liked Melodie—she had been the most pious and devout person she'd ever known, always present for church events, behind the scenes, humbly offering what she could. So Melodie's sudden disappearance from church had been puzzling and Penelope had meant to call her afterwards to see if she was okay, but had never gotten around to it. Now she felt ashamed—it made her sad to think how painful and lonely it must have been for Melodie if, in fact, what Martin said had actually happened.

She knew that Dorothy had been a friend of Melodie's and was still active in the church, so she had called her, saying she wanted to talk about something relating to the church and had been pleasantly surprised when Dorothy had invited her to come over that very afternoon.

Soon the two women were sipping tea in Dorothy's vine-shaded sunroom, talking about gardening, recipes, and shopping for bargains. Short and a little stocky, her strawberry blonde hair sprinkled with gray, Dorothy's freckled features were pinched and focused, eyes intent.

After a few minutes of social chatter, Penelope changed the subject to the church. "Dorothy, how long have you been teaching Sunday School at Hopeston church?"

"Oh, gosh!" Dorothy thought about it. "Twenty years, maybe."

"Have you been teaching the longest?"

"I don't know. I haven't thought about it, really. I just love working with the children. I don't *ever* get tired of it!"

Penelope smiled. "Is that the way all the teachers feel, do you think?"

"Well, some maybe. But really that love of teaching, loving the kids…isn't always there. I think only the best teachers have that."

"So, there have been others who love it as much as you do?"

"Only one."

"Who?"

"Melodie Farmer." Dorothy lowered her gaze and took a sip of tea. "I think she may have loved it more even! She adored the children. I think it was the combination of her being a wonderful storyteller and a truly devoted believer that captured their little hearts. The children felt her genuine love and loved her back!

"It was Melodie who got me interested in teaching Sunday School in the first place. We used to work on our lesson plans together and come up with craft projects that went along with the stories." She paused for a moment, remembering.

"Melodie was a very creative, fun person…kind of childlike herself. Maybe that's why she got along with the children so well. We had so much fun planning and teaching. *She* made it fun." Dorothy looked out the window, lost in thought and absentmindedly wiped at a tear that had trickled down her cheek.

"You miss her," said Penelope softly.

"Oh, yes." Dorothy turned back to Penelope, her face flushing pink. "It was never the same without her after she left."

Penelope watched her carefully, feeling a little guilty for traipsing around on such obviously tender ground. "Why did she leave?"

"Oh, I don't know." Dorothy said, pulling back. "But we kept things going. The program is as strong as ever. But enough about that. What church stuff did you want to talk about, Penelope? I do need to get going here pretty soon."

"Actually it's Melodie I wanted to talk about."

A shadow passed over Dorothy's face. "Oh, well…I can't…I…"

Penelope placed her hand on top of Dorothy's. "It's okay to miss her. It sounds like she was a close friend."

Dorothy retracted her arm and stood up. "I can't talk about this."

"You can't talk about what?"

"I can't tell you why Melodie left." Tears oozed from Dorothy's eyes and she turned her back on Penelope. A moment passed and then she sat back down. She took a deep breath—it was apparent she had changed her mind.

"I've never talked about this with anyone, but…he came to us and told us that Melodie was a sinful woman—that she had tried to seduce him. But I never believed it. Melodie would never have done that! She worshipped him. He was like Jesus to her!"

Heat rose up Penelope's neck. "Who was like Jesus to her, Dorothy?"

"The pastor was."

"Pastor…Lane?"

"Yes! He said he had to ask her to leave the church because she had refused to…to stop when he had asked her to." Dorothy began to cry.

"So, that was it? And poof, she was gone?"

"Yes. And he told us not to tell anyone. I feel uncomfortable even telling you now. He said he didn't want to ruin her reputation, but that it was best just to remove her before she infected others."

Penelope was incredulous. "He actually *said* that?"

"Yes! But it couldn't have been true. It's as though he was talking about somebody we didn't even know. I was in such shock I didn't know what to do."

Penelope sighed, not sure she wanted to know the answer to her next question. "So, what do you think really happened?"

Dorothy glared at her, with anger in her eyes. "You *really* want to know what I think? I think it was the pastor who was too friendly with *Melodie*. She left because *she* was uncomfortable. He said something about letting unrepentant sinners walk their own dark paths, but I think when he told us not to tell anyone, he was covering up his *own* behavior."

Penelope had held out some hope that what Martin had said wasn't true, but now, in her gut, she knew that it was.

"Did you ever contact her?"

"No. I never did." Dorothy began to sob. "I wanted to, but I felt I would be betraying the pastor's trust so I never did."

After a moment, she wiped her eyes and looked at Penelope. "Why are you asking about Melodie now? That was a long time ago."

"Well, Dorothy, I recently received information about what may have caused her to leave the church, and I wanted to know what you knew."

"What information?"

"I have reason to believe that Melodie wasn't just uncomfortable. It appears that Pastor Lane may have done something awful to her."

"Like what?" asked Dorothy, watching her closely while blowing her nose in a tissue.

"I want to be careful here, because we have no real proof, but let's just say I don't think Melodie Farmer was the one who was guilty of seduction."

"I knew it! I suspected that he did something to her! After she left, I watched him. I think he has a problem, a thing about women."

"Really?" Penelope was intrigued. "What makes you say that?"

"He touches women a lot. He was always kissing and hugging the women in the congregation. There were other Bible Series teachers who left the church too. Something was just not right."

Martin stood at his workbench repairing the mower, concentrating so thoroughly that he didn't hear the car drive up his lane. It wasn't until the shadow fell across the bench that he realized someone was present.

He turned his head to see a woman standing silhouetted in the light of the doorway. Though she greeted him, he still did not recognize her.

"Can I help you?" he said, wiping his hands off on a rag. Each waited for the other to say something else to break the awkward silence.

"I'm Penelope…Johnston. Mike's wife."

"Oh."

"Do you have a minute, Martin?"

"Yup."

"I'd like to talk. Can we go somewhere to sit down?"

Martin saw Penelope's discomfort, but not knowing her agenda, he was unwilling to make whatever this was too easy for her. He motioned for them to move out into the yard, and as he walked along the drive to the porch on the front of the house he could hear the crunch of her shoes on the dirt as she followed him. He mounted the steps and motioned for her to sit, and stood, in courtesy, as she took the wicker chair.

"Would you like something to drink?"

"Oh, don't go to any trouble for me."

"It's no trouble."

"Okay, water with ice. Thank you."

Martin turned without another word and disappeared into the house.

Penelope's heart pounded violently in her chest. She looked out at the meadow and breathed deeply, hoping to regain a sense of peace.

Martin took his time in the kitchen. He washed his hands thoroughly so as to collect himself and filled two glasses with ice and water from the tap. Then he made his way slowly back out to the porch. Penelope took the glass with a nod and a slight smile.

Martin sat down, a safe distance from her, in another wicker chair. "So, what brings you by?"

"I wanted to talk to you…after Mike…" She stumbled over her words, and blushed bright red with embarrassment.

Martin said nothing.

"Martin, I don't know how to begin. But since Mike spoke with you about… about Lillie and Joshua and…Melodie…I felt the need to talk with you myself."

"Okay."

"Would you tell *me* what happened?"

"What happened to Melodie, you mean?"

"Yes, please. Why she left the church."

"Your husband didn't tell you?"

"He didn't share details."

Wrinkles formed on Martin's forehead and he gave her a hard look. He considered the woman in front of him for a long time, trying to discern her motives, and then decided to just lay it on the line.

"She left because the pastor molested her and then finally raped her." He would spare no detail if that's what Penelope wanted. He was no longer willing to use careful language about what the pastor had done to his wife.

Penelope felt the force of his words like a slap on the face, and she forced herself to repeat his words. "Your wife was *raped* by Pastor Lane?"

"Yes." Martin took a gulp of water.

"Oh, that's awful, Martin. I...I am so sorry!" Penelope's throat constricted with emotion.

Martin looked out over the meadow.

"Did you know her?" he asked, sadness filling his eyes.

"Yes, though, I admit, not really well. I knew her well enough to know that she was devout, faithful, and hard-working; a woman who lived the Christian values genuinely."

A tear trickled down Martin's cheek.

Penelope coughed, working hard to clear her throat. "I was surprised when she left the church. I always meant to call her." The silence thundered between them.

"As hard as it is to imagine the pastor doing such a thing," she continued, "it's even harder to imagine Melodie trying to seduce the pastor, which is what he told the people at the church."

Penelope now let her own tears flow. "I'm so sorry I never called her. I should have reached out to her, but I didn't."

Martin turned to look at her. "I'm not sure it would have done her any good. She was so closed down after that...I'm afraid she couldn't receive our help."

"She needed support, Martin. That's a horrible thing to go through! But when it's your pastor, that's worse. Much worse!"

"And not one of her friends from the church called her."

"He told them not to."

Martin nodded. "That's what I've heard. What I don't understand is why there is such loyalty to the man."

"He's the best, Martin...in everything. There isn't a better pastor than Pastor Lane Richardson!" She told him how Pastor Lane had close relationships with those he served, how he was really a good counselor and preacher.

Everything suddenly made sense. "So that's why Joshua Crumley and your Lillie walked out of Delbert's funeral."

"Yes, and because he violated Joshua, too."

Penelope's mind whirred. "What do you mean? When he was just a boy?"

Martin nodded. "He was trying to stop the pastor from hurting Melodie."

Fear flooded Penelope's heart. She had boys of her own, now men off living their adult lives. But they had once been trusting, awkward adolescents too. How in the world would she have handled it if such a thing had happened to one of her sons? If the world was a place where gentle, devout, Christian women were destroyed by rape, and where young boys were chewed up trying to do the right thing, if it was a place where trusted spiritual leaders robbed boys and women of their innocence and purity of heart, then it was a dark world indeed.

"Oh, Martin!" she gasped. "He's a monster!"

Martin turned slowly and looked at her, with an unfathomable sadness. "It helps that you believe me."

Penelope was in a fog all the way home. How could her world be so different from what she had believed it to be all these years? If she had been so oblivious to what Pastor Lane was doing, then what else had she been blind to? What other falsehoods and lies were being perpetrated right under her nose without her having even the slightest clue?

As Dorothy said, she had thought the pastor overly affectionate with the women of his congregation, but had explained it away as nothing. She had wondered why so many women tended to leave the church and not return, but had thought nothing more of it at the time. Now, she thought, if Melodie and Joshua had been caught in the pastor's web, perhaps there were others.

She recalled Pastor Lane's face during Delbert's funeral when Joshua had stood and walked out. The pastor had been startled and then angry—but there was something else too.

Penelope pulled into her driveway and turned off the engine, but remained in the car.

From the kitchen window, Mike watched his wife. She had seemed distracted since he'd visited Martin Farmer. Though she had tried to talk with him about what he'd learned, he hadn't been able to come to grips with it himself, much less talk with her about it.

He felt sure nothing good could come of putting more energy into the now decade-old saga of Melodie Farmer and Pastor Lane. Hadn't Penelope been the one to suggest that he stay out of it in the first place?

After he'd gone to see Martin, he had decided to do just that. Though he'd agreed to call Pastor Lane after, he hadn't done it. He had decided that if the pastor wanted to talk to him, he would have to do the calling. So now what was going on with Penelope?

He opened the back door and crossed the yard to tap gently on the window. When she opened the door, he leaned in. "Are you okay?"

Penelope glanced up at her husband and reached for her purse before getting out. "No, I'm *not* okay."

"What's wrong, sweetheart?"

Ignoring his question, she turned and walked slowly into the house. Her husband followed her, dread creeping into his heart. When they reached the kitchen, she faced him and spoke.

"I know you don't want to talk about what happened to Melodie Farmer, but I'm going to need to." When she saw his face harden, she added, "Not now, I'm too tired to talk about it now. But, Mike, whether you like it or not, we're going to have to face this."

She turned and headed upstairs. When she reached the top, she called down to him. "I'm going to take a nap. Order pizza for supper and wake me in an hour."

He was stunned. He didn't want to go where Penelope planned to make him go, but he had long since learned not to cross her when she was adamant about something. She was usually right about stuff like this—he had to admit that his wife had always had good instincts. Not knowing what else to do with himself, he retrieved a beer from the refrigerator and switched on the TV.

Upstairs, Penelope lay on her bed, exhausted, but her mind would not shut down. She thought of Melodie—delicate, naïve Melodie. A kinship had developed between them now. If one woman could be treated with such horrifying violence, *all* could be.

67

When Mike awoke, the sunlight was gone, and the TV was blaring the news. He reached for the remote control and quickly turned it off. Looking at his watch, he realized that he hadn't ordered the pizza Penelope had requested and went into the kitchen to make the call.

Once the order was placed, he made himself climb the stairs to wake his wife—he was not looking forward to the discussion he knew was coming.

When he rounded the corner of the bedroom door, he stopped. The woman he knew so well, with whom he had shared many years of life—relationship, parenting, lovemaking, and arguments—lay fast asleep, vulnerable before him. Unbidden, an image passed before his eyes, a flash in which he saw Penelope raped by Pastor Lane. He shook his head trying to dispel the mental picture in his mind and knelt by the bedside.

Just then Penelope stirred and opened her eyes. She stretched like a kitten napping in the sun. "Is the pizza here?"

"Soon."

"Okay, let me wash up and I'll be right down." Mike left the room.

After changing into her robe and slippers, Penelope went down to the den to curl up in her recliner. A glass of red wine awaited her.

Mike called from the kitchen. "The pizza should be here in a few minutes. Where do you want to eat it?"

"I'm not moving from this chair!"

Mike grimaced to himself. "Gosh, Pen, this isn't like you."

He grabbed another beer and sat down on the couch next to her chair. They sat quietly watching TV until the doorbell rang and they both jumped. Mike answered the door, paid for the pizza and took it to the kitchen. Soon he appeared with a plate for each of them.

Penelope took her plate and set it down on the coffee table beside her. It was time to get this over with. "Since you wouldn't talk to me about it, Mike, I had to find out for myself what happened to Melodie Farmer."

Mike finished chewing. "What's that going to solve?"

"I don't know. But I had to find out. So I went to visit Dorothy Banks from church. She used to work closely with Melodie in the Sunday School program."

"Yeah? What did she have to say?"

"That she has always suspected Melodie left so suddenly because of something the pastor did to her."

"She doesn't know what, does she?"

"No, but she said the pastor told them Melodie had tried to seduce him and wouldn't take no for an answer. That he made her leave the church."

Mike took a bite of pizza. "Well, that matches what Pastor Lane told me."

"Haven't you ever wondered about the way he behaves around women, Mike?"

"What do you mean?"

"The way he hugs and kisses us all the time."

"Oh, for goodness sake, Pen, he's a friendly guy! Everybody knows that about Pastor Lane. That's one of the things people like about him." Mike set his plate down hard on the table beside him. "Is it a sin to be friendly?"

"No. But I think his boundaries stink!"

"Poor boundaries don't make you a rapist!" Mike froze, realizing he'd said the word aloud.

Seeing his expression, Penelope looked him in the eye. "It's okay, honey. Dorothy's not the only person I visited. I went to talk to Martin too."

Mike clenched his teeth in frustration. "Who gave you the job of snooping into this, Pen? You're just going to get caught in the middle of something!"

"So, you *do* think something happened!"

"Yes. But we have two opposing stories and no witnesses."

"That's not true. What about Joshua Crumley? Martin said he tried to stop the pastor from hurting Melodie."

Mike sat in silence and sipped his beer.

"Joshua and Lillie left that funeral for a reason, Mike. I don't believe they would *ever* have done such a thing unless they had a darn good reason."

Mike closed his eyes for a moment, resigning himself to the fact that there was nothing he could do to dissuade her.

"So where are you taking this investigation of yours next?"

"I want to talk to Joshua and Lillie. I want to know what they're thinking."

"Are you sure you want to get involved? You're going to get in over your head, you know."

"I'm already involved, Mike. I can't sit by and allow such violence toward women and children without doing something. I did nothing before when Melodie left the church and I'd give anything right now to be able to apologize to her for that." A sob caught in her throat.

Mike swigged the last of his beer and crumpled the can. "You know there will be hell to pay if this gets out," he said, anger evident in his voice.

"I can't believe you are more concerned about the hell to pay for facing the truth than you are about the truth itself."

"I'm not like you, Pen. I don't have a need to always speak the truth," said Mike, regretting his words as soon as he uttered them. "And plus, I'm concerned about what this'll do to you."

"What are you saying?"

"Just that sometimes it's okay to stay out of it and fade into the background and go on with your own life and not get mixed up in stuff like this."

"I can't do that. I have to stand up against this! What if it had been me, or one of our boys, Mike? If this is true, and I believe it is, then Pastor Lane must be held accountable!"

"Okay, Pen, I surrender." He raised up his arms palms facing her. "Go ahead if you must."

"Do I have your support? Or are you going to allow this to drive a wedge between us?"

"You know I'll always be here for you, Pen. But don't expect me to go traipsing around with you knocking on doors."

"Fair enough."

Rising from her chair, Penelope placed her empty wine glass beside her untouched pizza and, crossing the room, kissed her husband gently on the forehead and headed upstairs to bed.

68

In the haze of early morning, Joshua walked quietly down the lane to the Farmer house, listening to the crunch of gravel under his feet. He was alert and aware of the sounds of nature around him—the incessant peep of the chickadee at the edge of the woods, the bouncing scale of the field sparrow in the tall meadow grass. He loved seeing the sunlight bathe the treetops in golden light, promising the advent of a warm, clear day.

Since meeting Abigail and spending time with Lillie, Joshua had come to love being in nature. He now preferred to park his car on the dirt road and walk down the long driveway when he visited Lillie.

When he reached the yard, he saw no one was on the porch, so he made his way to the back of the house. Lillie squealed when she saw Joshua's face appear in the doorway. "What are you doing here?"

"Thought I'd come see the two of you." Joshua smiled, gesturing at both Martin and Lillie as he entered the kitchen.

Martin stood mixing a batch of muffins. "You're mighty stealthy."

"Yeah, well, I love it out here. Don't want to disturb the peace."

Lillie reached for the teakettle. "Want some tea?"

"Sure." Joshua pulled out a chair and sat down.

"You're just in time for Dad's award-winning banana apple walnut muffins!"

Joshua watched father and daughter work together for a minute. Martin poured the batter into a tin.

Joshua cleared his throat. "I came to talk to you about something."

Both Lillie and Martin turned to look at him, and Joshua laughed—they were in identical positions, the same expectant expressions on their faces.

"Boy, you two sure are cut from the same cloth. You should see yourselves." Father and daughter looked at each other and grinned.

Joshua went on. "I got a call yesterday from Penelope Johnston. She said she wanted to talk to you and me, Lillie, and asked if I would set up a time for us to get together."

"Really?" Martin said, bending to put the muffins in the oven.

"Yeah. Who is she? I know she goes to Hopeston Church but I can't come up with anything else."

Martin spoke without turning around. "Her husband is the chairman of the board."

"Oh. Wow," Joshua said. "So she was at the funeral probably."

"Yes," Lillie responded. "She and her husband were sitting near us."

Joshua squinted. "Is she a good guy or a bad guy?"

Lillie shrugged her shoulders and looked at her father. Martin sat down at the table, and took a sip of his tea. "If I had to guess, I'd think good. She came to see me the other day, here."

"She did? Mike Johnston came to see you too. Right, Dad?"

"Yes." Martin thought about his not-so-satisfactory visit with Mike, which had left him unsettled. His conversation with Penelope had gone quite differently. "She was really sad to hear what happened to Melodie, and to you, Joshua."

"If she knows what happened, why does she want to talk to *us*?" asked Lillie.

"I don't know, hon, but I have to say it made me feel better just having her believe me."

The timer on the stove went off, signaling that the muffins were done and Martin got up, dumped them from the tin, and placed them, steaming hot, with butter melting on top, on plates before each of them. They all ate ravenously, groaning with delight. Joshua sat back from his empty plate. "I give you first place for these muffins, Martin!"

Martin chuckled and then shifted in his chair. "So, Joshua, are you going to do it? Set up a time to talk to her?"

Joshua shrugged his shoulders. "I don't see why not. Do you, Lillie?"

"No. In fact, I'd like to see what she wants. Maybe her husband's sending her to get more information."

"Or maybe she doesn't like what he's telling her," Martin added.

Joshua and Lillie were sitting on the porch when Penelope Johnston drove up the lane in her sedan. They watched as she stepped out into the hot sun and approached the porch, hesitating at the bottom step.

"Hello, Joshua, Lillie," she said. "Thank you for agreeing to talk with me."

"You're welcome," Joshua said, rising and gesturing for her to come up and take a seat.

Lillie smiled politely but remained silent, watching the woman intently.

Penelope suddenly felt unsure of why she had come. "Again, I thank you for being willing to see me." A long, awkward silence followed.

"I was curious about why you two walked out at Delbert's funeral. It looked very intentional," she added.

Lillie spoke first. "You talked to my dad, right? So you know why."

Penelope felt the accusation of Lillie's words. What had she expected?

"Yes. But I was wondering if you would be willing to tell me yourselves."

"Why? Don't you believe my dad?"

"Yes, I do. But he didn't walk out of the funeral—*you* did. I would like to hear it from the horse's mouth." Her temper was rising to match Lillie's.

Joshua placed his hand gently on Lillie's arm. "Let me do this. Mrs. Johnston, we felt the need to walk out on a man who has done untold amounts of damage to me and to Lillie's family and many others. We felt he didn't deserve our respect or our willingness to listen to his words."

Penelope's eyes were wide. "You believe Pastor Lane abused others too?"

"Not *believe*, Mrs. Johnston. Know. As a matter of fact, we've met several victims."

"This is awful! Joshua you were just a boy!"

"Yes. I was thirteen."

"May I ask what he did to you?"

Joshua nervously glanced at Lillie. Did he want to tell the details of what happened to him? He knew that what he said might find its way all over town, but he decided to answer.

"The pastor molested me."

Penelope closed her eyes and shook her head. "It must have deeply affected you all these years."

"I'm only just beginning to see how much," Joshua said softly. Lillie slipped her hand into his.

Joshua took courage from Lillie's support. "He's been abusing people—women mostly—for years. The most recent case we know of took place just weeks ago, but we know of another case that happened thirty years ago."

Penelope covered her mouth with her hand. "Oh, my God!"

Lillie observed that although the woman before them was well-dressed, her hands were not the delicate hands of a pampered woman, and relaxed. She was beginning to like her, in spite of her initial reaction.

"Has anyone ever tried to stop him?" asked Penelope after a moment.

"Not as far as we know," responded Lillie, her initial irritation gone.

"Why not? How could he get away with this much abuse and never get caught?"

Joshua answered. "We're asking the same thing. We don't know! People seem to look the other way."

"Well, I personally would like to find out who knows about this. Somebody knows something and has never said anything!"

Lillie smiled at her for the first time. "Will you help us?"

"Yes. Tell me what I can do."

"Well," said Lillie, "we want to know who else has been victimized by Pastor Lane, who might have known what was going on, and who was on the church board at the time this happened to my mother and Joshua. Could you help us gather that information?"

Penelope's eyes hardened. "Yes, and anything else I can!"

Joshua and Lillie watched Penelope's sedan disappear down the driveway and basked in the realization that they had been given a gift—an ally. "She gets it, Lillie," he said.

"Yeah, and she could be quite helpful too, being the chairman's wife."

"Where did she come from? Are there more of her out there?"

"I bet there are." Lillie stood and pulled Joshua up and into her arms.

He wrapped his arms around her. "This is a good thing, huh?"

"Yes, it is." She leaned her head against his chest, pushing against his solidness. "If we can get names of people who knew Mother…" she paused as a few tears fell onto his shirt, "who were upset when she left, then we may be able to gather even more support for our efforts."

Joshua rested his chin on her head and looked out over the meadow, now so familiar to him. "I wonder what Mrs. Johnston's husband will think of this," he said finally.

✿

Penelope stood in the parking lot of the church, looking at the building where she and her husband had worshipped for years—where potlucks and Bible studies, silent auctions and Christmas plays had taken place. She had helped prepare meals and sewn costumes, sung in the choir and helped decorate the sanctuary for holidays.

Much of her spiritual life had taken place in this little church. It was where her community—her church family—gathered, where their babies were baptized, pre-teens confirmed, young couples married and friends memorialized. It was a place where a lot of good had been done.

But today she saw it with new eyes. Even the building seemed different. It was now the site of horrific acts of abuse, where the minister she had most loved and trusted had violated members of his flock. In so doing, he had violated and betrayed them all. A shiver ran through her as she imagined Melodie Farmer and Joshua Crumley trapped in the pastor's office.

Penelope cleared her throat and moved into action. She had come for a purpose and she would carry it out.

As she entered the church office, Pastor Terry was disappearing into his study to get some work done. He caught her eye and nodded before shutting the door—he would leave the wife of the chairman of the board to Marie.

Penelope greeted the secretary warmly. "Hello Marie, how are you today?"

"Fine thanks. What can I do for you?"

"I need some information."

"What sort of information?"

"Mike asked me to get past records of board meetings. He wants records from 1983 and 1985."

"The minutes, you mean?"

"Yes. He's trying to remember who was on the board back then."

"Okay. Let me see." Marie got up, opened a file drawer, and began fingering through the files. "Nineteen eighty nine, nineteen eighty six, here it is, nineteen eighty five, and…here, nineteen eighty three."

She brought the two files to her desk and opened them to look through their contents. "Would you like copies?" she asked.

"Yes, please."

"Is that it?" Marie said as she handed Penelope a brand new manila folder with the copies inside.

"Yes, I think that covers it. If Mike wants more, I'll let you know. Thanks."

"You're welcome."

Penelope tried not to seem hurried as she left, but she felt as though staying a moment longer would suffocate her. Once outside, she took a deep breath of fresh air and caught a whiff of fragrance from the flower garden. She smiled to herself as she climbed back into her car and drove away.

Mission accomplished.

69

Pastor Terry slowly made his way down the Farmers' lane. Hearing the car, Martin came out of the barn to greet him, wiping his hands on an old rag. "Hello, Pastor. Welcome." He reached out to shake Terry's hand.

"Thank you for agreeing to meet with me, Mr. Farmer."

Martin led the pastor into the kitchen. "Would you like some coffee?"

"Sure, that would be great."

Martin poured and handed him a mug and led him out to the porch.

After sitting in silence and taking in the beauty of the place, Pastor Terry summoned his courage. "I'm sure you know that your daughter and Joshua Crumley have created quite a stir in town. As a relative newcomer to the community, I came to try to understand why they interrupted the Nelson funeral the way they did."

Martin chuckled sarcastically. "Well, Pastor, I'm glad you came here rather than just listening to all the rumors. I believe I can shed some light on the subject."

He lit his pipe and took a long drag. "My wife, who passed away two years ago, was a devoted member of the Hopeston Church for years."

"I'm sorry for your loss."

Martin nodded, grateful for the pastor's compassionate words. "She and Lillie attended together—I never was interested much in church. I get my religion right here." He reached his arm out to indicate the woods and the field in front of them.

The pastor nodded in understanding. He'd heard from many men through the years that the out-of-doors, with all its beauty, spoke to their spirits better than church's liturgy and structures.

Martin continued. "Pastor Lane was the minister at Hopeston at the time Melodie and Lillie stopped going." He took a puff. "They both loved him. Everybody did. I don't envy your position—he is probably the most beloved pastor Hopeston has ever had."

Pastor Terry thought of the Nelson family. "I'm quite aware of what you mean, Mr. Farmer."

"Lane Richardson apparently developed a pattern of taking women under his wing and mentoring them to assist him in teaching the Summer Bible Series and the Sunday School Program at the church. In 1983, he asked Melodie to assist him with SBS.

"She had years of experience teaching in the children's Sunday School program, which she loved, and she was thrilled with the chance to extend her work into the summer months. I guess it was considered quite an honor to be mentored directly by him." He turned to look at Pastor Terry. "But it turns out that our beloved Pastor Lane abused his power. And my wife was one of his victims."

Pastor Terry was confused. "One of his victims? What do you mean?"

"I mean the pastor sexually violated my wife. I came home from work one day and found her locked in our bedroom, unwilling to come out. In the eight years she lived after that, she never once spoke of it to me."

The pastor listened in shock. It was not what he'd expected.

"All any of us knew was that she withdrew from the church and from us as well. We all lost her, especially Lillie, who is my youngest."

"Then how did you find out?"

"Melodie kept diaries. She wrote in them the whole time we were married. After her death, I read about it in one."

"Does your daughter know? Is that why she walked out?"

"Yes."

"But what of Joshua?"

"He knows too."

"Does anyone else know about this?"

"Probably more than are willing to say."

Terry sat quietly, musing over what Martin had said. "You said victims—plural not singular. Were there others?"

"Yes. We're discovering now that there are quite a few."

"I have only one more question, Mr. Farmer. Why didn't *you* walk out?"

"They felt a need to make a statement—to protest outwardly, publicly. I supported their actions, of course, but it wasn't my need to do likewise."

By the time Terry got in his car to leave, he was nauseous. He didn't want to believe that his predecessor had used his position and influence in such an offensive way, but if it was true, he could not sit on the information now that he'd been told and do nothing. As a clergyman, he was obligated to report abuse, to give credence to all who believed themselves victims of abuse. He was compelled to reach out to other members of his congregation who might have been affected by the abuse as well.

Nothing he had encountered was as serious as this situation. Anything he'd been called to do before paled in comparison. How does one proceed, he thought, knowing how much people loved the man he'd been told was an abuser, a sexual predator?

He already knew he was less popular than Pastor Lane had been—this certainly wouldn't help. Tears spilled down his cheeks as he drove and he began to pray aloud. *"Help me, Lord! Please show me what to do! Clearly people have suffered as a result of this man's behavior—I don't even know how many! Why, Lord, did you put me in this position to follow such a man...why have you given me the obligation to reveal such a horror?"*

He pulled to the side of the road and wept—for Melodie Farmer, for Martin and Lillie, and for all those victims still unknown to him. And then, he wept for himself.

70

Penelope spread the board minutes out on her dining room table. She scanned the names of the board members: *Mr. Jerry Bomont, Mr. Delbert Nelson, Mr. Ralph Stacey, Mr. Richard Powers, Mr. Stan Vets, and Mr. Marvin Melville.*

She flipped through the rest of the papers, until a section on the SBS session caught her attention.

> "The Summer Bible Series was once again a big success. Fifteen children attended and Pastor Lane was initially assisted by Melodie Farmer. Her experience and gifts as a Sunday School teacher were an advantage, but her departure from the program necessitated a replacement. Barbara Stacey magnanimously stepped in to assist the pastor and the SBS program proceeded without flaw."

Penelope lingered over the phrases "her departure" and "necessitated a replacement." Delbert was gone, so there was no way to find out what he knew. Ralph Stacey had been on the board—it was his wife who'd been called on to finish the session. And then there was Jerry Bomont. If Jerry knew something, Julia certainly knew it as well.

She wondered if Melodie Farmer had ever returned to church at all. Records of attendance are kept, she thought. Then she recalled her conversation with Dorothy Banks, who'd suggested that Melodie had long been a mainstay year after year as a Sunday school teacher. If Melodie had gone missing from the list of Sunday School teachers that fall as well, her departure that summer would have suggested a change more abrupt than had ever been intimated in the minutes. She looked at the names of those serving on the church board one more time: *Nelson, Bomont, Stacey*…It was time to pay a few more visits.

Penelope approached the Bomont's front door, butterflies in her stomach.

"What brings you here?" Julia said, eyes darting, as she opened it.

"Julia, I need to talk with someone about Delbert's funeral and I think it too early to talk to Pamela, so I thought of you."

"Well, yes. Come in. We'll talk over coffee." Julia exhibited an instant change of demeanor. She ushered Penelope into the living room, eyeing her suit and pumps from behind. "Make yourself comfortable while I get a tray of goodies. Cream and sugar for your coffee?" She disappeared into the kitchen, leaving Penelope to herself in the formal living room.

"No. Black, please," Penelope called, as she scanned the room. Julia kept a spotless house with knickknacks that seemed to come straight out of *Better Homes and Gardens*: frosted fruit in bowls that matched the carpet, vases with dried flower arrangements to set off corners, a large painting of the seashore over the couch in colors that matched the living room drapes. Nothing was unique or homemade. Penelope sensed that Julia's home reflected her personal style—a façade worn in an attempt to communicate perfection.

She stood examining a portrait of the family as Julia returned carrying coffee and an etched glass plate bearing store-bought cookies. Sitting, Penelope took a cookie, nibbled on it and then washed it down with a sip of coffee, glancing down to be sure there were no crumbs on her blouse. "I've been thinking about Pamela and her family ever since the funeral. Have you been in touch with them?"

"Of course I have."

"Good. Mike and I have wondered how Pamela felt about the funeral." Penelope hoped, by mentioning him, the visit might seem more official.

"Oh, what a mess that was!" exclaimed Julia. "If it hadn't been for dear Pastor Lane offering his words of comfort, I think the whole thing would have been an inexcusable waste of time! That young pastor of ours has a lot to learn—he should have stepped aside and let Pastor Lane officiate. That's what Pamela wanted, you know."

"No, I didn't realize that. But I do know how close Delbert was to Pastor Lane, so I wasn't surprised to see him there."

Julia continued her diatribe. "And then when those two kids so rudely disrupted the most tender part of his message…"

She stopped. "You know, they should be severely disciplined!"

Penelope remained nonchalant. "I hadn't seen Joshua in years, but Lillie Farmer was raised by good Christian parents, Julia. I don't think she would have done that without a reason."

"Christian? The Farmers? Oh, for goodness sake! Martin Farmer has never before darkened the door of our church, except, of course, when his wife died! And as for his wife, well...that's *another* story!"

Penelope's eyes narrowed. "What do you mean? I recall Melodie being very active in the church when our children were young. She taught Sunday School for years." She paused so as not to seem so eager to ask the next question. "Whatever happened to her anyway?"

Julia smirked. "She made a mess of things—that's what happened. She behaved poorly, so she was told to leave the church. I guess she found somewhere else to cause trouble."

"Cause trouble? What sort of trouble?"

"Penelope, you know our Pastor Lane has always been very loving and patient with needy women. He often got them involved in church life as a way of giving them a place to belong and a way to feel useful. But his kindness backfired in that case."

Penelope was beginning to prickle. "What do you mean? I can't imagine sweet Melodie doing anything wrong."

"She tried to seduce him! Can you imagine that? I know he's a good-looking, wonderful, kind man, but that doesn't excuse such behavior. Apparently he couldn't get her to leave him alone." Julia sat back and crossed her arms, quite satisfied with herself.

Penelope feigned surprise. "How do you know this?"

Eyes flashing, Julia leaned forward in her chair. "Because Jerry was chairman of the board at the time! The pastor brought it up at one of the meetings. It happened during Jerry's first year."

"So this was all kept quiet? And Melodie just left the church?"

"Yes. She left so suddenly the supplies weren't even put away the day he told her she would have to leave."

"But did the pastor ever say what she did? I mean, was it sexual?" Penelope wondered just how far Julia would go.

"Well, I'm not exactly sure. Jerry always leaves out details. But apparently it involved kissing and…more. That's what I heard anyway."

"Well, maybe the pastor encouraged that. He tends to be awfully affectionate with the women in the church."

Julia bristled with indignation. "Oh for goodness sakes, Penelope! Since when was being affectionate a sin? And how can you say that a pastor's warm nature is a come-on to a whore?"

Penelope acted as if she were thinking. "Perhaps Melodie's daughter has never understood why the pastor removed her mother from the church, and there's still bad blood between him and the Farmer family. That might explain her actions at the funeral."

Julia's self-restraint had dissolved. "That girl is no better than her mother! As far as I'm concerned she's a whore too…and now she's hanging around with that Jew!"

Penelope pretended ignorance. "Who? Joshua Crumley? Are they an item?"

Julia gloated. "Oh yes! I've seen them at Betty's Café as thick as thieves."

"But why would Joshua walk out of the funeral? He went first."

"I have no idea about that. All I know is he's a good-for-nothing Jew with no parental guidance. He's fatherless and his mother is a recluse. *They* don't live by Christian values."

Penelope winced at Julia's bigotry. "Let me understand this. You think Joshua took the risk of disrupting the most well-attended funeral of the decade just to support Lillie in an old case of resentment regarding her mother's being kicked out of the church? I don't know a young man who would go to such lengths for a girlfriend." Penelope watched Julia's face closely.

Julia set her coffee cup down on its saucer, and leaned forward in her chair. "He would if he was put up to it by an angry girlfriend who could never appreciate the nature of her mother's violation of sanctity or the inappropriateness of her behavior."

"But why would Lillie dare to put herself or her boyfriend under such public scrutiny if the fault lay clearly with her mother?"

"It wasn't so clear as all that," Julia blurted, realizing her mistake as soon as she said it.

"What do you mean it wasn't clear, Julia?"

"Well, I...I..." stammered Julia. "I mean most people didn't know...it was handled so carefully and quietly."

"Do you mean to suggest that there is some question about what exactly happened between Melodie and the pastor?"

"No," said Julia, collecting herself. "The pastor told the board! He told them what had happened!"

Penelope responded calmly but firmly. "Your husband was on the board, Julia, and you said he was vague about the details. You weren't there yourself, were you?"

Julia's eyes narrowed into slits. "Are you calling me a liar?"

"No, Julia. I just find it hard to believe that a woman as sweet and hardworking as Melodie Farmer was for all those years would seduce her pastor."

"Well, that's what he told us!"

"It's what he told your *husband*, Julia. You just said you weren't there." Penelope took a sip of her coffee, raising a shield to Julia's glare.

"Why have you really come here today, Penelope? It is obvious that the funeral is not the issue that concerns you."

For a moment, Penelope admired Julia's spunk—she was not easily intimidated. "I am trying to put together the pieces of a puzzle. I've learned some interesting bits of information since the funeral."

"What sort of information?"

"Information that contradicts what you've told me. The evidence is mounting that Melodie Farmer wasn't to blame for what happened during SBS the summer of nineteen-eighty-three." Penelope paused and looked Julia straight in the eye.

"You and I both know something happened, Julia. We also know that Melodie left never to return to Hopeston Church, a puzzling fact considering her devotion and level of involvement in the church for years prior to that. She faithfully brought Lillie to church and to SBS. And as you will recall, Lillie stopped coming to church then, too."

Julia opened her mouth to speak but stopped at Penelope's upheld hand.

"We have now seen Lillie Farmer and Joshua Crumley, who also attended faithfully as a boy, despite his Jewish heritage, deliberately disrupt Delbert's funeral precisely when Pastor Lane was speaking." Penelope took a sip of coffee and watched Julia, who remained silent, though it was clear from her body language that it was difficult for her to do.

"I am privy to three sources of information that suggest the version of what happened as you've told me. But I am also privy to a very different version that is, perhaps, even more plausible."

Julia could no longer stay silent. "Who have you been talking to about this?" Her eyes flashed with anger.

"Who told me will remain confidential," Penelope said. "But what I have heard is that it was the pastor who abused his position and seduced Melodie. And that she left the church a devastated woman."

Julia rolled her eyes. "That's preposterous!"

"Is it? You've been at the church long enough to see a number of women work closely with Pastor Lane and then abruptly leave, just as Melodie did."

"People come and go all the time from churches. That isn't the pastor's fault."

"You're right. But there's a pattern here. Pastor takes woman under his wing, they lead SBS together, woman mysteriously leaves the church. It has happened many times at Hopeston Church."

"I don't see how this proves any wrongdoing on the pastor's part."

"No, but you said yourself that the incident with Melodie Farmer was handled very quietly by the board. They had only the pastor's version of what happened. Did anyone ever ask the women for their side of the story?"

"Well, good luck getting Melodie Farmer to tell you hers." Julia's disdain was palpable.

Penelope winced at the cruelty of the statement. "You're right, Julia, Melodie cannot tell us. But perhaps her family is telling us now."

Julia sneered. "And you believe them over the word of our good pastor?"

"They're not the only ones, Julia. There are others in the community who know what happened and were told to keep silent. I suspect there are many members of this church who have remained silent in order to cover up the pastor's behavior. And I believe you're one of them."

Julia rose and moved towards Penelope as if to strike a blow. "Get out! Get out of my house!"

Penelope picked up her purse and headed for the door. Turning to face the older woman, she smiled. "Thank you for the coffee and cookies." The door slammed in her face.

As soon as Julia saw Penelope drive away, she headed for her phone.

"Barb?"

"Julia!" said Barbara Stacey.

"We have a problem, a big problem!"

"What is it?"

"People are talking. Ever since Delbert's funeral, this town has been upset, but some people aren't talking about what happened at the funeral. They're talking about Lane...and what he did."

Barbara was flabbergasted. "You mean his...um...indiscretions?"

"Apparently so. I don't know who's talking exactly, but Penelope Johnston has been snooping around. She was just here asking questions."

"Why would people be talking about it now?"

"I suppose something was triggered when Melodie's daughter and that Joshua Crumley disrupted the funeral. I think maybe Martin is talking."

"Oh for goodness sakes! We can't let this get out. We'll have to figure out who's said what. I'm sure whoever it is has some of their own skeletons. We can start a few rumors of our own."

Barbara seemed so sure of herself that Julia relaxed. "I'm sure you're right. Think about it and we'll talk soon." Julia thought for a moment. "But in the meantime shouldn't there be a board meeting? They would want to know, I'm sure."

"The next meeting isn't for another few weeks."

"Yes, but Barb, your husband is the vice chairman and when there's a need for an emergency board meeting, he and the chairman have equal authority to call one."

"Penelope's husband is the chairman! Who says he'll cooperate with this?"

"He'll have to. The vice chairman has the authority to call a meeting even without the consent of the chairman." Julia replied. "So you need to tell your husband to call an emergency board meeting in order to address the problem of what happened at Delbert's funeral. Then they can handle this other matter at the same time. I'll talk to Jerry, so he knows what needs to be done."

"Okay, I'll tell Ralph."

"What would this church do without us, Barb?"

71

Terry Bunker drove slowly home to the small house he shared with Hannah, his wife of three years, and their young son, Jacob. He and Hannah had met and married while attending seminary as classmates. She had abandoned her studies two years later, just short of their final year, in order to give birth and rear their child. Terry had received his first call as pastor of the Hopeston church.

They had moved into a friendly neighborhood a few blocks from the church and Hannah had fallen into the tasks of caring for the house and garden as well as their son, all with surprising ease given that she had had aspirations of becoming a minister herself.

Terry had always appreciated Hannah's sacrifice and her commitment to being a stay-at-home mom so he could focus on what he quickly realized was more than a full time job. Being responsible for a congregation of believers was harder than he had ever imagined.

As he drove home on this particular evening, he was more despondent than usual about what he felt was his inability to handle the growing storm of controversy and anger that raged in his church. With head down, he made his way up the walk to his front door, and it flew open. He smiled in spite of himself—there stood his wife, smiling broadly. His son stood beside her, holding her pant leg and mouthing "Dada" with the slimy face of a teething toddler.

Jacob fell to his padded bottom and quickly turned around to crawl backwards down the front steps to his father. Terry waited for his curly-headed boy to arrive, struggle to a standing position by pulling himself up on the leg of his pants, and reach up with sticky hands that opened and closed like pudgy lobster claws.

Terry dropped his briefcase and the toy in his hand, and scooped up his eager little boy. "How's my Jacob?" he asked, lifting him up into the air. A long string of drool fell onto Terry's face.

With Jacob under his arm like a sack of potatoes, he bounded up the steps and reached his face to Hannah's for a kiss, who, laughing stepped aside. After changing out of his suit, Terry took Jacob in for his bath, where they splashed and played in the soapy water with their funnels and toy boats. Hannah smiled, as she worked in the kitchen, at the little-boy shrieks and deep throaty laughter coming from down the hall.

Hannah had set the table for two with wine glasses and a candle. Jacob now safely in bed, she and Terry sat together sharing about their days.

"You seem tired," Hannah observed.

Terry nodded. "I am, I guess. This job is too much some days." He looked up at his wife, not sure where to begin, and then decided to just tell her. "I'm discovering bits and pieces of a sinister tale. It appears that members of the congregation have for years covered up some indiscretions of Lane Richardson."

"Really?"

"No one in the congregation has come out and said anything directly. They've all ended the conversations abruptly or remained silent. They haven't confirmed anything, but they haven't refuted what I've said either. They hint at indiscretions on his part and tell stories of certain people who have been subsequently and abruptly removed from the church." Terry sighed and took a sip of wine.

He looked up at Hannah again as the candle flickered at the center of the table, casting shadows in the darkening kitchen. "Because of what happened at the Nelson funeral, I'm afraid I've stumbled on something horrible. I'm beginning to see the real power structure in this church. It appears that if people threatened to reveal any details about what Pastor Lane did they were intimidated until they left."

Hannah appeared confused. "You keep talking about indiscretions. What kind of indiscretions?"

Terry took a deep breath. "Melodie Farmer's husband told me that Lane Richardson sexually assaulted her, but no one wants to talk about it. The church custodian even told me not to stick my nose where it doesn't belong."

"Whoa! Sexually assaulted her? I'd call that more than an indiscretion!"

Hannah sat back in her chair and thought for a moment. "Well, that certainly explains Lillie Farmer's walking out of the funeral. But what about Joshua Crumley? He left first."

Terry shrugged. "I'm not totally sure. From what Mr. Farmer said, Joshua may have known about what happened to Melodie. It appears he attended the summer Bible program and she took him under her wing. People seem to remember him as an awkward, introverted kid who was often under foot, and she was the only one who took time with him."

He tried to imagine what Melodie Farmer had been like. "She must have really loved children," he said, "but after what happened with Lane, she never came back to church."

Hannah stood and began to clear their plates from the table. "Have you spoken with any of those children that she loved and taught? They're probably all young adults by now."

"Well, many of them no longer attend the church even though their parents are active, long-time members. But I think you've got a point. It would be interesting to see what their perspective reveals." Terry drained the last drop of wine from his glass and took it with Hannah's to the kitchen sink. He grabbed the sponge and wiped the table while his wife washed the dishes and placed them in the drainer to dry.

72

lizabeth Hallman sat in an armchair in her bedroom, warmed by sunlight through curtains fluttering at the open window. Encased in her terrycloth robe and fuzzy slippers, she sipped her morning tea. It had been two weeks since she had come home from the hospital.

Allowing her thoughts to flow, a pastime learned during her convalescence, she found them return over and over to the group at the Crumley house. She had been stunned that these strangers had understood and been ready to support her—it was so foreign a feeling that she had, in a sense, gone through a free fall. Now she was emerging on the other side.

A blue jay called as it flew by. Elizabeth felt a gentle breeze against her neck. She breathed in deeply, recalling Joshua's solemn face and quiet presence. His was a different kind of support—he had said little to her but his presence had been a palpable comfort to her. It was humbling to her to find that a person could offer so much to another without uttering a word. His own story, his depth of understanding of the pain and fear she felt, his kindness, expressed through the subtleties of his body language and facial expressions and the selflessness in remaining present to her, had offered her love and she felt it still.

She had never known a man capable of such sensitivity and compassion. Her husband, to whom she had been married so many years, had not been, and now he expected her to be someone she no longer recognized. She had taken care of their household and their daughter Chelsea and had dutifully shared his bed but she didn't know who she was. All her years of marriage had been focused on the needs of others and she had molded her persona around those needs. Even her appearance had been crafted to please others.

Now, as she sat in her robe and slippers, she felt stripped of all those personas and shaky in the newness of it. She hadn't dressed for days, and now she wasn't sure what to wear. Nothing in her wardrobe reflected the new feeling she had about herself, a feeling she couldn't yet name. She wondered how long she would have to stay in a bathrobe.

Elizabeth's sister had been with her for the early days of her recovery, but had gone home. Lonely and scared, Elizabeth wondered how she would be able to carry on. She wasn't even sure she could go downstairs—the needs of her family overwhelmed her. For two weeks, her sister had taken care of all that and in so doing, had carved out a protected space, a bubble of peace, around her.

But, now, her protector was gone and she had to face life again. If she struggled with the simple task of dressing herself, how would she face dishes and laundry, the kids' troubles, and most of all, giving her body to her husband again?

Lost in her thoughts, Elizabeth failed to hear the tentative knock on her bedroom door. The footsteps and quiet voice of her daughter finally drew her attention out of herself.

"Mom?" Chelsea whispered.

Elizabeth responded shakily, wiping her eyes with the back of her hand and reaching for her daughter. "Hi, honey."

Chelsea took her mother's hand, aware of its limpness and the lack of its usual warmth. She held on, frightened by the fear she saw in her mother's eyes. "Are you okay?"

Elizabeth thought for a long moment before answering. In the past she might have said something to reassure her daughter, but now she felt compelled to be honest. Though she knew it would be jarring for them, it was necessary to her recovery, which she needed so desperately now. She had no option but to tell the truth, however raw it might be.

"No, sweetie, I'm *not* okay." She was amazed at the way the answer rose up from her depths, from the place where her heart had its roots. Seeing Chelsea's anxious expression, she quickly added, "But seeing you helps."

Elizabeth squeezed her daughter's hand and drew her closer. "Come, sit with me."

Chelsea sat on the chair's edge watching her mother's face. "Are you gonna come down? Daddy's making pancakes."

Elizabeth looked at her thirteen-year-old daughter's eager face. She took in the loveliness of Chelsea's silky hair pulled into a ponytail, her hazel eyes that spoke so loudly in their intensity. "Maybe in a few minutes." She looked away unwilling to let Chelsea see the fear in her own eyes. "You go on, honey. I'll be down soon." Chelsea rose obediently and started towards the door. "Okay, but don't forget."

"Wait...Chelsea!" Elizabeth called out, changing her mind.

"Yeah, Mom?"

"Wait. I'll come with you." She set aside her teacup and rose from the comfort of her armchair. Chelsea put her arm around her mother and walked with her all the way to the kitchen.

Al looked up from the frying pan. There was his wife, pale as a ghost. "Hello, Elizabeth. You come for nourishment?" he asked, forcing a smile.

Elizabeth's face showed an array of feelings. "Yes. I hear you're making pancakes." She lowered herself cautiously into a chair at the kitchen table. Chelsea set a plate and fork before her.

Al tried not to stare, sensing it made her uncomfortable. Never before had he paid such close attention to his wife's feelings and needs as during these weeks following her breakdown. Focusing on the pancake in the pan, he watched out of the corner of his eye while Chelsea deftly moved around the kitchen serving her mother. He saw her pour a small glass of orange juice, and collect a linen napkin and a tiny pitcher of syrup, and place them daintily on the table. The air was thick with expectation and hope.

Elizabeth remained silent, wondering if she would be able to eat. Faced with the choice of pleasing either her family or herself, she realized how often she had been confronted by this same dilemma. "Okay," she said, deciding to compromise. "Let me try one of your pancakes."

The tension lifted and Al personally delivered a sizzling pancake straight from the frying pan to her plate. "I hope you like it," he said, smiling.

Elizabeth returned his smile. The pancake before her was browned to perfection and formed a perfect circle. Taking butter on her knife, she deposited it into the center of the circle and watched it melt and slide to the edge. As she pushed the butter, aware of its diminishing size and changing shape as it melted, she saw it as a symbol that mirrored her own internal changes. Looking up, she wondered if Al and Chelsea had heard her thoughts.

Her husband and daughter turned away—they had been watching like hawks to see what she would do.

Elizabeth sighed and noticed they ate at the kitchen counter. "Will you come sit with me?"

Once rearranged, they ate in silence, Al and Chelsea trying hard not to watch as Elizabeth fiddled with her food. Finally she took a bite, and Al looked up to see delight make its way across her face. He was glad to see her happy—it struck him how much little pleasures meant in tough situations.

"This is good!" Elizabeth exclaimed, returning his gaze with a shy grin.

Elizabeth's sister's presence had served as a barrier that kept them from the need to communicate, both of them grateful for an excuse to avoid the inevitable. But now decisions would have to be made, and Elizabeth needed her husband's support and understanding. She wasn't the same strong person she had seemed, and she was now no longer capable of living the lie. The idea frightened her as much as the prospect of having to pry true feelings out of her husband.

They had rarely talked about how they felt. On an emotional level, they were as unfamiliar with one another as strangers. They knew one another's habits, traits, even smells. But each knew little of the inner workings of the other's heart, mind and soul.

After Chelsea washed the dishes and tidied up the kitchen with her father, she excused herself and ran off, leaving her parents alone together.

"Al?"

"Hmmm?" He continued with his cleaning.

"Will you sit a little longer with me?"

Laying the cloth over the edge of the sink, he came to the table and sat looking like a schoolboy being punished.

"You don't need to be afraid."

"No?" he said.

"Well, maybe…but I think we need to talk."

"Okay," he said, his voice trembling. "Talk."

Elizabeth waited a long time, unsure of her ability to put things into words that made sense and afraid of her husband's quick temper and impatience.

"I need you, Al. I need…" It was her turn to see the array of feelings play across his face. "I'm still unsure of myself. I guess I've changed." She was amazed at the genuineness of the words coming out of her mouth.

"I can see that," he said. "And, frankly, it *does* scare me."

"Me too," she said, with relief. "I feel like I've been stripped down to nothing and I have to start all over."

Al's eyes were not accusing, as she'd expected. Instead, they were open, calm and intense. He leaned back in his chair. "I suppose that means I have to change too."

Now that the door had been opened, he continued. "Honey, I've been a jerk. I've never before worried about losing you. I guess I've taken things for granted." She smiled at him and sent a hand slowly creeping across the table.

"Whatever we do, I have to continue counseling. I have to face this thing or it will eat me alive."

"I guess so." His face softened. "We'll do whatever it takes, Elizabeth, to make you better."

Tears filled her eyes and she saw the glitter reflected in his.

"Thanks." She started to pull her hand back, but he quickly reached out and covered it with his own.

73

At seven, the women began to arrive. Each took their seats quickly, now comfortable in the familiarity of Miriam's living room. By 7:15 Heidi, Rebecca, and Ruth were settled and waiting. At 7:20, the doorbell rang and Joshua opened the door to see Elizabeth, dressed in a pair of khaki slacks and a light sweater. There was something different about her—she seemed more at peace than she had when they'd met before. He smiled and gestured for her to come in.

They began with prayer. Gail bustled in, apologetic and disruptive, and everyone shifted to allow her to join them. Finally when things had settled down again, and introductions had been made, Elizabeth told them about her time in the hospital and that she had entered counseling with her husband.

"He's really changed," she said. "He realized he might lose me. Guess it woke him up."

"Was it that bad?" asked Heidi.

"Yes, it was. I feel I've been stripped down. It's scary, but feels good too." Elizabeth said softly.

Everyone sat silently for a moment taking in the enormity of the transformation Elizabeth was undergoing.

Rebecca would be the one to break the silence. "It really helps to have all of you to talk to. I'm not nearly as afraid as I was before, not nearly as alone."

At the half-way point of the evening, Joshua spoke. "Lillie and I see a counselor. And on our last visit, when we told her about this group, she issued me a challenge. I want to ask you the question she asked me. What is our goal in having these gatherings?"

After a long silence Ruth spoke softly, "It helps me to tell what happened. I wouldn't have been able to talk about it with anyone else."

"It helps us get over it," Elizabeth offered.

"I think we need to do something to stop the jerk from hunting down others!" Rebecca said with passion in her voice.

392

"I agree!" Lillie said.

"And I want him to apologize for what he's done. We deserve an apology!" added Heidi.

Joshua nodded and cleared his throat. "I've wanted revenge," he admitted. "But our counselor says we need to vent our anger and move beyond revenge."

Heidi looked at Joshua but asked the question of the whole group, "Don't you want to go after him?"

"I want him brought down!" said Gail.

"Me too." Though Ruth's voice was soft, her feelings were clear.

Everyone looked at her with surprise. Even Ruth felt the revenge of which Joshua spoke.

Gail looked around the circle. "Why do we have to move beyond revenge?"

"What good would that accomplish?" asked Lillie. "Wouldn't that just make us as bad as he is?"

"Maybe. But it would stop him from finding more victims." said Rebecca. "And, besides, it would sure feel good!" Everyone laughed.

"So hurting one person is okay but hurting many is not?"

"But we were innocent and he's not," Ruth said finally.

Heidi voiced the sentiment of the room. "How can we stop him without hurting him?"

Elizabeth sat with arms crossed. "I don't know but he needs to be held accountable for what he's done, that's for damn sure!"

"Okay, so, no bodily harm!" said Rebecca and everyone laughed again. "But seriously, what? Do we take him to court?"

The lawyer in the room took control. "That would be very long and complicated," he said. "We'd have to go through a long, drawn out legal process and focus in on only one case at a time, probably."

"Is there an easier, quicker, more effective way to get through to him?" Heidi asked.

"That's it!" Elizabeth's face lit up. "We should appeal directly to him."

"Yeah, without hurting him," Gail said sarcastically.

"That may be the only way to not hurt him," Elizabeth said, thoughtfully.

"By treating him with compassion, even as we hold him accountable."

Gail glared at the group. "I don't know if I can do that. I fucking hate the guy! He screwed up my life! Why are we trying to be so careful not to hurt the goddamn son-of-a-bitch?"

Rebecca stood up and paced around the room. "I agree! Why does he deserve such careful treatment? Isn't it his turn?"

Lillie was adamant. "Whatever we do, I want it to be effective. I want him stopped, I want him to recognize what he's done and apologize, as Heidi said."

"How do we get him to stop without killing him or putting him in jail for life?" asked Gail.

Heidi, the social worker responded. "How about therapy?"

"Oh, yeah," said Gail, again sarcastic, "you think he'll just say, 'Oh, I'm sorry, I goofed. Let me go to therapy and it'll be all better'?"

"Well not exactly. But we could appeal to him, to his better instincts."

"Do you think he *has* any? Heidi, the man is evil! Come on, we all know that!"

"Yes, we do," said Rebecca finally. "But he *is* a pastor and a good one at that. There has to be a part of him that knows good and decency and the importance of making amends."

"Yeah. We all know that side of him too." Lillie said. "That's why we got hooked in."

Elizabeth shook her head. "So, what is this guy? How can somebody turn out so Doctor Jekyll and Mister Hyde?"

Joshua looked around the room and sighed. "That's actually the classic sex offender scenario. It's denial that keeps them from seeing the evil side of their behavior. Sometimes they don't even remember what they've done."

"You mean they can keep that out of their minds so effectively they don't know they've done it?" Rebecca was incredulous.

"Yeah," Joshua said, nodding.

"So, we're supposed to appeal to a guy with a split personality that doesn't even know the damage he's done?" asked Gail.

"Maybe if we bring it to his attention, we'll make him think about it and maybe he'll begin to realize what he's done." Lillie said.

Gail threw up her arms. "But how? I for sure do not want to be anywhere near the asshole!"

Ruth agreed. "I don't want to see him. I don't think I could ever..." she said, fear evident in her eyes.

"Me neither," said Heidi, reaching out to pat Ruth on the shoulder.

Elizabeth shrugged her shoulders. "We could write to him."

Everyone looked at each her.

Lillie jumped up and grinned. "Wow, that's a good idea!"

"Yeah, we could each write a letter to him." added Heidi.

"And ask him to apologize." Elizabeth added.

"And tell him to fucking stop hurting people!" Gail said.

"We could tell him to get help—therapy, I mean." Rebecca added.

"And we could send our letters all together...in one package." Lillie was elated.

The room was quiet for a moment and then Heidi spoke again. "I've suggested to some of my clients that they write letters to people who've hurt them. It would be helpful for us too. It helps to tell a person who abuses you what you think."

Ruth looked down. "I don't know if I can..."

Heidi touched Ruth on the shoulder. "Do what you can, Ruth. All we can do is what we can do."

A peaceful feeling descended on the room—something had shifted, and a path had opened before them.

"Pamela."

"Hello, Lane."

"I just wanted to check in and see how you're doing, my dear. How's the family?"

"We're doing as well as can be expected, I guess—there's no easy way to deal with loss. But it was a big help to have you be a part of Delbert's funeral. Thank you again, for everything."

"You're welcome, Pamela. I wouldn't have had it any other way. Is there anything I can do for you at this point? Any way I can be of help now?"

"I don't think so, Lane. We just have to keep putting one foot in front of the other. The kids have gone back home, but they call me everyday and the girls stop over all the time. They've been wonderful, keeping an eye on me, getting me out to do things. I guess that's the only way to get through this." Pamela sounded melancholy.

The pastor hesitated before making his request, and then elected to proceed. "Pamela, I don't mean to add to your burden right now, but I wonder if I might ask a favor of you."

"Of course, Lane, what is it?"

"Remember those two kids who walked out at Delbert's funeral?"

"Of course I do!"

"Well, apparently they have started a rumor about me. They claim I did something to the girl's mother—Melodie, I think it is. I don't even remember her, really. Martin Farmer is telling people I abused his wife and Penelope Johnston is snooping around too. I am so sad that they feel they need to ruin my good name like this. Can you help me, Pamela?"

Pamela considered what the pastor was saying in silence and then made up her mind. "Of course I will speak on your behalf, Lane. Tell me who to call, what to say. I will help you. You have helped me and mine all these years. This is the least I can do. Just tell me what to say."

Lane smiled. Pamela Nelson would be a strong ally.

Pouring a snifter of brandy, Barbara retreated to her back porch. Staring out at her garden, she recalled all the family events they'd attended at the church. She recalled Mike Johnston's roles through the years—as usher captain, board member at Hopeston Church and now chairman of the board.

Then she began to think about the Johnston boys. Each off living independently as adults now. The older of the two Johnston brothers was more slight and gentle than the other. He had been a sweet boy as a child. He'd always been very helpful at church and loved to play with the children, who'd followed him around as if he'd been the pied piper.

She went into the house and called Julia Bomont. "Have you ever seen Carlton Johnston with a girl?"

"No...not that I can think of. Why?"

"Don't you see?" Barb said.

"See what?"

"He must be a homosexual!"

"Do you think so—that he's a...queer?" Julia began to see where Barb was going.

"What else could it be?"

"That's an abomination!"

"Exactly." The bloodhound had found the scent. "And not only that—but his father is the chairman of our church board. We can't have the chairman of the board and his wife allowing their son to be an abomination, can we? Our board members need to be above sin."

Julia smiled to herself. "Oh, Barb, this is good! How about I have another conversation with Penelope? We'll see how much she wants to continue to tarnish our pastor's good reputation."

Within minutes Julia was dialing the Johnston house.

"Penelope, this is Julia Bomont. I will get right to the point. If you don't stop sticking your nose into places it doesn't belong—if you don't leave Pastor Lane alone—I will send out a letter calling for your husband's resignation as chairman of the board."

"On what grounds, Julia?"

"On the grounds that you and he contaminate our church by allowing your son Carl to fornicate with homosexuals."

"What in the world are you talking about?"

"Come on, Penelope, you know homosexuality is an abomination to our Lord. We can't allow such sinful behavior to exist in our world. You and your husband have a duty to set your son straight."

Penelope was speechless. "First of all, my son is not a homosexual and second, if he were it wouldn't be any of your business."

"Here's, the deal, Penelope. I won't say anything about this, if you will promise to drop all your efforts to look into things...if you know what I mean."

Penelope hung up the phone with a slam. She knew Julia would ensure that the rumor about her son would be out before night fell. She would tell Mike when he got home from work, but she decided she needed to call her son. Hesitantly, she picked the receiver back up.

"Hi, Mom," said Carl. "What's up?"

"I need to talk to you about something." She told him about the events in Hopeston—what had happened at the Nelson funeral, and what she'd discovered since.

"I always did think Pastor Lane was a dirty old man!"

"What do you mean?"

"Just that. He was always doing weird things, touching us too much, being too friendly. We used to talk about it after Sunday school. None of us felt comfortable alone with him. We always stuck together."

Penelope was astonished. "Why didn't you ever tell me about this?"

"I don't know, I guess I felt I was safe and didn't feel the need to say anything. Why?"

Penelope told her son about all the conversations she'd had and the battle heating up between members of the church. Then she told him of Julia's accusation.

Carl chuckled sadly. "Mom, if you worry about what other people say, you'll never get anywhere in life. I've been dealing with that rumor all my life. "Fuck it! Let 'em talk. Don't let them get to you, okay?"

"Okay, son. Thanks. I love you."

"Me too. I'm proud of you, by the way. Go get 'em!"

"I love you, no matter what. You know that…right?"

"Yes, Mom, I know," he said.

She replaced the phone in its cradle with a prayer in her heart. *Bless you, God, for giving me sons!*

74

Three weeks passed and the support group gathered once again at Joshua's house, each with her letter in hand. Some read their letters out loud—others just sealed them and handed them to Joshua for safekeeping. They shared the experiences they'd had in writing their letters and what the process had done for them. The cathartic effect it had had was immense—it was clear to all that the venting of their rage and pain in this way had helped them move beyond the need for revenge. Lillie wanted to share her letter with the group, so they settled down to listen as she read.

Pastor Lane,

I grew up attending your church with my mother who was a devoted believer and a faithful Sunday school teacher. Her modeling taught me a lot but it was from you that I learned about God and faith. You taught me I was loved and safe in God's care, and under your teaching I came to believe in the security of an eternity in heaven with my Savior. These things you made clear to my young heart through your preaching and your kind care as my pastor. You are a gifted man and minister and you have impacted the lives of many.

But one day, when I was thirteen, I came home from school to find my mother cowering in fear, locked in her bedroom. She never recovered from what happened.

That day I lost my mother and with her my sense of direction, hope and security. She never returned to church after that and so neither did I. I have struggled with depression for years since because of the trauma of losing my mother's ability to be present to me anymore. All that I had learned from you in church began to unravel. I lost all sense of faith in life and other people. It was only months ago I finally found out what happened to my mother that day. After her early death, a couple of years ago, we discovered she had written about it in her diary. In reading her diary account I found out that it was you who had shattered our lives.

By luring her and convincing her of your innocent intent and caring concern for the state of her marriage you trapped her into becoming your victim. On that fateful day you raped my mother on the floor of your office. You so shattered her trust and her sense of reality that she was never able to reconcile your abuse with your compassionate pastoral care. She was never able to feel the love and care of her God, her church, her pastor or her family after that day.

Due to her courage in writing about what happened my mother, Melodie Farmer, has given me the chance to complete my own recovery from years of suicidal depression. The truth has been essential for me to finally put the pieces back together in my life. What I have discovered, however, as I sort through the pieces, is that there were other victims, other people who trusted and believed in you, who followed you and learned from you, whom you have also violated and betrayed.

Pastor Lane you are a sick man with a serious problem. Part of what makes you so dangerous is your ability to get people to listen to you, to trust you and to open up to you. The gifted side of you is what allows you to line up your victims. You have left a path of devastation behind you. This path is made up of not only the people whom you actually violated but also people like me related to them and under your care who have been deeply disillusioned by what you've done.

You have violated the trust and faith, the fundamental sense of security and salvation of countless individuals, congregations, and whole communities of people. For years people who love you have excused your behavior and covered up for you. So within the fabric of the very communities you purport to love and serve, as a man of God, are woven the deadly dynamics of deceit and distrust, of fear and betrayal. The true legacy of your work, Pastor, is not the good results of a faithful, godly ministry. Instead it is this awful picture that I describe to you now.

There are countless people who deserve your apology and potential victims who need you to find a way to face your problems and stop this diabolical behavior. You need help. I ask you to take an honest look at your life, at what you've done, and then take steps to change the course of the remaining years you have to live. If you can do this, make amends and seek help to stop this evil pattern of abuse and betrayal, you will restore hope in the lives of many and offer countless a chance at healing. Please consider this with careful, heartfelt attention.

> *Sincerely,*
> *Lillie Farmer*

Everyone in the room sat weeping silently. The fullness of the silence stayed with them. The letters had turned out to be a powerful tool of recovery for all of them. Joshua noted within his heart how wise the healer Abigail was and said a silent prayer of thanks for her counsel.

75

It was Friday evening and Bill Hadley's store was busy. Mike Johnston stood patiently in line.

A second checkout opened after a young woman answered Bill's call over the intercom for help up front. Just as he was moving his cart over to the new line, Mike heard his name called out behind him.

Mike turned to see Jerry Bomont approaching him, pushing a cart.

"Hello, Jerry, how're you this evening?"

"Just fine. The wife has me getting a few things. You too?"

"Yeah, I shop Fridays for our weekly ration. I guess it's my job now."

"Penelope busy with other things, eh?"

"Yep."

"A little too busy, maybe?"

"Nothing unusual. She's always involved in a lot of things. I can never keep up."

"Like getting into other people's business?" Jerry said, avoiding eye contact.

Mike was taken aback. "What do you mean?"

"You know how women gossip, Mike. I suggest you keep your wife on a shorter leash, that's all. She's liable to get herself into trouble, and we wouldn't want that, would we?"

Mike stared at the wizened old man in front of him and considered how he should respond. He might not agree with Penelope's decision to investigate what happened to Melodie Farmer but he had no right to tell her what to do—theirs had always been a relationship of equal power and mutual respect.

"I don't know about your wife, Jerry, but mine is not a pet to be kept on a leash. Whatever it is you're talking about, I suggest you take your threats somewhere else."

"Okay, Mike. I'm just trying to help—a warning from a friend, that's all." Jerry said. "Maybe you should consider calling a board meeting. Things are getting a little out of control and it's our job to guide who says what around here." He waved his hand with a flourish and walked away.

The table was set when Mike Johnston pulled his car into the garage. He brought the bags of groceries into the kitchen and placed them on the counter. Turning without a word, he took Penelope into his arms.

"Hello, there." Penelope leaned back to look at him.

"Hello, Pen. Have I told you how much I love you?"

"Not lately."

He leaned in and kissed her.

She blushed and smiled. "What's gotten into you?"

"Oh, I don't know. I just think you're amazing." He kissed her again.

"Wait a minute there, Romeo. You've been mad at me for days. Why all of a sudden the change of heart?"

Mike leaned against the counter and sighed. "You're right. I am mad. But not at you, Pen. Not anymore. I ran into Jerry Bomont in the grocery store just now, and I tell you, sometimes people just cross the line!"

"Why? What happened? What did he do?"

"He told me you were out of control and he threatened that…"

"What? Threatened what?"

"He said that because you're sticking your nose into other people's business, you're asking for trouble."

"Oh, he *did*, did he?"

"Pen, I thought at first you were getting into something that would only bring trouble. But now, I think you're onto something. Why else would Jerry feel the need to threaten me if you hadn't stepped into something he—or should I say Julia—wants kept quiet?"

Penelope nodded. "We're right, I'm sure. They're covering up what Pastor Lane has done. They know what happened. Julia said as much."

"She did?"

"Yes. When I went to see her, she admitted that the board had secretly handled the situation back then."

Mike shook his head. "Wow, Pen, you *are* amazing! You went to Julia Bomont's home and she spilled her guts to you?"

"Pretty much." Penelope beamed at him.

"I didn't want to get involved, but no one calls my wife a gossip or threatens us like that. I don't care who the Bomonts think they are! Perhaps it's time to have a board meeting about all this. What do you think?"

"I don't know, Mike. But it makes sense to try it, I suppose." She grabbed his hand and took him into the dining room. "But first, I have something else to tell you. While you were at the grocery store, I got a call from Julia, threatening me…and you, too. Let's talk while we eat."

76

The men arrived in dribbles and took their seats at the large round table in the fellowship hall of the church. All board members were present, as well as Pastor Terry.

Once seated, Mike opened the meeting with the usual prayer: *"Dear Lord, we have gathered as your ambassadors, leaders of this church and as we deliberate, help us to demonstrate the Christian values in our interactions with each other. In Jesus' name we pray. Amen."*

Mike lifted his head and began the meeting. "Thank you all for coming on such short notice. I guess we have a situation on our hands, here in Hopeston. People are angry about what happened at the Nelson funeral and there are things being said and done that are perhaps not so Christian. I thought we should come together to decide how we as a church want to handle this."

There was silence. The men all looked at one another. No one seemed to want to speak first.

"Well, I think there should be some consequence for doing something like that at a funeral," said a balding middle-aged man finally. Like most men in the church, Daniel Cross had served on the church board before. "Someone from the board, an elder of the church, ought to go talk to those kids and reprimand them."

Another long-standing member of the congregation spoke up. "Shouldn't they be made to apologize to Pamela and the Nelson family?"

Terry cleared his throat. "May I say something here?" The room quieted. "Ought we to find out why those kids did it before we do anything else?"

Ralph Stacey shook his head. "Why, for God's sake? Does it matter? It was wrong and they shouldn't have done it. Period."

"But there may be something behind their actions that we ought to be aware of as a board. This may not just be about two kids being rude."

Jerry Bomont, who was sitting next to Ralph, chimed in. "Pastor, with all due respect, you're new here. This is *not* something we need to go digging into.

405

The best way to handle this is to get them to make amends and be done with it. Otherwise we are creating a mountain out of a mole hill."

Terry asserted himself. "Jerry, with all due respect to you, you may have been here too long to see the forest for the trees. We have a responsibility to check this thing out. Have any of you spoken to members of either of those families? The Farmers or the Crumleys?"

The men all looked at one another again.

"No," replied Ralph. "Like you said, this is just rude teenage behavior, nothing more. There's no reason to go investigating it as though there is any merit to their actions."

Mike, who was seated next to the pastor, disagreed. "Those two are not teenagers. They're adults now, working and living in the city from what I understand."

"So what?" replied Jerry. "Does that make this any less offensive and rude?"

"Not necessarily, but it does indicate that there may be more maturity behind their actions than just two kids walking out 'cause they're bored and don't give a damn."

Terry cleared his throat. "Well, I have spoken with Martin Farmer about this."

Jerry Bomont looked at Ralph Stacey and smirked before responding. "Pastor, who said *you* could take this into your own hands? You don't know how we do things in this church, do you? The board is the body that decides how to handle disciplinary actions within the church."

"I wasn't taking any disciplinary action, Jerry. I couldn't have anyway, since neither of these young people are members of the church. I was simply visiting people in the community I serve."

Ralph raised his eyebrows. "You make a habit of visiting non-members?"

"Of course!" responded the pastor. "I am called to reach out to the un-churched as well as those in my congregation, and when there are people in my community that are in trouble, I am bound, by my role as a minister of God, to reach out to them."

"What makes you think someone's in trouble?" Jerry asked.

"I watched those two young people leave during the funeral, and I don't think it was boredom or immaturity that motivated them. There was a great deal of tension—something was driving their actions and I felt the need to follow up on that."

Jerry rolled his eyes. "So you went to talk to Lillie's father, like she's a kid?"

"I went to see what Mr. Farmer had to say that might shed some light on what his daughter did."

Mike encouraged the pastor to continue. "And what, if anything, did you find?"

Tension crackled in the room. This was indeed a much larger issue than anyone was willing to admit. Pastor Terry sat for a moment collecting his thoughts. "Apparently there are some deep concerns about…Pastor Lane."

Jerry Bomont turned to Mike. "Hold on, Mr. Chairman! We are not here to talk about Pastor Lane! We are here to discuss disciplinary action to be taken in terms of Lillie Farmer and Joshua Crumley."

"Jerry, you of all people know this is not that simple. Wasn't it you who accosted me in the grocery store the other day?"

The older man seethed. "I can't help it if your wife is out of control."

The muscles in Mike's jaw contracted and his eyes flashed. "My wife is the only other person I know, besides the pastor here, who cares enough about the people involved in this situation to have asked them what they have to say. And Jerry, you know very well, I think, that what they have to say is something that needs to be said."

"Well I don't think it's appropriate for *us* to discuss—we are here to talk about the funeral."

"And we're here because people are behaving in non-Christian ways in what they are saying and doing."

Daniel Cross, who had watched the latest exchange with renewed interest, coughed and then spoke. "I, for one, want to know what the pastor found out."

Everyone stared at him.

Pastor Terry looked down. "Well, Daniel, Martin Farmer says that Pastor Lane…abused his wife."

Jerry Bomont shifted in his seat. "We've dealt with this before."

Terry glanced up, a look of surprise on his face. "You have?"

"Yes, back in the eighties, Melodie Farmer and Pastor Lane had a problem, and the pastor came to the board. He wasn't sure how to handle her insistence on being so close to him and he had to ask her to leave the church. She did—so it was taken care of back then."

"Well," said Terry, "that's not how Martin tells it."

"Of course not! He's angry. And now that his wife is gone…you know people say all manner of things in their grief."

Mike had waited long enough. "Jerry, I think you are wrong," he said. "I too went to speak with Martin—at Pastor *Lane's* request, by the way. And if you heard his version of what happened you wouldn't be…"

"Wouldn't be what, Mike? Defending the reputation of a servant of God? Pastor Lane has been there for all of us, at one time or another, over the years. He's the best pastor I've ever known. You would ruin his reputation on the word of one angry, grieving man? Where is your loyalty, man—your gratitude?" Jerry was almost rabid.

Mike held his ground. "My loyalty is to the truth. My wife has…"

Before he could finish, Jerry was on his feet. "Your wife has been snooping around in other people's business and making a royal nuisance of herself!"

Though irritated, Mike steeled himself. "My wife has had the courage to find out what happened and gather the facts, Jerry. It's *your* wife who has been a royal nuisance! She called my wife threatening to call for my resignation if Penelope didn't stop 'snooping around,' as you say!"

"Well, *my* wife has the best interest of the church in mind. Your wife is…"

Mike stood, eyes blazing, and took a step towards Jerry. "Is what?"

"Well, if she were taking care of her own family instead of being a bloodhound for intrigue, you wouldn't have a homo in the house."

Terry grimaced. "Now, gentlemen…"

Mike would not be deterred. "You need to take that back right now, Jerry. I will not stand here and let you defame my family."

"What," snarled Jerry, "you suddenly found your loyalty and now you want to silence *me*?"

"Take it back, Jerry." The two men were now face to face. Stunned, the other men in the room all watched the drama play out in front of them without moving.

"I, too, am loyal to the truth, Mike! Your son is a homosexual and an abomination to this church!"

In an instant, the older man was lying on the floor, hand over one eye. Terry rounded the table and helped get Jerry back to his feet. No one else moved.

Mike stepped back, rubbing his knuckles, and glanced around the table. "I believe this meeting is adjourned."

One by one the men rose, and left the room. Terry retrieved an ice-filled cloth for Jerry, whose face was beginning to swell. The older man took the ice and held it to his face. Muttering, he left the church.

After a minute or so, only the pastor and Mike remained. Mike chuckled nervously. "I'm not sure we accomplished much here tonight."

Feeling the weariness settle over him, Terry shook his head. "No, but the lid is sure off the can of worms now." He glanced at Mike and smiled weakly. "And in church on Sunday, people will be wondering who gave Jerry Bomont a shiner."

"Sorry about that, Pastor. I'm not even sure what got into me exactly. I'd just had it, I guess." He paused. "You know, it's not that I'd care if my son were gay. It was the way Jerry went after my family," he said, as he turned to leave. "I guess I'm not the Christian you are, Pastor."

77

M artin Farmer headed out of the Hopeston post office to find Ralph Stacey blocking the doorway.

"I don't know what your problem is, Martin, but I think you'd better consider the consequences of spreading such falsehoods about the pastor."

The hair on Martin's neck stood up. "Excuse me?"

"You heard me. It will not be pretty if you continue to spread lies about the pastor, I can assure you. There's the law, Martin. A man cannot just go around saying whatever he pleases about another man without having to face legal consequences."

"If what he says is true, he can. There's a law that says we have freedom of speech in this country, unless you've forgotten."

"Not when it's a lie!"

Audrey Powers stood watching the two gentlemen from behind the counter. Seeing that other customers were approaching the building, Martin waved his hand at her and stepped outside the doorway. Ralph continued to block the door.

Martin could feel the heat in his face. "What exactly am I saying…that you're calling a lie?"

"You claim the pastor did something to your wife…*rape* is the word I heard, to be exact." Ralph's eyes narrowed.

"And how would you know it isn't the truth?"

Ralph's face contorted into a sneer. "This is a man who has served almost everyone in this community. He has been there at their birthing beds, their sick beds and their deathbeds. How can you accuse him of such a horrible thing?"

"Because I know what he's done and when people ask me about it, I'm going to tell them the truth. You can threaten me all you want with the law, but there isn't one that says I am not within my rights to speak the truth."

"You're asking for a legal battle, Martin. You better watch out—there are a lot of people in this town who would be glad to hang you for this." Ralph turned and walked back into the post office, leaving Martin standing alone.

Mike Johnston picked up the phone and dialed the church. Marie transferred his call to the pastor.

"I've been thinking, Pastor Terry. Maybe we should gather the whole community—have a meeting at the church and talk about this. Let people speak their minds. What do you think?"

"Gosh, Mike, I don't know." Terry thought for a moment. "But then, what do we have to lose? We could just say that people have been talking since the funeral and we figured it would be best to…" He paused. "I don't know. Do you think it would fly?"

"Maybe, maybe not. But like you say, we have nothing to lose."

"What exactly would it accomplish?"

"My wife would say it'll help people get it out, whatever they feel the need to say. It would be better than going around threatening people in dark corners like some people are doing."

Terry responded. "Yeah, you're right. I *am* appalled that people have known about this and done nothing all these years. And then, at the board meeting, it was obvious that no one was willing to deal with the truth."

"We don't want to believe it, I suppose," said Mike, taking the criticism personally. "If we just leave it be, it'll go away—that's what we do. But I think it's time to address this somehow."

Terry nodded in response. "How do we go about getting the word out about a meeting?"

"Well, we could print an announcement in the newspaper and invite everyone to come."

"And what will be the subject?"

Mike chuckled. "Proper behavior at funerals? It got the board there."

"Yeah, that'll do it, I think. People would want to come to the meeting out of curiosity, if nothing else. And I suppose the church ought to be about dealing with behavior like people disrupting funerals."

Terry thought for another moment. "I think this is good, Mike. People have asked me to address this. I think this may be the way to do it."

The next morning, an announcement appeared in the Hopeston Gazette:

A town meeting will be held at Hopeston Church on Saturday, October 7 at six pm. The subject of concern regards recent events at the funeral of our former city clerk, Delbert Nelson. The pastor and chairman of the board of Hopeston Church would like to address issues that pertain to members of the community at large. All are welcome and encouraged to attend and share thoughts and opinions. Respectfully, Reverend Terry Bunker and Mike Johnston, Hopeston Church Board Chair.

78

A udrey Powers, the postmistress, called to her husband in his study. "Hey, Richard, did you see this announcement in the paper?"

"What announcement?"

"The church is having a town meeting…"

"Really…what for?" Richard Powers entered the living room where Audrey sat in her recliner reading the paper. She held her cup of coffee close to her chest.

"It says 'the subject of concern regards recent events at the funeral…' blah, blah, blah…'to address issues that pertain to members of the community at large…'" She looked up at her husband's face for a reaction.

He crossed the room to look over her shoulder. "Delbert's funeral?"

"Yeah."

"It's probably about what those kids did."

"Maybe so," Audrey replied, scanning the announcement again.

Richard sat down on the couch across from his wife. "But, why?"

"To make it clear you don't do that at a funeral…? They really struck a nerve walking out like that."

"So, calling a church meeting is a way of letting the town know what not to do?" Richard thought for a moment. "That would be dumb. Things happen— you don't tell a whole town how to behave. That would be a case of the church going too far!"

"So why else would they do this?"

"Maybe there's more to it. You heard the talk in the luncheon afterwards. People were really angry about the way it affected Pastor Lane. Maybe this has more to do with him."

"Like what?" Audrey said, looking up. "He came back to give a eulogy, and a prayer. Some kids walked out when he was doing that. What's the big deal?"

"Exactly. It *is* a big deal for some reason—big enough to get the town together."

Audrey thought for a moment. "You think Pastor Lane is behind this?"

"I don't know. But I do recall issues coming up about him in the past."

"You mean the controversy over his SBS program?"

"Yeah. Remember that big fuss over whether or not to continue it after he left? There were people who wanted it gone immediately and others who felt very strongly we should continue it. There was a fairly major split in the congregation over it, though I admit I never really understood why a program was all that important."

"You're right. It *was* a big deal. People got really upset. There was something about his mishandling...the teachers...or the curriculum...I don't remember exactly."

"What I remember is how much people missed the pastor when he left. They still haven't gotten over it." Richard stood and shoved his hands in his pockets.

Audrey shrugged. "Maybe *that's* what this is about. Maybe Pastor Terry wants people to get over their attachment to Pastor Lane." She looked back at the paper.

Richard shook his head. "Why would he put himself in that position, though, with a meeting like this and the whole town there?"

"There must be some reason, or he wouldn't be doing it. And it's not just him. Mike Johnston's in on this too." Audrey paused. There was something in the back of her mind. "You know, the other day Ralph Stacey got into it with Martin Farmer right outside the post office. I wonder if there's a connection..."

"We'll have to go to find out. When is the meeting?"

"Saturday at six," Audrey answered. "We don't have anything planned, do we?"

"Not that I know of," said Richard, grinning, as he walked back toward his study.

Debra Hundley sat at the counter. "Hey, Betty, did ya read about the town meeting being held at the church?"

"Sure did! That ought to be a dandy!"

Debra lit a cigarette and took a puff. "So, what do ya think really happened? I've been hearing all sorts of stories."

"There are some that want to crucify the man—the poor guy. The pastor, I mean."

"Yeah, but if what they say is true, I say hang 'im!"

"I'm not sure what to think. I still can't believe he could do such a thing." Betty set the coffee pot back on the brewer and leaned on the counter.

Debra took another drag on her cigarette and laid it in the ashtray in front of her. "Oh, you'd be surprised what the nicest guys are really doing behind everybody's back. There's a lot of fakers in this world. I'm tellin' you, I know this for a fact!" She took a sip of coffee. "You gonna go?"

"Of course I'm gonna go!" said Betty. "I wouldn't miss it! Can you imagine this town getting together to talk about something like *this* and my not being there?"

Sunlight slanted in the windows of the small room next to the fellowship hall, casting its warmth on the ladies as they sat in a circle sewing quilt squares for a local charity. The conversation ebbed and flowed as they concentrated on their work. The content ranged from recipes to grandchildren, from hats to who'd recently given birth, from husbands to trips in the planning and their favorite TV shows. The chatter had a happy feeling to it.

Faith bustled in from the adjacent kitchen with a tray of cups, a pitcher of coffee and an assortment of homemade cookies. She poured herself a cup of coffee, and selected a cookie before taking a seat.

"Julia, I spoke to Pastor Terry after worship the other day, like you asked."

A thought popped into Julia's mind. "I wonder if your conversation with the pastor is the reason they are having this meeting at the church?"

"What do you suppose they have in mind?" asked Letty, oblivious as usual.

"I don't know," said Judith, "but I think they should leave things alone. What do they think they're going to accomplish by having a meeting like this?"

"It *is* a little risky." said Faith.

"What do you mean?" asked Letty.

"There are some things that are better left untouched."

"Like what?"

"The pastor doesn't need this kind of attention."

"Who? Pastor Terry?"

"No," replied Faith, shaking her head. "Pastor Lane."

Fran, who'd been quiet to this point piped up. "Who said anything about Pastor Lane?"

Faith puffed herself up. "Don't you think that's what this meeting is about? I mean, with all the rumors going around…"

Letty looked around in confusion. "I thought this was just about the funeral."

Julia started to speak again, but was interrupted by a host of women talking all at once. "Ladies! Please! Let me explain!"

The room quieted immediately and everyone looked at their leader.

"As you know, the funeral incident, which is what this meeting is undoubtedly about, was very upsetting to everyone, especially to the Nelsons. And ever since people have been trying to figure out why those kids walked out. Once people start speculating, things get a little out of hand and rumors start to fly."

Fran was confused. "But what's this about Pastor Lane? What's *he* have to do with it?"

"Nothing. There have just been rumors. That's all."

Letty's face brightened. "Don't you remember when Pastor Lane left Hopeston? There was an uproar over the SBS program and rumors were going around then."

"Oh for goodness sake! Why do people always bring that up?" responded Julia, her eyes shooting darts. "Pastor Lane is a wonderful man. Not a *perfect* one but we don't care what he's done on a personal level. We loved him as our pastor. And we still do!"

Judith nodded. "What matters is how you do the job. Your personal life is your own business." She turned to the others. "Would you want people snooping into your private life?"

"Does that count if you're a pastor?" asked Letty.

Julia got up to pour herself another cup of coffee. "Of course, we shouldn't violate a pastor's privacy. That's why I want to know what this meeting's about. I'm concerned that Pastor Lane's personal life will be brought up and that must not happen!"

"Well, what do we do?" asked Faith.

Before Julia could respond, Judith spoke up again. "Maybe we could find out what Pastor Terry has in mind. We could ask Marie—she might know the agenda for the meeting."

Julia smiled. "That's a great idea. I'll go talk to her. Keep sewing. I'll be right back." She set her cup aside and headed for the church office.

Marie sat behind her desk typing. "Hello Julia," she said, looking up at the sound of the door opening. "How's it going in there?"

"Where's the pastor?" Julia asked, ignoring her question.

"He's out on a church visit. What do you need?"

"I need to know why he's having this meeting."

Marie frowned. "The town meeting?"

"Yes. What's it about?"

Marie went back to her typing. "You'll want to come and find out."

Julia's face was red. "Marie, I want to know what that meeting is about!"

Marie looked up. "And I have indicated that you will have to come to the meeting to find out what it's about along with everyone else, Julia."

The office door opened and Penelope Johnston peered in. "I can come back later."

"No, it's okay," Marie said, frowning at Julia. "We were just finished."

Julia wheeled around to face Penelope. "It's you, isn't it? What have you done?"

"I don't know what you're talking about, Julia."

"You're behind it. I know you are!"

"Behind what?"

"You convinced your husband and that pastor of ours to have this little meeting, didn't you?"

Penelope looked from Julia to Marie, who shrugged, and back again. "Before you go accusing people of things, Julia, you might want to be clear about what you're saying."

Julia was livid. "Oh, I'm clear about this! You are the force behind your husband and now you've gone and told the pastor the things you've heard."

A hint of a smile appeared on Penelope's face. "You think *I* asked for this meeting?"

"Oh, I have no doubt." Julia wagged her finger in Penelope's face and stomped out of the office.

"Honey, I need to talk to you about something," said Pamela when her daughter, Mary Anne, answered the phone.

"What is it, Mom?"

"I just got off the phone with Lane Richardson. And…well, I feel strange."

"Strange about what?"

"About what he asked me to do."

"Do what? What are you talking about?"

"Lane says that people are spreading bad rumors about him and he wants me to make phone calls to get them to stop. I don't think I can do that."

"What sort of rumors?"

"About abuse."

"Oh." Here we go again, thought Mary Anne.

Her mother continued. "Apparently word has gotten out about his past. And Lane wants me to do something about it."

"Why you, Mom?"

"I don't know, honey. I think he's desperate. Delbert used to handle a lot of this for Lane. I don't think he has anybody else."

"But he can't expect you to take this on, especially now. You're in no condition to deal with his baggage. You're dealing with your own stuff."

"I'm glad you said that. I think this is too much to ask of me right now. I feel bad because he's done so much for us. I *know* his past is a problem for him. But I just can't..."

"No, you can't." Mary Anne was adamant.

"So, what do I do? I told him I would help."

"What's he going to do if he finds out you've done nothing? You can just say it was too much right now." Mary Anne thought for a moment. "By the way, did you see the announcement in the paper today?"

"No. I haven't read it yet. What announcement?"

"Well, apparently the church is having a town meeting of sorts, to discuss what happened at Dad's funeral."

"Really?"

"I guess we're going to see how our new pastor handles this one. Maybe this'll take care of it, Mom. Maybe there will be enough distraction with this meeting that the pastor's issues will be lost in the shuffle."

"Yeah, but that may be what he's worried about. People might bring some of those issues up at the meeting."

"So? Tell me how that's *your* problem."

"It's not, really, but you know your dad would have gone to bat for him without skipping a beat. I feel a little obligated..."

"That was Dad and this is you. I know you love Lane, Mom, but you don't have to take on all his stuff just because Dad's not here anymore."

"Lane thinks I do."

"But that doesn't mean you *do*. If you don't feel right about this, then maybe you should tell him that. You can be his friend, but he'll have to find other people to be his bodyguards."

There was a long silence as Pamela thought through what her daughter had said. "I think you're right, honey. It always helps to talk to you."

Mary Anne paused. "You know, Mom, maybe Dad took on more than he should have. It's almost like he protected Lane *too* much. Maybe it's good for him to have to face this finally."

"I don't know," replied Pamela. "But it's clear that it's out of *my* hands."

❧

Dorothy Banks lowered the newspaper into her lap. Never before had the church offered an opportunity for the whole community to come and air its grievances. It made her nervous.

She thought about the funeral, and her shock when Lillie Farmer and Joshua Crumley had walked out in the middle of it. But she had to admit, as she thought about it now, a part of her was glad they had done it—she, too, had been unpleasantly surprised when Pastor Lane had appeared.

Her face burning, Dorothy recalled Penelope's questions about Melodie and what had happened to her. Would this come out at the meeting? Would Penelope reveal what she had said? Then again, maybe it *was* time for all of it to come out. Maybe this meeting would allow the people of Hopeston to finally know the truth.

Dorothy began to pace the room. To busy herself, she went into the kitchen to check on dinner. She grabbed the oven mitt and stood, wringing it in her hands. Why had she kept quiet all these years? Why had she so obediently done as the pastor requested? Her best friend had suddenly left the church and her beloved work without an explanation and she had done nothing about it. She had known something was terribly wrong, but yet she had totally abandoned Melodie in her time of greatest need.

"Enough!" she said out loud. Looking around the kitchen to make sure no one had heard her, she giggled and then spoke out loud again. "That's right, you heard me! I will *not* let Lane Richardson or anyone else keep me from doing what I believe!" She stooped to pick up the mitt she'd dropped and slammed it, hard, onto the counter. "I will go to that meeting! And if I want to, I will speak my mind!"

Since their wedding, the Parks had subscribed to the Hopeston Gazette as a way of keeping in touch with the goings-on in Violet's hometown and the business of the world in which her father lived. Kevin sat reading the paper after supper, and came upon the announcement.

"Vi, look at this. There's gonna be a meeting at the church in Hopeston." He handed her the paper.

Violet read the announcement and looked up at her husband. "What do you think it's about?"

Kevin thought for a moment. "They went to that funeral—your Dad and Lillie and Joshua and his mother—right?"

"Yes."

"And that pastor, the one who...you know...was there." It was still hard for Kevin to say out loud what had happened to his mother-in-law.

Violet mused. "Yes, he was. He did the eulogy and they weren't expecting him to be there at all. It was a real shock to them." Martin had told her later how difficult it had been for all of them, and that Joshua and Lillie had walked out. "It sounds like what happened at the funeral has become an issue for the whole town."

Kevin looked up from the sports page. "Why don't you call your Dad and see what's going on?"

"I think I will."

"Dad? This is Vi. We just saw the announcement about the church meeting in the paper. Any idea what it's about?"

"Well, when the kids walked out, they humiliated Pastor Lane in front of the entire town. Courageous, those two."

Martin chuckled and then turned serious. "People *are* upset, though—Miriam and I have had people threaten us and, in the meantime..." he paused for a moment and cleared his throat. "...some other victims have shown up."

"Oh, my God. Really?"

"Yes, we know of several victims now. Lillie started a support group for them, she and Joshua together. The group meets at Joshua's house every three weeks."

"So, at this meeting...what are they going to talk about?"

"I don't know any more than you do. I suppose they want to address the rumors. Mike Johnston, the chairman of the board, came to see me to ask that I be quiet about what Lane did to your mother. And then the new pastor came to see me too."

"You're kidding!" Vi was aghast.

Martin stopped, realizing that once again, he'd kept Violet in the dark.

"I'm sorry, honey, I meant to call you. It's been a little crazy around here lately. Anyway, I told Mike what the pastor did to your mom and he believed me. I know he did—I saw it in his eyes.

"But since then we've been getting attacked. The word is out as to what Lane Richardson did and the town is not happy about it. I think maybe this meeting is intended to address some of that."

"Are you going?" asked Violet.

Martin paused before responding. "I'm not sure yet."

"Dad, I think we need to represent Mom as a family. I don't care what people think of what Lillie and Joshua did. That's nothing compared to what that pastor did to Mom! I'll come with you—I'll even call Bruce and get him there too."

"Honey…" replied Martin, "I think you're right. We *all* need to be there. I'll let Lillie know—it'll mean a lot to her. And to Joshua."

"Lane, this is Pamela."

"Pamela!"

"I'm afraid I have to tell you…"

"Pamela…"

"No, Lane, let me finish. Delbert was a dear friend to you, I know. He did a lot to help when things got…sticky for you…but I can't fill in for him. Not now. I hope you'll understand."

"You think I *did* the things they're saying?"

"No, I'm not saying that. I'm saying that my energy is low these days… and I'm barely able to take care of myself. I can't take on your stuff too."

"*My* stuff?"

"Yes, Lane. No one is perfect, but…I'm afraid I can't help you. I'm *so* sorry, but I have to go."

Lane attempted to sound more chipper than he felt. "What have you found out, guy?"

Ralph Stacey sighed into the phone. "Martin Farmer's smarter than we thought, Pastor. He's not scared."

"What do you mean? Smarter how?"

"He knows we have no case."

"Of course we do!"

"He's no dummy, Pastor."

"I have nothing to hide. What can he possibly be saying that is true?"

Ralph paused. "Are you sure about that, Pastor? I think we need to be realistic here. We all know *something* happened with Melodie Farmer. Are you sure you want this brought out in the open for the whole town to see?"

Lane was silent.

Ralph continued. "Pastor, with all due respect, your past…is a problem. This meeting will be the perfect opportunity for people to bring things up again. I'm not sure you want to risk it."

"You must think the worst of me, Ralph." The pastor's voice had lost all its forcefulness.

"No, Pastor," said Ralph. "I think of you as a man…just like the rest of us, who can't afford to be in the spotlight right now. I suggest you just lay low and let this pass."

"You think it will?" Pastor Lane searched for a straw of hope.

"Yeah, with time. And if we don't do anything to piss anyone off right now. It did before."

The pastor was quiet for a long time, and then spoke again. "Okay, I'll lay low, as you say. Thanks, Ralph, you're a good friend."

Lane hung up the phone and sat down heavily in his chair. His friends were slipping away. Mike Johnston hadn't called him back and now he and the new pastor at Hopeston had called for a town meeting. Pamela Nelson had declined to help him. And now even Ralph had told him to back off.

He went into his study and opened the cabinet behind his desk. This called for whiskey.

79

A week had passed since the package had arrived in the mail and Lane sat at his desk, looking out the window at the barrenness of the landscape outside. Fall had come early and the first frost had left its damage. The field that stretched beyond his carefully manicured lawn was a wild tangle of browning meadow grasses and wildflowers. Overnight, it seemed, the once vibrant colors of the landscape had taken on muted tones of burnt umber, sienna, chocolate brown and rust.

The vibrancy of his own life had been sucked out of him too—he was dead and frozen, his internal life like a winter landscape waiting for spring. People he had depended on for support were drifting away, his sermons were not nearly as well-received as they once had been, and he no longer saw adoration in the eyes of his congregants.

He felt a growing urge to do something, anything that would make him feel more in control. There was something gnawing at him—something he couldn't put his finger on.

What was it? Was there a reason for his inner discomfort? He tried to focus on the work before him but ultimately pushed his chair away from his desk and threw down his pen. He opened the drawer to his desk and took out the package.

It contained a stack of unopened letters rubber-banded together. He did not recognize all of the names, but he knew two of them—Joshua Crumley and Lillie Farmer.

What could the letters possibly say? He was ashamed that he had been afraid to open them—he had always prided himself on never allowing fear to rule him. Removing the rubber band, he allowed the letters to spill across the desk, and sat looking at them for a long time, until finally he picked up the one from the Crumley boy.

He opened the letter and began to read.

"Dear Reverend Richardson,

I am the young man who stood and walked out of Mr. Nelson's funeral. That was personally a necessary act of protest.

I do not know if you remember me as the thirteen-year-old boy who helped with the SBS in 1983. I have grown up and stayed away from Hopeston until recently.

Delbert Nelson's funeral was the first time I've been back to Hopeston Church since my childhood. When I saw you there I could not sit and act as though nothing had happened between us. When I was a boy..."

Red hot shame spread from Lane's neck to his cheeks, and he saw, in his mind's eye, a small boy sitting in an office, waiting in a chair, full of apprehension and a flutter of excitement. Then the image disappeared. He wiped perspiration from his brow and lowered his eyes to the pages before him.

"...Mrs. Farmer was the Bible Teacher that summer and she was my friend. I helped her clean up. You used to make her come to see you in your office. One day you were molesting her when I came to the door and tried to stop you. But that day you..."

Lane slammed the letter down onto the desk and fiercely covered it with his hand. His breathing jagged, he loosened his collar. Again the boy in the office appeared in his mind. This time a man came in, and smiled down at him, and Lane saw the joy the boy felt at the man's approval and attention.

He stumbled to the kitchen for a glass of water and drank it down while standing at the sink. What was happening to him? He paced the house, trying to focus on things that comforted him—his leather armchair, the grandfather clock in the hall that marked the hours, the brandy bottle and glasses in the den—but nothing offered him relief. He returned to his desk and picked up the letter again and read. *"...that day you raped her and you molested me..."*

The boy in his mind's eye looked up at the man as he reached out his hand to touch the boy's cheek and stroke his neck. The boy's joy turned to fear—he wanted to tell the man to stop but nothing came out of his mouth. The man's hand slid down the boy's chest to his waist and he crouched down in front of him.

Lane shook his head, trying to dispel the images appearing in his mind. He looked at the letter again and reread the words "you molested me" and pain suddenly pierced his chest. Was he having a heart attack?

His mind raced, trying to think of someone he could call, but no one came to mind. He needed company—someone to be with him and help him. He felt vulnerable and small, but he had no friends who had ever seen him in this condition.

Finally, in desperation, Lane stood up from his chair, put the letter roughly away in its envelope and stashed the packet away in its hiding place. Exhausted, he made his way into the darkness of his den and poured himself a glass of whiskey, and after downing a couple more, he sat down and drifted into a fitful sleep.

80

Jerry Bomont sat in his chair trying to read the paper. His wife Julia stood in front of him, hands on her hips. "The Johnstons are out to get him, Jerry, I'm telling you!"

He sighed and lowered the paper to his lap. "The announcement *did* come out after I ran into Mike at the grocery store."

"So, your threat made no difference. Mike punched you at the board meeting, for God's sake, and Penelope is still up to no good. I saw her at the church the day of the circle."

Jerry looked up at his wife, reaching up to touch his still tender eye. "And?"

"And I lost my temper."

"No surprise there," said Jerry under his breath.

Exasperated at her husband's apparent disinterest, she shook his shoulder. "What are we going to do?"

"Julia, I'm not sure there is anything we can do, other than attend the meeting and speak up if we need to. The pastor would do well to keep a low profile for now. That's all I can say."

"But that only makes him look guilty."

"Well…?" Jerry said, tipping his head forward and looking at her over his reading glasses.

"Well what, Gerald Bomont?!"

"I just wish you would leave it alone. It's best if we just don't get into this all over again. The man has an issue—leave it be. I don't think the meeting will be that bad—we've been through worse."

Julia fumed. Defeated for the moment, she turned and stomped off into the kitchen to clean up. The meeting would be a nightmare and yet, somehow, she couldn't wait for the day to come.

Unable to keep the letters out of his thoughts, Lane went to his desk and again removed them from their hiding place. Setting aside Joshua's letter, this time he chose one with more delicate handwriting on the envelope.

> *Reverend Richardson,*
> *I must tell you that what you did to me has destroyed my life. I have not been able to have a single relationship with a man since the day you raped me. I trusted you. I loved you. You said you loved me and that you wanted to marry me. I have never been able to trust again, and I am alone.*
> *Ruth*

Lane put down the letter. He felt strangely embarrassed—he didn't recall a Ruth in his life, yet this woman said he'd destroyed her.

An image of the boy flashed across his mind again. This time the boy was sitting on a couch and the man with a minister's collar was kneeling in front of him. What was happening to him? Where were these flashes coming from?

Though he worried that whiskey had become a daily habit, he poured a glass and drank it. He sat down in the den and closed his eyes.

A long line of big black Carpenter ants was coming towards him. He was pinned, like a specimen, to the wall and the ants were climbing the wall and swarming all over him. He was covered with a moving mass except for his mouth. Just as the ants were about to close in, he screamed and they began to fall away.

Lane sat up with a start, his heart pounding. As much as he feared the content of the letters, he was drawn to them, and he returned to his desk.

The letter now on top was from a member of his current congregation. Fear gripped him as he opened her letter and began to read, hands shaking so that he laid it on the desk in front of him.

Pastor Lane,

I must tell you how I feel about the events that have transpired between us. You have been a very attentive and kind pastor to me, counseling me during my darkest hours, making me feel safe and understood and reassured, giving me hope that my life would right itself after my painful divorce. I came to you in complete trust, as a member of a church ought to be able to do with her pastor. For many months, during our counseling sessions, I had no cause to fear that you would violate my trust. I poured out my heart and my soul to you as I sought to put back their broken pieces. I told you so much and I felt safe in doing so.

Then, when my nephew was in the car accident and I called for your help, you came to me and you broke all my trust and shattered my sense of safety by your behavior. I feel you took advantage of my increased vulnerability due to my fear and grief over my nephew. All my defenses were down and I counted on the pastor I had come to trust so completely. I put myself totally into your care.

I see now that I made a mistake in giving you that much power. But you abused that power when you molested me on my own couch in my own living room that day. You frightened me, offended me, violated me and betrayed me by your abusive actions. Then when I told you to leave, repeatedly, you refused to go and kept telling me there was no reason to be upset by what you'd done.

You have become a predator to me whom I fear and cannot trust. My fear has persisted. You are no longer my kind, gentle, understanding pastor. Your behavior has caused me to question my faith, to not be able to return to church, and to avoid religion entirely for fear of being abused and hurt again. I can't even talk to God anymore since somehow He allowed this to happen, you being his chosen representative.

I am now a mess and feel that you have caused lasting damage to my person, to my life. I have come to find out that I am not the only one you have sexually violated. In fact, my case is mild compared to those of other victims of your abuse. I am horrified to find that you are a dangerous sexual predator that has perpetrated your abuse over many years and in many incidents.

While I trusted you with my personal life, my healing and my future you had already brutally abused many others. Now I am filled with questions and self-doubt about how you could be so diabolical and so good at the same time. I wonder how you are able to appear so wonderful when secretly you are a violent *sexual criminal. How many people have trusted in your goodness and been led to believe in your ministry and sermons about life? How many people have you betrayed with your false life, your lies? Whole congregations, whole communities of people have allowed your influence, your guidance, your charisma to mold their lives and to inform their choices.*

How could you do this? How could you live this double life and carry on as though nothing was amiss? How can you live with yourself? You are a very sick man and you need help. You must be stopped from abusing again. Get help, Pastor Lane. Call a therapist.

Rebecca

It had suddenly become stifling inside. Lane carefully folded the letter and returned it to its envelope before placing it in the drawer. Donning a light jacket and cap, he walked out the front door and down his driveway toward the main road.

The whistle of the teakettle woke Abigail from her snooze on the porch. As she reached for a cup from the shelf she hesitated, hand outstretched—something tugged at her inside. She cocked her head and then moved her hand to the center of her shelf where the jewel of her teacups sat nestled in front of its rose-painted saucer. *Melodie's teacup.*

Taking it gently into her hands, she admired the delicate painting and felt the tugging again. She poured her tea and went back to the porch. Once settled in her chair she lit the center candle on her altar and immediately went into prayer.

As Abigail felt her spirit find its center, she was aware of images already crossing her mind: *A circle of women. Many people. A young couple. A man in his study slumped in his armchair. Tears. Fear. A gathering.*

Abigail wasn't sure of the specifics of the messages she was receiving, but she had a good idea that it had to do with the work she'd been doing with Lillie and Joshua. Her heart ached with the pain that came through for all concerned.

"Holy Mother," she prayed. *"I ask that thee come forth for this town. They are in pain and struggle and they need thy clear thinking for this time, this gathering. There are tears and arguments, many people. Thee knows what this is about, Holy Mother. I lift my soul and heart to thee now, holding within me the fears, the love, and the pain of these people. May they find their way through this."*

A sharp pain in her chest made Abigail gasp. The pain went quickly away and an image came to her: *a man in his chair, afraid and alone, the same man stumbling through the forest, searching for peace.* She lifted her thoughts up for him and in a wordless prayer gave him to the Divine Mother.

After a long, silent meditation, Abigail opened her eyes and saw the sunlight glint on the surface of the lake before her. The cry of an eagle rang out, echoed a few times and then silence returned.

Miriam opened the door to the first of the support group members to arrive. Before long all seven were seated in her living room. As in the past, Lillie opened the meeting with prayer. "You all know there's going to be a meeting at the Hopeston church this Saturday evening, right?"

Murmurs passed through the group.

Gail nodded. "Yeah, I read about that. What's it about? Anyone know?"

"We think the pastor wants to address the town about proper behavior at funerals," said Joshua, chuckling.

Everyone laughed.

"Will this be an opportunity for us to say something about Pastor Lane?" asked Elizabeth. The group members all looked at her. Again, murmurs.

"Well," Joshua said, "there are people who want to know why we walked out..."

"So, there's more to this meeting than just funeral etiquette..." said Gail.

Lillie nodded. "We think so. In the paper, Mike Johnston—the chairman of the church board—was listed as running this meeting. He and his wife have both spoken to my dad."

Heidi had said little until this point. "Did your dad tell them what happened?"

"Yes," Lillie replied. "We had decided that it was time to tell the truth, especially if asked."

Everyone sat in silence, thinking. Rebecca shifted in her chair and crossed her legs. "Wow, this could be ugly."

"God, I hope so!" Gail said. "It would serve the bastard right!"

Lillie glanced around the room. "Joshua and I are going to the meeting, along with his mother and my dad. Is anyone interested in going with us?"

Ruth spoke for the first time. "What do you think it will be like?"

Rebecca answered her. "Well, the chairman of the board will probably run it and he and the pastor will make statements and then…they'll probably open it up for people to speak."

"It's probably an opportunity for people to get things off their chests." Gail said.

Heidi stared at Joshua and Lillie, eyebrows raised. "And you two are going? Aren't people going to really let you have it for what you did at the funeral?"

"Probably," said Joshua. "But it wouldn't be very brave to stay home."

"Besides," interjected Lillie, "like Elizabeth said, this may well be a chance to tell the community what Pastor Lane did."

"You *are* brave," Ruth said softly.

Elizabeth leaned forward in her seat and looked around the room and then at Lillie and Joshua. "If you're going and putting yourselves out there like this, then I think we should all go and support each other."

The group sat for a bit and then Heidi nodded. "I'm going."

"Me too," said Rebecca.

"Ditto," said Gail.

Elizabeth turned to Ruth. "We can all sit together."

Ruth bit her lip. "I'm afraid."

Elizabeth patted the older woman's arm. "We all are. But this is part of healing—facing the truth and the consequences of being willing to speak the truth…finally."

Ruth thought for a moment, "Okay. I'll go. Only don't expect me to say anything."

"Only if you wish," replied Lillie.

81

The Saturday of the town meeting finally arrived, and everyone was prepared for a confrontation. Terry Bunker's wife, Hannah, had arranged for a babysitter so she could attend the meeting, which made him feel better—having his wife present would be calming. Mike and Penelope had talked for hours about what might be brought up at the meeting. They were clear that the behavior of Pastor Lane was the core issue and were prepared to speak about it, but decided they would not initiate the conversation unless no one else did. The town had to deal with the truth and do something—as much as they loved Pastor Lane they now knew he had a serious problem and were compelled to do what had to be done.

Violet and Bruce had arranged to meet and drive together. Their sister and father needed them there for support, but mostly they were coming to represent their mother and the lost parts of themselves. What had happened to Melodie was now part of their own stories and they intended to be present for every moment.

As they had at the funeral, Martin, Lillie, Joshua and Miriam would face the community as a united front. They knew that the focus of the meeting would be on Joshua and Lillie, but agreed that the reasons behind their behavior would be revealed as well. Each had rehearsed what he or she would say and felt as ready as they ever would.

The importance of support from Heidi and Elizabeth and the others in the group was immeasurable. They somehow knew that as hard as it would be, as contentious as it was likely to become, God would use them somehow as instruments in the healing of Hopeston and all whom Pastor Lane might have wounded.

Lane's mind was numb. In an emotional fog, he was unable to see what was around him. When he reached the edge of town on foot, he neither noticed the doe that came to the edge of the woods and silently watched him pass nor did he see the shadow of a large bird of prey circling overhead. He was completely oblivious to the cawing fest of a murder of crows deep in the forest.

Images continued to pass through his mind—a little boy squirming to get free and the iron hand of a man holding him down, Rebecca on her couch, Joshua as a young boy. He could see Joshua squirming to free himself as well.

Lane came to a trail that led into the woods and turned, without thinking, into darkness under the canopy of trees. The gloom of the forest matched his deadened mood.

The letter from the woman named Ruth came to his mind. Who was this delicate lady that claimed he had destroyed her life? Then, unbidden, he saw the face of the man in his daydreams, filled with desire. Flooded with a sense of shame, he stopped on the trail, and then, suddenly, the memory came fully into his consciousness. The face he'd been seeing was the face of his own childhood pastor—*and he was the little boy.*

Memory after memory came crashing. He'd been molested over and over again from when he'd been 13 years old until he had finally left for college. After that, though he had tried, he had not been able to form normal relationships. Sexual pleasure had become inextricably interwoven with the emotional effects of the abuse he had experienced—and his arousal connected to secret trysts and coercion of his partners.

In college, he'd found he was no longer satisfied with easy sex—he'd needed the aggression, the satisfaction of taking the innocence of his partners. No longer had he been turned on by willing sex partners—the excitement of the conquest had become an addiction.

Images from the past began to flash through his mind in rapid succession—people he had long forgotten came back to him, untold numbers of women he had lured and abused. He saw the innocent, naïve boy he had once been, trapped in the lure of the odd combination of pleasure and fear that had been forced upon him.

Then Joshua Crumley came to mind. He had never intended to hurt the boy—that was far too close to the source of his own wounds. But Joshua had threatened the success of his carefully planned seduction and taking of Melodie Farmer. *No predator will be dissuaded from his prey.*

To keep the boy from blowing his cover, he'd molested him and then forced him to watch, aroused, while he'd raped her. He could see Joshua's face in his mind as he'd unzipped his pants and stroked him, and he saw there the same mixture of pleasure and fear and shame that he'd seen on the face of the boy of his daydreams in the weeks past—the boy he now knew was himself.

All the good he'd done, all the years he had been an effective and loving pastor to his congregations were suddenly for naught, and he felt the weight of his wrongdoing press down on him.

Stumbling, he came to a clearing and realized that he had reached the river. Head spinning, he felt his way to a flat rock near the edge of the water. Mesmerized by the ripples and the purity of the crystal clear water before him, he knew it would be silent and peaceful under there.

He stood. Now feeling a strange calm descend upon him, he reached for a branch from a tree that had fallen into the river. Using it to steady himself, he made his way into the deepest part—finally surrendering his legs to the current. Eyes open as it dragged him under, he watched as the final bubbles escaped his mouth and felt the pressure on his chest as breath began to leave him.

Darkness came and enveloped him completely.

82

The chairs in the fellowship hall filled quickly as the people of Hopeston arrived. Pastor Terry and Mike Johnston sat up front. They had met briefly to talk about procedure and had agreed that Mike would lead the meeting. Anticipation filled the air when he finally stood and rapped on the lectern.

"Welcome, folks. Thank you all for coming this evening. Reverend Bunker and I talked and agreed that we should have an opportunity, as a community, to address the issues that have come up as a result of the circumstances of Delbert Nelson's funeral.

"There is a great deal of talk going around and people seem to have things to say, so we thought we would bring it here, to the church, to be aired and dealt with directly and honestly. I will be facilitating the discussion—anyone who wishes to speak should raise his or her hand and I will give you the floor. Please stand up so everyone can hear you."

Mike turned to Pastor Terry. "The pastor would like to begin with a prayer." Many people bowed their heads.

"Lord," began Pastor Terry, *"we ask you to be with us this evening as we seek to communicate with one another about some difficult matters. We are merely human beings and we do not always know the best way to do things. Help us to listen to one another and to solve the problems that have come up. We are all your precious ones and so we need your blessings and guidance now. In Jesus' name we pray. Amen."*

Mike stepped to the lectern again. "Now, who would like to speak first?"

At first no one made a move. For a moment everyone wondered if anyone would speak.

Daniel Cross raised his hand and stood. "I want to know what made Joshua Crumley and Lillie Farmer interrupt Delbert's funeral and walk out like they did."

Lillie's stomach churned. Right off the bat.

Mike glanced in the direction where he'd seen the Crumleys and Farmers sit. "They're here. It would be best for us to hear it from them."

436

Joshua looked at Lillie and took her hand. They stood together. Violet grabbed her brother's arm and squeezed. Bruce looked at her and winked.

Someone in the crowd yelled out of turn. "What does it matter why they did it? It was wrong!"

"If you have something to say please identify yourself and stand so we can hear you."

"You heard me just fine, Mike." Jerry Bomont's voice was loud enough for all to hear.

Pastor Terry stood up again. "Please, let the young people speak. They have the floor."

Joshua cleared his throat. "First, I would like to apologize to Pamela Nelson and the Nelson family." He turned to face them. "I did not intend to offend or hurt any of you by my actions at the funeral. I'm afraid I wasn't able to think of the consequences at the time. Please forgive me." He bowed his head ever so slightly to Pamela and turned back to the front.

Pamela smiled.

"I was taken off guard by Reverend Lane Richardson's appearance at the funeral. Once I saw him, he was all I could think about. The paper said nothing about his having a part in the service—had I known he would be there, I would not have attended."

He looked around the room and took a deep breath before continuing. "You see, twelve years ago, Pastor Lane nearly destroyed Lillie's family and me." Gasps could be heard rustling through the room.

"I could not stay there and listen to him and so I was forced to follow my conscience and walk out."

"I too was unable to stay," said Lillie, glancing over at the Nelson family. "And I too am sorry, Mrs. Nelson. We both loved your husband. This was not something we planned. We simply could not stay."

Joshua and Lillie both sat down. Violet leaned forward and gently touched each on the shoulder.

Richard Powers stood and turned toward Joshua and Lillie. "What do you mean, destroyed? Destroyed how?" Martin rose to his feet.

Upon seeing him, Jerry Bomont stood up. "Wait a minute now, Martin. Let's not get carried away. Pastor Lane is an honorable man with many wonderful years of service behind him. Let's not start getting out the man's dirty laundry."

Anger rose quickly in Violet's face. Bruce placed his hand on hers.

Daniel Cross spoke again. "But that's what started this whole thing, Jerry. If those kids left the funeral because of the pastor's behavior, I think we need to hear what Martin has to say."

The crowd murmured. Mike put up his hands to silence them. "Martin, did you have something to say?"

"Yes, Mike. As I've told some of you, my wife left record of a life-changing incident with Pastor Lane. During the summer of 1983, while they led SBS together, the pastor took advantage of my wife. He…violated her…sexually."

Another round of gasps traveled across the room.

Jerry Bomont jumped back to his feet. "Your wife left record? What does *that* mean? Anyone could 'leave record' of something and we wouldn't automatically assume it was true."

Martin turned to face the older man. "Jerry, Melodie was destroyed by what happened. The pastor took away all her trust and faith and any sense of self she had. You couldn't recognize her after that. She went into a shell and never came out again."

Barbara Stacey raised her hand. "That's because the pastor rejected her advances. He told her to leave the church. It was her own fault! No one made her come on to the pastor like she did."

"That's right!" Julia Bomont yelled. "The pastor told us. He tried to handle it quietly and discreetly. You have your facts wrong, Martin."

Martin turned to face Julia. "And how do you know my facts are wrong?"

"Because Pastor Lane told us what happened and there is no way he would do what you've said. How could that be the way it happened? Maybe your wife had to make up a story to feel better. It's disgraceful of you to try to put this on the pastor!"

Dorothy Banks' heart started to pound violently in her chest. She wanted to hide but something made her stand up instead. Mike saw her rise.

"Mrs. Banks, you have the floor."

Dorothy nodded and took a breath to calm her nerves. "I knew Melodie Farmer very well. She would never have done what Barbara and Julia are saying. She was a dedicated Sunday School teacher and a devout Christian. Anyone who knew her at all knows that.

"I know that the pastor did something to her. He told us never to talk to her after she left the church. There's no other explanation but that he was trying to keep us from finding out what really happened between them."

"Dorothy, you're just guessing," said Barbara Stacey.

Embarrassed, Dorothy nearly sat down, but something made her turn in the direction of her detractors. "No, Barbara, *you're* wrong. I *know* it wasn't Melodie's fault. The pastor did something to her, just as Martin and Joshua have said, and then tried to keep it all under wraps so no one else would know."

Stan Vets, another member of the board, rose to his feet. "This is all hearsay. No one can prove the pastor did anything wrong. All we have is his word and this record Martin says his wife kept. It's his word against hers. I'll take the word of a pastor any day."

A noise was heard in the back of the hall. The room turned to see Debra Hundley struggle to her feet. Swaying and grabbing the back of the pew to steady herself, she laughed sarcastically.

"Oh, don't think you can trust a man's word just because he's a minister! There are plenty of men who look like they're the most wonderful people... and when you really know...you'll see despicable behavior! Just because a man's a minister doesn't mean you can trust him!"

Betty put a hand on her arm and tried to quiet her, and Debra whispered back too loudly to Betty to keep her hands off.

Joe Bendler stood and shook his head in disgust. "What's that have to do with it? This is Pastor Lane we're talking about here! Come on people, hasn't he proven himself long enough in this community for us to know the man to be an honorable servant of God?" Murmurs shot through the room again.

Ralph Stacey raised his hand and turned toward Martin. "I guess we'll never really know what happened. Sorry, Martin, but your wife is not here to tell us what happened and there are no witnesses. So, I think we just need to accept Joshua and Lillie's explanation of their behavior at the funeral and their apology to the Nelson family and move on. There's no need to take this any further."

Joshua stood again. Everyone quieted and looked at him.

"You're wrong, Mr. Stacey. There *was* a witness."

The crowd was stunned.

"You want to know what destroyed means?" asked Joshua, in his most confident attorney's voice. "It means violated, betrayed, abused. I can tell you because I was there the day Pastor Lane assaulted Melodie Farmer. He raped her in front of me, and molested me while he was at it. I saw what he was doing and I tried to stop him. But I was just a kid and he took me down too."

All eyes were on Joshua as he continued.

"I've kept this to myself all these years because I was sure no one would believe me. You people of Hopeston have been so naïve! The man you so love and trust has been systematically using his position to seduce and abuse women right under your noses." He glanced in the direction of the Bomonts and Staceys. "And then some of you even knew it and covered it up!"

He reached down and took Lillie's hand. "This woman right here helped me to finally tell what happened. Martin shared Mrs. Farmer's diary account of what happened that day with Lillie and she, in turn, shared it with me. Mrs. Farmer wrote about *me* in her diary too—and she wrote me a letter that she could never bring herself to send."

He turned toward Ralph Stacey. "So, yes, Mr. Stacey, there *is* a record and there *is* a witness. And that is the truth." Ashen-faced, Joshua sat down and Lillie squeezed his hand.

The Bomonts stood almost in unison. "Just a minute here, Pastor. Before we get all touchy feely about this," sneered Jerry, "we still have no way of knowing what *really* happened. You're all going to just take this disrupter's word for it? Where *is* this diary? How do we know Joshua is a true witness and not just making things up?" Julia nodded her head vigorously.

One woman after another began to stand, and the crowd murmured. When all was done, the five women of the support group stood together side by side.

Mike turned toward them. "Is there something one of you wishes to say?"

Gail spoke first. "Yes. We are here to bear witness to the abuses of Pastor Lane. We are *all* his victims."

Julia was beside herself. "Who *are* these women? Where did they come from?"

Penelope, who had watched the volleys, raised her hand and stood to speak. "I've been checking church records and there is evidence of women leaving the church abruptly after working with the pastor on SBS for years." She glanced toward the group. "Are you ladies some of those women?"

"Yes," Heidi said. "Two of us worked with him in SBS."

"But he found other ways to abuse, too," said Gail. "I was the church secretary at the time of my experience. *You* remember me." She looked around and several people nodded. "We had an affair," she said. "I'm not proud of it, but in looking back I see how he sought after me. I didn't have a chance."

"Are there any other women who want to claim their sin was the pastor's fault?" Julia blurted. "I can't believe what we're hearing! Are you people going to just sit here and let these people say anything they want and do nothing?"

Someone yelled from the other side of the room. "Julia, shut up!"

"Yeah, we've heard enough from you!" To everyone's astonishment, the second voice was that of the postmistress, Audrey Powers. "Julia, you have done more damage in this church than anyone."

The place was suddenly in an uproar. It was not until Delbert Nelson's daughter, Mary Anne, stood that the room went quiet. Everyone's eyes were fixed on her as she spoke. "I personally would like to hear what these women have to say."

Elizabeth tipped her head to Mary Anne and stepped forward. "I was a young woman when the pastor molested me and it has taken me all this time to recover. He took my dignity, my faith—he took my life from me. I have pretended all these years that I was okay but I lived a lie to cover the pain. Now, with the help of these women and that of Lillie and Joshua, I have finally been able to face what happened and have begun to heal."

Rebecca took it from there. "I'm a member of Pastor Lane's current church in Broadley. He molested me..." she said, coughing to clear the emotion that came suddenly, "...just a month ago. In my own home."

"It's not over, people—he's still abusing. You here in Hopeston and we in Broadley have to face what he's done and deal with it or else he will continue to hurt women...people..." She corrected herself, looking at Joshua. "This takes a lot for me, for all of us, to be here tonight and tell you this. Please don't show us disrespect by not believing us."

Heidi squeezed Rebecca's hand and spoke again. "We thought long and hard about what to do and how to approach this problem. We finally decided to communicate with the pastor himself and ask him, with compassion, to stop, apologize for his behavior and get help. We've all written him letters. If you love him as much as you claim, you should want to help him. He's in deep trouble and he needs your help." The women sat down.

Violet suddenly stood and waited for her shaking to subside. She looked around the room at people she'd been friends with as a girl, and nodded at them in recognition. Mike gestured for her to speak.

"When my father told me he'd found out that my mother was raped twelve years ago, I was so stuck in disbelief that I initially blamed Joshua for what happened. I had poison in my heart for him." She turned to look at him and apologized with her eyes.

"But, I've come to realize that disbelief—failure to truly listen and trust each other—causes us sometimes to blame each other for things not done. Our relationships become contaminated with hatred and distrust and pretty soon family, community, church members are fighting with one another like enemies."

Violet waved her arm around the room. "Take a look around—this is what the abusive behavior of one influential man can do. It can rip the fabric that holds a community together.

"To save our families and ourselves, we *must* believe what these women and Joshua have told us. We have to face what Pastor Lane has done, and like these brave women before us, show the love of Christ to him—which is the only power that can burn away this poisonous infection." The only sound was a cough from the back of the room.

"All we ask is that you accept the truth of what you've been told here and recognize the abuse that has occurred for what it is. By facing it, we can refuse to accept it in our midst and protect this community from further damage. Then, and only then, will we begin to heal."

After looking around the room one more time, she sat down. Bruce put his arm around her shoulders and Martin took his daughter's hand.

Pastor Terry stepped to the podium beside Mike. "We do, indeed, have an example of the love of Christ before us here. These women...and man...have confronted Rev. Richardson in love, seeking to offer their help by asking him to face what he's done. We could all stand to do that.

"We are all sinners and must go before our Lord in confession. How is a pastor any different? As with all of us, his sin must be acknowledged and corrected. Let us each search our hearts for what we should do."

A few sniffles were heard. Mike, who had listened quietly to Pastor Terry's words, took a deep breath and turned again toward the crowd.

"I think that will be our last word for tonight. Thank you, Pastor Bunker. And thank you all for coming."

An hour later, the church fellowship hall stood empty.

83

"Come on, young fella, whatcha tryin' ta do, kill ya self?"

Lane sputtered and his chest was on fire. He gasped for air, and opened his eyes to find himself looking into a leathery face covered with a scraggly grey beard. He tried to speak but found he couldn't utter a word.

"S'okay. Don' try ta talk. Jus' catch yer breath."

Lane felt stiff and cold and wondered where he was.

The old man seemed to understand the questioning look in the younger man's eyes. "I found ya in the water o'er there." He pointed at a large boulder in the river. "Got the water outta ya and now we're warmin' yer up."

Lane felt the blanket around him for the first time and began to shiver.

"I know," continued the man. "Tried to do misself in once too. Didn' wanna live. I killed too many...in the war. Couldna live with it, wanted out."

Lane tried to sit up. As he struggled, he felt the strong arms of the old man lifting him. When he was settled with the blanket wrapped securely around him, the man handed him a cup of hot coffee. "Here, drink this. It'll warm yer up."

The two men sat in silence side by side on the river bank, one wrapped in a wool Army-Navy blanket and the other dressed in waders.

"Why'd you take me out?" Lane finally croaked to his companion, feeling the warmth of the drink unlock his vocal cords.

"Someone saved me once upon a time," the man said, looking at the river. "I guess this time I was 'spose ta do the savin'." After a pause the old man went on. "That's not how we're 'spose ta go," he said, licking his lips. "There are reasons ta keep on livin'."

Lane fought the tears welling in his eyes. "And reasons not to."

The old man kept his eyes averted. "Hey, yer already wet, tears ain't gonna hurt none."

A great blue heron flew by, its huge wings beating slowly like a heartbeat. The old man looked up and followed the bird's flight. "Ain't she pretty!"

Tears now flowed down Lane's face. "How can I ever atone for what I've done?"

"By not tryin' ta ditch it all for starters."

"How can I ever face anyone again?"

"Ya take each day at a time. And ya let the beauty round here keep ya afloat." The man motioned in the direction the heron had gone. Lane followed the man's arm with his eyes, realizing just how much of the beauty of life he had missed seeing.

They sat in silence again, but this time, Lane was aware of the sounds all around him—the lap of the water on the shore, the breeze in the leaves overhead, the rustle of small animals in the underbrush, the twitter of birds. This was very different from the muted silence under the water. This was *alive*. *He* was alive.

"Whatcha do that's so bad?" the old man asked.

Lane couldn't say it aloud. He wasn't sure he could talk about any of it with anyone, couldn't yet fully admit to himself what he had done.

The man peered at him from under bushy eyebrows. "Is it worse than slaughterin' innocent women and children like pigs in their beds?"

Lane was stunned by the man's confession, but still could say nothing.

"Did ya force your way into their homes and rape any woman ya could find? They were jus' the enemy anyway, right? What did it matter?"

Lane listened, horrified, as the older man continued.

"We'd joke about it. After the first time, one guy vomited and tried to get us all to stop but we beat the shit outta him. He shut up after that." The man picked up a stone and threw it hard into the river. "The worst part was the fear in their eyes. I still see it now, as clear as if it was yesterday."

Lane sipped his coffee, oddly calmed by what he was hearing. It was as if he were listening to a congregant in counseling, but in this case he was the congregant.

"So, when I came back stateside, I couldna forgit, couldna git rid of it. It followed me ev'rywhere, to my bed, to my job, into my dreams, even my sex. Ev'rytime I had a woman all I could see were them faces.

"I could never keep a job. I was too bothered. So I drank. Thirty years of staying drunk to forgit, to block it all out. Had blackouts too, ended up in weird places. It was useless, why live, eh?" He glanced at Lane and shook his head. "I wasna any good to anyone, 'specially not to misself. I figured the world was better off without me."

Lane hoped the man would go on, but finally gave in and asked the obvious. "What made you change your mind?"

"The man who found me was a minister. He told me there was things I could do to help others hurtin' as bad as me. So, I volunteered at a vet'rin's halfway house. It went on from there, I guess."

The irony of the situation was almost too much to contain. Lane stifled a chuckle before responding. "So, you stopped drinking. Have the thoughts stopped too?"

"No booze, but I'll never git away from the faces."

"How can you stand it?'

The old man sighed. "Kinda made friends with 'em, I guess. They keep me going. They remind me of my work here now." The man motioned to the river with his head. "But it's here I get peace. I come out here fishin' to git filled up agin."

Lane put down his empty mug. The man filled it back up from his large thermos. "Keep takin' that warmth into ya. Once ya stop shivr'in' I'll take ya home."

"You don't need to do that."

"If ya think I'm gonna jus' leave ya stay here by this river, yer crazy!" The two men drifted into silence again.

"Did you say a *minister* saved you?"

"Yup."

Lane laughed out loud.

They sat together in silence until finally the older man helped the younger to his pick-up truck and drove him home. As they came to the end of the street on which he lived, Lane opened his mouth to thank his guardian angel and realized that he didn't know his name.

"Ned," said the old man, when Lane asked. "You?"

"I'm Lane," he said simply.

They came to a stop in front of the house and Ned turned to Lane. "Whaddaya do? For a livin', I mean?"

The pastor got out of the truck, folded the blanket he'd been wrapped in and laid it on the seat before answering. "I'm a minister."

Ned nodded and grinned.

Lane stuck his head in the door. "Made friends with 'em, huh?"

"Yep!" said Ned. "Steady companions." He waved his hand and drove away, leaving Lane standing on the curb in front of his house.

On the way down the driveway, Lane noticed every detail he had missed before—the helicopter seed pods collected by the door, the coo of the mourning dove overhead, the whistle of the wind around the shutters.

He opened the door and went into his den and sat down. Exhausted, but strangely lighter, he was struck that the presence of the old man was still with him. After bathing and donning warm clothes, he ate a simple meal and wandered into his study, and took out the packet of letters. One by one, he opened and read each one. And his tears flowed.

He'd preached it many times, but now it was his to do. Atonement and redemption lay in his own hands. Though the church taught that Christ's death on the cross paid for all our sins, he knew now that his desire to escape responsibility for his actions had been *his* ultimate sin. Killing himself to avoid the consequences of his behavior would have been an unforgivable cowardice. If alive, he had an opportunity to make amends—to repent, turn his life around, and stop hurting others.

He thought of the old man at the river and it renewed his resolve. If Ned could face what he had done, learn to live with it and find a way to turn the sins of his past into something good, then surely he could do the same. He could confess his sins, make amends, and claim redemption for himself.

He sat in the silence for a long time, and then opened another drawer in his desk and pulled out a phone book. Flipping through the pages until he found the number he was looking for, he picked up the phone and dialed.

"Hello," he said, as the face of the boy he had once been flashed across his mind. "I need help."

Abigail Speaks

I have seen a great change in my town. From my vantage point I see the struggles and battles fought to find what's right. In my role as healer in this region, it is my job to interpret and share the visions that come to me.

People are motivated by a desire for meaning. Some are led astray to seek it in power, others in false love. A few find it in the real thing of mucking around in our humanness together. Out of our brokenness, we are both perpetrators and abettors of the perpetrations of others and, as a result, we stand aside, allowing abuse, injustice and violence to occur.

We stop looking and bury our heads in the stuff of our individual lives as if we can avoid or deny the thread that connects us all. We lie to ourselves and thus to one another and a stink is allowed to go unchecked in our midst—the proverbial elephant in the room. It takes brave, and often wounded, individuals to break the spell by facing the truth and delivering it into the light. We must, finally, face the truth of who we are and what we've done—all of us. Then, and only then, can we, as a community, begin to heal our wounds, right the wrongs and choose love.

This story of Hopeston reveals that one person's awakening is an opportunity for others to awaken. Martin, with Melodie's help, led his family into a new level of cohesion that brought them healing and growth and caused them to become closer with one another. Violet discovered forgiveness and healing and it has transformed her into a warrior for peace. Bruce rediscovered his love for family and his own big heart and, as you know, Lillie found her soul, its path and its mate.

Miriam and Samuel (yes) continue to surround their son with love. Joshua, who is healing nicely, holds his head high and has embraced his ability to lead with the love and support of Lillie, his lover and friend.

Together these two young people are a powerful force. This will not be the only Holy War they fight—they are only just getting started with what they will do in the world. Their love is strong and infectious—and inspires others to seek their own purpose and meaning. Lillie is a healer and Joshua supports her unwaveringly in her mission. And the victims who met for support and told their stories are now strong enough to share what they've learned and guide others in doing the same.

But perhaps the biggest miracle of all is what has happened to the pastor. Lane Richardson, in recognizing his own painful wounds, has finally been able to move beyond denial and face what he has done. All aspects of his character have now been bared and he is ready to face the truth and seek help in making amends and ceasing to hurt others.

Why has he not been punished for his transgressions? I assure you he has been and will be. He will never be free from the horrific consequences of his actions, there will never truly be relief for him in this life. But, like Ned, he will learn to live with it and carry on, accepting the altered condition of his own existence.

No matter what, there is always hope for human beings to find the best in our *selves* and in one another. The shining reality of our potential lingers around every corner. The choice to claim it and grasp hold of it for dear life, however, requires a corporate effort, for without one another we cannot prevail.

Once a community captive to the darkness of ignorance and denial, this town squandered its birthright. But by responding to the call upon her heart to speak the truth, even in death, Melodie Farmer aided it in doing so as well. If we each do our part, others will be inspired to do theirs. So goes the ripple effect of transformation.

Now it's up to every soul here to grapple with his or her own inner sense of calling to a higher purpose. The town is now surrounded with a new light—a positive energy emanates from it. It can become a haven for the truth—a beacon of the freedom it brings. And by the grace of the Divine Spirit, Hopeston will finally live up to its name.

That same Spirit calls all who will hear to a journey toward wholeness and to an awakening to opportunities for second chances. "Complete" healing isn't the goal—we will never be completely healed because it is the process of healing itself that gives us hope, peace and the ability to engage in Love. It is when we choose life, in all its humanness, that we find…redemption.

Lillie's
Redemption

To order additional copies
please visit:

www.LaLobaInc.Com

La Loba, Inc.
Soul Groups
Wilderness Retreats
Spiritual Direction

To schedule a book signing, an author visit to your group or
book club, or to arrange a speaking engagement
contact:

Lydia Waring Meyer, MSW, MDiv
P.O. Box 26
Grand Haven, MI 49417
lydia@lalobainc.com

Volume Discounts Available